When Violence Begins at Home

How to Identify a Potential Batterer

- Jealousy
- Controlling behavior
- Quick involvement
- Unrealistic expectations
- Isolation
- Blames others for his problems
- Blames others for his feelings
- Hypersensitivity
- Cruelty to animals or children
- "Playful" use of force in sex
- Verbal abuse
- Rigid sex roles
- Jekyll-and-Hyde personality
- Past battering
- Threats of violence
- Breaking or striking objects
- Any force during an argument

If your partner exhibits more than three of these warning signs, there is a strong potential for abuse in the relationship. Without effective early intervention, abuse can escalate in severity and sometimes lead to death. If you believe you are in danger, please call:

National Domestic Violence Hotline
800-799-SAFE

All calls are handled in strict confidence.

This book is lovingly dedicated
to my sisters and brothers
in the battered women's movement.

And to the phenomenal women.

When VIOLENCE Begins at HOME

A Comprehensive Guide to Understanding and Ending Domestic Abuse

K. J. Wilson, Ed.D.

Hunter House Inc. Publishers
P.O. Box 2914
Alameda CA 94501-0914

Library of Congress Cataloging-in-Publication Data
Wilson, K. J.
When violence begins at home : a comprehensive guide to understanding and ending domestic abuse / by K. J. Wilson.
p. cm.
Includes bibliographical references and index.
ISBN 0-89793-228-5
ISBN 0-89793-227-7 (pbk.)
1. Wife abuse—United States. 2. Wife abuse—United States—Prevention. 3. Family violence—United States. I. Title.
HV6626.2.W55 1997
362.82'927'0973—dc21 97-18270
CIP

Ordering
Trade bookstores and wholesalers in the U.S. and Canada, please contact
Publishers Group West 1-800-788-3123 Fax (510) 658-1834

Hunter House books are available for textbook/course adoptions, and are sold at bulk discounts to qualifying community and health care organizations for resale or for special promotions and fundraising. For details please contact:

Marketing Department
Hunter House Inc., P.O. Box 2914, Alameda CA 94501-0914
Tel. (510) 865-5282 Fax (510) 865-4295
e-mail: marketing@hunterhouse.com

Individuals can order our books from most bookstores or by calling toll-free:
1-800-266-5592

Cover Design: Jil Weil Graphic Design, Oakland
Book Design: *Qalagraphia*
Project Editor: Dana Weissman
Editorial Coordinator: Belinda Breyer
Production Coordinator: Wendy Low
Copyeditor: Mali Apple
Indexing: Alta Indexing Services
Proofreader: Susan Burckhard
Marketing Director: Corrine M. Sahli
Marketing Associate: Susan Markey
Customer Support: Christina Arciniega, Edgar M. Estavilla, Jr.
Business Management: Mike Nealy
Order Fulfillment: A & A Quality Shipping
Publisher: Kiran S. Rana

Printed and bound by Publishers Press, Salt Lake City, UT
Manufactured in the United States of America

9 8 7 6 5 4 3 2 1 First edition

9/98

Contents

Quick Contents

A listing of sections that may be of immediate importance to some readers, arranged alphabetically

Foreword

Every January, I receive requests from the media for statistics on the increase of domestic violence on Super Bowl Sunday. Many shelters for battered women have reported such an increase, but there are no hard data. I remember that one year a public service announcement concerning domestic violence was aired during the television broadcast of the football game. That announcement should be repeated every year.

Without a doubt, one can say that watching games of heated competition arouses strong emotions that can lead to violence. Witness the riots that have occurred at some soccer games and the fights in the stands at baseball and football games. In her work counseling batterers, Anne Ganley found that these men were unable to distinguish their emotions, that arousal was almost inevitably expressed as anger.

For the first time in the United States, a major athletic organization, the Seattle Mariners baseball team, has joined the Washington State Coalition Against Domestic Violence and KIRO-TV for a statewide, season-long educational campaign "Refuse to Abuse."

The National Advertising Council and the Family Violence Prevention Fund have collaborated on a national publicity campaign, "There is no excuse for domestic violence," which has had an impact on government and the corporate world.

There is hope.

Dr. Wilson undertook a monumental task when she decided to write *When Violence Begins at Home: A Comprehensive Guide to Understanding and Ending Domestic Abuse.* She traces the origins of violence against women from its roots in patriarchal society dating back thousands of years to the beginnings of the grassroots battered women's movement in the 1970s. Until then, the existence of domestic violence had been either denied or tacitly approved by law and custom.

Since then, the private practice of beating women into submission in the home has been publicized as a threat to the welfare of society as a whole. A network of shelters for battered women and their children has been established. Domestic violence has been defined as a crime and penal codes have been revised. Advocacy and support groups for victims/survivors have been formed. Public and private service agencies have developed programs to educate personnel and the community about the dynamics of domestic violence, its effects, and its treatments.

Twenty years seems like a long time. Advocates sometimes despair that despite all of these efforts to overcome violence in the home, it appears to be increasing. But domestic violence is not on the increase; it is the reporting of its incidence that has increased—a sign that our outreach has been successful. Women are breaking away from the abuse of their husbands and partners, and we need to protect them in the process and help them reconstruct their lives. Domestic violence is a social disease for which we as a society must take responsibility.

Twenty years is but a moment in time considering the thousands of years that made violence against women a worldwide tradition. We need to acknowledge the great strides that have been made to date. Grassroots organizing has been successful in bringing about change at local, state, national, and international levels. The Violence Against Women Act of 1994, passed by Congress and signed into law by President Bill Clinton, will have far-reaching effects in our struggle against domestic violence. As I write this foreword, the Second World Congress on Family Law and the Rights of Children and Youth is meeting in San Francisco. A key topic of the conference is domestic violence and its profound effect on all dimensions of a child's development. The latest effort at outreach has been made by the U.S. Postal Service, which has put the toll-free National Domestic Violence Hotline number (800-799-SAFE) on the covers of two hundred million thirty-two-cent stamp booklets.

There is hope.

In this book, Dr. Wilson has done a superb job in summarizing what we have learned and what we have accomplished over the last twenty years in responding to domestic violence. She speaks from her own experience as a survivor of violence and stalking, and describes the period in her own life when she went underground. She also speaks as an authority from her experience working with battered women's centers and her comprehensive knowledge of research on the subject. Her simple, straightforward style of writing is refreshing and easily understood. This book answers once and for all every question people have asked about the dynamics of abusive relationships.

Although my book *Battered Wives* has been credited as the catalyst for the battered women's shelter movement, I chose two arenas with which I was already involved as my personal commitment in creating change: the criminal justice system and politics. In San Francisco, we (attorneys, law students, advocates, and service providers—all women) formed the Coalition for Justice for Battered Women to take on the male bastion of law enforcement. Our objective was to establish that *domestic violence is a crime* and to make radical changes in police procedures in response to domestic violence calls. We had the backing of then Mayor Diane Feinstein who directed her police chief to work with us on a new general order, which includes provisions that Dr. Wilson describes in her chapter on the legal system.

Changes in police policy necessitated reevaluation of the prosecutor's handling of spouse abuse cases. Having the district attorney file charges of abuse as a crime against the state reduces the potential for recrimination by the defendant and increases the likelihood that the battered woman will cooperate with the prosecution. Expert witnesses can dispel misconceptions the jury may have about battered women. It took twenty years, but now we have a domestic violence unit within the San Francisco Police Department to investigate cases. We also have a specialized domestic violence unit in the district attorney's office providing vertical prosecution (one attorney handling the case throughout).

The role of the judiciary must not be minimized. Educating judges can be a problem because of their discretionary power and the assumption that they are above public reproach. Last year, the *San Francisco Examiner* revealed that San Francisco municipal court judges were using "civil compromise" in domestic violence misdemeanor cases. Defendants were being let off with an apology and a few hours of counseling. Those of us who had orchestrated changes in policies of the criminal justice system were shocked.

Supervisor Barbara Kaufman called for public hearings, and the judges were outraged that we dared to challenge their discretionary privilege. But the civil compromise clause is a legal option for cases involving neighborhood disputes, property damage, or petty theft. It was never meant to be used in the disposition of domestic violence caseloads. The California legislature backed our position and passed a bill to prohibit the misuse of civil compromise in domestic violence cases. As this is being written, activists are working with the legislature to cover child and elder abuse as well.

The California legislature also eliminated the option of diversion to a counseling program for defendants in domestic violence misdemeanor cases on the basis that it was too lenient. The law now requires that a defendant who is placed on probation for committing a crime against an intimate partner shall be subject to certain conditions: completion of a year of specialized counseling for batterers, a minimum period of thirty-six months on probation, and automatic issuance of a protective order.

Dr. Wilson states that the Texas Council on Family Violence considers traditional counseling, family therapy, and mediation inappropriate in a battering intervention. Mandating couple's counseling or mediation places the battered woman at a disadvantage and in further jeopardy.

We are not dealing with domestic disputes or communication problems. The batterer communicates quite clearly that he is the head of the household and will use force to maintain that power over family members. We are dealing with abject, unreasonable *violence.* Not having dinner ready on time can trigger a severe violent episode. Appropriate intervention must deal with the batterer's violent behavior. *You cannot mediate violence.* This bears repeating over and over again.

Unfortunately, the California legislature has not yet understood that message. Despite the 1990 recommendation of the National Council of Juvenile and Family Court Judges that no judge mandate mediation in cases in which family violence has occurred, California's judiciary persists in blocking attempts to exempt domestic violence cases from our mandated mediation of child custody and visitation "disputes." The best we have been able to get is the right of the battered woman to have a separate hearing without the presence of her battering spouse, to have a supporter accompany her during the hearing, and to presume that mediators and judges will be trained in the dynamics of domestic violence. If the latter were true, judges and mediators would understand the danger they are courting. Sheila Kuehl and Lisa Lerman warn that the battered spouse should have her attorney, or one recommended by an advocate, review any agreement reached in a mediation process before signing it. Agreements under this mandate have a greater potential for a breakdown.

It took years for battered women's advocates to add consideration of spousal abuse as a policy (along with child abuse) for determining custody. But the plea that the father have unsupervised visitation "is in the best interests of the child" still prevails, no matter how violent his nature. There are enough reported incidents where battered women *and* their children are killed during the process of separation or divorce. What else do we need to convince the legislature of the mediation folly?

San Francisco's Commission on the Status of Women created a subcommittee to look at a citywide response to domestic violence following the murder of Veena Charan by her husband in 1990. Except for one thing, she had done everything by the book over a period of fifteen months. She obtained a restraining order and was awarded temporary physical custody of her nine-year-old son. She sought a divorce and participated in mediation through Family Court Services as mandated by California law. She cooperated with the prosecution of her husband on felony wife beating. The one thing she didn't do was to avail herself of the safety of a shelter for battered women and their children.

Joseph Charan was sentenced to twelve months in jail. The sentence was suspended, however, in lieu of conditional probation: domestic violence counseling, a stay-away order, and thirty days in jail. A few days later, before reporting to probation, he murdered his wife in front of teachers and schoolchildren before killing himself.

The investigation showed that the judge was not informed of the many police contacts the defendant had prior to the current criminal charge. Joseph Charan had violated the restraining order both in San Mateo County where his wife worked and in San Francisco where she resided. He had also vandalized her home, scrawled graffiti, and rammed his car through the garage door. He made several attempts to kidnap their son at school.

Judges need to have a complete file on prior incident reports as they can be an indicator of homicide risk. The defendant should be taken into custody immediately after sentencing and processed by the probation department. The delay because of case overload can, and did, result in a death sentence for Veena Charan despite the stay-away order. All governmental departments that were involved in any way were cooperative in tracing Veena Charan through the system to determine what went wrong. All except the Family Court Services director, who claimed immunity because of client confidentiality. The presiding judge of Family Court and the city attorney backed her position. Members of the investigating committee were frustrated. They needed to know what impact mediation had on Veena Charan.

Since then, unsuccessful attempts have been made to amend the mediation clause in the law to exempt cases in which there is a history of violent episodes. A father's rights still prevail over the endangerment of wife and child. But each time a bill is introduced, more legislators become sensitive to the issue.

There is hope.

The latest ploy in the struggle to explore and prevent domestic homicides is the California state law that permits counties to create Domestic Violence Fatality Review Teams. The legislation is fashioned pretty much by guidelines for existing Child Fatality Review Teams, but it left out one very essential piece of the legislation—how to deal with confidentiality. Already San Francisco's Mental Health Department has declared that information from client files cannot be shared with the death review team without a waiver.

The problem of confidentiality can be resolved by requiring each committee member to sign a confidentiality agreement that information provided the review team will remain confidential and will not be used for any reason other than that for which it is intended. A violation of the agreement would constitute a misdemeanor. The law could state that this statute overrides contradictory codes of ethics from individual professions. The identity of the person is not the interest of the review team. Seeking clues based on the experience of the individuals to find the gaps in our response systems, recognizing signs of homicidal risk, and preventing fatalities is the mission of the death review teams.

Successful prosecution depends not only on the education of all branches of the legal system (both civil and criminal), but also on the battered woman herself. They all need to know that violence unchecked increases in frequency and severity, and sometimes leads to murder. With the cooperation of law enforcement officers, the Family Violence Prevention Fund in San Francisco has produced and made available manuals on procedures (including custody and visitation) for police, district attorneys, and judges.

Unless your local criminal justice system is enlightened about the lethality of domestic violence, is willing to adopt new and revised criminal justice policies, or you have enough political clout to get the state legislature to mandate these changes, then perhaps the protection order is the route to go. Either way it is necessary to watchdog the system and see that these orders are enforced. Personnel changes make education a never-ending process.

I remember the time in the early 1980s when politicians in San Francisco discussed issues instead of launching personal attacks on each other. No politician then dared to omit support of shelters for battered women as a key campaign issue. If laws in your state are obstructive rather than productive in dealing with domestic violence, it will be necessary to form political coalitions to publicize the problem and urge passage of remedial legislation at the state level. Funding for domestic violence programs was a key campaign issue in the last election for governor of California.

If we are to make substantive changes in the law, we have to be more involved in electoral politics. It isn't enough to form a Coalition Against Domestic Violence to lobby the state legislature: we need to change its makeup. We need to educate candidates for office and get commitments or planks in their campaign platforms to further efforts toward *prevention* of domestic violence. We need to elect more women who will challenge the status quo and push issues not always embraced by their male counterparts. Mayor Rita Mullins of Palatine, Illinois, was newly elected chair of the Women's Caucus of the U.S. Conference of Mayors in San Francisco this month. During her two-year term she intends to focus on combating domestic violence, increasing affordable child care, and creating a mentoring program for women who are, or who want to be, mayors. The gender gap in elections is growing.

There is hope.

In counseling battered women, there is a fine line between warning them and frightening them. Women should not be discouraged from leaving a dangerous situation. They should be educated regarding the inevitable escalation of the violence and offered help in putting together a safety plan. Although great strides have been made to provide recourse and safety to battered women, the systems we have developed are not uniform nor fail proof. But with persistence and continued advocacy, public awareness, and support, we shall overcome the obstacles we have encountered.

I was lucky to have had Eleanor Roosevelt as a role model. Her words have been an inspiration. "You gain strength, courage and confidence by every experience in which you really stop to look fear in the face. . . . You must do the thing you think you cannot do."

Dr. K. J. Wilson did. Her contribution is immeasurable. This book will be the bible of domestic violence advocates for years to come.

Del Martin
San Francisco, June 1997

Preface

I am honored to introduce you to a book that will provide an overview of what we have learned about ending violence against women in the family. The author is the director of training at the Austin Center for Battered Women (CBW). I served as the center's first director from 1977 to 1982, leaving to become the executive director of the Texas Council on Family Violence. In that role, I have continued to support the development of the Austin center and others throughout Texas, as well as assisting to found the National Network to End Domestic Violence, which led the effort to pass the Violence Against Women Act of 1994. From those vantage points, I am able to assure you that the philosophy of the Austin center has remained, since its inception, one of listening to battered women in order to design programs and services for them. Battered women's experiences have dictated the advocacy approaches in public policy and professional practice to ensure that governmental and private helping agencies are truly responsive to the needs of battered women as they express them, and not as we may have been taught in our brief examination of family violence in most institutions of higher education. By keeping the focus on listening and learning from battered women, and never assuming that something cannot be changed or improved, the Austin center has been and continues to be a model and to provide leadership to the battered women's movement as a whole.

The goal of this book is to share what has been learned in almost twenty-five years of dedicated work by volunteers, staff, and the board of CBW. Dr. Wilson has taken the task of putting to paper the accumulated knowledge in an effort to assist others throughout the country who seek to design responsive programs or who wish to understand the myriad of methods that we must employ if we are indeed to stop the violence. While it is hoped that the full knowledge gained can be shared, it is actually an impossible goal, in that certain skills must accompany knowledge to achieve the quality of programs and services that the Austin center has. The willingness to take risks, creativity, the skill of receptivity to new information, and the maturity to admit when something is not working as ectively as hoped are all necessary as well. The leadership of the Austin nter throughout its history has had the necessary skills, openness to owledge, and the grounding in the philosophy that "there but for the ıce of God go I." This means that any woman can be in a battering relanship, that violence against a woman is not about the woman herself, but that helping a woman to successfully live violence free must be about supporting her choices, having shared what information and services we can to assist her. Replication in other communities is possible, but only if accompanied by the skills and philosophy that form the infrastructure upon which to build similarly effective programs.

In saying this to you so strongly, I suspect that you may question my objectivity. Granted, I am inordinately proud of the Austin center and of knowing that it has remained true to battered women as it has grown to be one of the largest of the programs in our state. Many of us worry that when our organizations succeed and grow, the essence of our beliefs can be lost. Isn't the true success of a movement recruiting others to participate in the work with the same commitment as early founders? Isn't true success possible only when we acknowledge that if the work were easy, those who came before us would have answered so many of the tough questions already and that we must be willing to remain open and continue to learn as we go? I believe that in this context, success means ever-striving to find the answers, knowing full well that the complexity of family violence and its pervasive nature in our culture and the world will not permit us to see its end during our lifetimes. But in every way that those of us doing this work and sharing in a desire to build safe, supportive families can share what we have and ask for what we need, we can all make a contribution to that eventuality.

Deborah D. Tucker
Former Executive Director, Texas Council on Family Violence
Vice-chair, National Network to End Domestic Violence

Acknowledgements

In the course of writing this book, I had the pleasure of talking with numerous women and men in Texas and across this nation. One thing became abundantly clear to me as a result of our discussions: these incredible people diligently work to end violence in the home because of their desire for justice and their respect for humanity. While their contributions are frequently unrecognized, they continue their quest with a compassion and a willingness to share that is nothing less than remarkable. This book is the product of their wisdom, passion, and guidance. To the many people who so willingly shared their gifts with me, I offer you my gratitude and appreciation.

I am continually touched by the support and encouragement I receive from the dedicated staff, board of directors, and volunteers at the Austin Center for Battered Women (CBW). I find that the company of these fine individuals has enriched my life in more ways than I could ever express. Their relentless, loving efforts to end domestic violence continue to motivate and inspire me. I consider it an honor and a privilege to stand with the CBW family in our struggle.

I would like to extend a special thank you to my friends and coworkers who so generously offered their insight and support on this project. My gratitude goes out to Erin Clark, Pat Clark, Lucy Muñoz, Barri Rosenbluth, Sara Slater, Kelly Sullivan Garcia, Kalpana Sutaria, Betty Davis, Vivian Rogers, Julia Spann, Joan Carter, Mary Kay Sicola, Gin Keller, Murilyn Pinkosky, Holly, Martha Peine, Anne Spellacy, Theresa Pritchard, Stephanie Horgan, Margaret Young, Rose Hernandez, Angela Atwood, Darlene Strayn, Dana Little, Wicket Davidson, and Lisa Rivera Capper. Several members of the CBW family, including Laura Hopingardner, Patsy Flores, Dina Ortiz, Sarah Hauck Seaton, Kim Cox, and Sara Sloan, helped research materials for this project.

Kelly Rountree, CBW executive director, generously offers her faith and trust in my abilities. She encourages me to thoughtfulness, to action, and to grow. For this, and so much more, I am most grateful.

The staff and volunteers at the Texas Council on Family Violence and the National Domestic Violence Hotline provided immeasurable support and assistance. I wish to extend a special thank you to Ellen Fisher, Cyndy Perkins, D'An Anders, Susan Mathis, Diane Schultz, Tony Switzer, Anna Belle Burleson, Diane Perez, Sonia Benavides, Karen Buck, and Shaun Thompson.

I also wish to thank Kiran Rana and Dana Weissman at Hunter House and Kathleen Niendorff for their dedication to this important issue and their faith in my abilities.

That I am alive and able to write this book is due, in part, to the support and assistance of my family and friends. My parents, Calvin and Carrie Wilson, gave me all the encouragement, support, and assistance I needed while respecting and honoring my need to find my own path. My brother, Billy Gage, and my nephew, Henry Goode, offered their assistance at a time when I was barely able to help myself. My dear uncle, Allen Hesser, gave me a safe haven and a loving heart at a time when I thought I'd never be safe again. My sister, Jan Conner, provided immeasurable love, support, and kindness. It is to all of these dear people that I extend my love and my gratitude.

Barbara Stone, my teacher, my mentor, and my friend, always knew I could and helped me get there. Paulette Beatty, Nancy Sawtelle, and Rhonda Snider gave of themselves in such a way as to help me find the strength within me. To all of you, I offer my appreciation.

I am also blessed with the love and support of my chosen family. I am especially grateful to my sisters, Janeen Ashton, Terri Leeth, and Abba Anderson, who have traveled many miles with me. I am blessed with their company and their love. To Joel Maiorano, I wish to express my gratitude and deep affection for his faith, humor, and support. I have learned much from this kind man. Melinda Cantu and Margaret Bassett fill my life with an abundance of love, laughter, and encouragement; they are the sisters of my heart. Miz Gail Rice moves me with her compassion and challenges me to action. Diane Rhodes never fails to tap my shoulder when I need it and lends hers for my tears and my laughter. I cannot begin to offer Juanita Salinas enough thanks for all that she is and all that she gives, but I hope my love will do.

Lastly, to the many women who have so willingly shared their pain and their triumphs with me, I offer my grateful appreciation. You have taught me more than you will ever, ever know.

When Violence Begins at Home

Introduction

I first became involved with the battered women's movement in 1978 when I was working for a newly funded displaced homemaker's program in a small rural community in Texas. Displaced homemaker's programs, which evolved from the women's movement, were created to empower divorced, widowed, and separated women.

Although the late seventies was a period of newfound growth for battered women's centers, many communities lacked organization for abused women. Since the city in which I resided was one such community, many of those who turned to us for help were battered women. Almost twenty years later, I can still vividly recall the first "unofficial" hotline call I took. With no shelter in our community and few or no services available to battered women, I remember my sense of helplessness and frustration. By 1979 I had begun researching the battered women's movement in Texas. By 1980 I had developed a passion for this work.

I would like to say that my involvement in the battered women's movement has been consistent for the last twenty years. In truth, however, it has not. My growth and empowerment has taken a winding path, including my own involvement in abusive relationships and my turn at burnout.

However, I keep returning to the movement. And, as a result of my experiences and growth, each time I return I find that I am a better advocate. I have come to truly appreciate the importance of not only "talking the talk," but "walking the walk" as well.

Along the way, my commitment to ending domestic violence has deepened. I am fortunate to be able to fulfill my passion through the educational programs that I offer to community groups, volunteers, advocates, and abused women. We share, we learn, we grow, and we struggle together for change. And we are better people because of this process.

In the summer of 1994 I presented a workshop at the 6th National Conference on Domestic Violence, sponsored by the National Coalition Against Domestic Violence. I returned home with a strong need to write about the women whom I had come to know and love, who dedicate their lives to this movement. Upon receiving approval from the Austin Center for Battered Women (CBW) executive director Kelly Rountree and the

CBW board, I began this endeavor. For the next year, I struggled to balance my work at CBW with my attempts to write.

In the fall of 1995, former CBW board member Kathleen Niendorff met with Kelly Rountree and Ellen Rubenstein Fisher, then associate director at TCFV, about the possibility of writing a comprehensive summary of what we have learned about domestic violence in the last twenty years. Both women liked the idea and when asked who would be willing to tackle this formidable task, Kelly mentioned my name. The rest of the story is a blur of late nights, too much coffee, and little rest. Luckily, I was guided by an unequivocal understanding that this book would reflect my passion and that it would be a part of my own learning, growth, and empowerment as a formerly battered woman.

When Violence Begins At Home approaches domestic violence with the understanding that it does not occur in a vacuum. The effects of abuse on women and children touch every aspect of their lives as well as the lives of those around them. Domestic abuse is a complex social problem that must be understood and seriously addressed by all community members if we truly expect to create a peaceful future for everyone.

Chapter 1 (The Dynamics of Abusive Relationships) defines domestic abuse and explores the myths and realities surrounding violent relationships. In Chapter 2 (The Effects of Family Violence on Children) I examine the behavioral and psychological effects of growing up in and withstanding an abusive family. Chapter 3 (Teen Dating Violence) describes the frightening phenomenon of dating violence among adolescents. It also explains how programs implemented by the Austin Center for Battered Women can serve as a model for addressing this problem.

Chapter 4 (The Intimate Relationship Between Substance Abuse and Domestic Violence) examines the complex connection between two present-day plagues and identifies effective intervention strategies. In Chapter 5 (Battered Women and the Legal System), I explore the legal options and roadblocks many women encounter when appealing to the judicial system.

Many women live in such fear of their batterers that they feel their only chance for survival is to live in hiding. Chapter 6 (Living Underground) describes how women can successfully plan for and endure a life in hiding.

Chapter 7 (The Oppression that Binds: Barriers to Living Violence Free) concerns the different challenges that confront women of color, lesbians, undocumented women, women with disabilities, older women, women in prison, and women residing in rural areas.

The impact of domestic violence extends far beyond the walls of the family home. Friends, family members, co-workers, supervisors, physicians, nurses, religious leaders, and congregation members all have an important role to play in the lives of women suffering abuse. The community that seriously expects to eliminate this vicious problem must take an active stance against domestic violence *as a community.*

The question, "How do you help someone in an abusive relationship?" is answered in Chapter 8 (Friends, Family, and Loved Ones: When Someone You Know Is Being Hurt). In addition, this chapter provides a series of sensitive questions that concerned individuals can ask to determine if an abusive relationship exists. Chapter 9 (Domestic Violence and the Workplace) explores the impact of domestic abuse on the workplace as well as the employer's role in helping to make the work environment safe for abused employees.

In Chapter 10 (Battered Women and Their Health: The Response of the Medical Community), I discuss the responses and responsibilities of the medical community to abused women. Chapter 11 (Battered Women and Communities of Faith) outlines specific strategies the religious community can use to provide battered women with wise counsel and practical care. Chapter 12 (Creating a Community Response to Domestic Violence) discusses strategies for developing a collaborative response to domestic abuse and highlights the Austin, Texas community's efforts to address this problem.

Intervention on behalf of abusive families can take a variety of forms. Chapter 13 (Intervention Strategies for Battered Women and Their Children), discusses support groups and counseling options for women and children. In Chapter 14 (Intervention and Prevention Programs for Batterers), I examine the variety of treatment programs available for batterers. I also establish important guidelines for choosing a program that addresses the safety needs of women and children.

Individuals who share their lives in an effort to end domestic violence do so because they have a passion for peace. Too often, however, the nature of our work wears away our energy and defeats our ability to share our passion over an extended period of time. In Chapter 15 (Loving Ourselves: Self-Care for Helpers), I explore what it means to "burn out" and how we can successfully avoid this path.

Chapter 16 (The National Domestic Violence Hotline) describes the history and the services of the NDVH, which was recently revived as a result of hard won federal funds and the careful stewardship of the Texas Council on Family Violence. In Chapter 17 (A History of Violence Against Women), I trace the history of domestic abuse from its origins in patriarchal society to the birth of the grassroots battered women's movement in the 1970s.

In 95 percent of reported domestic violence cases, these crimes are committed by men against women. This statistic is reflected throughout this book in my reference to the batterer as "he."

However, I do not wish to give the impression that lesbian and gay battering does not exist or is of lesser importance than nongay battering. Same sex battering is as detrimental to the lives it touches as battering in any nongay relationship. As the Texas Council on Family Violence Lesbian Task Force explains, *The Pain Is the Same.* I apologize for any misunderstanding this may create and ask for your patience in my continued use of "he" to describe batterers and "she" to describe survivors.

• • •

In writing this book, I had to wrestle with many old demons and I am proud to say that I have won. Safety concerns continue to be paramount for me, however. You may notice that I do not use my full name, and you will see no picture of me on the jacket of this book.

Although I have concerns for my safety, I am also committed to helping others better understand domestic violence so that we may all do our part to end this problem. I will address my safety concerns but I will not be silenced. We have been forced into silence and shame for far too long. Never again, my sisters, never again.

CHAPTER 1

The Dynamics of Abusive Relationships

FAMILY VIOLENCE is a simple phrase, but it encompasses a horrifying list of abusive behaviors, both physical and psychological, inflicted by one family member on another . . . . The list is endless. There is seemingly no end to the horrors some human beings can inflict on those whom this society calls their 'loved ones.'

—The American Medical News, *January 6, 1992*

Martha was twenty-seven when she met Phillip. The manager of a small business in a rural community, Martha was also attending night classes in order to complete a graduate degree. Phillip was self-employed and was well known in the community. He was handsome, charming, and witty. Unfortunately, he was also married.

Three years passed and Phillip got a divorce. During this three-year period Phillip spent a lot of time around Martha's place of business. He would drop by to see the owner of the company and inevitably end up in her office. When Martha learned of his divorce, she was secretly pleased. Here was her opportunity to go out with the man she was so drawn to. When Phillip asked her to lunch, she didn't hesitate.

They immediately began to see each other every day. Martha was so thrilled with all the attention that she didn't notice Phillip's irritation when she occasionally turned down lunch dates with him in order to meet with her girlfriends.

The first few months of their relationship were exciting and romantic. Phillip showered her with gifts and affection. Toward the end of this early courtship, however, Martha began to feel smothered with Phillip's constant demands on her time and attention. When Martha told Phillip she could no longer see him, he was furious and vowed to win her back. Thus began a flood of flowers, gifts, telephone calls, and letters. Martha stood firm with her decision for a while, but eventually began to miss Phillip. She finally agreed to see him again.

Shortly after their reunion Phillip moved in with Martha, and things began to escalate. Phillip began telling Martha what he considered appropriate dress. He encouraged her to gain weight because he liked women with "meat on their bones" and would then make fun of her because her clothes were becoming tight. His constant phone calls continued, but now he required her to outline her whereabouts on a minute-by-minute basis. If she told him she would be home at five o'clock, the phone would be ringing as she walked in the door. If she was late, even only a few minutes, he would interrogate her. He began accusing her of having affairs.

Two years later Martha was ready to end the relationship. Phillip, however, wanted to marry her, and her refusals sent him into rages. Initially he threw or hit things, but eventually he began to push and shove her. Martha begged Phillip to leave. He moved in and out of her house so many times that Martha lost count. Each time he left, however, he would harass her at home and at work so persistently that she would give in and let him return. Martha found herself growing more and more afraid of him.

As Martha continued to refuse Phillip's proposals, he became increasingly abusive. Holidays were the worst. The last Christmas Eve they spent together, Martha found herself trapped under a seven-foot Christmas tree. While he held the tree on top of her, Martha felt the lights burning her arms. She silently prayed that she would never have to spend another holiday in fear.

Martha considered herself an intelligent, responsible woman. She maintained a professional position, attended graduate school, and was well respected in her field. Privately, she was embarrassed and humiliated.

Phillip had been born and raised in the area and was well liked in their community. He had friends in the police department and the county attorney's office, so Martha didn't feel safe approaching them about her situation. She thought about contacting the local battered women's shelter, but Phillip's cousin worked there and Martha was afraid she would tell him. Her shame and fear prevented her from seeking help.

During the fourth, and final, year of their relationship, Phillip's abusive behavior reached its height. One evening, after another refused proposal of marriage, Phillip drove his truck into the back of Martha's car, pushing it into the closed garage door. It was three in the morning and the crash could be heard throughout the neighborhood, though no one called the police. Phillip was now telling Martha that she would never be able to leave him. He threatened to kill her and then himself if she tried to leave. He taunted her and said that if she tried to get a restraining order against him, he would ignore it. Nothing would keep him from her.

Being abused and humiliated had become a way of life for Martha, but the final straw was the last time Phillip attacked her. Dragging her across the kitchen floor, he repeatedly kicked her with his steel-toed boots. Martha found herself being kicked in the stomach, back, legs, and arms. Picking her up and throwing her into the kitchen table, Phillip then held her down while he stomped on her hands.

When his rage had passed, Martha was left crumpled on the floor, bruised and bloodied. Phillip quietly approached her, crying, and said that if she had just done what he had wanted this wouldn't have happened. "You made me do this," was Phillip's explanation for his behavior. "If you don't marry me, I'll have to kill you. If I can't have you, no one else can either!"

Martha was now sure that if she didn't do something, Phillip would kill her. Afraid to go to the local authorities, she decided to take matters into her own hands—she would literally run away. For the next few months Martha secretly planned her escape. She found the courage to tell her friends, family, and coworkers about her abusive relationship. Thankfully, all were supportive and offered help.

Finally, after months of planning, Martha secretly packed a bag, got into her car, and drove away. She left her home, her friends, her job, and her possessions. She had her life, however, and she was safe. She lived on the run for the next few months, living out of a suitcase. Looking for a job was difficult, but she eventually found employment in another part of the country. Today Martha celebrates her new life and her peace. She knows what it is like to live in fear and has vowed never to live that way again.

What Is Abuse?

Every fifteen seconds in the United States a woman is battered by someone who tells her he loves her. Research indicates that half of all women in this country will experience some form of violence from their partners during their relationship and that more than one-third are battered repeatedly every year. In 95 percent of these assaults, the crimes are committed by men against women.[1]

Most people do not clearly understand the word *abuse*. Visions of broken bones and black eyes are the generally held impressions. Certainly these severe physical indicators are signs of abuse; however, abuse can be much less noticeable and much more insidious. It is not uncommon for women who have completed the Austin Center for Battered Women's classes on domestic violence to approach me and confide that they have just realized that their ex-partners were abusive. They knew something was terribly wrong—they just didn't have a name for it.

To be effective advocates for battered women, we must have a working understanding of exactly what constitutes abuse. For our purposes abuse can be considered any attempt to control, manipulate, or demean another individual using physical, emotional, or sexual tactics. The terms *abuse, battering, family violence,* and *domestic violence* will be used interchangeably in this book.

Physical Abuse

Physical abuse is any use of size, strength, or presence to hurt or control someone else. Although some of these behaviors are clearly more dangerous than others, all show a lack of respect and an attempt to control the other's behavior. It is not necessary to use physical violence often to keep a partner in a constant state of fear. A batterer may actually use violence infrequently, as a last resort.

Abuse Involving Physical Contact Between People

pushing
pulling
slapping
biting

choking
shoving
grabbing
pinching
spanking
kicking
spitting
hair pulling
arm twisting
forced kneeling
burning
shooting
stabbing
restraining
backhanding
pushing into/pulling out of a car
banging partner's head on wall or floor
abuse of children
abuse of animals
hitting partner while she's pregnant
standing or sitting on partner
pinning partner against wall
forcibly carrying partner
punching with a fist
attacking with an object or a weapon
murder

Abuse Involving the Use of an Object

throwing things
breaking personal items
driving recklessly
trying to hit partner with car
slamming doors
tearing clothes
breaking objects
punching walls or doors
sweeping things off tables or from drawers
kicking furniture, car, or walls
threatening with an object
threatening with a weapon

Abuse Involving the Use of Size or Presence

chasing
unplugging phone
stalking
standing behind car to prevent driving away
taking car keys
sabotaging car
taking credit cards, money, or checkbook
trapping
clenching fists as a threat
standing in doorway to prevent exit
locking partner out of house
abandoning partner in dangerous places
refusing to help partner when she is sick, injured, or pregnant

Emotional Abuse

Emotional abuse is any use of words, voice, action, or lack of action meant to control, hurt, or demean another person. This type of abuse is usually harder to define than physical abuse. At some time in their relationship almost all couples shout or scream things that they later regret. Emotionally abusive relationships, however, are defined as involving repeated hurtful exchanges with a disregard for the partner's feelings.

While some emotionally abusive relationships do not involve physical abuse, all physically abusive relationships contain some emotional abuse. Emotional abuse is so much more than name-calling. One of the dangers of this type of abuse is that it is frequently subtle and insidious.

Many battered women describe emotional abuse as equally as, if not more, damaging as physical abuse. According to one battered woman, "If you get beaten you at least have the bruises to prove it. With emotional abuse all you know is how much it hurts inside. That's where the scars are. How can you show that to someone? It comes down to your word against his."

Types of Verbal Abuse

threatening to kill
threatening to use violence
making threats to children
accusing partner of unfaithfulness
calling names like whore, bitch, and slut
leaving nasty messages on answering machine
making insinuations
making statements like:
"You're dumb."
"You're stupid."
"You're ugly."
"You can't do anything right."
"No one else would have you."
"Whose baby is it?"
yelling
using insults
being sarcastic
name calling
withholding approval, appreciation, or affection as a punishment
sneering
growling
criticizing
ignoring
humiliating
laughing at partner
insulting family or friends
threatening family or friends

Emotionally Abusive Actions

being irresponsible with money
controlling access to money
displaying intense jealousy
isolating partner from friends and family
keeping partner up all night
checking up on partner
taking others' possessions
making faces
manipulating with lies

threatening to divorce
having affairs
constantly questioning partner about activities
not working
keeping partner from working
threatening to take custody of children
denying access to phone
threatening suicide
threatening to harm self

Sexual Abuse

Sexual abuse is any sexual behavior meant to control, manipulate, humiliate, or demean another person. This is a confusing area for many people. For too long women have been taught that sexually submitting to the husband is a wife's duty. Historically, women have had little say as to when, where, how, and with whom they engaged in sex.

Sexual violence is common in abusive relationships. Sex in these relationships is often used as a means to exert power over the female partner and to further shame and humiliate her. Frequently women are raped after a beating. Sexual deviancy, too, often occurs in these relationships. One battered woman reported being tied and bound with barbed wire while her husband and his friends repeatedly raped her.

Types of Sexual Abuse

unwanted touching
sexual name calling
unfaithfulness
false accusations
withholding sex as a punishment
forced sex with partner
hurtful sex
insisting partner dress in a more sexual way than she wants
forcing partner to strip when she doesn't want to
forced sex with someone other than partner

forcing partner to watch others
rape with object
forced sex with animals
unwanted sadistic sexual acts

Dispelling the Myths

Domestic violence, like other forms of violence against women, has long been shrouded in myths and fallacies. Many of these myths focus on the misconception that the woman has somehow caused her battering. They also serve to protect and isolate others who feel that "domestic violence could never happen to me." In addition, these myths sometimes offer comfort to rescuers who have been thwarted in their efforts to help battered women.

One of the problems for couples in abusive relationships is that they, like the general populace, believe and promote these fallacies. Dispelling these myths helps couples understand the realities of their relationship and helps abused women begin to understand how they have been blamed for their own abuse. We must shatter these myths if we hope to understand abusive relationships and to help battered women to empower themselves.

MYTH 1:

Battered women are helpless, passive, and fragile; have little or no education, no job skills, and numerous children; and are usually women of color.

FACT:

Our extensive work with battered women teaches us that, while the above may be true for some women, it is not applicable to all battered women. If anything is truly equal opportunity, it is battering. Domestic violence crosses all socioeconomic, ethnic, racial, educational, age, and religious lines.

MYTH 2:

If a battered woman doesn't leave her partner, it must be because she enjoys the abuse.

FACT:

Inherent in this myth is the notion that the battered woman is masochistic. Originating with Freud, the misconception is that the woman is receiving some sort of sexual gratification from the battering. A classic form of "victim blaming," this myth takes all responsibility for the abusive behavior from the batterer and unjustly places it upon the woman.

As a former battered woman and having worked many years with battered women, it has been my experience that battered women neither enjoy nor receive any type of sexual gratification from battering. This much we know: broken bones, bruises, shame, fear, and humiliation are not sexy!

MYTH 3:

Battered women are mentally unstable if they choose to stay in abusive relationships.

FACT:

Another form of "victim blaming," this myth oversimplifies the reasons women remain with their abusive partners. As we shall see later in this chapter, the dynamics of abusive relationships are complex and intense. And, while some battered women have mental health issues that influence their situations, this does not guarantee that they will stay with their partners.

Many battered women do exhibit behaviors that, to those of us outside the intimate relationship, may seem unusual or even bizarre. It is important to remember that, as an outsider to the abusive relationship, we are not living with the daily threat and fear of abuse or death. *These women are.* The constant threat of violence will begin to affect how a woman thinks, feels, and acts. What appear to be bizarre behaviors to us are often survival strategies women use to keep themselves safe and to control their environment to the best of their perceived abilities.

MYTH 4:

Battered women have done something to cause the battering.

FACT:

Another "victim blaming" statement, this myth places responsibility for the batterer's behavior squarely on the woman's shoulders. Most battered women spend inordinate amounts of energy trying to placate and please their abusive partners. The reality of the situation is that no one else, including the woman, is responsible for the abusive partner's behavior. Though he is unwilling to accept it, the batterer alone has that responsibility. The batterer *chooses* to abuse his partner, regardless of the woman's behavior.

MYTH 5:

Men who batter their partners are socially inept, socially inappropriate, or violent in all their relationships.

FACT:

It is a common misconception that the batterer treats people outside the abusive relationship the same as he does his partner. This is typically not the case. Many batterers exhibit a Jekyll-and-Hyde personality. Batterers can be quite charming and delightful when they want to be. This is how so many women get pulled into these relationships. Initially, the batterer may seem loving and attentive; eventually, however, his behavior becomes abusive.

This Jekyll-and-Hyde behavior also contributes to the confusion of Myth 3. If a woman gathers the courage to reach out to a friend, family member, or coworker, and that person has seen only the charming side of the batterer, the listener may find the woman's stories of abuse and terror difficult to understand. Consequently, people in whom a woman confides may experience disbelief or think there is something wrong with her. It is noteworthy that a batterer's behavior outside the abusive relationship is a good indicator of his potential for violent behavior with his partner. If he is violent with someone other than his partner, the chances of her getting seriously hurt rise tremendously.

MYTH 6:

Alcohol and drug use cause battering behavior.

FACT:

For many years it was believed that if an abusive partner curtailed his alcohol or drug use, the battering would cease. These substances were blamed for the batterer's behavior. We now know that being intoxicated or high is simply an excuse for abusive behavior, not its cause.

Certainly, many abusive relationships involve alcohol and chemical-dependency issues. Battering and chemical dependency, however, are two separate issues. Research indicates that even when a batterer quits drinking or using drugs, the battering continues.[2] He will simply find something or someone else to blame for his behavior.

MYTH 7:

Abusive relationships will never change for the better.

FACT:

The key to changing an abusive relationship is the batterer's willingness to accept responsibility for his actions. If the batterer admits to the inappropriateness of his actions, wants to change, and seeks counseling, then he has a chance to recover. If the batterer will not accept this responsibility and refuses to change, the woman's greatest chance for living nonviolently is to flee the relationship. If the woman is willing to set appropriate boundaries for herself, believes in her value and worth as a human being, and develops and utilizes the resources and support systems available to her, she has taken a giant leap toward finding peace in her life.

A word of caution to anyone who thinks she may be in an abusive relationship: abuse, whether emotional, physical, or sexual, does not just stop. In fact, unless there is some type of intervention and change, abuse will actually escalate over time, becoming more and more severe and perhaps even lethal.

MYTH 8:

Battered women grew up in abusive families.

FACT:

Many women who find themselves in abusive relationships did not grow up in violent households. Often these women come from gentle, loving families. What tends to be the standard, however, is that their families were traditionalist with a strongly held belief in prescribed feminine sexual stereotypes. And, while not all battered women saw their mothers battered or were battered as children, we are beginning to learn that a high percentage of battered women are incest survivors.

Research indicates, however, that many men who batter lived in a childhood home where violence was present. In fact, witnessing domestic violence as a child has been identified as the most common risk factor for becoming a batterer.[3] These men either saw their mothers being battered or experienced the battering themselves. They also learned, through childhood and societal conditioning, that it is acceptable to use violence against women.

The Truth About Abusive Relationships

In her book *Trauma and Recovery,* Judith Herman explains that the methods used to coerce hostages, political prisoners, survivors of concentration camps, and battered women are surprisingly similar. Batterers use a number of tactics beyond physical abuse to hold women in abusive relationships. According to Dr. Herman, the methods of establishing control over another person are grounded on the "systematic, repetitive infliction of psychological trauma." These methods of psychological control are intended to instill fear and a sense of helplessness and lower a woman's sense of self.[4]

One of the primary motivators for using abusive behaviors is to maintain power and control in the relationship. Ellen Pence, in her work *In Our Best Interest: A Process for Personal and Social Change,* outlines a series of abusive behaviors used by batterers to maintain power and control in their relationships.[5] This list of abusive behaviors includes the following:

Economic Abuse

Trying to keep her from getting or keeping a job
Making her ask for money, giving her an allowance, or taking her money

Sexual Abuse

Making her do sexual things against her will
Physically attacking the sexual parts of her body
Treating her like a sex object

Using the Children

Making her feel guilty about the children
Using the children to deliver messages
Using visitation as a way to harass her

Threats

Making or carrying out threats to do something to hurt her
Threatening to take the children, commit suicide, or report her to child welfare

Using Male Privilege

Treating her like a servant
Making all the decisions
Acting like the "king of the castle"

Intimidation

Making her fearful by using looks, actions, gestures, a loud voice, or by smashing things or destroying her property

Isolation

Controlling what she does, who she sees and talks to, or where she goes

Emotional Abuse

Putting her down or making her feel bad about herself
Calling her names
Making her think she's crazy
Playing mind games

Based on the input of more than two hundred battered women, these abusive behaviors work together to shame, humiliate, and instill fear in women so that they become less and less able to act on their own behalf.[6]

Who Is the Battered Woman?

The effects of abuse on battered women include psychological characteristics that greatly resemble those of hostages.[7] The implication here is that these characteristics are the *result of being in a life-threatening relationship*, not the reason for being in an abusive relationship.

Battering affects all types of women. However, there are some general characteristics that battered women develop in response to the abuse they suffer. Some of these are lowered self-esteem; accepting responsibility for the partner's actions; guilt; feelings of helplessness that affect how the women think, feel, and act; and denial, a survival strategy.

Lowered Self-Esteem

For many women, maintaining a positive sense of self is a daily effort. Women often begin to internalize the sexism that permeates our society and to discount their accomplishments, abilities, and self-worth. Adrienne Rich, author of *On Lies, Secrets, and Silence*, refers to this internalized sexism as self-trivialization.[8]

For women with abusive partners, this struggle with self-trivialization becomes even harder. One of the primary ways batterers maintain power and control in the relationship is by devaluing and shaming the female partner. She may begin to believe that she deserves no better because the batterer tells her exactly that. Even for women with a relatively strong sense of self, living with ongoing devaluation begins to take its toll. The female partner will eventually begin to internalize her partner's criticisms and to believe them herself.

Accepts Blame for Her Abuse

As the woman's self-esteem erodes, she is also faced with a partner who is constantly blaming her for his abusive behavior. The batterer works hard to convince the woman that the abuse is her fault. I have known women who were beaten because dinner was late, dinner was early, children were crying, children were asleep, laundry was cleaned, laundry was cleaned but not folded correctly, and a multitude of other excuses.

She increasingly accepts responsibility for her abusive partner's actions. As she may already be experiencing self-trivialization, it becomes relatively easy for her to believe that she can alter her partner's behavior if she will only change—if she can only become a better wife, mother, cook, maid, lover, or mind reader.

In reality, a woman has no control over her abusive partner's behavior. No matter what she does or does not do, the batterer *chooses* to hurt her. As she tries to appease and please her abusive partner, all to no avail, her sense of failure and hopelessness will continue to increase. Regrettably, this sense of failure further contributes to her lowered sense of self.

Guilt

A battered woman's feelings of failure contribute to and enhance her feelings of guilt. Battered women continually ask themselves, "Have I done everything I can do to make him change? Is there anything I could have done that I didn't?" Complicating this sense of failure is the fact that battered women are not allowed to express their feelings and frustrations or, if they do, they are discounted. This inability to express themselves makes abused women angry. Anger, however, is just another feeling that they are not allowed to express.

What women begin to do, then, is to internalize these feelings of anger. This volcano of feelings does not simply lie dormant. Women will begin to actually turn this anger on themselves, and it is manifested as guilt. These feelings of guilt then further erode their self-esteem, producing a vicious cycle of low self-esteem, blame, anger, and guilt.

Feelings of Helplessness and Passivity

With continued abuse women may begin to exhibit characteristics such as submissiveness, passivity, docility, dependency, and an inability to act, make decisions, or even think. Adoption of these postures is an instinctive response to a life-threatening situation. They are, in reality, survival strategies. Battered women are not really passive but, rather, develop strategies for staying alive. These survival strategies include denial, attentiveness to the batterer's wants, fondness for the batterer (accompanied by fear), fear of interference by authorities, and adoption of the batterer's perspective.

Denial and Minimization of Abuse

The battered woman's feelings of anger and fear may become so overwhelming that she turns them off in order to cope with her everyday life. She may begin to deny the seriousness of her situation or minimize the abuse she faces. Denial is a survival strategy that helps the woman cope with her abusive situation. Such denial may include these components:[9]

- Assumption that the batterer is a good man whose actions stem from problems that she can help him solve

- Denial that the abuse ever occurred
- Denial that the batterer is responsible for the abuse, which instead is attributed to external forces
- Belief that she is the instigator of the abuse and thus deserves the punishment
- Denial that she would be able to survive without the batterer's support (emotional or financial)
- Belief that marriage and/or following the beliefs of her religion, which may tell her to obey her husband, are more important than her personal welfare

We frequently talk to women who claim they are not battered women because the abuse they suffered didn't require a trip to the hospital. In one case, I spoke with a woman whose husband had pointed a loaded gun to her head. She minimized the violence of this act by explaining that because he hadn't hit her she really wasn't an abused woman.

Who Is the Batterer?

We know that batterers come in all shapes and sizes, professions, educational backgrounds, religious affiliations, and ethnic backgrounds. However, batterers do have some characteristics in common, including a belief in the use of violence, the use of defense mechanisms to justify abusive behaviors, pathological jealousy, and a dual personality.

Belief in the Use of Violence

Men who batter do so because they can and it works. Abusive men have received the message that violence against women is acceptable behavior. This message may come from a variety of sources including the childhood family and our society. When societal institutions such as the judicial system do not hold men accountable for their violence, they actually collude with the batterers to perpetuate the violence.

Defense Mechanisms

Typically, the batterer will not accept responsibility for his actions and develops a number of defense mechanisms to explain why he batters. These defense mechanisms include the following:

- *Rationalization*
  "I just wanted her to listen to me."
- *Denial—Minimizing*
  "I only pushed her."
- *Denial—Claiming loss of control*
  "A man can only take so much."
- *Blaming*
  "If she hadn't provoked me . . ."

Batterers not only deny responsibility for their actions, but they also often deny that any type of abusive behavior has taken place. It is not unusual to hear women say that after a severe beating they were told that it never happened and that they had imagined the whole thing. Women are encouraged by their batterers to question their own judgments and realities. "Don't you remember falling down the stairs?" a batterer may ask. Batterers will tell them they must be losing their minds. After awhile, they begin to feel like they are.

Jealousy

The abusive partner is jealous of any relationships the woman has, including those with other men, women, children, and even pets. Anything that takes time away from him is seen as a threat. One of the greatest fears a batterer has is the fear that his partner will abandon him. This manifests itself in extreme jealousy and possessiveness. He believes that if he can completely control her, she won't leave. Batterers rely so heavily on their partners that they are willing to do anything to keep them from leaving—even maiming or killing them. It is not uncommon for batterers to become severely depressed, even suicidal, if they think their partner is going to leave.

To feel secure, the batterer must be overly involved with his partner. Constantly monitoring her time, not allowing her free time to be with others, and questioning her about her whereabouts are just a few of the ways a batterer will monitor his partner. Women have shared stories with me about batterers who would take them to work, pick them up for lunch, pick them up after work, and call throughout the day to make sure they were there. And, although they may be constantly monitored, abused women are still accused of being unfaithful.

In one particularly brutal relationship, a batterer placed a tape recorder under their bed so he could monitor his wife while he was out of town. There was a television in their bedroom, and the recorder picked up the sitcom the woman watched. When the batterer returned from his trip and listened to the recording, he didn't hear the television show; rather, he heard her with another man. Although she desperately tried to make him realize it was the television he was hearing, he refused to be convinced. She received several severe batterings because of her "infidelity."

Another reason for such constant manipulation of the woman's time and energy is the batterer's need to isolate her and make her dependent on him. If the woman's support system is reduced, or even destroyed, her dependency on him increases. The more she is tied to him, the greater her dependency and the less likely she is to leave him. Remember, this is one of his greatest fears.

Dual Personality

Batterers typically present a different personality outside the home than they do inside, which complicates a woman's ability to describe her experiences to people outside the relationship. It also helps to keep her tied to the relationship. The batterer does not always batter: many have periods when they can be very generous with their affection. The woman has seen this and knows that her partner is capable of being loving to her. If she could only get him to change and maintain this loving side on a constant basis, she may reason, their relationship would be better. Thus, much of her time is spent trying to be the "perfect" wife and mother so that the batterer will continually exhibit his loving side. Unfortunately, this is a setup for her; the batterer will choose or choose not to batter her, regardless of her actions.

The Cycle of Abuse

According to Lenore Walker, author of *The Battered Woman,* violent relationships are not always violent but, rather, often follow a three-phase cycle: tension-building, acute-battering, and what I call "remorseful." Unless the cycle is broken, the violence will escalate, in both frequency and severity. The following is a description of the cycle:[10]

PHASE I—The Tension-Building Phase

- Less lethal forms of battering occur.
- The woman senses the tension and tries to placate the abusive partner to prevent the abuse.
- The woman minimizes the minor incidents and blames herself for her partner's behavior.
- The woman denies that the tension will escalate to more severe battering although it may have happened before.

PHASE II—The Acute-Battering Phase

- The batter's rage escalates dramatically.
- Both the batterer and the woman accept the myth that he can't control his anger.
- Severe injuries occur as a result of the battering.
- The woman experiences shock and disbelief that the incident has occurred.

PHASE III—The Remorseful Phase

- The batterer expresses contrition over his behavior and makes promises to change.
- The batterer is charming and loving.
- The batterer offers gifts (flowers, jewelry, perfume, candy) to apologize for his behavior.
- The batterer begins to elicit feelings of guilt and sympathy from the woman.
- The batterer generates confirmation of his loving behavior from others.

- The woman's desire to believe he will change and the batterer's temporarily changed behavior reinforce her desire to stay in the relationship.

It is important to note that this cycle is not present in all violent relationships. When present, however, these three phases of abuse vary from couple to couple in terms of intensity and length of time in each phase. It is the third phase, however, that tends to be the most insidious, as it is in this phase that the woman is given false hope. The abused woman wants to believe that her partner can and will change. He is giving her every indication, both verbally and through his actions, that he intends to change. It is during this phase that batterers often agree to counseling, only to claim they are "fixed" after attending a few sessions. Unfortunately, unless the batterer makes a conscious effort to change or the woman flees the relationship, the abuse will continue.

How to Identify a Potential Batterer

I am often asked how a woman can determine whether the man she is involved with is potentially abusive. Following is a list of behaviors that are seen in people who abuse their intimate partners. The last four behaviors are almost always seen in batterers. If the person exhibits more than three of these warning signs, there is a strong potential for abuse in the relationship. A batterer may exhibit only a couple of these behaviors, but they may be quite exaggerated. For example, the person may demonstrate extreme jealousy over a woman's relationship with her sister.

1. JEALOUSY
   A batterer will say that his jealousy is a sign of love. In reality, jealousy has nothing to do with love. It is a sign of insecurity and possessiveness. A batterer may question the woman about who she talks to, accuse her of flirting, or be jealous of the time she spends with family, friends, or children. As the jealousy progresses, he may call her frequently during the day or drop by unexpectedly at her home or office. He may refuse to let her work for fear she will meet someone, and he may even go so far as to check her car mileage or ask friends and coworkers to watch her.

2. CONTROLLING BEHAVIOR

   The batterer will claim that his controlling behavior is due to his concern for the woman's welfare. He will be angry if the woman is "late" and question her closely about where she went and whom she talked to. As this behavior worsens, he may not let the woman make personal decisions about the house, her appearance, the children, or going to church. He may keep all the money or even make her ask permission to leave the house or use the telephone.

3. QUICK INVOLVEMENT

   Many battered women dated or knew their abuser for less than six months before they were engaged or living together. The batterer comes on quickly, claiming "love at first sight," and will tell the woman flattering things such as "You're the only person I could ever love." He needs someone desperately and will pressure the woman to commit to him.

4. UNREALISTIC EXPECTATIONS

   The batterer is dependent on the woman for all his needs. He expects her to be the perfect wife, mother, lover, and friend. He will say things like, "You're the only person I need in my life." She is expected to take care of everything for him, both emotionally and in the home.

5. ISOLATION

   The batterer will attempt to diminish and destroy the woman's support system. If she has male friends, she is accused of being a "whore." If she has female friends, she is accused of being a "lesbian." If she is close to her family, she is accused of being "tied to the apron strings." He will accuse people who are close to her of "causing trouble." He may want to isolate her geographically by moving far into the country and not having a telephone. He may not let her use the car or may try to keep her from working or attending school.

6. BLAMES OTHERS FOR HIS PROBLEMS

   If the batterer is chronically unemployed, he will accuse others of doing him wrong. He may make mistakes and then blame the woman for upsetting him and keeping him from concentrating or doing his job. For almost anything that goes wrong, he will tell the woman she is to blame.

7. BLAMES OTHERS FOR HIS FEELINGS

   The batterer will tell the woman, "You made me mad," "You're hurting me when you don't do what I ask," or "I can't help being angry." He actually makes the decision about what he thinks and feels, but he uses those feelings to manipulate the woman.

8. HYPERSENSITIVITY

   The batterer is easily insulted. He claims his "feelings are hurt" when he's really angry. He takes the slightest setbacks as personal attacks. He will rage about the injustices that happen to him, things that actually are a part of life, such as being asked to work overtime, getting a traffic ticket, or being asked to help around the house.

9. CRUELTY TO ANIMALS OR CHILDREN

   The batterer may brutally punish animals or be insensitive to their pain or suffering. He may expect children to be capable of doing things far beyond their ability and then punish them when they do not meet his expectations. For example, he may spank a two-year-old for wetting a diaper. He may tease children until they cry. He may not want the children to eat at the table or expect them to stay in their rooms while he is at home.

10. "PLAYFUL" USE OF FORCE IN SEX

    The batterer may like to throw the woman down and hold her during sex. He may want to act out sexual fantasies in which the woman is helpless. He may show little concern about whether the woman wants to have sex and use sulking or anger to manipulate her into compliance. He may start having sex with the woman while she is sleeping or demand sex when she is ill or tired.

11. VERBAL ABUSE

    In additional to saying things that are meant to be cruel and hurtful, verbal abuse includes degrading the woman, cursing her, or discounting her accomplishments. The batterer may tell the woman that she's stupid and unable to function without him. He may wake her up to verbally abuse her or not allow her to go to sleep.

12. RIGID SEX ROLES

The batterer may expect the woman to serve and obey him. The batterer will view women as inferior to men and believe that a woman is not a whole person without a relationship with a man.

13. JEKYLL-AND-HYDE PERSONALITY

Many women are confused by their batterers' mood changes. One minute he's nice; the next he explodes. This does not necessarily mean he has mental problems. Explosiveness and mood swings are typical of men who abuse their partners, and these behaviors are related to such other characteristics as hypersensitivity.

14. PAST BATTERING

The batterer may say he has hit women in the past but that they made him do it. The woman may hear from relatives or ex-partners that the man is abusive. A batterer who minimizes what he has done to a previous partner is likely to be violent with his current partner. Battering behavior does not just go away.

15. THREATS OF VIOLENCE

Threats of violence include any threat of physical force meant to control the woman. Most men do not threaten their partners, but a batterer will try to excuse this behavior by saying that "everybody talks like that."

16. BREAKING OR STRIKING OBJECTS

The batterer may break things, beat on tables or walls with his fist, or throw objects around or near the woman. Such behavior is used as a punishment, but its primarily function is to terrorize the woman into submission.

17. ANY FORCE DURING AN ARGUMENT

The batterer may use force during arguments, including holding the woman down, physically restraining her from leaving the room, and pushing and shoving. For example, he may hold her against a wall and say, "You're going to listen to me."[11]

The Lethal Nature of Abusive Relationships

Without effective early intervention, abuse in relationships can escalate in severity and sometimes lead to death. When domestic violence results in murder, it is often a reflection of the community's failure to recognize the severity and potential fatal consequences of the problem and to address its role in early intervention.

When battered women are killed by their partners, it frequently occurs after they have been separated from them or have taken other action to end the relationship. Women who leave their abusive partners are at a 75 percent greater risk of being killed than those who stay.[12]

Since our society continues to question why women stay in abusive relationships, it is crucial that we consider how dangerous and difficult it is for a battered woman to leave. Many women stay because of a reasonable fear that they will suffer severe injury or death if they attempt to end the relationship.

Unfortunately, when a batterer murders his partner, the tragedy is often portrayed as an unintentional "crime of passion" caused by the man's overwhelming love for the woman. Murder is, however, the ultimate expression of the batterer's need to control his partner's behavior.

Research indicates that when women kill it is much more likely to be in self-defense than when men kill.[13] Battered women who resort to homicide have tried, often repeatedly and unsuccessfully, to obtain protection from their batterers. Only a very small percent of battered women kill their abusers to end the violence.

CHAPTER 2

The Effects of Family Violence on Children

Children who live in homes where there is family violence live in fear, confusion and pain. A lot of our work is to help create a sense of safety for these children—safety to express themselves, safety to be themselves, and safety from abuse and fear. My hope is to give these things to them so that they may give it to their children and stop the cycle.

—Melinda Cantu, Director of Children's Services,
Austin Center for Battered Women

If the family household is a nightmare for abused women, it is even more so for their children. For any child living in violence the basic need for a safe, secure home goes unmet. Children of battered women are victims, regardless of whether or not they are the direct recipients of violent acts. It is estimated that approximately 3.3 million children in the United States between three and seventeen years of age are at risk of exposure to family violence.[1]

The violence that children are exposed to can take several forms. One form of abuse often seen in children from violent families is sexual abuse. This type of abuse has been explored at length by numerous authors and will not be discussed in this chapter. A variety of readings on this subject can be found in the *Additional Resources* section of this book.

Children may also be physically abused by their parents. Approximately 70 percent of the men who abuse their female partners also abuse their children. As violence against women becomes more severe and frequent in the home, children experience a 300 percent increase in physical violence by the male batterer.[2] In fact, the breaking point for many battered women is when the batterer begins abusing the children. At this point, many women attempt to leave.[3]

Reports by battered mothers indicate that 87 percent of children witness the abuse.[4] Events can be witnessed in many ways. Children may hear their mother's screams or crying, the batterer's threats, glass breaking, or wood splintering. They may see the aftermath of abuse in the form of torn clothes, their mother's injuries, broken furniture, or wounded animals. Children who witness abuse suffer extreme emotional trauma and react with shock, fear, and guilt.

Children's lives are frequently disrupted by moves to escape domestic violence. They may lose considerable school time; flee their homes without taking books, money, or clothing; and live in the family car when shelters are unavailable. Many children of battered women who move to new school districts are unable to enroll in school if they lack birth certificates, immunization records, and other paperwork that was left behind when they and their mothers fled. Batterers, as part of their control of the family, frequently destroy such documents.

Characteristics of Children Living in Violent Homes

Children raised in violent homes learn many lessons. They learn how to keep family secrets. They learn how to get what they want through aggression and manipulation. They learn that people who love you hurt you. They learn that violence, albeit painful, is an acceptable part of life.

Children's responses to living with violence will vary according to their age, gender, stage of development, and role in the family. Many other factors play a part, such as the extent and frequency of the violence, repeated separations and moves, socioeconomic status, and special needs of the children independent of the violence. We do know, however, that the reactions of children exposed to family violence may include disruptions of normal developmental patterns that result in emotional, behavioral, and cognitive problems.[5]

General Characteristics

Regardless of their age, children living with domestic violence tend to have a strong sense of isolation and helplessness. Their initial method of solving problems is by hitting. They suffer from an extremely high level of anxiety and tend to have developmental delays. As the children mature, their degree of sympathy toward the mother diminishes and may be replaced by overt hostility.

In their book *Children of Battered Women,* Peter Jaffe, David Wolfe, and Susan Wilson list a series of behaviors that can be found in children who witness domestic violence. These characteristics include the following:[6]

1. A combination of limited tolerance for frustration, poor impulse control, and externalized or internalized anger
2. Sadness, depression, stress disorders, and psychosomatic complaints
3. Absences from school, pre-delinquent and delinquent behavior
4. Sexual acting out, running away, isolation, loneliness and fear
5. A combination of poor impulse control and continual hopefulness that the situation will improve
6. Poor definition of self or a definition of self in parenting role (role reversal)
7. Low self-esteem; sees self and siblings with few options or expectations to succeed
8. Increased social isolation, increased peer isolation, or complete identification with peers
9. Poor social skills
10. Feelings of powerlessness
11. Constant fear and terror for their life as well as for their parents
12. Confusion and insecurity
13. Increasing deception including lying, stealing, and cheating
14. Poor definition of personal boundaries and of others' personal boundaries
15. Little or no understanding of the dynamics of violence and, often, an assumption that violence is the norm
16. Self-blame (depending on the age) for family violence, separations, divorce, and internal conflicts
17. Frequent participation in maiming or killing animals or battering siblings

18. May use violence as a problem-solving technique in school, with peers, and with family
19. Poor sexual image, uncertainty about appropriate behavior, and immaturity in peer relationships
20. Heightened suicide risks and attempts including increased thoughts of suicide or of murdering parents

Infants

An infant who is raised in a violent family has the basic need for attachment to the mother seriously disrupted. Routines around sleeping and feeding may be anything but normal. The abused mother may be unable to handle the stressful demands of her infant. This distancing is recognized by the child and causes serious separation anxiety.

The early parent-child relationship sets the stage for the child's future relationships. If this early relationship is characterized by trust, consistency, and nurturing, the child's ability to develop positive relationships with others is greatly enhanced. If, however, early parent-child relationships are marked by fear, inconsistency, and unmet physical and psychological needs, the child's future relationships are likely to be poorly formed. Such children also exhibit a higher frequency of behavioral and emotional problems.[7]

Infants and young toddlers may be injured in a battering incident by being caught between their parents. They may be accidentally hit, pushed, or dropped during a violent episode. The mother may hold an infant for his or her own safety, but quickly discover that the batterer has no regard for the baby's physical or emotional safety.

Physical symptoms displayed by infants from violent homes often include a propensity for illnesses, irritability, and difficulty sleeping.

Toddlers and Preschool Age Children

Small children may feel responsible for the violence that is occurring in their home, and yet be open to discuss this violence. They may suffer severe separation anxiety and be reluctant to leave their mother. These children are often irritable, express somatic complaints, and are fearful of being alone. They may also regress to earlier stages of functioning.

Elementary School Age Children

By elementary school, gender-related differences in children's reactions to family violence begin to emerge. These children look to their parents as role models. Boys who witness violence quickly learn that violence is an appropriate way of resolving conflict. Boys from violent homes are frequently described as being disruptive, acting aggressively toward objects and people, and throwing severe temper tantrums.[8]

Girls may learn that victimization is inevitable and that no one can help change this vicious pattern. They develop an increasing assortment of somatic complaints and are more likely to display withdrawn, passive, clinging, and dependent behavior.[9]

Children may practice what they have learned at home by fighting at school or in the neighborhood. These externalized behavior problems will undermine their adjustment to school and create consequences that will serve to aggravate an already volatile home environment.

For elementary school age children, exposure to abuse may also lead to significant emotional difficulties. These children may live in shame, embarrassed by the family secret. Their experiences may undermine their self-esteem and confidence. And they may have few opportunities for activities outside the family because of the batterer's domination and control.

These children may experience guilt out of a belief that perhaps they could prevent the violence. If only they were better children, maybe their father wouldn't be so upset with their mother. They are often confused by the violence and have a divided sense of loyalty in desiring to protect their mother, but still respecting and fearing their father.

When children reach school age, teachers may recognize one or more of the following warning signs of physical abuse. While one or two of these signs are not necessarily an indication of abuse at home, a child displaying several of these signs should make a teacher suspicious.[10]

- Having dirty clothing, body odor, or an unkempt appearance
- Having an unexplained injury
- Acting shy, withdrawn, or too eager to cooperate
- Arriving at school early and leaving late
- Not wanting to go home

- Wearing long-sleeved clothes in warm weather
- Talking about abuse
- Acting nervous, too active, or destructive
- Acting fearful of being touched by an adult
- Being absent from school with poor or no excuses
- Showing little hope of being comforted when in trouble
- Always searching for favors, food, or services
- Having difficulty in getting along with other children

Teenagers

During adolescence, children begin to develop intimate relationships outside their families and can practice the communication patterns they have learned. For some teenagers it is the beginning of violence within their own dating relationships. For adolescent girls it may be a turning point in which they start to accept threats and violence from boyfriends.

Many teenagers have lived with violence in their families for years. In seeking independence and relief from family violence, some teenagers decide that running away may be an escape. Most interviews with runaway children and teenagers point to family violence as a major factor in the decision to leave home.[11]

Some teenagers begin to act out their anger and frustration in ways that result in delinquencies and the interventions of the juvenile justice system. Some teenage boys handle their frustrations by exhibiting the behavior that has been most clearly modeled for them, that is, by battering their mothers or siblings.

Other teenagers take on additional responsibilities to keep the peace and provide safety for their families. Older teens, especially girls and those with younger siblings, may assume parenting responsibility. They may protect younger siblings during violent episodes and offer reassurance in the aftermath of the violence. These adolescents may feel they cannot leave home because they must protect their mothers and siblings. Obviously, such responsibilities are a heavy burden for these youngsters.

Behaviors to Expect from Children in Crisis

Children exposed to family violence may or may not be able to talk about their feelings and concerns. Children's behaviors are, however, good indicators of how well they are coping. New problem behaviors are not unusual for children in crisis. All children exhibit these behaviors at some time; however, concern for the child is necessary if the level of the behavior is extreme.

Some behaviors to look for in a child in crisis include the following:[12]

- Loss of appetite or any change in eating patterns
- Sleep disturbances such as nightmares and restlessness
- School problems such as refusing to attend, truancy, or a drop in performance
- Withdrawal
- Clinging to mother or siblings
- Shyness
- Fear of the dark
- Increased violent behavior such as kicking, hitting, and fighting
- Verbal abuse or talking back
- Regression such as bed-wetting, wanting a bottle, baby talk, and thumb sucking
- Inappropriate responses to discipline
- Temper tantrums
- Whining
- Oversensitivity
- Role reversal such as taking on a parenting role
- Testing and pushing limits as far as possible
- Stealing
- Lying
- Irregularity or diarrhea

Post-traumatic Stress Disorder in Children

Children exposed to family violence exhibit symptoms similar to those suffering from post-traumatic stress disorder. PTSD is classified as a type of anxiety disorder by the American Psychiatric Association. The disorder may have an onset at any age following exposure to a psychologically traumatic event that is generally outside the range of typical human experience.

Criteria for PTSD include the following:[13]

1. Existence of a stress or that would create significant symptoms of distress in almost anyone
2. Reexperiencing the trauma as evidenced by a least one of the following: recurrent recollections of the event, recurrent dreams of the event, sudden acting or feeling as if the traumatic event were recurring because of an association with an environmental stimulus
3. Numbing of responsiveness to or reduced involvement with the external world, beginning some time after the trauma, as shown by at least one of the following: markedly diminished interest in one or more significant activities, feeling of detachment or estrangement from others
4. At least two of the following symptoms that were not present before the trauma: hyperalertness or exaggerated startle response, sleep disturbances, guilt about surviving when others have not or about behavior required for survival, memory impairment or trouble concentrating, avoidance of activities that arouse recollection of the traumatic event, intensification of symptoms by exposure to events that symbolize or resemble the traumatic event

Information presented throughout this chapter indicates that many of the reactions of children from violent families can be classified as responses to trauma. Children who live with violence may also display emotional symptoms that are quite removed from the initial trauma. Such symptoms may not be readily detectable as PTSD because they may be expressed in a manner that disguises their origin such as running away, truancy, or dating violence.

Children's emotional development is closely connected to the safety and nurturing provided by the family environment. Children of violent families suffer a loss of faith that there is order and continuity in their lives. Normally, the family plays a crucial role in protecting children from traumatization and assisting in recovery when necessary. Children of violent families, however, are traumatized *because* of the family environment.

Positive Adjustment in Children

Not all children who live with violence exhibit developmental difficulties. Research indicates that several factors contribute to a child's resiliency in coping with family violence. These factors can be grouped into three areas:[14]

1. Dispositional attributes of the child (such as the ability to adjust to new situations)
2. Support within the family system (as from relatives or among siblings)
3. Support persons outside the family system (as from neighbors or teachers)

There is also evidence that children's coping reactions can vary as a function of their developmental stage. Research with toddlers and preschoolers indicates that disruptions in their normal family functioning are associated with problem behaviors inside and outside the home.[15] While family disruption certainly has a negative influence on older children's social interactions, it has been suggested that these children are better able to cope with the stress because of their use of peers and schools as sources of information and support.[16]

CHAPTER 3

Teen Dating Violence

Eddie's got a fast car.
And he drives me to school.
My friends think he's cool.
And they wish they were me.
But they don't see when he hits me.
Or screams and calls me names.
Eddie's got a fast car.
Today he picked me up for school.
And we had another fight.
And he pushed my face into the dash.
And I'm confused and I'm scared.
Because tomorrow morning I'll wake up.
And I'll look out my window.
And he'll be sitting there.
And I'll have to get in.
Eddie's got a fast car.[1]

Battering finally received recognition as a serious social problem in the 1970s. Almost nothing was known, however, about teen dating violence. In her book *Dating Violence: Young Women in Danger*, therapist and battered women's advocate Barrie Levy explains that when she talked about violence as something teenagers "might encounter when they grew up and had intimate relationships or got married, or about violence they may have witnessed between their parents, some of the young women revealed they currently or had already experienced violence from their adolescent boyfriends."[2]

Numerous studies in the 1980s confirmed what Levy suspected. Young women were in danger from their teenage boyfriends and in such high numbers as to elicit shock from the research community. Approximately one out of ten high school students experiences physical violence in dating relationships. Among college students, the figure rises to 22 percent.[3]

Levy defines abuse in teenage dating relationships as "a pattern of repeated actual or threatened acts that physically, sexually or verbally abuse a member of an unmarried heterosexual or homosexual couple in which one or both partners is between thirteen and twenty years old."[4] Dating violence is not unique to any particular class, community, or ethnic group or to heterosexual women. It appears to be prevalent in all communities.

Nor is dating violence a new phenomenon. As early as 1957, Eugene Kanin reported that 62 percent of women surveyed had been victims of sexually aggressive acts during their last year of high school dating. In 44 percent of those cases, the offender was either her steady boyfriend or her fiancé. For 21 percent of those women, the sexually aggressive act was attempted or completed rape.[5]

Among high school and college students, abuse is more likely in a serious, rather than a casual, dating relationship.[6] The violence often begins when the couple perceives that they have entered into a monogamous relationship. This stage of the relationship appears to elicit expectations tied to sexual stereotypes, including the male's right to control his partner and the female's obligation to yield to his wishes. Teenagers involved in violent dating relationships also appear to express a greater acceptance of violence in marriages.[7]

Abusive Versus Healthy Dating Relationships

Many teenagers perceive jealousy, possessiveness, and abuse as "normal" in intimate relationships. Normal, that is, to the extent that abuse happens so often that it is an expected or accepted way to express love.[8] And many teenagers actually consider sexual coercion or hitting justifiable under certain circumstances.[9] In several studies, young men reported that their violence served the purpose to "intimidate," "frighten," or "force the other to give me something."[10] These claims are much bolder than those of violent adult men. Violent husbands, for example, rarely admit that their aggression is manipulative, but rely heavily on "out of control" justifications such as alcohol, drugs, anger, and stress.[11]

There is some indication that young women think violence has a bad effect on their relationships, whether they are hit or the ones who do the hitting. Young men, whether they are the abusers or the abused, believe that violence has either a positive effect or no impact at all on their relationships.[12]

According to Patricia Occhiuzzo Giggans, executive director of the Los Angeles Commission on Assaults Against Women, "Dating and courtship among teenagers today have an injurious and at times, potentially lethal, dimension. It has become evident that one of the main reasons for this [development] is that our children do not have a clear sense of what constitutes a 'healthy relationship.' It is frightening to hear how many teens, from all economic, racial and cultural backgrounds express how 'normal' physical, psychological and sexual control is within their own dating relationships and in those of their friends."[13]

Nurturing love incorporates a wish that the loved one will grow, flourish, and develop to his or her fullest potential. This implies that each partner receives and encourages pleasure in other close friendships and independent activities. In unhealthy love, one or both partners believe they cannot survive without the other. The desire to be together every minute develops into a need or demand for the partner to be continually available.[14]

Teenagers often mistake jealousy as a sign of love. There appears to be some confusion about the difference between jealousy and concern. Concern refers to caring for another person and focusing on the partner's well-being and needs. Concern does not involve controlling behaviors. Jealousy, on the other hand, refers to suspicions about rivalry and infidelity. Jealousy involves the fear of losing something, which implies ownership—and people do not own one another. Jealousy can lead to inappropriate and abusive behaviors in the attempt to guard a possession. If a person is viewed as a possession, that person is not being respected as a human being.[15]

A healthy relationship is an ongoing process involving commitment, flexibility, respect, and honesty. When someone chooses to share his or her life with us, we are being offered a gift. We should value this gift and all the beauty and challenges that accompany it.

Similarities to Adult Abusive Relationships

Patterns of abuse in teen dating relationships are similar to those in adult battering relationships. They involve the same elements of control and jealousy, enforced by emotional and physical abuse. Teenagers and adult battered women describe the same range of violent experiences, from slaps and shoves to beatings and attacks with weapons.

Each year, an alarming number of young women are murdered by their boyfriends. Approximately 20 percent of female homicide victims are between the ages of fifteen and twenty-four. Typically, after these tragedies occur, investigation into the dating relationships reveals patterns of control and physical abuse.[16]

The violence in teen dating relationships, however, is not always physical. Many young women are severely emotionally damaged by partners who continually demean and control them. Teenage batterers use a variety of threats to enforce their demands. Direct threats are made against the girlfriend or her family. A batterer's suicide threats can be terrifying to a young woman, especially when the abusive partner has made previous attempts. Batterers may intimidate their partners by threatening to expose embarrassing secrets, often regarding her sexual behavior.

A batterer may force his girlfriend to steal money from her parents or give him money she has earned. Some young women have been coerced by boyfriends to engage in illegal acts, such as shoplifting, prostitution, and drug dealing. Threats to report her illegal activity add to the batterer's ability to control the young woman.[17]

Teenage batterers, like their adult counterparts, refuse to accept responsibility for their actions and blame their partners for the abuse. Often the teenager's behavior is blamed on jealousy. Almost any action on the young woman's part—whether talking to another young man, not being home when the boyfriend calls, or going out with girlfriends—is labeled as provocative. Both high school and college students view jealousy as a major cause of dating violence. Uncontrollable anger has also been cited as a primary cause of dating violence.[18]

Teenagers report that conflicts about sex often lead to violence.[19] Date rape accounts for 67 percent of the sexual assaults reported by high school and college women. Young women between the ages of fourteen and seventeen represent an estimated 38 percent of those victimized by date rape.[20] Repeated sexual assault and sexual coercion in intimate relationships contributes to feelings of worthlessness, humiliation, and shame that gradually undermine a young woman's ability to escape.

It is often difficult for young women to even identify sexual abuse in their relationships. This may be due to their inexperience and limited education about sexuality. This lack of recognition may also be a result of a tolerance for sexual assault when it is associated with romantic involvement.

Young women with more traditional values have reported that they are more accepting of forcible rape as well as less sure of what constitutes rape.[21] Young women may also feel that it is useless to try to stop a partner intent on rape. One study found that one of every six women interviewed reported that they believed that when a man became sexually aroused, it was impossible to stop him or for him to stop himself.[22]

Unique Aspects of Teen Dating Violence

While young couples in violent relationships share some commonalties with their older counterparts, there are several youth-specific aspects to their relationships. Pressure to conform to peer group norms contributes to an emphasis on having a dating partner. Peer pressure can be intense, and the fear of being different or of violating peer group norms can create rigid conformity or enormous stress.

Definitions of what is "normal" masculine or feminine behavior are often extreme and fit stereotyped patterns of dominance and passivity.[23] Frequently, teenage boys will begin to establish such patterns when their violent dating behaviors are reinforced by members of their peer group and society as a whole.

Expectations of a girlfriend may include that the young woman give up activities and other relationships in order to give priority to her boyfriend. Female socialization may also lead a young woman to assume responsibility for solving problems within the relationship.[24] Expectations of a boyfriend may include that he be sexually aggressive, make all the decisions in the relationship, and control his girlfriend's activities and behavior.

Teenagers have fewer resources and much less mobility than do most adults. If they are members of a minority group or are poor, their lack of power and access to resources is compounded. Young women are often unable to avoid the abusers because they attend the same school. They are not free to move out of their neighborhoods or change schools. This contributes to a young woman's feelings of fear and entrapment.

While young women are more likely than young men to talk to someone about their violent relationships, there is a hesitancy to talk to teachers, counselors, clergy members, and law enforcement officers. Instead, young women tend to seek out friends and, to a lesser degree, family members for help. In one study, 25 percent of high school students told no one, only 26 percent told their parents, and 66 percent reported the abuse to friends.[25]

Young women may feel that seeking help from adults would be pointless, especially when societal institutions have not addressed the problem or communicated a willingness or ability to respond. Teenage hesitancy to seek help from parents may be due to the fact that they are struggling for independence and want to solve problems themselves or with their peers. They may fear, justified or not, that if told of the abuse, their parents would curtail their independence and control future decisions about their relationships or other aspects of their lives. In addition, the isolation, shame, and fear a young woman experiences may also prevent her from reaching out to those who could help.

Barri Rosenbluth, coordinator of the Teen Dating Violence Project at the Austin Center for Battered Women, explains that even when young women do reach out, some families do not take the problem seriously. Sometimes they will pressure the young couple to stay together, especially if they have a child. Other adults may assume that their daughters are overreacting, acting out, or going through a phase. Some parents minimize the bonding that takes place between teenagers and expect them to easily break off a dating relationship. School personnel may become impatient with their misbehavior and, without recognizing the danger the young woman faces, insist that such behavior not be displayed at school.[26]

Adults have access to legal and social services that may be unavailable to teenagers. If available, they may be accessed only if parents or guardians are involved in the action. This is a barrier for many youth who resist telling their parents or other adults about the abuse. Many battered women's centers cannot shelter teenagers unless they are emancipated. *Emancipation* is usually defined as maintaining a separate residence from the parents or having a child.

Teenagers may not take legal action in their own name, and few states permit minors to use civil and criminal laws that specifically relate to domestic violence. In other states, such general laws as civil harassment statutes can sometimes be applied. Few laws exist, however, that protect teenagers from abusive dating relationships. Temporary restraining orders may be unavailable to young women unless the application is made by the parents.

Special At-Risk Populations

Special circumstances exist for many young women that make them vulnerable to dating violence. Pregnant teenagers, young women of color, and gay and lesbian youth are especially at risk for relationship violence.

Pregnant Teens

Both adult and teenage women are at greater risk for violence when they are pregnant.[27] Studies of battered women report that from 25 to 60 percent of the women were abused during pregnancy.[28] In an informal survey of more than two hundred pregnant teenagers in several large metropolitan areas, 26 percent reported they were in a relationship with a male partner who was physically abusive. Sixty-five percent of those abused had not talked with anyone about the abuse, and none had reported the abuse to law enforcement agencies.[29]

Abuse during pregnancy includes blows to the abdomen, injuries to the breasts and genitals, and sexual assault. Abused women suffer a higher number of miscarriages than do nonbattered women. Batterers may even prevent or sabotage their partners from obtaining appropriate medical care.

In addition to the injuries young women sustain, negative health effects are visible in low infant birthweight. The percentage of low birthweight infants is approximately twice as high among battered women as compared to nonbattered women.[30]

Teens of Color

Evelyn White, author of *Chain Chain Change: For Black Women Dealing with Physical and Emotional Abuse,* explains that young women of color are especially vulnerable to dating violence.[31] According to White, "Young black girls get conflicting messages about their identities. A girl's identity is not just based on who or what she believes she is, but also what society tells black girls they are. This is extremely painful because I believe that the first message black girls get is that they aren't good enough. . . . It is the rare black girl who can develop her own identity outside the external societal forces, both black and white, that tell her what she should be. . . . I think that this inability to find our own voice, our own being, keeps black girls vulnerable to the demands and expectations of others that are so prevalent in abusive relationships."[32]

If a young woman feels that her options for success are limited by racism, she may depend on the dating relationship to define her future. These feelings may keep her tied to her abusive partner. If she does seek help, she may expect to be blamed or not taken seriously. In addition, she may be unwilling to discuss her problems because of the protectiveness that comes from understanding the struggles of her boyfriend in a racist society.[33]

Young women from Asian and Pacific Island communities, in which dating and sexuality are possible sources of shame, are also vulnerable to dating violence. According to Mieko Yoshihama, Asha Parekh, and Doris Boyington, "The low status they hold in the traditional Asian/Pacific family hierarchy as children and as females, compounded with a culturally based emphasis on maintaining harmony even if it is at the cost of the individual's well-being, continues to discourage these teenagers from asserting their rights and needs. Because of their powerless position, their needs as victims may remain unaddressed."[34]

Like their Anglo peers, Asian/Pacific teenagers often remain silent regarding their violent relationships. Young women who do seek help are often assaulted a second time because of the insensitivity and discriminatory behavior of their families, their communities, and the professionals they turn to for help.[35]

In most Asian/Pacific cultures, dating issues and sexuality are considered taboo and are not discussed. A young woman who has been dating or has been sexually active loses her respectability according to the traditional values of her community. These teenagers face the burden of keeping both the violence and the dating relationship secret from their parents. The shame and guilt associated with dating intensifies the teenagers' feelings of being responsible for the violence.[36]

Not only is it difficult for them to turn to the family for support, but many young women may believe that seeking professional help will only create problems by bringing more shame to their families. A cultural value that is shared by most Asian/Pacific cultures is that of enduring and suffering without complaint. Both men and women value silence and acceptance as a way of handling difficulties with pride. There is pressure to keep silent in order to prevent family shame. This presents a dilemma for young women for whom the pains and concerns of the moment are demanding. Teenagers may minimize the violence in their lives and believe that they should not be reacting so intensely to their trauma.

Other factors contributing to a young women's entrapment include a fear of exposure and lowered self-concept. In an effort to control his partner, the abusive young man may threaten to tell her family about her dating relationship. In addition, sexual violence further affects the young woman's feelings of self-worth.[37]

Gay and Lesbian Teens

Another group at risk for dating violence is teenage gays and lesbians. These teenagers often do not recognize the problem of relationship violence and may even deny its very existence. Lesbian and gay teenagers may not define the relationship they have with a person of the same gender as a dating relationship. Therefore, the term *dating violence* may seem irrelevant to them.

The confusion about norms and roles that characterizes nongay teenage relationships is even more bewildering in teenage gay and lesbian relationships. A lack of visible role models and relationships adds to the uncertainty. Without role models, a partner's control and abuse may be accepted as normal.

It requires a lot of courage to come out, or identify oneself as gay or lesbian, to friends and family. Fear of identifying as gay or lesbian, or fear of homophobic responses from parents, peers, and others, may keep teenagers from telling anyone about their relationship and seeking help.[38]

If teenage gays and lesbians are not out, the secrecy of their relationship adds to their low self-esteem and vulnerability to isolation and abuse. It may also make them unable to trust anyone outside the relationship, making it difficult to seek support if a partner is abusive. While nongay teens often have trouble reaching out to adults for support, gay and lesbian teenage couples may be as isolated from their peers as they are from adults. The secrecy of the relationship also allows the threat of exposure to be used as a weapon to intimidate and maintain control. Such unwanted exposure is known as "outing."[39]

The Effects of Teen Dating Abuse

While both young men and women report having inflicted and received physical abuse, the experiences and consequences are not the same. And, in nongay relationships, females are more likely to be the victims of severe forms of physical and sexual violence.[40]

Young women respond to the trauma of dating violence with anger, fear, and surprise. The major emotional response batterers exhibit, however, is sorrow. Women outnumber men by almost a three-to-one margin in cases in which severe emotional trauma is reported.[41]

Rape has a devastating impact on the mental health of survivors, with nearly one-third of all rape victims developing rape-related post-traumatic stress disorder sometime in their lifetimes.[42] Some of the most common responses following rape or battering (which may or may not be symptomatic of rape-related PTSD) are anxiety, depression, disruption of social functioning, problems in sexual functioning, suicide attempts, sleep disturbances, hostility, somatic complaints, and obsessive-compulsive symptoms.[43] In addition, young women often experience confusion combined with feelings of helplessness and powerlessness.[44]

Symptoms unique to teenage survivors are sudden personality changes, drops in school performance, withdrawal from school or social activities, flagrant promiscuous behavior, sudden phobic behavior, self-destructive or risk-taking behavior, drug or alcohol abuse, development of eating disorders such as bulimia and anorexia, and alienation from peers or family.[45]

Teenage rape survivors face four major issues. First, there is a sense of loss of personal integrity. This can be devastating to a young woman who is still in the process of defining who she is and separating from her parents. When this work is interrupted, there is often a regression to the safety of earlier stages of development.

Second, teenagers have a need to believe that they can control their environments. Rape or battering upsets a teenager's perception of her ability to control her world and affects her ability to trust in herself, others, and the world around her.

A third issue is the damage to a teenager's emerging sexual identity. A rape experience may have serious repercussions for future sexual encounters, as later sex may be coupled with the feeling of violation.

The fourth issue deals with the damage done to a young woman's self-esteem. A young woman is likely to internalize blame for the rape or battering. False assumptions, such as "I am bad" or "I deserve to be raped or battered," reinforce an already shaky sense of self and can lead to severe self-esteem problems.[46]

If Someone Is Hurting You or Someone You Love

It can be very difficult for teenagers to determine whether a relationship is abusive. In addition, many barriers make it hard for parents to help teenagers who are in abusive situations. The questionnaires that follow can help teenagers and parents to make assessments and get help.

Are You in an Abusive Relationship?

If you are dating someone and are unsure if your relationship is abusive, ask yourself the questions below.[47]

Are you dating someone who . . .

- Is jealous and possessive toward you, won't let you have friends, checks up on you, or won't accept breaking up?
- Tries to control you, is bossy, gives orders, makes all the decisions, or doesn't take your opinion seriously?
- Is scary, threatens you, or uses or owns weapons?
- Is violent, has a history of fighting, loses his or her temper quickly, or brags about mistreating others?
- Pressures you for sex, is forceful or scary around sex, thinks women are sex objects, tries to manipulate you into having sex by saying things like "If you really loved me, you would . . .," or gets too serious about the relationship too fast?
- Abuses drugs or alcohol and pressures you to use them?
- Blames you when he or she mistreats you? Says you provoked them, pressed their buttons, made them do it, led them on?
- Has a history of bad relationships and blames the other people for all the problems?
- Believes that men should be in control and powerful and that women should be passive and submissive?
- Makes your family or friends worry about your safety?

If you answered yes to several of these questions, chances are you're in an abusive relationship. Another good measurement for this is simply to ask yourself, "Do I feel like I'm being mistreated?" If you answer yes to this question, then you are.

There are many kinds of abuse, from "joking" remarks about women to tickling, forced sex, slapping, pushing, and threatening with weapons. Emotional abuse can be particularly confusing, especially when it takes the form of friendly playing around. Teasing is a good example. If you feel embarrassed, hurt, humiliated, or inadequate as a result of your partner's comments, you are being emotionally abused.

If your dating partner has slapped, pushed, or threatened you, it's important to take it seriously. It means he or she is trying to control you, and there's a good chance it will get worse unless you do something about it.

Every teenager has certain rights and responsibilities in a dating relationship. These rights are a part of all nurturing, loving, and caring relationships. Some of these rights and responsibilities are listed below.[48]

Your Rights

- To refuse a date without feeling guilty
- To ask for a date and accept no as an answer
- To say no to physical closeness
- To end a relationship
- To have an equal relationship
- To have friends other than your dating partner
- To participate in activities that don't include your dating partner
- To have your own feelings and be able to express them
- To set limits—that is, to say yes or no or to change your mind if you choose
- To have your limits, values, feelings, and beliefs respected
- To say "I love you" without having sex
- To be heard
- To be yourself, even if it is different from everyone else or from what others want you to be

Your Responsibilities

- To determine your limits and values
- To respect the limits, values, feelings, and beliefs of others
- To communicate clearly and honestly
- To ask for help when you need it
- To be considerate
- To check your actions and decisions to determine whether they are good or bad for you

If your partner is hurting you and you're not sure what to do about it, an excellent first step is to reach out to people who can help you. Battered women's centers throughout the country help teenagers just like you. No matter how alone you may feel, there are lots and lots of people out there who have gone through what you're going through. They understand how hard this may be for you and all the confusion you may feel.

The telephone number for the National Domestic Violence Hotline is (800) 799-SAFE. Call the hotline and they will give you the telephone number of the center nearest you. When you make these calls, you won't have to give your name unless you want to. Making these calls requires a lot of courage. Remember that the people at the center will work with you to help you get safe and stay safe.

Is Your Teenager in an Abusive Relationship?

If you are a parent and think your child is in an abusive relationship, there are steps you can take to help her. Young adults are more willing to talk about their relationship if they feel safe and supported.

Asking your daughter the following questions in a warm, supportive manner may help her open up to you about her situation.[49]

- What happens when your partner doesn't get his or her way?
- Is your partner extremely jealous?
- Does your partner ever threaten you?
- Does your partner ever tell you what to wear, how to do your hair, or how to wear your makeup?

- Does your partner ever hold you down, push you, or hit you?
- Does your partner ever try to keep you from seeing other friends or from doing things you'd like to do?

Really try to listen to your daughter without judging, assuming, or giving advice, and try to believe what she tells you. Let her talk about her partner, and don't let your anger get the best of you when she tells you what a wonderful or loving person her partner is. Try to understand that she can both love and hate her dating partner.

If you are unable to listen without getting angry, blaming her, or trying to tell her what to do, chances are she will be unwilling to have further conversations with you about her relationship. Realize, too, that the possibility of her listening to your advice is slim. The bottom line is that the more she becomes isolated from you, the more dependent she will be on her abusive partner for emotional support. The more emotionally connected she is to her partner, the harder it will be for her to get help.

Let her know you love and support her. Tell her you are concerned about her safety, but try not to be critical of her partner, no matter how terrible you think the person is. Make sure she knows that no one has the right to hurt her, no matter what she thinks she has done to deserve it. Offer to go with her to get help, or give her the number for the National Domestic Violence Hotline.

When you have an opportunity to be with your daughter, try to arrange some of the time alone with her and some of the time with her friends and loved ones. Opportunities to be with people that are loving and nonviolent toward your daughter will remind her that she can be loved without being abused.

There will be times when it's appropriate to put your energies into rescuing your child. You may feel, however, that you must continue your rescue effort, even when it becomes counterproductive. For example, a parent's continued insistence that her daughter stop seeing her partner is likely to lead to no-win arguments and the daughter's refusal to discuss the situation. This helps neither person and shuts down the lines of communication. Try to resist the temptation to continue when it seems harmful to you or to her. As difficult as this may be, try to go about your usual activities and keep in touch with people you can rely on for support, including your local battered women's center.

There may come a time when the stress of your daughter's relationship is more than you can handle. If so, you may need to limit your discussions with your daughter. If you find yourself too angry, critical, or depressed to be supportive, ask another trusted family member or friend to stand in for you. Explain to your child, in the most loving way possible, that you need a break. Be sure to make it very clear that you love her and want her to be safe, but that your feelings of helplessness, fear, or anger make it impossible for you to help at this point. Let her know you will resume discussions about her relationship as soon as possible, and be sure she has other support people she can rely on.

If your son is the violent person, do everything possible to get him into a family violence program or to a counselor. Be a positive role model for your child, and actively demonstrate equality and respect through your own relationships with others. Identify to your child the negative consequences of his behavior. Let his girlfriend know that you understand that he is in the wrong and that she should not stay with an abusive partner, even if he is your son.[50]

What Teenagers Do and Don't Need from Family and Friends

As a parent or other concerned adult, remember that young people do not easily reach out to adults. Adults must not hold back or wait for them to ask for help, but we must actively help teenagers define healthy and abusive relationships. Our youth need us to be supportive and honest, not minimizing, blaming, or punitive.

The lists below will help adults to relate to and assist teenagers in abusive relationships.[53]

In relating to a teenager, don't:

- Be critical of the teenager or her partner
- Ask blaming questions such as, "What did you do to make him hit you?" or "Why don't you just break up?"
- Pressure her to make decisions
- Forbid the couple to see each other (the abused partner is likely to secretly see her abuser anyway, and secrecy further entrenches her in the relationship)

- Talk to both teenagers together (the abused partner will not feel free to say what she feels)
- Assume that she wants to end the relationship or that you know what's best for her

In relating to a teenager, do:

- Listen to and believe her
- Take her relationship seriously
- Offer to go with her to get help or to talk to a professional
- Let her know that violence under any circumstances is unacceptable
- Let her know she has the right to be loved without violence
- Be a role model for healthy relationships
- Help her obtain legal and other protection (such as getting a restraining order, filing charges, or changing phone numbers)

Intervention and Prevention Strategies

To reduce teen dating violence in our communities, a comprehensive prevention and intervention response must be developed. Programs must be funded and implemented in schools, health clinics, battered women's shelters, and the courts. Programs should be coordinated efforts that involve everyone coming in contact with teenagers, including school personnel, counselors, health care practitioners, police, parents, and other teenagers.

These comprehensive prevention and intervention strategies must occur at several levels. Barrie Levy explains, "Like other kinds of violence against women, abuse in adolescent dating relationships must be dealt with at multiple levels because it is caused by a set of interacting societal/ institutional, community, family and personal factors."[52]

Beginning at the "macro" level, social institutions that both support and promote male domination should be called to account and changed. For example, the media and entertainment industries, which so often target our youth, must be held accountable for their objectification of women and their ever-increasing tendency to glorify violence.

Attempts should be made not only to educate couples in violent relationships, but to educate all youth. Educational programs should be directed at elementary school, middle school, high school, and college students. Information about dating violence should emphasize the importance of peers in supporting nonviolent relationships.

School personnel should also be educated about dating violence and trained in intervention strategies. Health and counseling personnel should be trained to question students about dating violence.

Campus resources, including intervention programs and support groups, should be made available to teenagers in abusive relationships. Every effort should be made to publicize these services in order to increase their utilization. As teenagers involved in violent dating relationships tend to seek out peers for assistance, efforts should be directed at informing the peer group about the availability of these programs.[53]

Education about dating violence is needed by all populations, regardless of race or class. However, vast differences exist between and within populations, and generic messages and programs can often be ineffective. Special populations such as lesbian and gay youth, young men and women of color, and pregnant and parenting teenagers should be reached with messages that are targeted specifically to them.

Teenagers must also be educated and empowered to carry out their own educational prevention activities. In some schools, students have organized campus speakouts and public forums. Students should be trained as peer leaders and challenged to engage in activities designed to change social policies that perpetuate violence.

Some school systems have begun to implement these and many other strategies. School policies have been developed to reinforce the message that dating violence is unacceptable. Personnel have been educated about the issue and trained in intervention strategies, and intervention policies have been established for personnel witnessing violence among young couples.

The Teen Dating Violence Project

Great numbers of teenagers can be reached through schools and, because of this, intervention and prevention programs have begun to make their appearance on school campuses. One of the early leaders is the Teen Dating Violence Project.

The TDVP had a modest beginning in 1988 when a teacher at a nearby high school asked the Austin Center for Battered Women (CBW) to help do something about teenage dating violence. Today the TDVP is a rapidly growing peer support and educational project dedicated to helping teenagers establish safe and healthy dating relationships and addressing the needs of youth-at-risk due to family violence.

CBW volunteers facilitate a fifty-minute workshop at middle schools and high schools to promote awareness of dating violence and to encourage young people to get help for themselves or their peers in the event of abuse. CBW counselors conduct weekly support groups to address the special needs of teenagers who have experienced violent behavior in dating relationships (as victim or abuser) or have witnessed domestic violence in their families.

Young men and women are referred to CBW support groups by principals, teachers, school nurses, and counselors. Many adult women who use CBW services have referred their daughters to the support groups. Other teenagers are self-referred or come at the urging of their friends. Those interested sign up for the groups voluntarily. The groups are run separately by gender and are limited to approximately twelve students. Except for cases of child abuse and homicidal or suicidal threat, information shared in the support groups remains confidential.

A combination of educational and group-counseling methods are used to examine the types of abusive relationships, their underlying dynamics, and the characteristics of healthy relationships. The TDVP uses a four-phase curriculum. In the first phase, group members learn how to define their experiences and name (acknowledge) the abuse. In the second phase, members discuss their personal experiences with the goal of confronting their beliefs about the abuse and affirming their rights to respect and safety. In the third phase, facilitators present information regarding such topics as recognizing controlling behavior, effective communication, assertiveness training, and conflict resolution without violence. The fourth phase involves bringing closure to the support group and evaluating its effectiveness using feedback from group members and school staff .[54]

The TDVP teaches young people several basic truths about intimate relationships, including the following:

1. You have a right to be treated with respect. No one deserves to be abused.
2. You define what is abusive. If it feels abusive, it is.
3. People who abuse their partners want power and control over another person.
4. Both partners suffer in an abusive relationship.
5. Violence is always a choice.

Barri Rosenbluth, coordinator for the TDVP, has developed *Expect Respect,* two curriculum manuals designed to help other programs replicate this model.[55] Written specifically for school counselors, these manuals can be used by other youth service providers in a variety of settings. The support group manual features instructions for twenty-four one-hour group sessions on such topics as dating rights and responsibilities, jealousy, communicating assertively, fair fighting, and ending a relationship. The classroom presentation manual, coauthored with Dana Bartels, CBW abuse education specialist, includes a script for a one-hour presentation, instructions for trainers, and guidelines for implementing the program.

Recognized nationally as a model violence prevention program, the TDVP (as of 1996) has provided classroom presentations to 12,500 students in thirteen schools. More than 1,054 young men and women have participated in the TDVP support groups. Not only has the TDVP been active in virtually every school in Austin, but the program has expanded its services to reach young adults in churches, juvenile detention centers, substance abuse programs, and other nonprofit agencies.

The TDVP helps teenagers better understand their rights and responsibilities so that they may avert the suffering that comes from years of abuse in violent relationships. Mary, a fifteen-year-old participant, says it best. "I was scared to talk about it at first, but now I know I didn't do anything wrong—that it wasn't my fault at all. Now I'm going to help others who may have the same fears I had."

CHAPTER 4

The Intimate Relationship Between Substance Abuse and Domestic Violence

The social expectations about drinking and drinking behavior in our society teach people that if they want to avoid being held responsible for their violence, they can either drink before they are violent or at least say they were drunk.

—Richard J. Gelles[1]

Considerable evidence supports the contention that alcohol abuse and violence are related, both within and outside the family. Studies have consistently found alcohol to be involved in one-half to two-thirds of homicides, one-fourth to nearly one-half of serious assaults, and more than one-fourth of rapes.[2]

Substance Abuse and Violent Men

Depending on the study, reported alcohol abuse among batterers varies from 16 percent to 79 percent.[3] Abusive men with severe alcohol problems are just as likely to abuse their partners when drunk as when sober. They are, however, more likely to inflict serious injuries on their partners than abusive men who do not have a history of substance abuse. In addition, substance abusers are more likely to sexually attack their partners and to be violent outside the home.[4]

Reported drug abuse among batterers ranges from 8 percent to 30 percent.[5] Many drugs have been implicated in acts of violence, and each has a different physiological effect. Some of these drugs are marijuana, cocaine, opiates, hallucinogens (such as LSD), and stimulants.[6]

Evidence suggests that, of these drugs, amphetamines may be the only substance that serves as a possible cause of violent behavior. Amphetamines heighten excitability and muscle tension and may lead to impulsive acts. The behavior that follows from amphetamine use is related to both the dosage and the personality of the user prior to taking the drug. High-dosage users who already have aggressive personalities are likely to become more aggressive when using amphetamines.[7]

Does Substance Abuse Cause Family Violence?

Although there is a substantiated connection between substance abuse and family violence, we should not make the assumption that substance abuse *causes* domestic and child abuse. According to Del Martin, author of *Battered Wives,* "Alcohol is one of several factors that often contribute to the circumstances in which marital violence occurs. It may be used as an excuse for violence and it may trigger arguments that lead to violence. But, contrary to conventional beliefs, it is not necessarily a direct cause of violence and therefore does not help to explain the causes of wife-beating."[8]

The relationship between alcohol abuse and domestic violence is both confusing and complex. Edward Gondolf, a psychiatric research fellow at the University of Pittsburgh and a sociology professor at Indiana University of Pennsylvania, explains that three theories currently surround this association.[9] The first, the "disinhibition" theory, states that drinking breaks down people's inhibitions and leads to antisocial behavior. The evidence for this theory is that people often behave differently when they are drinking than when they are sober. The implication is that violence is caused by alcohol abuse.

The "disavowal" theory emphasizes the role of social learning in the alcohol/violence relationship. Substance abuse, accompanied by violence, provides the opportunity for socially learned rationalizations, or excuses, for the violent behavior. In this theory substance abuse is used as an excuse for deliberate acts of violence.

The third explanation, the "interaction" theory, suggests that the interaction of a variety of physiological, psychological, and social factors explains the relationship of alcohol abuse and violence. That is to say, the combination of these influences on an individual determines the degree to which he will be violent when drinking.

Perhaps the best evidence against the disinhibition theory comes from cross-cultural studies of drinking behavior. Craig MacAndrew and Robert Edgerton reviewed cross-cultural evidence regarding how people react to alcohol. They proposed that if the pharmacological properties of alcohol are the direct causes of drinking behavior, then there should be very little variation in drinking behavior across cultures.[10]

Contrary to what they expected, MacAndrew and Edgerton found that drinking behavior varies greatly from culture to culture. In some cultures individuals become passive; in others they become aggressive. What is noteworthy in their study is the discovery that the difference in behavior appears to be related to what people in each society believe about alcohol. If the cultural belief is that alcohol is a disinhibitor, people who drink tend to become disinhibited. If the cultural belief is that alcohol is a depressant, drinkers become passive and depressed.

In our society there is a widespread belief that alcohol releases violent tendencies. According to MacAndrew and Edgerton, when people are drinking they are given a time-out from the normal rules of social behavior. The denial of family violence, not only within the family but by society at large, and the belief that alcohol is a disinhibitor combine to provide a socially acceptable explanation for violence. In essence, being intoxicated gives the batterer something to blame, other than himself, for his behavior.

Alan Lang and his colleagues tested this cross-cultural research.[11] College student subjects were randomly assigned to one of four groups. Two groups received tonic water, and two groups received tonic water and vodka. One group receiving tonic water only and one receiving vodka and tonic were accurately told what they were drinking. The other two groups were misled: the tonic-water-only drinkers were told they were drinking vodka and tonic, and the vodka-and-tonic drinkers believed they were drinking tonic water that had been decarbonated.

Aggression was measured by assessing the intensity and duration of shocks subjects believed they were administering to Lang's associates. Fine motor skills were also measured by having subjects place objects of various shapes into shaped holes.

The researchers found that drinking alcohol, regardless of whether the subjects knew they were drinking or not, was related to fine motor skills.

They also discovered that the most aggressive subjects were those who thought they were drinking, regardless of whether their glasses actually contained alcohol.

Morton Bard and Joseph Zacker report that in 1,388 cases of domestic assault, nearly half of the abusive men said they were drinking at the time of the assault. When blood-alcohol tests were administered, however, less than 20 percent of the men were legally intoxicated.[12]

Despite the evidence against the disinhibition theory, some researchers persist in asserting that alcohol and drugs cause violent behavior.[13] This perception is also common among the general public. It appears that, in our society, domestic violence is more comprehensible when inflicted by a person who is intoxicated. An abused woman can avoid seeing her partner as abusive, instead thinking of him as a heavy drinker or an alcoholic. For the abused woman, the link between alcohol consumption and violence often offers a way for her to understand her partner's abusive behavior and gives her false hope that, if the man would only stop drinking, the violence would cease.[14]

Families that interpret their domestic problems in this way usually focus on the husband's drinking problem rather than on his abusive behavior. The conception of alcohol as the problem also appears to contribute to violence not being followed up in evaluation interviews, not being adequately described in case reports, and not being addressed in treatment programs.[15]

Battered women with substance-abusing partners consistently report that during recovery the abuse not only continues but often escalates, creating greater levels of danger. In cases in which battered women report that the level of physical abuse decreases, they often report a corresponding increase in other forms of abuse such as threats, manipulation, and isolation.[16]

Edward Gondolf suggests that both alcohol abuse and domestic violence may be caused by underlying needs for power and control associated with distorted perceptions of masculinity.[17] Heavy drinking among men has been shown to represent toughness, risk-taking, virility, and sexual prowess in American culture. Women, however, drink for quite different reasons. Heavy drinking among women is more likely to be related to depression and to be used to sedate the emotional trauma associated with battering.[18]

Ascribing causality to substance abuse and domestic violence simplifies a highly dynamic and complicated relationship. Sociologist Richard Gelles explains, "Except for the evidence that appears to link amphetamine use to family violence, the portrait of the alcohol and drug crazed partner or parent who impulsively and violently abuses a family member is a distortion. If substances are linked to violence at all, it is through a complicated set of individual, situational, and social factors."[19]

Battered Women and Substance Abuse

The batterer is not always the alcoholic. Battered women, too, may have substance-abuse problems. While women may drink less than men, they appear to be more susceptible to the physical consequences of drinking.[20]

Women are more likely to develop liver disease with a lower level of alcohol consumption than men. Native American women aged fifteen to thirty-four are thirty-six times more likely than white women to have cirrhosis of the liver. Although African American women tend to drink less than white women, they are more than six times as likely to develop liver disease. Women are twice as likely as men to develop and die from cirrhosis, pneumonia, and other alcohol-related diseases. In addition, female alcoholics die at rates fifty to one hundred times higher than do male alcoholics.[21]

Low self-esteem, feelings of inadequacy, and depression consistently appear in women with substance-abuse problems. They often feel lonely, isolated from positive support networks, and less worthy of help than do men in similar conditions.[22]

Domestic violence increases women's risk of addiction, depression, attempted suicide, and a range of other health and mental health problems. Results of a study of 481 identified battered women seeking emergency room services indicated that battered women have a relative risk of attempting suicide that is eight times as great as for nonbattered women, a risk of drug abuse six times as great, and a rate of alcohol abuse fifteen times as great.[23]

Approximately 7 to 14 percent of battered women have alcohol abuse problems.[24] Women's substance abuse problems do not cause their physical abuse, although some women may be using alcohol to self-medicate against the emotional and physical pain associated with battering. Self-medication with legal or illegal drugs is an expression of personal control as well as an attempt to numb the pain of the experience.[25] Judith Herman, author of *Trauma and Recovery*, explains that "Traumatized people who cannot spontaneously dissociate [a self-induced hypnotic trance state] may attempt to produce similar numbing effects by using alcohol or narcotics."[26]

Battered women's exposure to these secondary problems is partially a result of their feelings of entrapment, which are reinforced from both within and outside the relationship. From within, the batterer's coercive control exercised over a wide range of the woman's activities severely affects her sense of personal freedom and heightens her feelings of fear and frustration. From outside the relationship, ineffective, inappropriate, or blaming responses from those to whom the woman reaches for help also contribute to her feelings of entrapment in a relationship wrought with escalating violence. Isolated within the relationship and blocked from without, the battered woman seeks to meet her needs to the best of her perceived abilities. Self-medication may seem her best alternative. When that no longer offers sufficient relief, she may attempt suicide.[27]

Tragically, in attempting to ease her pain, a chemically addicted battered woman may actually be increasing the danger she is exposed to. Drugs and alcohol make her less aware of, and less responsive to, cues of forthcoming violence. Less able to escape, she is more likely to fight back, thus increasing the likelihood of serious injury. She may also be less aware of injuries she has suffered.[28]

Many battered women report that their chemically dependent partners initiated them into drug use and then sabotaged their efforts to quit. Threats to disclose her substance abuse to local authorities or significant others is another tactic the batterer may use to control his partner.[29] According to one battered woman, "He would buy my drugs for me because he said he liked me better when I was stoned. When he got mad at me, though, he'd flush my dope down the toilet and threaten to tell my boss I was a junkie."

Women's substance abuse problems are frequently viewed as less serious than men's, and their condition may be more frequently misdiagnosed. Many chemically dependent battered women are addicted to drugs that were prescribed by health care providers from whom they sought help.[30]

The most commonly prescribed medications for post-traumatic stress disorder, as well as for a variety of other ills, are tranquilizers such as benzodiazepines. These are effective for short-term use in the immediate aftermath of a traumatic event. Long-term use, however, carries some risk of addiction.[31]

Battered women with chronic tranquilizer or analgesic use, chronic symptoms unresponsive to treatment, vague complaints, and frequent clinic visits may be burdened with a variety of psychiatric labels that identify them as difficult, demanding, or noncompliant patients who do not deserve serious attention. Labeling, and the resulting ineffective responses, illustrates the importance of properly identifying domestic violence in female patients.

A Comparison of Alcoholism and Battering

Although substance abuse and domestic violence are related, they are separate issues with several crucial differences. While substance abuse is primarily harmful to the user, domestic violence is primarily harmful to the person being abused. The greatest physical danger in the chemically dependent family is to the user, while the greatest danger in the violent family is to the person being abused.

While equal numbers of men and women may be chemically dependent, men are overwhelmingly the perpetrators and women are overwhelmingly the recipients of violence. Ninety-five percent of the victims of domestic violence are women.

Domestic violence services have a longer history of responding to children than do chemical dependency services. Children comprise about two-thirds of the residents in most battered women's shelters. In contrast, most treatment programs for women are not equipped to serve mothers with children.

A disease model is preferred for chemical dependency, while a sociopolitical analysis is frequently applied to domestic violence. Battering is not a disease but, rather, a deliberate and intentional behavior. Many alcohol treatment programs operate from a "sobriety first" philosophy, while battered women's shelters operate from a "safety first" philosophy.

While domestic violence is a criminal act, chemical dependency is criminal only in specific situations. There has been a stronger criminal-justice response to drunk driving and drug abuse than to the battering of women.[32]

The batterer and the alcoholic are alike in some respects. One important similarity is the tendency for the perpetrators to discount their behavior and to minimize the severity of their drunkenness or battering. Batterers and alcoholics blame others, make excuses rather than accept responsibility for their behavior, and exhibit Jekyll-and-Hyde personality changes.

Violence and drinking occur more and more frequently as these unhealthful lifestyles progress. Inevitably, the drinking and the violence begin to cause greater trauma and more problems in almost all areas of family and personal life. Alcoholics and batterers frequently attempt to regain control, make empty promises, and create false hopes.

Partners of alcoholics and batterers often minimize the impact of drinking and violence on the family. The denial process of not feeling, not trusting, and not talking dominate the family. Alcoholism, when coupled with violence, doubles the need for denial and creates an even greater sense of hopelessness for family members.[33] Claudia Black, author of *It Will Never Happen to Me,* explains it this way: "Remember, the goal of family members in attempting to live through these problems is the same—minimize the conflict, adjust, placate, act-out, drop-out—do anything, but be sure to survive."[34]

Recovery Programs

Anyone working with families in which both domestic violence and substance abuse are present must recognize that full recovery for the family will not usually occur unless both issues are addressed. For the dually affected family, the reemergence or continuation of violence or substance abuse can act as a trigger for the onset of the other problem. Studies have consistently shown alcohol abuse to be a major predictor of dropout from batterer's treatment programs. It has also been shown that domestic violence contributes to alcohol relapse.[35]

Recognizing the complex relationship between domestic violence and substance abuse is a first step toward the provision of effective services, for both battered women and their partners. It is crucial that battered women's advocates and substance abuse counselors recognize the similarities and differences between these two problems. Advocates in both fields should familiarize themselves with the philosophy, strategies, and assumptions of the other.[36] This understanding will enhance the development of an effective collaboration.

Self-help programs such as Alcoholics Anonymous (AA) promote and support emotional and spiritual health and have helped countless numbers of alcoholics get sober.[37] These programs, however, were not designed to address battering and are thus ineffective in assisting batterers to change their abusive behavior. A treatment program for substance abusers who batter must include attendance at a program designed specifically to address the attitudes and beliefs that support batterers' behavior.

In cases of both substance abuse and wife abuse, the pattern seems to be to give first priority to providing treatment for the substance abuse. In AA, this is known as "sobriety first." Substance abuse programs, in fact, often neglect relationship violence. This may occur because of the erroneous assumption that the violence will subside with sobriety. Some municipal courts overwhelmingly refer domestic violence cases to substance abuse treatment programs rather than to batterer's treatment programs.[38]

In batterer's treatment programs men who are chemically dependent are frequently referred to alcohol rehabilitation programs, AA, or Narcotics Anonymous as a prerequisite to their participation. There is no assurance, however, that the two programs will reinforce each other.

In fact, approaches and assumptions in conventional recovery programs often contradict the counseling provided in most batterer's treatment programs. In AA the focus is primarily on one's self. Batterer's treatment programs, in contrast, emphasize the impact of the batterer's behavior on his family. The objective in such programs is for the batterer to become less self-centered.

AA recovery programs often implicate the batterer's partner as codependent or coalcoholic and utilize family treatment strategies that may put an abused partner in a dangerous position. Batterer's treatment programs view the partner as caught in an enforced state of compliance and dependency. Abuse and threats force her into submission.

AA emphasizes that alcohol abuse is a disease. Batterer's treatment programs emphasize that violence is a choice. AA emphasizes the number of sober days and meetings attended. Batterer's treatment programs are concerned with the abused woman's feelings of safety as a result of her partner's treatment.

While there are certainly distinct differences between these programs, there are several important similarities as well. Both AA and batterer's treatment programs confront denial and minimization of destructive behaviors. Both address rationalizations used to justify behaviors, and both urge men to take personal responsibility for their behavior. Both emphasize the personal change that is necessary on a daily basis over the long term. These programs also promote mutual support that breaks down social isolation. Finally, both assert that men can and should change their destructive and dangerous behaviors.[39]

Batterers who are involved with alcohol or other drugs need to address both problems directly and concurrently. This is absolutely critical, not only to maximize their families' safety but also to lessen the possibility of relapse. True recovery requires much more than abstinence. It includes adopting a lifestyle that enhances all aspects of emotional well-being. This goal cannot be achieved as long as the battering continues.

Recovery programs for family violence and substance abuse must begin with screening and assessment for both problems. According to Gondolf, "Decisively addressing alcohol abuse may be essential to increasing the effectiveness of wife assault programs, and confronting wife assault may improve the effectiveness of alcohol treatment programs."[40]

Helping professionals need to ask direct questions of clients to determine whether domestic violence has occurred. As with any sensitive issue that has been perpetuated by denial, questions should begin with the least threatening and lead to the more direct. The following is an example:[41]

- Do you and your partner argue often?
- If either of you drink, are your personalities different when drinking?
- Does your partner ever lose his or her temper, throw things, or threaten you?
- Do arguments ever end in pushing, shoving, or slapping?
- Has your partner ever used a fist or a weapon against you?
- Have you ever been concerned about the safety of your children?

The order of service delivery for dually affected families should be as follows: (1) address safety issues, (2) begin recovery for alcoholism and/or other drug abuse, (3) begin recovery for the violence before the alcohol program ends, and (4) provide ongoing support for both sobriety and the elimination of violent behavior.

Never assume that, once someone is clean and sober, problems associated with domestic violence will automatically cease. Unless the abuse is addressed, the underlying issues of power and control are still in place. If, by chance, the abuse ceases when the drinking stops, the fear, guilt, and anger experienced by those abused do not automatically disappear and should be addressed.

The Abused Partners of Men in Recovery

Often, partners of batterers in substance abuse recovery programs are directed into such self-help programs as Al-Anon and codependency groups.[42] Like other traditional treatment responses, however, these resources were not designed to meet the needs of battered women and often inadvertently set them up for further harm.

The goals of codependency treatment typically include helping family members get self-focused, practice emotional detachment from the substance abuser, and stop their enabling or codependent behaviors. Group members are encouraged to define their personal boundaries, set limits on their partners' behaviors, and stop protecting their partners from the harmful consequences of the addiction. These strategies can be very helpful for women whose partners are not abusive. For battered women, however, they will likely result in an escalation of the abuse, including physical violence.

Many battered women's advocates and substance abuse counselors are in disagreement concerning the labeling of battered women as codependent. Many domestic violence workers feel that this label is victim blaming. In battering relationships the behaviors described as enabling or codependent are often forced, coerced, and maintained by abuse. In addition, these behaviors often serve as battered women's survival strategies.

Battered women are often highly sensitive to their partners' moods as a way to determine levels of danger. They may focus on their partners' needs and cover up for them to avoid being beaten. Seen in this light, battered women's behaviors are not codependent, but are, instead, survival strategies necessary to maintain the women's safety and the safety of their children. When battered women are encouraged to stop these behaviors they are in essence being asked to stop doing what may be keeping them alive.[43]

Some of the concepts of codependency reflect valid concerns that can be helpful when placed in the proper context. Equally important, however, is the realization that attempts to eliminate a battered woman's survival strategies, without offering her viable alternatives, can and will endanger her life.

Some key points service providers should always remember when working with abused women whose partners are in recovery are the following:[44]

1. Guarantees for the woman's safety in the relationship can never be based upon the promises of her abusive partner.
2. If she is still in the battering relationship, she may deny or minimize the danger she is in. Family or couples counseling is not safe for the battered woman until the violence has been addressed.
3. Believe her and tell her the violence is not her fault. Do not join the batterer in his denial or minimization of the abuse.
4. Codependency concepts are not appropriate in trying to understand why women remain in violent relationships.
5. Dispel any belief that the violence will stop when she or the batterer becomes clean and sober.
6. Assess her safety with her and help her to develop a safety plan.
7. Share information with her about her options and resources, including battered women's services, protective intervention, and legal options.

Battered women need to understand the purposes and limitations of such resources as Al-Anon and codependency groups. It is equally important that they receive accurate and complete information about available resources, particularly domestic violence services, so that they can make informed choices and set realistic expectations.

Battered Women in Recovery

While nearly one-third of the estimated ten million alcoholics in America are women, less than a quarter of the patients at publicly funded alcohol treatment centers are women. At drug treatment centers, about 30 percent of the patients are women.[45] Battered women face several obstacles to their recovery including shame, fear, denial, and service systems ill-equipped to meet their special needs.

Shame is perhaps one of the hardest obstacles for women to overcome. In 1991 Sheila Blume summarized the differences commonly found between male and female alcoholics. One key difference is that women are more stigmatized for their substance use and abuse.[46] This stigmatization and the unwillingness of many physicians, mental health professionals, police, and courts to identify battered women as chemically dependent are detrimental to early intervention and treatment. Shame, too, may be a major contributor to women's denial. One of the main reasons Hispanic women alcoholics often do not acknowledge their problem is the strong sanctions within the Hispanic culture against women drinking.[47]

Fear is also a powerful motivator for chemically dependent battered women. Women often fear reprisal or abuse from their partners, not being able to take care of or to keep their children, and punishment from local authorities.

Batterers are often resistant to their partners' attempts to seek help, including substance abuse treatment. They may sabotage their partners' recovery by preventing them from attending meetings or appointments, or they may increase the violence or threats in order to reestablish control. Some substance-abusing battered women decide to leave treatment when their participation appears to compromise their safety.[48]

Most alcohol and drug treatment centers do not provide child care, much less allow women to bring their children with them if they are in need of in-patient treatment. This situation is a major deterrent to women seeking help. According to Diane Rhodes, shelter director for the Austin Center for Battered Women, "Taking their children with them is a first priority for many of our residents. They often feel there is no one they can trust with their children's safety. In these situations a woman will refuse treatment unless she is guaranteed that she can take her children with her."

Frequently, women have neither the money nor the insurance to pay for treatment. This disadvantage may keep them from seeking help or force them to accept the services they can afford rather than those they need.

One study reported that African American women face greater financial difficulties, are more likely to be multiple-drug abusers, and experience a greater sense of alienation than do white women.[49] These results suggest that black women and other women of color have more or different barriers to overcome in entering treatment than do white women.

In addition, women of color have fewer alcoholism services available to them than are available to African American, Hispanic, and Native American men. When a woman of color is also a lesbian, services specifically designed for her needs are almost nonexistent. Of 540 rehabilitation centers in Texas, only 17 are for females and only one is specifically for Hispanic females.[50]

One of the most difficult problems facing drug-addicted pregnant women is finding a treatment program that will accept them. There is a tremendous fear among service providers concerning liability issues associated with treating pregnant addicted women. In New York City, of seventy-eight drug treatment programs surveyed, 54 percent refused to admit pregnant addicts and 87 percent refused to take pregnant, crack-addicted women on Medicaid.[51]

Research shows that women receive the most benefit from drug treatment programs that provide comprehensive services for meeting their basic needs, including access to food, clothing, and shelter; transportation, job counseling and training, legal assistance, and educational opportunities; parenting training; family or individual therapy; medical care and child care; social services and social support; assertiveness training and family planning services.[52] Traditional male-oriented drug treatment programs may not be appropriate for women because they often do not provide these services.

Bringing women into treatment is not feasible until systems are in place that offer sensitive, effective, nonracist, and antihomophobic treatment. Failure to design programs and policies that meet women's needs results in treatment programs that are either underutilized or ineffective in their service delivery.

Approximately 30 percent of AA membership is female.[53] A substantial number of women drop out of AA due to frustration with the patriarchal model of the Twelve Step program. As an alternative to this program, women's groups have begun to form that take the Twelve Steps and adapt them to better meet women's well-being and spiritual needs.[54] These groups are providing a sensitive and effective alternative to the more traditional, male-oriented recovery programs.

Creating an Empowered Response to Substance Abuse

At the same time that chemically dependent battered women are confronting treatment programs not designed to meet their needs, they may also be dealing with domestic violence programs that are ill-prepared to serve them effectively.

Many battered women's shelters have strict rules forbidding the use of alcohol and other drugs in the shelter. These restrictions are necessary for providing a healthful environment for residents, both women and children. Offering chemically dependent battered women shelter without addressing their substance abuse, however, is setting them up to fail. In addition, refusing shelter to chemically addicted women sends a very clear message. Unfortunately, it is a message that may reinforce their depression, frustration, and desperation.

In some cases, once a battered woman finds safety, the substance abuse will subside. Some women will stop abusing because of a pregnancy. For truly addicted battered women, however, the same is not true. Expecting the chemically *addicted* battered woman to respond the same as the chemically *abusing* battered woman is unrealistic.

At the Austin Center for Battered Women, shelter advocates report that an increasing number of residents have substance abuse problems. According to one twenty-year veteran in the movement, "We do seem to be working with more chemically addicted women. We're also seeing a big difference in the drug of choice. Crack is definitely more popular and this is a particularly serious addiction to address."

One of the reasons CBW is serving more women with substance abuse problems may be because of a change in attitude among staff and volunteers over the last few years. Advocates are now more informed about substance abuse and have moved away from blaming and judging chemically addicted women. This nonjudgmental environment allows residents to be more open about their addictions and the problems they create.

CBW's admission policy has been changed to reflect these more empowering attitudes. All women seeking shelter continue to be screened for substance abuse during their initial assessment, but their addictions are not used against them. No woman is ever turned away because of a drug problem. Chemically addicted women are admitted to the shelter with the understanding that their substance use will be addressed with their counselor or advocate.

Residents are asked if they are interested in addressing and changing their drug-using behavior. If they express a desire to go into treatment, they are provided with the appropriate resources to best meet their needs. CBW works closely with the Austin Women's Addiction Referral and Education Center, a feminist counseling and educational program. CBW also works with Austin Family House, an in-patient and halfway house for women and their children.

Changes in attitudes and policies have greatly improved CBW's service delivery. Residents are now routinely given opportunities to address both their safety and recovery needs. According to one CBW advocate, "We've really gotten away from that 'bad girl' attitude that shames and blames the woman. Now we focus on the behavior, which is more consistent with the movement's empowering philosophy."

CHAPTER 5

Battered Women and the Legal System

Systemic solutions to domestic violence must be adopted. Policies that on their surface should be useful—that is, greater police arrests or enforced use of protective orders—have repeatedly floundered on the shoals of indifference by other critical actors.

—Eve and Carl Buzawa, authors of
Domestic Violence: The Criminal Justice Response[1]

Many attitudes of and responses by the justice system have historically prevented battered women from getting the help they need. The justice system's response has often been inadequate and has left survivors confused and discouraged. A lenient response by the court may encourage a batterer to believe that violence against a family member is acceptable. On the other hand, a jail sentence may punish not only the batterer but the family as well by depriving them of financial support.

Laws and law enforcement vary greatly from state to state and from city to city. It is often difficult for battered women to know what to expect if they turn to the justice system for help. Some women may get the assistance they need, while others may be further victimized. In addition, there are some women whom the law simply may not protect including undocumented women, women involved in crime, and lesbians.

Understanding the Justice System

The legal response to domestic violence consists of a complex network of processes, people, and laws. It has many different aspects, and a battered woman may become involved with any of them. Battered women are often implicitly expected to understand the legal system in order to access the help they need. That this system may seem intimidating and frightening is understandable considering that it often stumps the experts.

The justice system is a framework comprised of law enforcement officers, prosecutors, and the court system. To better understand the system, it is helpful to understand the distinction between the *criminal process* and the *civil process,* as the differences between them can have a profound effect upon battered women.

The criminal justice system deals only with crimes. A crime is an act in violation of penal law. It is considered an injury to the state and will be prosecuted as such. The rationale for treating a crime as an injury to the peace of the state is to protect all citizens from a criminal who may strike again and thus must be deterred or punished. The result is that crimes can be prosecuted regardless of whether battered women take action. In fact, women are not always able to make the prosecution process work, such as in the case of murder.

The civil system deals with all the legal processes and matters that are not criminal. These matters include breach of contract, divorce, custody, property rights, recovery of money for injury, and a variety of other issues. In these cases, one party may sue another party. The legal remedy is usually an order by a judge. The judge can order the second party to do certain things or to pay money to the first party. It is important to remember that no one can be sent to jail as part of the remedy in the civil process except through contempt proceedings. Contempt proceedings more closely resemble criminal proceedings than civil and they may involve a jail sentence or a fine.[2]

In most states women have a choice of three legal strategies to protect themselves against domestic violence:[3]

1. Divorce or legal separation from the abusive husband
2. A civil protection order that requires the batterer to stop abusing, threatening, or harassing the woman
3. Criminal prosecution of the batterer

In appropriate situations women may be able to get both criminal enforcement and civil protection orders.

Civil Protection Orders

A civil protection order, now available in all fifty states and the District of Columbia, is an order issued by a civil court judge in response to a written petition from a battered woman. The order may command the abusive partner (a spouse, former spouse, or lover) to stop abusing, harassing, or threatening the woman and to stay away from her. The order can also provide for custody, supervised or unsupervised visitation, and child and spousal support; the abuser's eviction from the family home (even if it is held in the batterer's name); prohibition of the batterer from contacting the woman at her residence, school, or place of employment; payment for the woman's moving, medical, and legal expenses; and a requirement that the batterer get counseling or participate in a substance abuse or batterer's treatment program. If the protection order is violated, courts may hold the violator in contempt, impose fines, or incarcerate the violator, depending on state laws.[4]

The remedies provided by protection order legislation are separate from and not replicated by existing divorce and separation procedures. Even if the woman plans to file for divorce, a civil protection order may be needed because her only recourse if the batterer violates the divorce conditions is to return to court to petition for a hearing. A violation of the civil protection order, however, would provide for his immediate arrest.

Civil protection orders are also distinct from criminal justice remedies. Other than in New York State, petitioning for a protection order does not prohibit a woman from bringing criminal charges against the offender at the same time. Some judges recommend that domestic violence survivors consider pursuing their cases both civilly and criminally, at least in cases involving aggravated assault and battery.[5]

In cases involving ongoing criminal prosecution, protection orders may help prevent the opportunity for retaliation, intimidation, or undue influence on the woman. The criminal defendant in a family-based crime will often have both a strong sense of having been wronged and easier means to retaliate against the woman.

In addition, long-standing emotional ties and socialization factors can interfere with the criminal justice goals of punishing the offender and deterring future crime. These factors may influence a woman, leading her to withdraw as a prosecution witness. By prohibiting contact and evicting the batterer from the home, civil protection orders can often address the unique circumstances of criminal assault between intimate partners and thus increase the likelihood that the criminal prosecution will proceed.

Many women, however, do not want the batterers charged criminally or jailed: they simply want the violence to stop. Other women are fearful of entering into an adversarial criminal procedure against their abusers. For these women, civil protection orders may offer the only form of legal protection.[6]

Obtaining a Protection Order

In some states, a woman may ask the court for an order herself, without the aid of a lawyer. This is called appearing pro se (meaning "for yourself"). In other states, an attorney must be present, whether a private attorney, a free legal services lawyer or representative from a law school clinic, or a government attorney.

Sometimes women may be able to get an immediate short-term emergency protection order, without the abuser being present, on the basis of their own testimony. This temporary order must then be served on the abusive partner and followed by a full court hearing, at which the batterer has an opportunity to appear, before it can be extended for a longer period. In some cases, it may take months to find and serve the batterer, hold a court hearing, and issue a longer-term protection order. These longer-term protection orders can be in effect for six months to two years.[7]

Limitations of Protection Orders

In addition to their potential benefits, protection orders have historically had several limitations. Until recently, a woman who moved to another state to escape an abusive partner sometimes found that the second state could not enforce the restraining order issued in the first state. To receive protection, the woman had to obtain a protection order in the new state.[8]

Another limitation is that it may be difficult for women to obtain an order. All states have mechanisms for issuing emergency protection orders and many have low filing fees, especially if the case involves a spouse or former spouse. In some situations, however, it may take several weeks for a woman to obtain a protection order, and the process sometimes involves prohibitively high lawyer fees and court costs.

Another factor to consider is that domestic violence frequently occurs during evenings or on weekends, when most courts are not in session. As of 1990, only twenty-three states provide for issuing emergency after-hours protection orders.[9]

The utility of protection orders may also depend on whether they provide the requested relief in specific detail. Unfortunately, there are few guidelines for judges to use in interpreting the statutes and determining which types of relief are authorized and appropriate for individual women.

In addition, civil protection orders have not always been consistently enforced. Few courts have developed guidelines or procedures for punishing violators. As a result, there remains a great deal of confusion in regard to arrest authority and appropriate sanctions for protection order violations.[10]

A 1991 study examined 355 temporary and permanent protection orders issued in courts in Denver and Boulder, Colorado. One year after the temporary order was issued, 60 percent of the women reported that their partners had violated the order at least once. Women who had obtained permanent orders were as likely as those without to report violations. The 355 women in the sample made a total of 290 separate calls to police; however, only 59 arrests were made in these incidents.

While women were very satisfied with the police response to the abusive incident that led them to seek a court order, their ratings of the police response to order violations fell drastically. Very few women returned to court to seek a violation hearing because of fear of retaliation, feelings that it would not help, and not realizing that this was an option.[11]

Law enforcement uncertainty about arrest in order-violations cases may stem from a long-standing, general legal prohibition against making a warrantless arrest for any misdemeanor unless it occurs in an officer's presence. In recent years, exceptions have been made by statute, allowing a warrantless arrest for misdemeanor domestic violence in twenty-three states.

By the early 1990s, in forty states, a violation of a protection order constitutes either a misdemeanor or criminal contempt. In these jurisdictions, police may arrest an offender for a violation of any aspect of a protection order that the officer witnesses. Despite these statutory changes, however, enforcement remains procedurally complex for both police and courts.[12]

Other limitations include limited funds for training and supervising clerks who assist battered women seeking an order; difficulty in serving protection orders thereby placing women in danger during the days and even weeks until service has been made; and ineffective or nonexistent monitoring systems to determine whether batterers are complying with the terms of the order.[13]

Positive Effects of Protection Orders

Despite these limitations, it appears that obtaining protection orders may have a positive impact on battered women's sense of personal control and self-confidence. Research surveying the experiences of seventy-five battered women using protective orders in Denton County, Texas, found that while women responding to the survey were generally very positive about the process of applying for and receiving the order, nearly half were dissatisfied with the enforcement process. Comments indicated that some law enforcement officers were reluctant to make arrests, seemed unfamiliar with the orders, or dismissed the women's fear and pleas for help. The orders did, however, appear to work well in the areas of protecting children, gaining a sense of control, reducing fear, and beginning the process of divorce.

The majority of women responding to the survey felt empowered by the protection order experience, describing positive changes in self-perception not necessarily tied to the practical effects of the orders. Acting on one's own behalf, moving away from helplessness, using the legal system, and sending a strong message to the abuser that abuse would not be tolerated were all mentioned as ways the process improved women's self-perception.[14]

Improving the Protection Order Experience

Regardless of their empowerment abilities, orders without enforcement offer little protection and often increase women's danger by creating a false sense of security. Batterers routinely violate orders, especially if they believe there is no real risk of being arrested. For enforcement to work, courts need to monitor compliance, women must report violations, and law enforcement officials, prosecutors, and judges should respond sternly to reported violations.

Domestic violence requires a coordinated response from each part of the justice system, acting in collaboration with local social service and advocacy group representatives. Civil protection orders, as part of the solution, cannot be used and enforced fully by any one of these groups without cooperation from the others. For example, law enforcement officers may be reluctant to file reports or make arrests if they do not believe the prosecutors will follow through or that the judge will impose appropriate sanctions.[15]

Courts should develop, publicize, and monitor a clear, formal policy regarding protection order violations in order to encourage respect for the court's order and to increase compliance. These court guidelines should specify the procedures that law enforcement officers are required and authorized to follow and the procedures that judges themselves will follow in holding violation hearings.[16]

Attitudes about domestic violence must also be challenged. Several judges interviewed for a study conducted by the National Institute of Justice reported that they first had to change their views of domestic abuse in order to respond to the issue effectively. While they originally thought of domestic violence as a relationship problem, they later came to see it as a complex problem of persistent intimidation and physical injury. In effect, they now view domestic violence as a violent crime and as serious as any other form of assault and battery.

In addition to changing their views about the nature and seriousness of domestic violence, judges reported a change in their perception of the court's proper approach to handling civil protection order petitions. They no longer view the hearings as an extension of divorce court, in which a negotiated settlement of a private problem is called for. Instead, these judges now view civil protection order proceedings as the application of an immediate civil remedy to criminal behavior.[17]

The Violence Against Women Act of 1994 actually strengthens protection orders and, if actively enforced, may help lessen battered women's struggles. Under the act's "full faith and credit" provision, states are required to enforce each other's civil protection orders. The act also makes it a federal crime for a person to cross state lines with the intent to engage in conduct that violates a protection order, and it prohibits anyone subject to an order that meets certain specifications from possessing a firearm.[18] Unfortunately, as of June 1996 there have been only fourteen prosecutions under the act's criminal provisions.[19]

Stalking

Stalking is a form of criminal activity composed of a series of actions. Removed from the domestic violence context, these actions might constitute legal behavior. For example, sending flowers and waiting for someone outside her place of work are actions that, on their own, are not criminal. Coupled with an intent to instill fear or injury, however, such actions may constitute a pattern of behavior that is illegal.[20] Each state has its own definition of stalking, and it is important for battered women to check their states' statutes on what definition is being used. Contact the National Domestic Violence Hotline at (800) 799-SAFE for the telephone number of your state's coalition on domestic violence. They should be able to explain your state's stalking laws.

Although every stalking case is different, a stalker's behavior typically grows more threatening and violent over time. The stalking activity generally escalates from what initially may be bothersome and annoying but legal behavior to obsessive, dangerous, violent, and potentially fatal acts.

Antistalking Legislation

The primary objective of antistalking legislation is to intervene in a suspected stalking case before the behavior results in physical harm. The two most immediate and typical interventions are arrest and protection orders.[21]

Stalking first drew widespread public concern when a popular young actress named Rebecca Shaeffer was shot to death in 1989 by an obsessed fan who had stalked her for two years. Although it was the death of a celebrity that first attracted media attention, stalking victims are women from all walks of life and most are trying to end a relationship with a man. Some battered women's advocates believe that up to 80 percent of stalking cases occur in a domestic violence context.

The initial publicity about Shaeffer's death resulted in a rush to pass antistalking legislation. California passed the first such legislation in 1990, and by 1992, twenty-seven states had enacted similar legislation. Today, forty-nine states and the District of Columbia have antistalking laws. (Maine uses an antiterrorizing statute. The state also amended its protective order statute in 1993, adding provisions for the employment of protective orders to prohibit stalking behavior.[22])

States designate as stalking a variety of acts, ranging from specifically defined actions such as nonconsensual communication to harassment. To be convicted of stalking in most states, the stalker must display a criminal intent to cause fear in the woman. The conduct of the stalker must be "willful," "purposeful," "intentional," or "knowing." Many states do not require proof that the defendant intended to cause fear as long as the stalker intended to commit the act that resulted in fear. In these states, if the woman is reasonably frightened by the stalker's conduct, the "intent" element of the crime has been met.

Many states have both misdemeanor and felony classifications for stalking. Misdemeanors generally carry a jail sentence of up to one year, while sentences from three to five years are typical for felony stalking offenses. Most state statutes contain sentence-enhancing provisions for the presence of one or more additional elements, such as if the stalker brandished a weapon or violated a protective order. Some states allow incarceration for as long as ten years for repeat offenses.[23]

Drafting effective antistalking legislation that withstands constitutional challenges is a difficult task. In some cases, the distinction between lawful activity and stalking activity is hazy. Defendants seeking to challenge antistalking laws usually argue that these statutes are constitutionally defective because they are so overly broad that they infringe upon constitutionally protected speech or activity.

By January 1996, the Justice Department had identified fifty-three constitutional challenges to stalking statutes in nineteen states. For the most part, courts are upholding the laws.[24] This was not the case in Texas, however, when, in September 1996, the Texas Court of Criminal Appeals threw out the state's three-year-old antistalking law, declaring it unconstitutionally vague. The court's written opinion said the law, as it was written, did not protect First Amendment rights.[25] Texas now has a more specific antistalking law.

Since the first antistalking legislation was passed, many states have amended their initial laws, in part due to concerns about constitutional challenges and other issues that arose in implementing the laws. Many of the initial statutes, for instance, did not specifically prohibit threats or assaults on non–family members, such as the woman's new intimate partner. In general, the revised laws include specific "intent" and "credible threat" requirements, broaden definitions, refine wording, stiffen penalties, and emphasize the suspect's pattern of activity.[26]

The effectiveness of stalking laws varies from state to state depending on the language of the law and the attitudes of those enforcing it. A detective's time and effort mean little if the city prosecutor won't take the case. A district attorney can't obtain a conviction if the law leaves gaping loopholes. For example, some states have overly specific stalking laws that allow stalkers to avoid specific items on the laundry list of stalking actions while continuing to terrorize women.

A shortcoming of nearly every stalking code is that penalties are not stiff enough. The National Institute of Justice has encouraged legislators to make aggravated first-time stalking a felony offense rather than a misdemeanor.[27] Most states have ignored the institute's recommendations. Even when a state's stalking laws are better written, the attitude of local law enforcement can prevent a case from ever reaching trial.

Making the Judicial System Accountable

For the most part, the burden of proof falls to the battered woman to show that she has indeed been victimized through the act of stalking. The National Coalition Against Domestic Violence has outlined the following suggestions, which can be helpful in attempts to make law enforcement agencies and the judicial system accountable to battered women.[28]

1. Keep detailed records on the reporting of the incident(s). A copy of the police report, statements of concern about the police or judicial system's treatment of the woman, what services were offered to the woman, the result of any court proceedings related to the incident, and details of the proceedings.
2. If the woman is not satisfied with the enforcement of the law or feels that the incident is not receiving the attention to which it is entitled, she should write a letter addressed to the chief of police, the state's attorney, the chief judge, the attorney general, and a crime victims advocacy group. This letter should clearly identify the following: whether the woman's life is in immediate danger, the nature of the problem, and facts about how and why the incidents fit the pattern of stalking as defined by that state's stalking law. Detailed information from the police or court reports and what action was not taken or enforced by law enforcement or the judicial system should also be included. The letter should clearly state a

request for appropriate action from the persons to whom the letter is addressed.

3. Fax or hand deliver the letters immediately. Copies of the letters should then be sent to all addressees by certified mail with return receipt.
4. A copy of the letters, in addition to copies of the dated return receipts, should be given to a trusted individual.
5. Seek legal counsel for possible legal action.[28]

If You Are Considering Taking Legal Action

When battered women try to access the justice system to protect themselves, they are often thrown into a strange and frightening world. When women do not have access to legal advocates, sensitized lawyers, clerks, police officers, or judges, they often give up in frustration and disgust. The following is offered as a guide for battered women who are considering taking legal action against their abusive partners.

First, I strongly encourage you to contact your local battered women's center to discuss your situation with a legal advocate. If your community does not have a center, advocates at the National Domestic Violence Hotline will be able to help you.

Protection Orders

After you have obtained protection orders, carry them with you *at all times.* Leave a certified copy at the local police precinct where you live or work, where the batterer lives, and where your children go to school or daycare. Make sure that wherever you are likely to encounter the batterer, the police in that area have been notified that an order is in effect.

When Children Are Involved

If at all possible, do not leave your children at home with the batterer. This is true even if they are not in danger, as this may weaken your custody case later. Immediately upon leaving your abusive partner, seek temporary custody of your children as part of the legal proceedings in your civil protection order. Ask your lawyer to arrange to have the court order provide that you will not have to be alone with the abuser when he picks up the children for a visit. Arrange pickups at a relative's home, a church, a public place, or other safe location. If possible, involve a third party in making arrangements and transferring the children for visits and, if necessary, in supervising visits.[29]

If your children are being abused, call your local shelter immediately to discuss the procedures for getting help from the child protection office.

Rehabilitative Maintenance

Also known as temporary alimony, rehabilitative maintenance is payments of support for a specified length of time after separation. You can request these payments in your protection order. Such payments can be used to help you finance your education, training, and therapy.[30]

Building Your Case

Whichever legal route you choose, the more evidence you have that shows you were subjected to abuse, the stronger your case. Police logs, medical records, photographs, and the testimony of those who heard a fight or saw your physical condition afterward can provide good courtroom evidence. Some formerly battered women who have kept journals describing the abuse, including dates and times, have found them to be very helpful.

To establish the evidence, call the police as soon as possible during or after an incident, and ask your neighbors to call too. Seek medical treatment and tell the doctor the full story. Ask your doctor to take photographs of your physical condition, or take them yourself. Torn or bloody clothing and anything used or threatened to be used as a weapon should be kept with the photographs in a secure place until they are turned over to a lawyer or prosecutor.[31]

Legal Procedures to Be Wary of

Two measures to be suspicious of are forced mediation for domestic violence complaints and mutual protection orders imposed on both parties. When domestic violence is present, the power structure of a relationship is not in equilibrium. This can seriously impede the mediation process.

Unfortunately, mediation is often suggested as a way to avoid "wasting" court time and resources. The National Council of Juvenile and Family Court Judges has recommended that no judge mandate mediation in cases in which family violence has occurred.[32]

Mutual protection orders have been discouraged by law in several states. Mutual orders are usually issued by a judge with the consent of the parties and include language that stipulates that both persons will refrain from harassing and assaulting the other. It sounds harmless until you are abused and call the police for help. They may refuse to help, and they may even arrest you because they cannot tell who the likely aggressor is given that both parties have been ordered not to harass the other. The mutual protection order keeps the police, the court, and the batterer from acknowledging that a criminal act has occurred. Avoid any such restraints on your behavior.[33]

Legal Recourses for Lesbians and Gays

Although most domestic violence programs are designed for nongay women, and police may be reluctant to intervene in a lesbian or gay relationship, there is hope. In about thirty states, domestic abuse laws cover unrelated adults of the same sex, so lesbians and gays can use these laws. In all states, criminal law prohibits physical assault and threats. Lesbians and gays interested in utilizing these laws can seek arrest and prosecution of abusive partners.[34]

Legal Recourses for Older Women

In addition to the domestic violence statutes that are available to all battered women, older women can often get help in the form of information or direct assistance from the state or local office on aging or the state protective service.

• • •

The most important goals of the justice system should be to assure both the short-term and long-term safety of battered women. The justice system must do everything it can to support battered women in every act that reduces their isolation and promotes safety and self-esteem.

Simultaneously, the justice system must understand why battered women find it so hard to realistically assess their situations and to regain control of their lives. Blame should not be shifted from the batterer to the woman, nor should her struggles be dismissed as masochistic enjoyment of the abuse.

CHAPTER 6

Living Underground

Getting started can be very hard for people who have trouble with beginnings. After all, where do beginnings begin?

—Dorothy Bryant[1]

In the early morning hours of July 28, 1991, I arose after having spent an exhausting evening of being harassed and threatened by my abusive boyfriend. I packed a small suitcase and waited for my mother, father, brother, and nephew who were soon to arrive. Upon seeing me, my brother confided to my mother that he had seen a lot of scared people in his life, but never anyone as scared as I. He was right. I was about to begin running for my life and I was terrified.

Before me lay a journey that was to prove both difficult and demanding. Living underground, however, was also the beginning of my new life. Several years later, while working at the Austin Center for Battered Women, I began receiving calls from women interested in how they could plan for and live underground. They had heard through the grapevine that I had done this and had survived to tell the tale. I found myself sharing my story with numerous women trying to survive in the same way I had.

Through the years I have had the pleasure to meet a few other women who have also lived underground. Our stories are surprisingly similar. We all made our plans and protected ourselves without the benefit of talking to anyone who had personally accomplished the feat. We gathered bits of information from various sources, including battered women's centers, lawyers, and loved ones. All of us used what we learned, coupled with our own common sense, to protect ourselves. That we are alive today is testimony to the effectiveness of our efforts.

The information in this chapter is based on those personal experiences and from information currently available to the public. Historically, the assumption has been that anything about living underground should not be in print because it will help a batterer find his partner. We have, however, reached a point where this logic no longer serves battered women. There are books available that outline, step-by-step, how to find someone's address, telephone number, and social security number.[2] In contrast, little information is available to help a battered woman thwart her partner's efforts to find her. The information provided in this chapter is intended to fill this void.

Making the Decision to Live Underground

Those of us who chose to live underground did so because we were terribly afraid that our batterers were either going to kill us or harm our children. Our decision represented the final effort to save ourselves and our families after many other strategies had failed. According to Holly, a volunteer at the Austin Center for Battered Women and survivor of an eighteen-year abusive marriage, "I wanted to begin living rather than surviving."

I strongly urge you to seriously consider your decision to go underground. It requires an incredible amount of planning and secrecy and can be very dangerous. You must be committed not only to ending your abusive relationship, but to severing ties with almost everything and everyone familiar to you. You are the best judge as to whether this is what you need to do. When considering this decision, please remember that with careful, thoughtful planning, it is possible to escape and to create the life you want.

All of us who have lived underground had access to trustworthy people and monetary resources to help us escape. If you are considering making this move, you will need to evaluate your own resources. If you do not have trustworthy friends, relatives, or adequate personal finances, do not despair. Contact your local battered women's shelter and ask for help. The people at the shelter are a valuable resource. They will help you address your safety needs and explore your options.

Those of us who successfully lived underground did so without children. Taking children underground is much harder than going by yourself, and there are some serious legal ramifications for taking children with you. All states have enacted criminal parental kidnapping statutes. These laws vary as to whether parental kidnapping is a felony or a misdemeanor. In some states, parental abduction becomes a felony only after the child is transported across state lines.

The criminal liability of unwed parents, joint-custodial parents, and sole-custodial parents varies from state to state. In some states there is no criminal violation if the abduction occurs prior to the issuance of a custody order.[3] If you are considering living underground with children, I encourage you to talk to both a lawyer and a legal advocate at your local battered women's center.

Changing Your Name or Social Security Number

One of the first questions I am asked when people discover that I have lived underground is, "Did you change your name?" Neither I nor any of the women who contributed to this chapter changed our names or social security numbers.

If you are considering a change of name or social security number, the following information may be beneficial, though it does not substitute for sound legal advice. I urge you to discuss these options with a trustworthy lawyer.

State statutes for name changes usually require publication of the change in order to notify creditors and others who have a right to know. To prevent your batterer from discovering your name change, a motion can be made to the court for you to directly notify all your creditors and other interested parties (such as the probation office, the Immigration and Naturalization Service, and the military). This alleviates the need to publicly announce your name change.

An alternative is to request that you be allowed publication of a notice that simply says that you are changing your name, without indicating your new name, and requests that anyone with questions contact your lawyer or the court. You must also ask the court to keep the records confidential or to sequester the file or any papers with the confidential information. This includes not listing anything on the docket sheet that would reveal your current address and new name. You will need to explain the danger you face and that you can keep this information from your batterer only if it is completely inaccessible to everyone.

If you are divorced or were never married to your batterer and have children with him, changing your name will be more difficult. The same procedure is followed, however. If you change your children's names, the father must be notified of the change so that he has an opportunity to argue against it if he so desires. Ask the court not to list the children's new names on your batterer's copy of the papers.[4]

To change your social security number, you must go to the Social Security Administration office and explain why you need to change your number. Be very specific in informing them that you are trying to protect yourself from being located by your batterer. You will have to promise never again to use or reveal your old social security number until the first time you claim benefits from the Social Security Administration. They will then cross-reference your old social security number to the new one so that you will receive your full benefits.[5]

Changing your social security number will not fully protect you, especially if you do not also change your name, and vice versa. Be aware that anything that connects you to your past may give your batterer a way to find you. Continuing to use the same credit cards, having your mail forwarded by the postal service, forwarding of school or medical records, telephone contact with persons from your past, or having money transferred from your old bank account to a new one could be used to locate you.

How You Can Be Found

If you fail to cover your tracks, there are a variety of ways your batterer can find you. This section will outline the ways you can be discovered. Do not be discouraged, however; later in this chapter we will discuss ways to conceal your location.

Information such as your address and social security number can often be obtained through a written request for your driver's license record. Your location can be traced through traffic violations and accident reports. Your batterer can request copies of tickets you have received, which may reveal your current address and telephone number.

States vary as to what information they will release to the public. Some states have instituted a policy of informing an individual that his or her driver's license record was pulled. You may want to check with your state's drivers' records bureau about the policies in your state.

In Texas, driver's license files are open record. The Texas Department of Public Safety must provide driver's record information to anyone making a request and paying the required fees. The department does not maintain a list of who has requested information or inform individuals that a copy of their record has been requested. The department has, however, implemented an Alternate Address Policy, which restricts public access to an individual's address as it appears on the Texas driver's license. If you wish to limit access to your home address, you will need to complete a short form requesting this service.

You can also be traced through motor vehicle registrations. Remember, motor vehicle records departments have varying policies regarding the information they make available to the public. Contact your state's Department of Transportation to learn about the policy in your state.

For example, the policy of the Texas Department of Transportation (TxDOT) is to release information by telephone only when the caller provides the Vehicle Identification Number (VIN). If someone has your license plate number, however, he can go to the county tax office or a TxDOT regional office, or can write to the department. The person making the request will pay a small fee for each inquiry and must sign a form stating that the information will not be used for unlawful purposes.

To avoid detection, a woman residing in Texas can obtain a court order stating that, for safety purposes, her license plate number is to be deleted from the computer system. In the future, she will need to remember when her license plates must be renewed because she will not receive a notice.

If your batterer has your social security number, he can trace you through a variety of places including voter registration records. He can also find the address that you have used for any dealings with certain businesses and credit card companies.[6]

Voter registration information is available upon request and can be accessed with either your name or your social security number. Your latest home address and your social security number may be listed on your registration record. Never reveal an unlisted telephone number. An unlisted telephone number that is part of your voter registration information is considered available to anyone as part of a public record.

Numerous public records can be accessed at the county level. The following is a brief list of records that will contain information about you that may disclose your location. Any of these records can be accessed with just your name. The address listed on these records should not be where you are living. Instead, use a post office box, preferably one in a city where you do not reside.

- Amended judgment
- Assumption agreement
- Assignment of mortgage
- Breach of lease
- Change of name
- Divorce
- Guardianship
- Involuntary bankruptcy
- Judgment
- Lien
- Power of attorney
- Revocation of power of attorney
- Separation
- Trust agreement
- Voluntary bankruptcy

Such licenses as pet, hunting, or fishing licenses are considered public record. Copies of them can be obtained by using only your name and will probably have your telephone number or address listed. Remember, if you put an unlisted number on a license, it becomes public information because you chose to put it on a public record.

If you request that the post office forward your mail, your batterer can obtain your forwarding address for a small fee. His request may be made by mail or in person. However, the postal service will not provide a street address for anyone who uses a post office box for personal mail.[7]

Planning Your Escape

It takes extensive planning and careful attention to detail to prepare to escape an abusive relationship and live underground. The women contributing to this chapter planned from four months to three years. This section outlines the preparations you will need to make including finding a contact person, finding a lawyer, and issues related to your finances, mail, moving, telephone, and house.

Under no circumstances should you tell your batterer you are leaving. If your relationship is so dangerous that you would consider living in hiding, revealing your plans will only jeopardize your safety. Your batterer must believe that life is proceeding as usual. Any suspicious questions or behavior on your part can lead to a fatal confrontation. According to one survivor, "You will never do anything more important than this escape. You can't afford to make a mistake."

Find a Contact Person

If you decide that living underground is what you need to do, the next step is to find a contact person. Carefully evaluate your existing relationships with family and friends to determine whether there is a person you can trust and who is willing to help you. You must be able to trust this person with your life.

Your contact person must be willing to help you through the long haul. Depending on the danger you face, you may need to live underground for a long time. Choose no more than two people to serve as your contacts. This contact person (or persons) should be the only individual who knows your whereabouts while you are underground.

Talk to a Lawyer

If it is safe, ask a close friend or relative for the name of a good lawyer. If you are not comfortable doing this, call your local battered women's shelter and ask if they can refer you to a lawyer. Another option is to call several lawyers listed in the telephone book until you find one you feel you can trust. One survivor recommends interviewing three attorneys. "They usually offer a free thirty-minute introductory session. Get an hour and a half of free legal advise as soon as possible."

A lawyer can provide information regarding stalking laws, civil protection orders, name and social security number changes, divorce, wills, and other legal avenues. If you are married, consider filing for divorce immediately. Before you depart, have the original request for divorce written. Ask your lawyer to have it arrive a few days after you leave. A strong message must be sent that this move and the divorce are ending the relationship.

Your Finances

As soon as you decide to go into hiding, begin saving money. Living underground is expensive. Eating out, even fast food, can cost up to twenty dollars per person, per day. You may need to borrow money from family or friends for your expenses. Several of us had to do this.

Do not leave a paper trail. Plan to take as much money in cash or traveler's checks as possible. Under no circumstances should you write checks or withdraw money from an old account or a joint account while you are underground. If you have a joint account, wait to withdraw money until immediately before your departure. If the account is in your name alone, you may want to close your savings account the day before you leave and wait until later to close your checking account. If your employer owes you money, have them send your checks to your contact person's post office box.

Your Telephone

When planning your move, do not make long-distance calls from your house to your new area or to family or friends or allow anyone else to. Your batterer can use the numbers listed on the telephone bill to discover your location. In addition, your abuser may start harassing your friends or family. Although my batterer and I were not married, he was able to obtain a copy of my last telephone bill. Fortunately, none of these people knew where I was. Regrettably, however, he used the telephone numbers to harass some of these people.

In addition, do not use a calling card if the monthly statement is mailed to your batterer's address. Instead, use a friend's telephone number and reimburse her. If your contact person needs to reach you, ask her to call you either at work or at specific times when your abuser is not around.

Your Mail

There are two ways you can have your mail forwarded. Both options require that all your mail be routed through your contact person. Make arrangements with this person to open a post office box for your mail. Ideally, the mailbox should be in a location other than the city where your contact resides, and it *must* be in a location different from where you are hiding. Your contact will need to collect your mail and forward it to you.

Once the box is established, call your creditors and have them forward your bills to it. The other option is to have the post office forward your mail to your contact's post office box. Remember, however, that if you go through the postal service, your batterer can get a copy of your forwarding address. If you do this, be absolutely certain that your contact person is using a post office box for your mail. Under no circumstances should your contact person use a home address for your forwarded mail.

Your House

When I made the decision to live underground, I resigned myself to abandoning my house and defaulting on my loan. After discussing this with my lawyer and contact person, however, I arranged to give my contact power of attorney to take care of the property for me.

Power of attorney is an excellent way to avoid detection and not lose property you own. It allows your contact to conduct business transactions on your behalf. I gave my contact power of attorney to conduct business transactions related only to the house I owned, allowing my contact person to take care of and to rent my house for me. The bottom line is that I did not default on my loan and ruin my credit.

If your contact does not want the responsibility of renting your house to someone, power of attorney will allow that person to turn the property over to a real estate agent who can rent your house. If you find yourself in a similar situation, talk to your contact person and your lawyer about using this strategy to protect property you own.

The Move

When planning your move, check and double-check the dates and times when your batterer will be out of the house for at least eight hours. A business trip or special meeting at work are safer days than most. One survivor reports, "Even knowing my ex-husband was meeting and entertaining out-of-town clients, he still came home four hours early. The movers and I missed him by forty-five minutes." Knowing that my batterer had a very unpredictable schedule, I made arrangements for family members to move my possessions into storage so I could leave immediately upon their arrival. This may have saved my life. My batterer showed up less than an hour after I left.

If you hire a moving company, do not give them your telephone number. Be very direct in telling them that this is a confidential move. Under no circumstances should the moving company call your house. Advise them that you will contact them to confirm the move.

If you use moving boxes, hide them in a safe place or store them at a trusted neighbor's. Breakables can be wrapped in clothing, towels, and sheets. Take as much out of your house as you can. It will be much easier to return something later than to get something you forgot. If in doubt, take it. Be sure to take anything that has sentimental value to you as this may be your last chance to save it.

Other Considerations

If you write down any of your plans, keep them where your batterer cannot find them, such as at work or with your contact person. Your contact person can help you check and double-check your plan.

In arranging for a place to live while in hiding, all of us initially stayed in locations distant from our contact person. Some women had found jobs before their moves; others had not. I lived with trusted relatives in various locations for three months before I found a job and was able to move my possessions to a semi-permanent location. Whether you immediately move to a new location or live on the run as I did, your contact person should be the only person who knows your whereabouts all the time.

Living in Hiding

Plan on living underground for at least a year. One former battered woman reported living underground for two and a half years. Once you have begun your new life, it is absolutely crucial that you continue to protect yourself and guard your location. This section discusses the ways you can keep yourself safe while you begin to rebuild your life.

Your Mail

During the entire time you live underground, continue to use your contact person's post office box for all credit card and other bills that may show up on a credit report. During this time, your contact will need to forward your mail to you. For local bills, such as gas and electricity bills, open a post office box in your community. Under no circumstances should you receive mail at your home address.

If you write to friends or relatives, place the addressed letter in another envelope and mail it to your contact person to mail it for you. If you mail it from your location, it will be postmarked with your city's name or that of a city close to you.

Your Finances

If you open a new savings account, the bank will require your social security number for income tax purposes. Don't forget that your batterer can find your location if he has access to your social security number. Consider opening a joint savings account with your contact person at a financial institution near the city in which your contact person resides. Give the bank your social security number; however, the address on the account should be your contact's post office box. If you need money, your contact can make the withdrawal and forward it to you.

When opening a new checking account, consider opening a joint account with your contact person and using that person's social security number. You will now have a checking account that you can use, but your batterer will not be able to trace your social security number to it. The only personal information that should appear on the checks is your name and mailing address. Your mailing address should be the post office box that you have opened in your new community.

Your Telephone

When setting up an account with your local telephone company, ask for an unlisted number. Explain your situation and discuss how you can make certain that your name and number are never disclosed in any manner to anyone. Stress the danger you face and your safety needs.

Avoid making calls to family or friends from your underground location. People with Caller ID on their telephones will then be able to discover your location. If you must call someone from your underground location, ask the telephone company for instructions on using Caller ID Blocking to prevent your number from being disclosed. One of the safest ways to contact anyone from your past is in writing in the manner previously discussed.

Personal Safety

While living underground it is best to act as though your batterer knows where you are. Keep all doors and windows securely locked. Carefully look outside before leaving your house. Drive by your house or look at your front door before entering. Change your coming and going times. Don't be predictable.

Consider renting a security apartment, which is a unit in a building with a front entrance and access from a hallway rather than from outside.

Show a picture of your batterer to as many neighbors as possible. Explain your situation and let them know he is dangerous. Ask them to call the police if they see him anywhere near your house.

Plan an escape route out of your house or apartment in the event that he breaks in. If you live in a two-story structure, buy a "fire ladder" at a hardware store and keep it under your bed.

Ask your local police department if they will send someone out to assess your home security and to point out what needs attention. Many police departments provide this service for members of their community. Also ask to speak to someone in the assault unit, and explain your situation to that person. Ask how the assault unit handles domestic violence calls. Get the person's name and make sure you give them your name. This groundwork may help if your batterer is able to find you.

Other Considerations

As you begin opening new accounts and establishing residence in your new community, be prepared to explain your situation to new neighbors, your employer, and others who need to know. Although it was embarrassing to reveal my situation to strangers, I found most people receptive and concerned for my safety.

Make sure your new employer understands why you are living underground, and ask that no information be given to anyone about you, regardless of the circumstances. Show your batterer's picture to your employer, and ask that the police be called if he appears at your place of employment.

Never forget how easy it is for someone to get your address, telephone number, and social security number. Use your post office box as little as possible. Always try to route your mail through your contact's post office box. Never give out your home address or telephone number.

It may help to try to think like your batterer in order to anticipate what he may do to find you. This will allow you to stay at least one step ahead of him.

After a year, consider finding a permanent place to live. Even if your batterer has not contacted you at your underground address, assume he has discovered your location. One more move will get you even farther from your batterer and will be well worth the work. And this time you will be moving toward something rather than running away from someone.

The Joys and Challenges of Living Underground

Initially, feelings of loneliness and isolation were very present in our lives. Not being able to entertain friends or family, giving up friendships, the fear of being located by our batterers, and living alone in a new city proved to be very challenging for all of us.

I was particularly angered by the fact that I was having to live my life as if I had done something wrong. I also became very tired of explaining my abusive relationship to strangers.

After a few months, however, something miraculous began to happen to all of us. We became aware of the peace and serenity in our lives. According to one survivor, "At one point I realized that my batterer wasn't going to call me on the phone or show up on my doorstep."

All of us used this time to begin healing from the years of abuse we had suffered. As we began to reclaim our lives, we experienced what I refer to as a rebirth. Not many people have this opportunity. Today, our lives are very different from those we once knew. Best of all, we now live with peace in our hearts and in our lives.

CHAPTER 7

The Oppression that Binds: Barriers to Living Violence Free

The oppression of women knows no ethnic nor racial boundaries, true, but that does not mean it is identical within those differences.

—Audre Lorde[1]

In the past twenty years, the battered women's movement in the United States has made enormous strides in establishing shelters and other domestic violence programs. In addition, a large number of social service agencies are addressing the problem of domestic violence.

To effectively advocate for battered women, domestic violence programs and other agencies must provide services that are culturally and group specific and operate from an understanding of women's diverse backgrounds. Insensitivity to these differences alienates battered women and fails to meet some of their very specific needs.

All women face barriers when trying to escape battering relationships. These barriers can be grouped into four basic categories.[2]

- **Personal barriers** such as shame, fear, lack of personal resources, and lack of emotional support
- **Relationship barriers** such as denied access to money, transportation, jobs, and the physical abuse itself
- **Institutional barriers** such as immigration policies, cultural insensitivity, a lack of services, discrimination, sexism, and other forms of oppression
- **Cultural barriers** such as language differences, beliefs about marriage and the family, gender roles, and religious beliefs

Combined, these barriers create formidable obstacles that women must address and overcome in order to live their lives violence free.

Two factors contribute to the ongoing maintenance of violent relationships. The first is the degree to which women are isolated from key support systems. Our society continues to not only marginalize, but to make invisible, women of color, older women, lesbians, women with disabilities, and other communities of women. When this is coupled with women's isolation from friends and family, their risk of being abused greatly increases.

Second, society's continued reluctance to provide opportunities for women to access such resources as education, skills, and jobs can foster women's dependency on their partners. Together, social isolation and dependency help keep women entrenched in violent relationships that may eventually cost them their lives.

The following summaries are a brief overview of the major barriers that women of color and other communities of women must address when confronting abusive relationships. Notice how these personal, relationship, institutional, and cultural barriers work to increase women's isolation and dependency.

Women of Color

Women of color comprise highly heterogeneous populations and make diverse choices in coping, functioning, and empowering themselves. The communities of women of color are highly diverse with regard to economic status, family structure, occupation, and lifestyle. In addition, differences exist among women from the same ethnic and racial group.[3]

Women of color also have different interpersonal styles. An *acculturated* woman of color is one who has chosen to assimilate into white society and has rejected the general attitudes, behavior, customs, and rituals of her culture of origin. A *bicultural* woman of color has pride in her racial and cultural identity and yet is comfortable operating in the white world. A *culturally immersed* woman of color has openly rejected white values, embracing the identity and traditions of her cultural group. Finally, a woman of color with a *traditional* interpersonal style usually has limited contact outside her community of color, may be older or newly immigrated, and speaks only the language of her traditional culture. Depending on a woman's place in the acculturation process, the challenges to helping her address her abuse vary.

While there is great diversity among women of color, one common barrier that all women of color face is the racism in our society. Racism, at both the individual and institutional levels, affects the quality of services and support battered women of color receive. In fact, the level of racism in any particular community will help determine whether any services are made available to battered women of color.

Battered African American Women

In addition to sexist and racist attitudes and practices, battered African American women face a number of other barriers that they must address to live violence free.

Internalized Societal Images

The image of African American women as long-suffering victims can create confusion about the abuse in their lives. According to Evelyn White, author of *Chain Chain Change: For Black Women Dealing with Physical and Emotional Abuse*, "The images and expectations of black women are actually both super and sub-human. . . . This conflict has created many myths and stereotypes that cause confusion about our own identity and make us targets for abuse." These negative and conflicting images may make women wonder who they really are and what their partners and society expect from them.[4]

The Family

Many African Americans have mothers, fathers, sisters, and brothers who are not blood relatives. These individuals are considered as much a part of the family as real family members. Socialization in the black family is an important part of understanding the identity of the abused woman. There may be intense loyalty to the extended family and strong vows of privacy and respect for the family unit.

While this support network enriches the black community, it can hinder women who approach family or friends about the violence in their lives. These support persons may have divided loyalties and feel they are being pressured to take sides.[5]

Religious Beliefs

Many African American women have strong religious beliefs dating back to early childhood and typically comprise about 70 percent of black congregations. Religious beliefs or fear of rejection from the church may keep women in abusive relationships.[6]

Conflicted Loyalty

According to White, because women and men live in the same racist society, women cannot help but be sympathetic to what African American men suffer. "We know that the black family has been damaged by slavery, lynchings and systematized social, economic and educational discrimination. Though we have surely been divided as black men and women, our mutual suffering has prevented us from completely turning our backs on each other."[7]

Many women in violent relationships fear that if they report an abusive partner, he will be treated more harshly by law enforcement officials because he is a man of color. This sense of conflicted loyalty may prevent many battered women from reaching for help.[8]

Shelter Services

Some women may be reluctant to leave a familiar network of neighbors, family, and friends to live in a shelter with a group of people they don't know. In addition, many shelters are predominantly staffed by persons that black women have learned to mistrust. If the shelter is located in a white neighborhood, this may create enhanced feelings of vulnerability, visibility, and exposure.

Regrettably, shelters are not immune to the racism that exists in society, and some can be run in ways that are insensitive to the needs or perspectives of black women.[9] According to Pat Clark, coordinator of women's advocacy for the Austin Center for Battered Women, "One of the hardest things for black women to deal with is to leave their homes and live in a shelter that is almost completely staffed by white women. It's definitely a trust issue. Our community believes that you don't put your trust in the white system. To do so implies you're turning against your own race."

Battered Latinas

Latinas are an extremely heterogeneous group with respect to country of origin, race, education, income, age, religion, marital status, years in the United States, language, acculturation, and cultural values. All these factors play a part in understanding the culture and the community of Latinas in abusive relationships.

Latina and *Hispanic* are general terms used to refer to Spanish-speaking women from Mexico, Puerto Rico, the Dominican Republic, Cuba, Guatemala, Nicaragua, El Salvador, the rest of Central America, and all the countries of South America. They also include generations who are born in the United States and call themselves Mexican Americans, Chicanas, Cuban Americans, and Nuyoricans (people of Puerto Rican descent who were born in New York). All have different histories and cultural backgrounds.[10]

Cultural Expectations

The Latino culture is a patriarchy with a long-established social system. Women are often relegated to the roles of wife and mother. It is not socially acceptable to be divorced, to marry several times, or to remain single and have children out of wedlock. For these reasons it may take some time for battered women to consider leaving their partners. According to Myrna M. Zambrano, author of *Mejor Sola Que Mal Acompañada: For the Latina in an Abusive Relationship*, "Latinas have little representation in political and economic arenas. We are not only denied equality by American society, but by our own Raza, by our own men. It is time that we demand and take the place we deserve, a seat beside them, with full voice and vote. Until we are recognized as true partners, we will not command the respect that is necessary to make rape and physical abuse a thing of the past."[11]

The Family

Latinas usually look toward the family as the center of culture. Being a woman in Latino culture implies responsibility to husbands or other significant males such as fathers and brothers. Family relationships are dictated by a definite authority structure of age, gender, and role.

The authority of the family is respected. Individual needs often defer to family unity and strength. For battered women this often means tolerating abuse for the sake of family pride and preservation. Problems are usually kept in the home. Counseling may be received from a priest or other respected authority, and help from outside agencies is rarely sought.[12]

Lucy Muñoz, a women's advocate with the Austin Center for Battered Women, explains that the people most important to battered Latinas—that is, their families—are also those least likely to support them if they leave. According to Muñoz, "When we marry we are supposed to stay married—no matter what happens. If we try to leave abusive marriages our families do not support us. In fact, they will often try to make us return."

Guarded Trust

Latinas are not accustomed to revealing their feelings to outsiders and may find it difficult to express themselves to strangers. If battered Latinas do seek help outside their family, they may be reluctant to discuss their abuse. Details about their personal lives are reserved for those they trust.

Financial Barriers

Latinas are more concentrated in low-paying, semiskilled occupations than the overall workforce. The money women need to move or to obtain a lawyer is not always available. For Latinas who drop out of school, poor education and lack of skills make it difficult to get better-paying jobs. Additionally, opportunities for job advancement are not always comparable to those of white women because of racial discrimination.[13]

Religious Beliefs

Latinas often accept their situations with resignation, believing their family life is the way God wants them to live. They may feel that the power to change is not in their hands and prefer to accept a bad situation rather than attempt to correct it because this is seen as arrogance before God.

In addition, limited access to birth control, lack of information about contraception, and Catholic doctrine often result in a larger family, which can make it difficult to move or to find affordable child care.

Language Barriers

Being abused is embarrassing to discuss, and talking about it is even more difficult when language and cultural barriers exist. Even if women speak English, it may not be a language in which they are comfortable expressing their feelings.

Battered Asian Women

Battered Asian women have a difficult legacy to bear. The abusive treatment they receive grows out of deeply rooted cultural and social values of both their country of origin and the United States. Although the Asian culture is the source of much strength, it also contributes to a tolerance of domestic violence. The unequal status of women and the right of men to beat them has been asserted throughout the centuries in Asia.[14]

The Family

Mutual obligation and self-reliance within the extended family structure are valued in Asian cultures. If there is a conflict between an individual's needs and the family's goals, the family's goals are given priority. Maintaining family harmony is often at the expense of women, particularly wives and daughters-in-law.

Interdependence of family members and the importance of mutual help and support are deeply ingrained values. Reporting the batterer's abuse to outsiders will frequently make an Asian woman feel disloyal. Her socialization in an Asian culture may make her feel that she has brought shame to her family, either because she believes she is in some way responsible for the abuse or because she reported it.

Support Systems

Asian families who resettle in the United States. frequently leave behind members of their extended family. The extended family, consisting of aunts, uncles, grandparents, and cousins, makes up the traditional Asian support system and acts as a mechanism for controlling domestic violence. With the loss of the extended family, this support and control is also lost.

Children

Some Asian women fear that moving away from their abusive husbands will mean losing their children or, at the least, stigmatizing their children. The Asian community reinforces the belief that women must not leave their family and community.[15]

Family Privacy

Another barrier for women who need help is the Asian attitude toward "private" issues. Most battered women feel ashamed about their abuse, but these feelings are even more pronounced for Asian women. It is considered inappropriate to discuss family matters outside the family as to do so brings shame to the family.

Self-Control

Emotional control is considered a mature trait in the Asian culture. Open displays of pain or anger are thought to be immature and unworthy of cultured adults, particularly women. For this reason, Asian women seldom express their true feelings and emotions, except among very close relatives or friends.

Assuming Responsibility

Assuming responsibility for problems is considered virtuous, and readiness for self-blame is particularly valued in women. While this tendency toward self-blame is similar to that experienced by American women, the Asian woman's self-blame should be considered in the context of her cultural socialization rather than as a manifestation of low self-esteem.

Resignation

Perseverance and the acceptance of suffering are highly valued virtues among Asian cultures. What appears to be the passivity and apathy of a battered Asian woman is often a culturally based response to adversity.

Respect for Authority

Asian women are socialized not to question the commands or decisions of persons in authority and not to express their own wishes or opinions. The Western values of direct self-expression and self-determination are unfamiliar concepts. This cultural conditioning may prevent her from asking for help or from questioning racist treatment by a service provider.

Immigration Barriers

Immigrating to the United States involves many adjustments. Women must deal with a new sociopolitical system and a new language. Some are not citizens and don't want to make trouble or bring attention to themselves for fear of being deported.

Lack of Information

Some battered Asian women don't seek help about their violent relationships because they don't know that it is wrong. Many do not even realize that battering is a crime and punishable by law or that they have legal rights and can press charges.[16]

Battered Asian Indian Women

South Asia includes the geographical area of the entire Indian subcontinent: India, Pakistan, Sri Lanka, Nepal, Bhutan, and Bangladesh. Although there are strong similarities among the social and cultural structures of the various South Asian nations, the region is not monolithic.[17]

In addition to fourteen official languages, Asian Indians speak hundreds of dialects that are nestled within each language. Although Hinduism is the most popular religion in India, there are a variety of other major religions such as Christianity, Islam, Jainism, Buddhism, Sikhism, Sufism, Zoroastrianism, and Judaism.[18]

Power relations between men and women are intertwined with other structures of social hierarchy such as class and caste. In addition, the relationship between two women of the same household is affected by their relations to the men in the household and by the men's relationship. Familial relations are also characterized by hierarchy of age.[19]

The Family

Group and family identity are emphasized in the Asian Indian culture. Family ties are further complicated by the tradition of extended family. Since group identity is given priority, battered women may hesitate to make decisions to end abusive relationships before they consider the feelings of other family members. Women may consider not only their parents' wishes, but those of their grandparents and other significant relatives.

Arranged marriage is still a norm in these cultures. The relationship between a man and a woman may initially begin with a relationship between the families. Separation, divorce, and remarriage may not be considered for fear of shaming and dishonoring the family. In addition, there may be pressure from the family to reconcile and continue living with the batterer.[20]

Family Privacy

Within the Asian Indian family, there are strict rules about privacy intended to maintain family honor. Family matters are not shared with individuals outside the family. Neighbors and friends may, however, gain the status of relatives by establishing kinship with a family.[21]

Isolation

Kalpana Sutaria, president and cofounder of Saheli, a support group for Asian battered women in Austin, Texas, explains that the fear of being isolated from the family is one of the greatest barriers for Asian Indian women to overcome. "Even more than a lack of resources, Asian Indian women's fear of loneliness and isolation keep them tied to abusive relationships. I continue to hear, over and over again, 'Who are going to be my friends? Am I going to be all alone?'"

The absence of a protective support system composed of family, friends, and neighbors increases women's social isolation. It also intensifies their dependency on the abusive relationship. In addition, many women are forbidden by their husbands to contact friends and family or to develop friendships. They may be denied access to postage, money, telephones, and transportation.[22]

Shelter Services

For Asian Indian women who are already feeling emotionally and culturally isolated, the unfamiliar nature of shelters may heighten their sense of alienation. Additional complications may arise from their unwillingness to trust shelter staff, police, and other support personnel.

Services considered standard for other groups of women may be both unfamiliar and uncomfortable for Asian Indian women. The food provided at the shelter may create problems, especially if the women are vegetarian. Most Asian Indian women are uncomfortable about undressing in front of anyone. The informal habits women often display in exclusively female surroundings can make Asian Indian women very ill at ease.[23]

Battered Native American Women

Like other communities of women of color, there is tremendous within-group diversity in the Native American culture. Native American women have different languages, traditions, and spiritual beliefs. There are 365 state-recognized Native American tribes with 200 distinct languages in the United States. Further complicating the issue of heterogeneity is the continuous migration between reservations and urban areas.[24] A battered Native American woman may have a different framework based on whether she grew up in an urban setting or on a reservation.

The Historical Context of Domestic Violence

Varying rates and patterns of abuse exist among different tribes. It is important to note, however, that domestic violence is a relatively new phenomenon in the Native American culture. Abuse of both Native American women and children by Native American men can be traced to the introduction of alcohol, Christianity, and the European hierarchical family structure. Women from the Sacred Shawl Women's Society on the Pine Ridge reservation in South Dakota report that while domestic violence existed in pre-reservation society, it was both rare and severely reprobated.[25]

Many traditional Native American histories indicate that when domestic violence did occur, the community responded. The batterer would be banished or ostracized, or retaliation was left to the male relatives of the victim.[26] Such traditional methods of addressing domestic violence were eliminated or limited with the advent of a Western European criminal justice process.

One possible reason abuse rarely occurred in pre-reservation society can be traced to traditional tribal legends that assert the sacredness and importance of women in a spiritual, economic, and political sense.[27]

Societal Oppression

Several factors have accompanied the increase in domestic violence in Native American communities. These include the removal of Native Americans from their ancestral lands, suppressed religious and cultural practices, forced removal of Native American children into foster homes and boarding schools, a disruption of traditional living patterns compounded by the poverty of reservation life, and a 90 percent reduction of the Native American population from the time of European contact to the establishment of reservations. These dramatic changes in social, spiritual, and economic structure have drastically undermined traditional ways of life.[28]

The Family

The Native American family is an extended one that includes aunts, uncles, grandparents, cousins, as well as adopted relatives. The nuclear family of mother, father, and children is considered a household within the family.[29]

Native American families are very close. If domestic violence occurs, the family is expected to take care of the problem. If a Native American woman goes outside the family for help, she is ostracized by her family and the batterer's family.

The Reservation

Some Native American women have resided on the same reservation for their entire lives. If a battered woman leaves her home to go to a shelter, she is forced to leave both familiar surroundings and her support system.

Many women residing on reservations live in such poverty that they do not have access to telephones, transportation, or child care. In many cases, the remote areas in which they live do not even have telephone lines or a transportation system. Some battered Native American women do not speak English. All these factors severely impact women's help-seeking behavior.[30]

Confidentiality

Confidentiality is a major issue in small communities. Sanctions within tribal or clan groups or other subgroups are often more severe in relation to an informant than to an abuser. Although the community may view the behavior of the batterer as undesirable, the decision to contact the external legal system or to reveal details of intimate family life is often viewed as disloyal. In addition, due to various group and subgroup relationships, outside intervention is often viewed by battered women as undesirable.[31]

Spirituality

Native American spirituality can be a source of profound support, comfort, and healing for many battered women. According to Karen Artichoker, coauthor of *Domestic Violence Is Not Lakota/Dakota Tradition,* it can also serve to keep them in abusive relationships. The idea of connectedness to the earth and to each other is frequently used by the batterer and other family members as a reason for the woman to remain in a violent relationship.

Trust

Many Native American women have a high level of mistrust for white agencies and helpers. This lack of trust is not difficult to understand given the historically oppressive way that white society has treated Native Americans. This mistrust may keep the battered woman from reaching out for help. In many cases, when battered Native American women do reach out, they are confronted with helpers who are insensitive to their unique lifeways and culture.

Battered Undocumented Immigrant Women

Despite the expanding awareness of the devastating consequences of domestic violence, battered undocumented immigrant women continue to be marginalized and out of reach of helpful services. Since the mid 1980s, there has been an increasing climate of racism and intolerance against immigrants, who have been portrayed as threatening economic, cultural, and political life in the United States, as well as being blamed for increased unemployment and crime. Caught up in this environment of intolerance, Congress, beginning in 1986, codified a number of measures that served to severely restrict immigration to the United States.[32]

Immigration laws and policies have never reflected the needs of women. Women were originally prevented from entering this country as separate entities due to the doctrine of coverture, which stated that the husband is the head of the household and that a woman's nationality and residence follows that of her husband.

Immigrant women are at risk from domestic violence because immigration laws have made them dependent on their husbands to achieve lawful residence in the United States. In 1986, the Immigration Marriage Fraud Act (IMFA) created additional obstacles for immigrant women seeking lawful permanent residence in the United States on the basis of their marriage to either a United States citizen or a lawful permanent resident. Although the harsh impact of the IMFA has been somewhat softened as a result of amendments to the act in 1990 and 1991, and despite the Violence Against Women Act legislation, battered undocumented women continue to remain largely out of reach and unable to access the help, services, and legal resources available to them.[33]

Legal Services

Family law practitioners who are competent to deal with domestic violence issues are often untrained in immigration practice. Immigration practitioners are able to assist with visa matters and applications for lawful permanent residence, but may lack knowledge of the domestic violence issues their clients face. As a result, recent amendments to immigration statutes that specifically apply to battered women may not be utilized because of the dichotomy between family law practitioners and immigration practitioners.

In addition, immigrant women may be unfamiliar with ways to access the legal system for any type of assistance. They may not realize that domestic violence is against the law. They may also be unaware that they have legal options and that there are agencies and community resources available to support them.

Obtaining Permanent Residence

Battered immigrant women are often faced with the threat of deportation not only from the Immigration and Naturalization Service (INS), but also from their spouses. This is a particularly effective way for batterers to maintain power and control over their wives.

If women try to escape abusive relationships, they may risk their ability to obtain lawful permanent residence, which may rely solely on their husbands' cooperation with the INS. They may face deportation to their country of origin. For women who have fled persecution in their home country, deportation could mean torture, jail, or death. For others, it can mean a return to a life of extreme poverty, disease, and little or no opportunity.

Perhaps the worst threat is that women may have to leave their U.S.-born children. Once deported, the women can be excluded from the United States for five years. Deportation is something most battered immigrant women are not willing to risk. If they are unaware that they may have other legal avenues to obtain lawful permanent residence, most will be reluctant to leave a violent relationship.[34]

Community Resources

In a 1992 study conducted by the Texas Department of Human Services and the Texas Council on Family Violence, shelters in Texas reported that the community resources most accessible to battered undocumented women are counseling, immigration information, and education. The community resources that are most difficult for battered undocumented women to utilize are employment and housing.[35]

Most family violence shelters are not providing battered undocumented women with unique services or services different from those provided to women who are United States citizens. Shelters may want to help, but have limited bilingual staff and a limited understanding of the unique needs of undocumented women and how to help them.

Language Barriers

Often, battered immigrant women are without sufficient English language skills to enable them to seek help or use resources. Women who cannot speak English cannot communicate with their neighbors, the police, lawyers, doctors, or advocates. They may even become alienated from family members as their children or working husbands gain fluency. Women may become more dependent on their husbands or other family members to interpret the culture for them.[36]

Cultural and Social Barriers

Cultural and social differences prevent many battered immigrant women from readily seeking help. When discussing immigrant women, we must consider their experiences in light of at least two sets of extended social relations, the current social relations in the United States and those in the women's countries of origin. Cultural norms concerning a woman's place, family, marriage, sex roles, and divorce may contribute to an environment in which an immigrant woman feels isolated and powerless to escape the violence.

Financial Barriers

Immigrant women are often economically dependent on their partners to a greater extent than most women who are citizens or lawful permanent residents. Economic dependence is intensified due to the impact of immigration laws concerning employer sanctions and hiring practices as well as immigration laws and regulations that may make immigrant women ineligible for most forms of public assistance or income entitlement programs.[37]

Health Services

Many battered immigrant women do not know how to gain access to health services. Even when they are able to access such services, language barriers make it difficult to discuss their health problems. Women may be reluctant to discuss certain aspects of their anatomy with male medical personnel, and they may not want their children to interpret for them.[38]

Battered Lesbians and Gays

Although the battered women's movement has been advocating for battered women and their children for many years, little has been done to address this problem in the lesbian and gay community. This is sadly ironic considering that lesbians have helped start many of the domestic violence programs in the United States.

Violence in lesbian relationships occurs at about the same frequency as violence in nongay relationships.[39] Battered lesbians and gays suffer from the same physical, emotional, and sexual abuse as their nongay counterparts. Gin, a volunteer at the Austin Center for Battered Women and a former battered lesbian, explains a particularly frightening incident she experienced. "She caught me off guard when she burst through the door and punched me in the stomach. She proceeded to punch me several more times, then she grabbed me by the neck and pushed me against the wall yelling, 'If you ever leave me I'll kill you and then kill myself.'"

Homophobia

Although lesbian and gay battering has definite similarities with nongay battering, there are some distinct barriers lesbians and gays must confront. Suzanne Pharr, writing in *Naming the Violence: Speaking Out About Lesbian Battering,* explains: "There is an important difference between the battered lesbian and the battered non-lesbian: the battered non-lesbian experiences violence within the context of a misogynist world; the lesbian experiences violence within the context of a world that is not only woman-hating, but is also homophobic. And that is a great difference."[40]

Pharr defines homophobia as the irrational fear and hatred of people who love and sexually desire those of the same sex.[41] The norm in most of the United States is that it is perfectly acceptable to be overtly homophobic. Unfortunately, battered lesbians and gays must overcome not only the fear of abuse from their partners, but also the possibility of added victimization by homophobic service providers, law enforcement agencies, prosecutors, and judges.

Myths and Stereotypes

While myths and stereotypes abound for nongay battered women, they are even more numerous for battered lesbians and gays. In attempting to ascertain the causes and contributing factors of same-sex abuse, many inaccurate stereotypes have evolved. One widespread misconception is that abusive women are stronger and characteristically more "butch" than battered women, who are stereotyped as more passive or "femme."

Another harmful myth surrounding same-sex battering is that of "mutual battering." This is an example of victim blaming and is simply another way to minimize and dismiss same-sex abuse. While some battered lesbians and gays have been violent toward their abusive partners, the violence is largely in self-defense and may be rage at past violence.[42]

These myths grow from misconceptions about lesbian and gay couples and a simplistic understanding of the factors that contribute to men's domination over women. As long as our society continues to perpetuate these myths and stereotypes, effective advocacy for battered lesbians and gays will be hindered. In addition, these myths frequently give batterers additional ammunition with which to further intimidate and control their partners.

The Lesbian and Gay Community

The lesbian and gay community's response to battering has also been impacted by homophobia. Denial, minimization, and rationalization about abuse has been the community's way to protect itself from a society that is looking for reasons to condemn lesbians and gays as sick and perverted. In addition, the lesbian community may minimize lesbian violence because it doesn't want to destroy the myth of a "lesbian utopia."[43]

According to Claire Renzetti, author of *Violent Betrayal: Partner Abuse in Lesbian Relationships,* "Acknowledging that lesbian battering is a serious problem may indeed be unpleasant, even painful, for the lesbian community. But until such acknowledgment is made, until victims' needs are effectively and sensitively met, and until batterers are challenged and held accountable for their behavior, all lesbians are unsafe and the struggle for the creation of a peaceful, egalitarian community of women is violently betrayed."[44]

Outing

One common intimidation and control tactic used by abusive lesbians and gays is the threat of "outing," the unwelcome disclosure of a person's sexual orientation. Batterers may threaten to "out" their partners to family, friends, employers, and church communities if they attempt to leave the relationship. Depending on the circumstances, outing can mean loss of a job, support systems, and even child custody.

Isolation

Lesbians and gays frequently obtain their emotional support from the lesbian and gay community. Many lesbian and gay couples share close friends. Battered lesbians and gays may experience conflicts about whom they can talk to. They may fear shaming their partners before mutual friends or fear that mutual friends will take the abusive partners' side.

It may be difficult for battered lesbians and gays who are not out to turn to relatives for support. In addition, many lesbians and gays have lost the support of relatives and nongay friends when they have come out.

Survivors of same-sex battering may be isolated from the lesbian and gay community because of geographic location, fear of coming out, or lack of knowledge about how to find other lesbians and gays. They may see their abusive partners as their only support system.[45]

In addition, the lesbian and gay community is frequently small, even in larger cities. In some cases the community is so small that anonymity and confidentiality cannot be assured.

Safety

Battered lesbians face safety issues quite different from those of their nongay sisters. Batterers may try to enter shelters and support groups, claiming they are the victims being battered, not their partners. If shelters do not screen female visitors as effectively as they do male visitors, a female batterer's access to her partner is made much easier.

Although shelter locations are often well-guarded secrets from men, they may be known to lesbian batterers if the batterers are a part of the women's movement in the community.[46]

The Legal System

In most states, domestic violence statutes do not explicitly apply to lesbian and gay couples, and in those states where they do apply, the police and the courts do not consistently or fairly enforce them in cases involving same-sex couples.[47]

Police officers frequently minimize the violence that battered lesbians and gays experience and do less to intervene. Minimizing the violence creates the potential for more mutual arrests and leads to arrests being wrongly categorized under disorderly conduct charges. The police frequently fail to inform battered lesbians and gays about local domestic violence programs that may be of assistance. The culmination of all these homophobic actions is that battered lesbians and gays and their abusive partners receive the message that violent behavior is not a serious criminal action.

Children

The homophobic fear of lesbians raising children may increase scrutiny by child protective services. In addition, a battered lesbian may face custody battles if she prosecutes her abusive female partner and the children's father is unaware of the fact that she is a lesbian.

Shelter Services

Shelter programs were designed and developed to respond to the needs of women who are being battered by men. This assumption influences everything from philosophy and policies to actual services. In the past, there has been a tremendous fear of addressing same-sex abuse. Many shelters fear they will jeopardize their programs' credibility or lose hard-won funding if they publicly acknowledge this problem. This is an example of *lesbian baiting*, or attempting to control women by accusing them of being lesbians when they engage in behavior considered inappropriate. It prevents many domestic violence programs from effectively meeting the needs of a population of women and men at risk for abuse.

If battered lesbians and gays do reach out to local domestic violence programs, there is no guarantee that advocates will be understanding or sensitive to their needs. Like other forms of oppression, homophobia can and does occur among shelter staff. In addition, battered lesbians may be entering a shelter where the residents are homophobic as well. For men in same-sex abusive relationships, there may be no shelter services available.

Battered Older Women

Domestic violence among our older population is a reality and, as the population continues to age, is a problem not likely to just disappear. There are more people sixty-five and older today than in any other period of history. In 1900, 4 percent of the United States population was age sixty-five or older, while people under age eighteen made up 40 percent of the population. By the year 2020, 22 percent of the population will be sixty-five or older and 21 percent will be under age eighteen.[48] As baby boomers continue to age, the need for services for battered older women is likely to increase.

Elder abuse is more frequently compared to child abuse than to spouse abuse within the context of family violence. This is due to the misconception that elder abuse is solely a problem of care giving. The parallel is, however, fundamentally flawed. First and foremost, older women are not children. To be compared as such is both paternalistic and condescending and ultimately demeans and devalues older women. Moreover, treating older women like children not only ignores differences between adults and children, it also ignores the range of abusive situations to which older women may be exposed.[49]

Secondly, elder abuse does not always occur by a caretaker against a dependent victim. In a survey of older adults living in the Boston area, results indicated that most mistreatment was committed by one spouse against another. Sixty-five percent of the abuse cases were between spouses, and only 23 percent involved an adult-child caregiver abusing a parent.[50]

Even when the older woman is dependent, the conditions of dependency are very different from those of children. Parents have a clear legal responsibility for children, unlike almost all caregivers of older adults. Unless proven otherwise, older women are considered to be competent, responsible individuals and are therefore responsible for decisions regarding their own lives.[51]

Who Is the Battered Older Woman?

In a study conducted by the Community Care Organization of Milwaukee and the Wisconsin Coalition Against Domestic Violence, twenty-one battered older women participated in in-depth interviews about the violence they had experienced. Most of the women were in relatively good health. Most of the women abused by their partners were abused for the entire length of the relationship. These women were extremely isolated and difficult to locate. The majority of these women did not want to discuss the abuse with anyone, and few contacted agencies for help.[52]

Ageism

Older adults are especially vulnerable to abuse because of the social status they occupy. Systematic stereotyping and discrimination against older adults contribute to their isolation and devaluation.

When battered older women reach out for help, service providers sometimes respond in an ageist manner. Ageism is a system of destructive, false beliefs about older adults. In addition, service providers may neglect to consider the needs of battered older women.

Internalized Social Expectations

Battered older women were raised at a time when they were expected to stay at home and care for their children. Divorce was not considered socially acceptable, and ending the relationship may mean failing in their primary role. Older women who have internalized rigid gender roles may be less willing to talk about their abuse or to seek help from community agencies.[53]

Self-Identification

Many older women do not identify themselves as abused. Some may see their relationship as normal. In addition, battered older women may believe that battered women are exclusively young women with children. This is especially true when media exposure is given predominantly to young women or to women with children. These images may leave society and older women with the impression that domestic violence doesn't occur in later life.[54]

The Family

Adult children are often not supportive of the change in their parents' relationship. If the abuse has been hidden from the children for years, they often refuse to believe it when they are told. In some cases the children have seen the mother suffering the abuse, have become accustomed to it, and resent her sudden rebellion.[55]

Financial Barriers

Fear of financial insecurity often keeps older women in abusive relationships. Many battered older women are financially dependent on their abusive partners. The economic reality for many older women is a choice between continued violence or assured poverty. Fourteen percent of women sixty-five years and older are poor.[56]

Some abused older women have no formal education or economic resources. Older women may find few employers willing to hire them, either for reasons of age discrimination or because many older women have been in low-paying or part-time jobs or have not worked outside the home.

Employed battered women may not earn enough to support themselves. Others may have no access to resources obtained during the relationship. Some women may not be eligible for social security because of their years of working at home. Women who are on their abusers' policies and have uninsurable pre-existing conditions may fear losing their insurance.[57]

Aging in Place

The gerontological term *aging in place* refers to public or private resources that are available to allow older adults to remain at home as they grow older. This is the desired alternative to entering institutions to receive needed care. For battered older women, however, aging in place may mean continued abuse and isolation.[58]

Many older women fear being placed in a nursing home if they leave their homes. Others are reluctant to give up a lifelong residence in exchange for a month or two in a shelter with no assurance of a permanent residence.

Shelters are frequently geared toward the needs of younger women. Women who have not lived with small children for many years may find the stress of dealing with youngsters too great. They may be in poor health and have special needs that go beyond what the shelter program is able to meet.[59]

Isolation

Battered older women may have lost contact with family and friends. Support persons may have died through the years and new friendships never developed. Retired abusers may go everywhere with their partners or may monitor telephone calls and mail. Battered women who do not drive or who are forbidden to drive may be dependent for transportation, mobility, and socialization.[60]

Health

Natural cognitive and physiological changes occur as we age. Changes in vision, hearing, touch, pain tolerance, and mobility may limit the ability to live independently. In addition, years of abuse can create physical problems that can cause battered older women to feel, or actually be, dependent upon their abusers. Some women feel obligated to take care of their abusers, who may have serious health problems themselves.[61]

Battered Women in Rural Areas

For our purposes, the term *rural battered women* refers to women outside major United States urban centers. It should be noted that distinct regional differences affect the experience of rural living. In some areas in the Northeast, rural communities are geographically closer to urban areas than are many rural areas in the Southwest. This can seriously affect the challenges that battered women face.

Availability of Services

Appropriate services for rural battered women and their abusive partners are sadly lacking. Funding agencies are often more inclined to allocate money to urban areas where reports of larger numbers of people served make a program appear more cost-effective.

Rural family violence programs have access to fewer local funding sources. In addition, many grants to these programs are funded for only one or two years.[62]

If women seek assistance from other social service programs, they are frequently confronted with staff who have little or no training in domestic violence and do not consider the social context of the woman's situation.[63] In many cases, it is necessary to refer battered women to services offered in urban areas. When a rural battered woman relocates to a shelter in an urban area, she often experiences an additional crisis because she is confronted with a strange environment and may be isolated from her local support network.

Conservative Attitudes

The attitudes and beliefs of the rural community often indicate a more traditional, conservative bias. Women may be financially dependent upon their abusive partners. The rural church frequently provides ideological support to old traditions by preaching the virtues of the dependent status of women.

Denial is often high in rural communities. The false ideology that domestic violence happens only in urban areas or to certain kinds of women is often present. Belief in the need to maintain family privacy at all costs and a lack of understanding regarding domestic violence also hinder rural women's ability to flee abusive relationships. Some rural areas put such emphasis on maintaining the family that separated or divorced women are excluded from positive social outlets and may even be socially ostracized.[64]

Transportation

A lack of adequate public transportation contributes to the isolation that rural battered women experience. Private transportation may also be limited. An abusive partner may limit access to car keys or may damage the automobile to prevent his partner from driving. Neighbors may live so far away that they cannot be readily accessed. Some women may never have learned to drive.

Rural battered women may be dependent upon family members or friends to provide transportation. Unfortunately, these relationships are often severed by a batterer or by the woman in an attempt to prevent further abuse.

Lack of Privacy

Many rural battered women lack the privacy of anonymity. This situation can intimidate a battered woman, who may decide against taking public action because she does not want the facts of her home life revealed to the residents of her small community.

In some instances, women may have too much anonymity. They may be so isolated, either geographically or by their abusive partners, that they are not known at all by other members of the community. If they are unaware of what is happening to victims of abuse, community members have no basis for offering help.[65]

Employment

Rural areas generally lack adequate job opportunities for women. In addition, conservative rural attitudes often make it difficult for a woman to seek and hold employment, particularly in nontraditional, higher-paying jobs. This leaves many battered women underemployed, if not unemployed and financially dependent.[66]

Child Care

For battered women trying to work outside the home, the lack of child care in rural areas is a major problem. Lack of affordable and accessible child care not only curtails battered women's involvement in the paid labor force, but it may also limit training opportunities.[67] Ultimately, this creates an additional burden for mothers attempting to work outside the home and support themselves independent of an abusive relationship.

Housing

The housing choices available to battered women who want to move out of their abusive households may be limited or inadequate. One-third of the people in the United States live in rural areas, but two-thirds of the substandard housing is located there.[68]

Communication

Many rural homes do not have telephones or access to direct dialing. It may be a long-distance call to reach the nearest town with a shelter or other services. Many battered women cannot afford long-distance calls and most probably do not want a record of such calls on the telephone bills for their batterers to see.

Party lines, which still exist in some rural areas, present their own problems. Women may fear that someone is listening when they are calling for help, and they may be unwilling to ask someone to get off the line so that they can make a private call.

Police

Rural police may have neither the time nor the resources to provide battered women with transportation or to stay with them to insure their safety. In addition, police response may be inconsistent. Various law enforcement agencies in an area may not be trained together, and individual police officers may be unfamiliar with new legal developments pertaining to family violence. Some rural communities have no local law enforcement body at all. Many have only one police officer, who may or may not be trained and certified. In some areas, the sheriff is located many miles away in the county seat.[69]

Battered Women with Disabilities

Comprehensive statistics about abuse of individuals with disabilities are almost nonexistent. Professionals working with this population report, however, that abuse among people with disabilities occurs at the same rate, or more frequently, than in the general population.[70]

Women with disabilities are often patronized and treated as children. They may be met with condescension and disbelief when they report abuse. Limited access to appropriate information about domestic violence, loss of a caregiver, isolation, and limited access to services are just a few of the barriers that keep women with disabilities trapped in relationships that endanger their lives.

Denial of the Problem

Few people want to admit that this problem exists. How can someone beat a woman who uses a wheelchair? The horrific nature of this abuse keeps many from effectively addressing the problem. It is precisely this denial that allows the abuse to continue unchecked. As a result, many police departments, social service agencies, and women's shelters are ill-prepared to deal with the violence that affects women with disabilities.

Physical Barriers

Although the passage of the Americans with Disabilities Act has sought to address the issue, many buildings continue to be inaccessible to people with disabilities. Some courtrooms, police stations, shelters, and other locales continue to have physical barriers that make it almost impossible for women to come forward.

Another physical barrier is the lack of interpreters and TTYs. TTYs are special telephone teletype systems for the deaf and hearing impaired. The omission of these necessary services often prevents women who are hearing impaired from obtaining and receiving help.

Lack of Information

The level of awareness about domestic violence is not nearly as high among women with disabilities as it is among the rest of the population. Although information on abuse is increasingly available to women with disabilities, there is a severe lack of educational materials on this subject that address the special needs and problems of this community.[71]

For the deaf and hearing impaired, much of the literature about domestic violence uses syntax too complex to be well understood. Vocabulary can also be a problem; words may have one meaning in English and another in sign. Even slight differences can create confusion, which further compounds the problem of discussing this sensitive subject. In addition, many English words do not have exact equivalents in sign.[72]

Isolation

Because no one wants to talk about sexuality to women with disabilities, women who have been sexually abused may go through life never fully understanding what has happened to them. Without appropriate information on domestic violence, battered women with disabilities are more likely than other women to assume that their experience is unique, and they are less likely to know where to go for help or that help is available to them.

When women are isolated, they are more likely to blame themselves. Even if a woman does decide to seek help, she will not be able to access the help she needs unless the services are barrier free.

Community Factors

The community of people with disabilities is extremely close, strong, and insulated. Its small-town atmosphere may limit a woman's chances of reporting her problem and maintaining confidentiality. This is an important need for most women, especially when they first seek help. The isolation of this community from the rest of society creates a greater dependence upon the partner, the family, and the community. A woman with disabilities may be more afraid of threatening this support system than an able-bodied woman who has more alternatives for establishing a new support system.

In addition, society's insensitivity to the problems of people with disabilities has fostered a mistrust about service providers and a fear of intervention into their personal lives.[73]

Loss of Caregiver

Getting help is often complicated by the fact that, in many cases, the batterer is providing care to the woman. When the person who is doing the abusing is also the caregiver, it becomes incredibly difficult to reach out for help. If the batterer is removed from the home, the woman may be faced with having no personal care at all.

In addition, seeking outside help may actually be life-threatening. Faced with the choice of enduring abuse or having no one to feed, cloth, and care for them, many women will choose to continue living with their batterers.[74]

Transportation Barriers

For battered women who are mobility impaired, transportation can become a major barrier to fleeing an abusive relationship. Many smaller communities have no special transit services and, although larger urban areas may have them, they are often inadequate. Most shelters do not have vehicles equipped to transport women using wheelchairs.

One former battered woman with a disability explains that in order to use the special transit service in her community, she had to call hours in advance of leaving her home. "When I was trying to leave my abusive boyfriend, I couldn't use this service. Waiting at the curb for hours would have made me an easy target for him. I had to wait at the curb, too. The van would not stop unless they saw me."

Battered Women in Prison

The last few years have witnessed an increasing awareness of the needs of battered women in prison. According to Suzanne Donovan, project specialist with the Texas Council on Family Violence, "Battered women in prison are no different than battered women seeking assistance through shelters or other domestic violence programs. In the last few years, advocates in the battered women's movement have come a long way in understanding the connections between women seeking shelter, those who are killed by their abusers, and those who kill their abusers, but much work remains to be done. Battered women in prison need support from their sisters outside."[75]

It's not easy to reach out to battered women in prison. Many people hold preconceptions about women who fight back. There are often logistical problems as well. Women's prisons are frequently located in remote areas. In addition, some women in prison do not readily identify themselves as battered.

Visiting a woman in prison can be intimidating, especially the first time. Ellen Fisher, executive director of the National Domestic Violence Hotline, explains, "The first day I went to the prison, I stayed up the night before. I was afraid I wouldn't have anything to say, or to offer. After just thirty minutes of talking to her, I knew she was the same as me."[76]

It is crucial that battered women in prison know that advocates and others outside are concerned about their well-being. We should provide support for any battered woman, regardless of whether she is charged, convicted, or acquitted of a crime. Battered women in prison face barriers distinct from those on the outside. As advocates for all battered women, it is our responsibility to provide the best service possible based on the needs of each individual woman, regardless of the circumstances in which she finds herself.

Battered Women Defendants

While many battered women defendants have needs specific to the criminal justice system, many of their needs lie outside the courtroom. They may need to make peace with the deceased, to deal with their partner's family, or to address their emotional pain and that of their children. Despite the trial and possible imprisonment, women need to go on with their everyday activities as best as they can. Like other women, they may require housing, public assistance, and other support services.[77]

Battered Women Who Kill

While women commit less than 15 percent of all homicides, they have historically received harsher sentences than do men for the same crime. In addition, homicides committed by women are seven times as likely to be in self-defense as those committed by men.[78]

Prior to the 1990s, it was not unusual for women to receive forty-five years to life sentences for killing their abusive partners. In stark contrast, abusive men who kill their partners serve an average of two- to six-year terms.[79] Fortunately, some progress has been made in the last few years. While some women continue to enter prison with twenty- to twenty-five-year sentences, in the last few years more are receiving lesser sentences.[80]

Women charged with homicide have the least extensive prior criminal records of any female offenders.[81] And, once released, women convicted of killing their abusive partners have an incredibly low return rate.

According to one former battered woman in prison, "Prison has been another form of a nightmare. It is degrading, dehumanizing, and definitely a battleground, where only the strong or determined survive. You are no longer a person, you are a number. You have no rights, no privacy. . . . It is a garden of negativeness and only self-motivation can help you reach toward a better existence."[82]

Sixty-five to 95 percent of incarcerated women are victims of prior abuse, and approximately 50 percent of female prison inmates are battered women. Many women incarcerated for felonies were acting in self-defense, were coerced into illegal acts by their abusive partners, or are taking the punishment for crimes committed by their abusers.[83] Despite the high percentage of abused women in prison, there is a shortage of battered women's support groups as well as classes to educate and inform the general prison population about abuse.[84]

According to one female inmate, "I am in a facility that vaguely addresses abuse of any kind. There are two programs that are occasionally offered. Both of these programs are very good; however, they are not offered enough to the inmates. There are 110 women in this facility, and classes are limited to ten inmates."

Incarcerated battered women frequently need help with appealing their sentences and applying for and processing clemencies when their appeals have been exhausted. If advocates do not make themselves available to these women, then who can they turn to for help?

Correctional and parole personnel frequently have little or no understanding of the dynamics of domestic violence. Without appropriate training, similar to that given by domestic violence programs that try to sensitize police, correctional and parole personnel can easily replicate the abusive behavior of a batterer.[85]

After Incarceration

When women leave prison, they are frequently unaware of services available in the communities to which they are paroled and have little or no support. Liaisons are needed between the women awaiting parole and organizations that provide services in a specific community.

Approximately 70 percent of incarcerated women are mothers. Many of these women lose their parental rights if their terms are longer than twelve to eighteen months.[86] Battered women released from prison need help in reuniting with their children. Numerous issues need to be addressed after such long separations.

One former inmate explains that women coming home after years in prison must work harder than men in the same position. "We have to work harder to prove ourselves worthy of a good job, trust, respect and love. It's easier for men who are ex-convicts because it is more acceptable for men to have committed a crime or to protect themselves than it is for women."[87]

Additional Considerations

Each community of women has unique barriers to face, and these barriers are multiplied for women who belong to more than one group or culture. For example, a battered lesbian residing in a rural area may not only have to deal with an openly homophobic community, she may also be confronted with a lack of services, communication barriers, and isolation.

Individually, these barriers have a considerable impact on women's abilities to escape battering relationships. In combination, they build a wall of oppression that helps maintain abusive relationships and keep women entrenched in situations that are both dangerous and life-threatening.

CHAPTER 8

Friends, Family, and Loved Ones: When Someone You Know Is Being Hurt

Helping a battered woman is a process that may take a long time. We have to realize that she needs to move according to her own timetable and not ours.

—Erin Clark
Hotline Coordinator, Austin Center for Battered Women

In 1996, approximately 20 percent of the calls received on the Austin Center for Battered Women Hotline were from friends, family members, and employers asking how to help someone they knew. Studies show that battered women often seek help from their informal support networks including relatives, friends, and neighbors. In fact, it appears that the greater the violence, the more likely women are to seek help.[1]

The manner in which we respond to those who turn to us for help can have a powerful impact on their lives. This impact can be positive or negative, depending on the nature of our response. According to Judith Herman, author of *Trauma and Recovery,* "A supportive response from other people may mitigate the impact of the event, while a hostile or negative response may compound the damage and aggravate the traumatic syndrome. In the aftermath of traumatic life events, survivors are highly vulnerable. Their sense of self has been shattered. That sense can be rebuilt only as it was built initially, in connection with others."[2]

There are several ways you can help an abused woman who has reached out to you. Before we explore these steps, however, we will examine how you can prepare yourself to be the best helper possible.

The Role of the Helper

In their concern for her well-being, many helpers advise a battered woman to "just leave." When she fails to heed this advice, helpers often turn away in frustration and anger. Don't make the assumption that the abused woman has not thought of "just leaving." It is quite possible that she has considered this option along with the major obstacles associated with her departure.

One likely obstacle is fear of retaliation from the batterer. A battered woman has just cause to fear for her safety. The highest risk for serious injury or death to a battered woman is when she is leaving or has left her violent partner. Battered women who leave are also at risk for harassment at work, homelessness, and an overall decrease in their standard of living.[3]

Try to imagine yourself in her situation. Imagine fleeing your home with nothing but the clothes on your back, the money in your pocket, and your children. If you are lucky, you will have a safe place to stay for the night and perhaps the next several weeks. Your children will be scared and confused. Not only are you removing them from their home, but they will probably need to change schools. If your partner is particularly violent, you may need to refrain from contacting family or friends who might reveal your location. If you are employed and your employer is insensitive to your safety needs, you may have to quit your job. If you are not employed, you may be worried about supporting yourself and your children.

Escaping a violent relationship is a complicated, arduous, and dangerous process. Don't expect immediate results from your efforts to help a battered woman. You will need to be patient with her and prepared for her to vacillate between leaving and staying as she reviews her options and their possible outcomes. Remember that, regardless of the decisions she ultimately makes, your support will have a subtle impact, even if you are unaware of it.

The ability to demonstrate unconditional acceptance is crucial in helping a battered woman to help herself. Try to suspend judgment when confronting behaviors and attitudes different from yours, and be flexible enough to accept her without imposing your values and ideals.

Helpers Versus Rescuers

In trying to be supportive, significant others can actually become overprotective. They may be so overprotective that they reinforce feelings of helplessness that the abused woman is trying to overcome. So-called rescuers may do more and more for the abused woman, rather than helping and supporting her to do for herself. Such behavior implies that the woman is not capable of acting on her own behalf. The more the rescuer accepts the idea that the abused woman is helpless, the more the abused woman is forced into that role. Rarely does rescuing result in improvement. On the contrary, the more helpless and dependent an abused woman feels, the less able she will be to act on her own behalf.[4]

Some key differences between helpers and rescuers are listed below.

A Helper

- Believes that a battered woman is in crisis, but with appropriate support, information, and resources can make her own decisions and determine her own fate
- Listens for requests for help
- Gives what the woman says she needs
- Checks in with the woman periodically
- Establishes and maintains appropriate boundaries
- Does most of the listening
- Supports the woman as she makes her own decisions and does her own work

A Rescuer

- Believes that a battered woman is helpless and needs someone to save her
- Gives help when it is not asked for
- Fails to find out whether the help is welcomed
- Gives advice instead of information
- Gives what he or she thinks the woman needs
- Does most of the talking and working

The goal in assisting a battered woman should be to help her empower herself to make the best decisions possible. Susan Schechter, author of *Women and Male Violence*, explains that "empowerment means gaining control over the decisions affecting one's life and finding access to the resources needed to live decently."[5] While you can certainly help a woman in crisis, it is ultimately up to her to change her own life and to create her own future.

Preparing to Be a Helper

Battered women have diverse backgrounds, personalities, and needs. As such, there is no single solution applicable to all battered women. Try to be sensitive to individual differences and avoid treating women categorically.[6]

Before you can offer help to an abused woman, you need some understanding of the resources available in her community. Is there a shelter in her town? Do they offer support groups? What is the policy of her local police department? How does she go about getting a restraining or protective order? Is there a batterer's treatment program in her community?[7] The National Domestic Violence Hotline, at (800) 799-SAFE, can help put you in touch with battered women's shelters and other agencies that can answer these questions.

Be aware that helping a battered woman often generates powerful feelings of anger, pity, fear, frustration, and sadness. In order to be helpful, you will need to be in touch with these feelings without being self-critical and without projecting them onto the woman you are trying to help. A positive self-image and a healthy sense of humor can help put these emotions into perspective.[8] In addition, seeking support, information, and ideas from your local battered women's shelter will help you address your frustrations and concerns as you help your friend.

Be very careful about directly intervening if you witness a woman being assaulted. Batterers can be incredibly dangerous, and jeopardizing yourself will not be of benefit to you or the woman you are trying to help. The most effective route you can take when you see or hear someone being abused is to call the police as quickly as possible.

How to Help a Battered Woman

If an abused woman has reached out to you for help, you will need to listen to her, talk with her, provide her with support and information, and offer to help in whatever way you can. In your role as a helper, let her take the lead. Let her tell you what she needs rather than assuming you know what's best for her.

One of the most important things you can do is to maintain some level of ongoing contact with the woman. Physical and psychological isolation are powerful control tactics used by batterers. An open line of communication between you and the battered woman can be a lifeline.

Let the abused woman know you are a nonthreatening, concerned ally who is able to see the reality of her situation and still respect her as a person. By all means, convey *respect* to her in every way possible. Do not admonish, patronize, or negatively judge her. Make and repeat clear statements about her value and rights as a person, such as "You don't deserve to be treated that way" and "No one, not even your husband, has the right to mistreat you."

Express disapproval of her partner's abusive behavior, but do not be critical of him. For example, instead of saying "John must be some kind of monster to hurt you like he did," a more appropriate response would be "I'm really concerned about the way John treats you. No one has the right to mistreat you." If you focus on the batterer rather than on his behavior, the woman may become defensive and try to make excuses for him.[9]

Convey your concern for the woman's safety if things continue unchecked, but stay away from advice giving. This may be difficult because of your desire to make sure she is safe. Advice giving falls into the rescuing category, and you will be more valuable to her if you maintain the helper's role.[10] According to Erin Clark, hotline coordinator for the Austin Center for Battered Women, "If you try to rescue her by giving her advice, you're actually setting her up to feel like she's disappointed you if she doesn't do what you've told her. These feelings may prevent her from reaching out to you again in the future." Instead of saying "You need to get out of that relationship before someone gets killed," a more appropriate remark would be "I'm really concerned about your safety and wonder what's going to happen to you if this hitting doesn't stop." Stay away from "you" statements such as "you should," "you need to," and "you have to." Instead, use "I" statements such as "I'm concerned," "I'm worried," and "I'm afraid."

Let the woman know that she does not have to endure her situation alone and that she deserves support. Offer her the telephone numbers of local resources such as a battered women's shelter, but don't force information on her if she doesn't want it. If she refuses your offer, let her know that you respect her wishes and that you will hold onto the information in case she becomes interested at any point in the future.

Your friend may need you to problem solve with her. She may be so entrenched in her crisis that she cannot see her options, such as staying at a shelter or another safe location; joining a support group; changing jobs; obtaining counseling, continuing education, or training; filing for separation or divorce; and getting legal counsel.[11]

Help her discover and develop her own resources, including money, friends, relatives, and employment. Encourage her to turn to others for support, people she can trust. Suggest that she assess each relationship she has as a potential source of protection, emotional support, or practical help, or as a potential source of danger.[12]

If she has children, ask how she thinks they are being affected. Support her concern about their emotional and physical welfare without blaming her. Point out that children are always deeply affected by domestic violence and deserve protection from it.[13]

The ideas listed below may be useful as you begin the helping process.[14]

Be Aware of Who She Is

Allow her to tell her story.

Let her know you believe her and want to hear about her experiences.

Let her know you care about her and are concerned about her safety.

Help her identify her feelings.

Support her right to be angry. Don't deny any of her feelings.

Be sensitive to the differences between women. Realize that no woman is a stereotype and that each has had different life experiences.

Respect the cultural values and beliefs that affect her behavior. Know that these beliefs may be a source of security for her and that their importance to her should not be minimized.

Know that she does not need rescuing.

Help her assess her own resources and support systems.

Be Aware of Who You Are

Be aware of your own attitudes, experiences, and reactions to violence.

Be honest about your own limits of time and energy.

Beware of your own need to be an expert.

Don't give advice. A battered woman has had numerous people tell her what to do.

She needs someone to listen to her and support her as she plans her own course of action.

Be conscious of your own cultural biases, beliefs, and prejudices.

Do not express disappointment if the woman decides not to leave her violent partner.

Be honest and explain your fear and concern, but let her know that you still care about and will support her.

You may be one of the first people in your friend's life to show her respect and support at a time when she most needs it. What you will receive in return is the opportunity to see strength and courage in action and the knowledge that you have helped a woman to help herself.

Listening with Love

One of the greatest gifts you can give an abused woman is to listen to her with love. Listening with love is different from other types of interaction. It requires more effort and concentration than needed for simple chatting. Listening with love is very different from discussions in which the listener is focused on what he or she is going to say or how he or she is going to react to what the speaker has said.

Listening with love is an act of will requiring choice and effort. First and foremost, you must make a conscious decision to *listen.* This means not only hearing what she says, but listening to her words and emotions with your entire being. This type of listening requires that you be completely present, clearing your mind of everything else and focusing on the person in front of you.

Listening with love is a gift because it goes against our natural tendency to talk and to establish our own position. Let the woman tell her story without interruptions, and don't fear silences that may occur. The woman will eventually break those silences. Use body language to indicate that you are listening. Lean toward her as she speaks and nod your head to indicate your understanding.

Listening with love occurs at two levels—words and feelings. The conversation will usually begin on the content, or words, level. Supporting the woman as she expresses her feelings, however, is the most important aspect of listening with love. Remember, this may be the first time she has had the opportunity to verbally express the range of emotions she has been experiencing.[15]

As the conversation progresses, try using a technique known as *reflecting*. As the woman shares her story, digest and filter her words and the feelings behind them, and then reflect back to her your interpretation of what she is saying. For example, if she says "John seems to be getting more and more violent with me," your response might be "That must be really frightening for you." She will then either confirm or deny what you have reflected.

One word of caution: reflecting does not mean repeating word for word what the woman has said. It does mean reflecting back to her your *interpretation* of her feelings and her words. Reflecting responses might begin with such phrases as "It sounds like," "It seems that," "In your situation," and "As you see it."

Don't worry about reflecting back the "wrong" thing. If you do, the woman will correct you. In the previous example the speaker could have responded, "No, I'm more confused than frightened." Whether you reflect accurately or not, the woman will know you are present for her. She will know you are listening to her with love, and there is much comfort to be gained from that.[16]

If you want to be an effective listener, there are some pitfalls to avoid. First, don't give advice. Our natural tendency is to tell people how they should solve their problems. Advice giving, however, will focus the conversation on you and will not help the woman make the best decision she can for herself.

You will also need to suspend your judgments and assumptions. Be as objective as possible, giving honest feedback that separates fact from your own subjective opinions and emotions. Objectivity does not mean that you must be emotionally neutral. It is possible to communicate feelings of empathy and acceptance without passing judgment.[17]

Listen without blaming, and believe what the woman tells you. Do not discount her fears that her partner may try to kill her if she leaves or that if she stays she may also be killed. Also, beware of the temptation to think she is exaggerating. Telling you her story is probably very embarrassing for her, and she is not likely to exaggerate. By offering a safe, accepting place to talk, you will help her begin to break the silence.

Battered women often express love for their abusive partners. They may hate his abusive behavior and know he can be dangerous, yet still have feelings for him. These confused feelings are a normal response for someone in this situation. Remember, many batterers are not abusive all the time. Rather than trying to convince her that she really doesn't love her partner, acknowledge, and validate her mixed feelings. According to Clark, "We find this really opens a door and allows us to make a connection with her." Validating rather than denying her feelings gives an abused woman a profound sense of relief and can help create a strong bond between you.

Be honest with the abused woman and with yourself. Do not pretend to have all the answers or deny that you are affected by your experiences with her. It is equally important, however, to be a warm, patient, and approachable listener who is sensitive to her feelings and needs.

Don't get ahead of the woman as she speaks. If you find yourself formulating your response before she has finished her thoughts, back up: you are not truly listening to her. You have begun to focus on you, not her.

This type of listening may at first seem strange and awkward. With time and practice, however, you will begin to feel this gift of love become a part of who you are. It is a privilege to share this gift with people we care about, and it is comforting to know that we are connecting with each other at a deeper and more meaningful level.

Creating a Safety Plan

The abused woman you are helping may not be ready to leave her abusive partner. Rather than trying to convince her otherwise, such comments as the following will convey your concern and encourage her to think more deeply about her situation.[18]

- "I'm afraid for your safety."
- "I'm afraid for the safety of your children."
- "I'm worried that it will only get worse."
- "I'm here for you when you are ready to leave."
- "You don't deserve to be abused."

The abused woman who decides to stay with her abusive partner may need a safety plan to help protect herself and her children from further violence. Ask the woman if she has thought about this and if she feels it would be helpful. If she expresses interest, ask whether she would like your help in creating such a plan.

First, she should be aware of warning signs or cues of forthcoming violence. She will probably be able to describe signs that are specific to her partner; however, some general warning signs are listed below.[19]

Physical Warning Signs

- Red face
- Clenched fists
- Clenched teeth
- Squinting eyes
- Glaring
- Heavy breathing
- Sweating
- Shaking or trembling of the arms, legs, or entire body

Behavioral Warning Signs

- Pacing
- Shouting
- Raising fist or leg as if to hit or kick
- Becoming argumentative
- Hitting objects

- Staring the woman down
- Physically cornering the woman

Verbal Warning Signs

- Yelling
- Name-calling
- Making ethnic slurs
- Using nicknames that she dislikes
- Making derogatory comments about her

Once she has identified the cues she needs to watch for, she can develop a step-by-step plan of action to help her protect herself and her children the next time she feels her partner escalating toward violence. Sample safety plans are listed in Appendix I.

When the abused woman sees her partner exhibiting any of the cues of forthcoming violence, it is advisable for her to leave the situation as quickly as possible. It is of no use to try to have a discussion with a batterer who is escalating toward violence. Having made a safety plan better enables the woman to take care of herself and her children when she feels she needs to escape a volatile situation.

Reaching Out to Someone You Think Is Abused

Do you suspect that someone you know is in an abusive relationship? Compare your observations about their relationship with the warning signs listed below.[20]

1. The couple avoids being around others, preferring to stay at home or to go out alone.
2. One person appears to do the decision making for both people.
3. The couple avoids discussing the relationship or focuses on only the good qualities and avoids discussing problems.

4. One person exhibits quick and inappropriate anger.
5. One person seems to be blamed for causing all the problems in the relationship.
6. Abuse, such as yelling and name-calling, is openly observed, and marks or bruises may be visible.
7. One partner exhibits violence toward objects or animals.
8. One person may exhibit obsessive jealousy toward the other and may accuse the other of infidelity.
9. The couple openly experiences intense and sometimes violent arguments.
10. One partner tries to isolate the other from significant others and may even sabotage friendships to prevent the other from receiving support.
11. The suspected batterer is secretive about his past.
12. One person's needs seem to be more important than the partner's needs.

In *Next Time She'll Be Dead*, Ann Jones warns women to "stay away from a man who disrespects any women, who wants or needs you intensely and exclusively, and who has a knack for getting his own way almost all the time. Any of the above should put you on guard. And if, when you back off, he turns on the solid gold charm, keep backing."[21]

If after reviewing these warning signs you still suspect that the woman is in danger, there are several steps you can take to reach out to her. Respectfully approach the woman and express your concern for her. It may be hard to break the taboo around privacy, especially if you don't know the woman well. You can initiate a conversation with her by saying something such as "I don't mean to pry, but I've noticed you seem really depressed lately. I just want you to know that if you ever want to talk, I'm available."

If the woman appears open to a conversation, you might want to gently ask her some nonthreatening questions to help her begin to talk about her abusive relationship. Some questions you might want to ask are the following:[22]

- Is your partner extremely possessive or jealous?
- Does your partner try to control your behavior by telling you where you can go or who you can associate with?
- Does your partner threaten or criticize you?
- Does your partner blame you for everything that goes wrong in the relationship?
- Does your partner treat you differently from the way he treats other people?
- Are you afraid when your partner gets angry?

If, in the course of the conversation with her, the woman continues to show signs of welcoming your help, continue in the ways discussed in this chapter. Don't be surprised, however, if she rebuffs you or denies her situation. If this happens, do not press her. Simply let her know you are available if she would like to talk.

Communication cannot be forced. Any relationship you develop with a suspected battered woman should occur naturally. Such a relationship can grow from a positive, friendly, and receptive attitude. You can be helpful to her simply by being available as a friend when and if she chooses to reach out for help.

CHAPTER 9

Domestic Violence and the Workplace

Domestic violence is not something we can simply ignore. It is not just a family problem. It is crime that is damaging to individuals and their families, as well as to productivity in the workplace. We in corporate America cannot afford to stand on the sidelines if we hope to protect the well-being of our employees and the health of our company.

—Jerome A. Chazen, Chairman Emeritus, Liz Claiborne[1]

Many battered women are working women. Domestic violence is a serious problem that does not disappear when women leave their homes and enter the workplace. Ninety-six percent of employed battered women experience problems at work due to the abuse they suffer.[2] The effects of domestic violence show in lost productivity, increased health care costs, absenteeism, turnover, workplace violence, and lawsuits. The cost of this crisis to United States companies is between $3 and $5 billion annually.[3]

In a study of fifty battered women by the Victims Service Agency of New York, half of the respondents missed an average of three days of work per month because of abuse at home. 64 percent reported being late to work because of their abusers, and 75 percent used company time to telephone friends, counselors, physicians, and lawyers because they could not do so at home.[4]

Domestic violence frequently affects women's health. Many battered women suffer from stress-related illnesses, depression, eating disorders, and substance abuse problems.[5] In turn, these health problems affect job performance.

Workplace violence is a realistic concern for battered women and their employers. Homicide is the leading cause of female workplace deaths.[6] In 1992, approximately 20 percent of the women killed in the workplace were murdered by a current or former male partner.[7]

Economic self-sufficiency is crucial for battered women. Maintaining a job, earning money, and receiving health care benefits are extremely important concerns to women trying to escape abusive relationships. In addition, many abused women find some level of support and achieve a positive sense of self through their work. It may be one of the few areas in their lives where they feel competent and are treated respectfully.

Batterers often jeopardize their partners' employment. A batterer may disrupt a woman at work by either constantly calling her or showing up at inappropriate times and demanding to see her. Seventy-four percent of employed battered women are harassed by their abusive partners at work, either in person or over the telephone.[8] A batterer may keep his partner up until early morning hours so that she either oversleeps or misses work altogether. He may contact his partner's employer or coworkers and falsely accuse her of stealing from the company, abusing drugs or alcohol, or suffering from a mental illness. When a batterer discloses this false information, he will express concern for his partner's well-being and the well-being of the company.

Such abusive behaviors affect not only battered women, but their coworkers as well. Although women are not responsible for the abusive behavior of their batterers, approximately 20 percent of employed battered women lose their jobs as a result.[9]

Corporate Responses to Domestic Violence

Despite the prevalence of domestic violence, the corporate community has not considered it a high-priority issue until relatively recently. Although women comprise almost half of the workforce in the United States, only a few corporations have taken leadership roles on the issue. This is beginning to change, however, as an increasing number of corporate leaders recognize the serious impact domestic violence has on both their employees' lives and their companies.

In a 1994 survey conducted on behalf of Liz Claiborne by Roper Starch Worldwide, one hundred senior executives in Fortune 1000 companies across the United States were interviewed about their perceptions of domestic violence and the workplace. Fifty-seven percent of the respondents believe domestic violence is a major problem in today's society and that it has had a negative impact on many aspects of their employees' performance, most notably psychological well-being (56%), productivity (49%) and attendance (47%). Equal numbers believe that domestic violence has had a harmful effect on the physical safety of their employees and insurance and medical costs (44% each).[10]

On a related note, 66 percent of the respondents believe that a company's financial performance will benefit from addressing the issue among its employees, while only 30 percent say domestic violence is not serious enough to merit a companywide response. These leaders are, however, least likely to cite corporations as institutions that should play a major role in addressing the issue of domestic violence: only 12 percent say they believe corporations should play a major role. Instead, they believe that responsibility for addressing the problem should fall to the family (96%), social service organizations (92%), and the court system (85%).

Esta Soler, executive director of the Family Violence Prevention Fund (a national, nonprofit organization that focuses on domestic violence education, prevention, and public policy reform) and the National Workplace Resource Center on Domestic Violence, responds. "Business leaders still feel that the responsibility for addressing domestic violence should fall to the family, despite the fact that the family's failure to deal with this problem has caused it to rise to crisis proportions. Abuse in the home is not just a private family matter. It is time for our society and corporate leaders to take responsibility for this problem."[11]

Recently, the Employee Assistance Professionals Association asked businesses with employee assistance divisions to track reports of domestic abuse among their employees so that the association can develop effective referral and training programs on the issue.[12]

Several corporations have made noble efforts to educate employees about the issue and to provide in-house assistance programs, including counseling and referrals to community domestic violence programs. Both Marshalls and Whirlpool Foundation have made the Family Violence Prevention Fund's Community Action Kit available to thousands of employees.[13] The kit includes referrals to coalitions against domestic violence in every state. Many corporations have also made domestic violence a priority in their corporate giving plans and have helped fund national and local efforts to prevent domestic violence.

Two corporations in particular, Liz Claiborne and Polaroid, have established themselves as leaders in the corporate battle against domestic violence.

Both continually seek new ways to have a positive impact on the problem and have developed some innovative programs and policies.

Liz Claiborne's Women's Work Program

Liz Claiborne's Women's Work program was created in 1991 with the mission of reaching out to women and their families to create positive social change on the issues affecting them. According to Wendy Banks, senior vice president, "Our 'Women's Work' program was always envisioned as a lightning rod for social change. We hope to not only educate the general public about domestic violence through the program, but also to raise corporate America's awareness of the need to deal with this problem."[14] To date, more than 320,000 educational brochures and 24,000 posters featuring antiviolence images and messages have been distributed, at no charge, to community groups, law enforcement agencies, and social service organizations.

At local levels, each year 10 percent of sales from Charity Shopping Days and profits from sales of commemorative items such as T-shirts and coffee mugs benefit local family violence organizations in October, National Domestic Violence Awareness Month. This month-long public education campaign, sponsored by the National Coalition Against Domestic Violence, involves efforts at the national, state, and local levels to heighten awareness and understanding of domestic violence. Billboard and radio public service campaigns have been developed in San Francisco, Boston, and Miami to help mobilize local community groups and retailers around the issue of domestic violence.[15] A pilot program of educational workshops is currently being developed at the University of Washington in Seattle, Washington University in St. Louis, and the University of Minnesota in Minneapolis.

The national campaign has sought to raise awareness of family violence among the general public as well as the following constituencies:

- *College students:* A survey was conducted in 1995 to determine their knowledge and perceptions of domestic violence and its impact on their lives.
- *Legal and medical establishments:* Programs have been designed to encourage awareness and intervention.

- *"Influentials":* Information on the issue of violence has been distributed to 1,500 politicians, celebrities, and business and community leaders.
- *Corporate sector:* A survey of Fortune 1000 CEOs was conducted in 1994 to determine their understanding of family violence, and materials for display in employee areas have been distributed.

In house, Liz Claiborne provides an employee assistance program nationwide to employees, their spouses, and anyone with whom they share a household. Employees can either walk into the health services department for assistance or, to maintain confidentiality, call a toll-free hotline and receive counseling and referrals. All division heads within Liz Claiborne are prepared to assist by referring an employee to health services or the hotline and allowing time off from work to seek help. Seminars on family stress have been instituted as a result of the Women's Work program and are open to all employees.

At an employee's request, the company tries to provide a parking space near the facilities and an escort to and from the employee's vehicle. The workplace is also secured by guards or receptionists equipped with panic buttons.[16]

Polaroid Corporation

Polaroid began to think about the connection between employee productivity and domestic violence about ten years ago through the company's employee assistance program. The performance of a female employee, a seventeen-year veteran, had begun to slide. In the course of a discussion with her supervisor and the EAP staff, the woman revealed that she was being battered and that she knew of several other females employees in similar situations. A counseling group was organized for the women.

Polaroid began looking not only at battered employees, but also at those they suspected might be batterers. According to Jim Hardeman, corporate EAP manager and a leading expert on domestic violence and the workplace, "We started looking at individuals who were violent at work and found over half were also violent at home."

As a result of Hardeman's concern and the corporation's willingness to address the issue, Polaroid has developed a variety of in-house services for their employees and initiatives at the local and national levels. The company's employee assistance program provides counseling and support to employees on various issues. EAP staff receive additional training to improve their ability to counsel victims of family violence and to provide community referral resources for batterers. Lunchtime seminars have been held throughout the company with guest speakers from local police departments and battered women's shelters.

Polaroid tries to accommodate employees affected by family violence who need time off to seek safety and protection, make court appearances, or arrange new housing. The company offers flexible work hours, short-term paid leaves of absence, and extended leaves without pay with the guarantee of the same position upon return.

Through an initiative called the CEO Project, Polaroid is attempting to influence and persuade companies in Massachusetts to take up the fight against domestic violence. The CEO Project encourages local businesses to adopt a women's shelter, providing financial support, in-kind assistance, volunteers, and advocacy. In turn, the shelters are able to offer educational seminars to employees and consultation in developing workplace policies and guidelines for battered employees.

In 1991 Polaroid began the Polaroid School of Law Enforcement Imaging, a seminar series designed to train law enforcement professionals in effective field and laboratory photography applications and techniques. Since 1991 more than 15,000 law enforcement professionals have attended Polaroid seminars around the country. Today, Polaroid offers law enforcement seminars on more than a dozen topics.

Polaroid has donated funds through the Polaroid Foundation, the company's independent philanthropic entity, to battered women's shelters in several communities throughout Massachusetts. In 1993 Polaroid donated "seed" money to the Massachusetts Coalition of Battered Women's Service Group to start the Jane Doe Safety Fund.

That same year, Polaroid responded to increased requests from the law enforcement community by adding a seminar on Domestic Violence Injury Documentation. This seminar covers such photographic essentials as lighting and composition techniques for photographing victim's injuries and crime scenes. Seminar attendees also receive information and training on the process of testifying in court with evidential photography.

In 1994 the Harvard School of Public Health's Injury Control Center received $48,000 in federal funding for a joint project with Polaroid to study how employee assistance programs work with women who have experienced domestic violence at home or work. Usually, EAPs provide short-term counseling and advocacy to employees and their families. They may also make referrals to other resource agencies. Through their research, the Injury Control Center hopes to identify effective strategies for preventing violence against women and to encourage organizations to adopt these strategies and develop additional ones.

In recognition of National Domestic Violence Awareness Month, Polaroid sponsored a symposium in October 1994. The event brought together people from such various disciplines as education, health care, business, and the judiciary to explore ways that companies can begin to mobilize to protect women against domestic violence. All proceeds from the event were forwarded to eight women's shelters in Massachusetts.[17]

Texas Council on Family Violence

In Texas, the Texas Council on Family Violence is making great strides in reaching out to the corporate community. In the summer of 1996, TCFV completed an eighteen-minute training video entitled *A Home Away from Home: The Impact of Domestic Violence on the Workplace.* In addition to the video, TCFV staff has developed a training manual that helps employers (1) effectively intervene when an employee is experiencing domestic violence, (2) design an organizational action plan to address domestic violence as it affects the workplace, and (3) educate corporate leaders about the financial, medical, and emotional costs of domestic violence on the workplace.

In September 1996, TCFV sponsored a half-day workshop for business professionals entitled "Domestic Violence Is a Workplace Issue." Featuring Jim Hardeman, corporate EAP manager for Polaroid, as the guest presenter, the workshop gave TCFV and Hardeman the opportunity to address this important issue and its impact on the Austin community.

A Proactive Response to Domestic Violence in the Workplace

Although many corporate leaders believe that addressing domestic violence should fall primarily to social service and other agencies, corporations do have a responsibility to support employees whose lives are affected by violence. While the Occupational Safety and Health Administration has no specific regulations for preventing workplace violence, the OSHA General Duty Clause does require employers to provide a safe and healthful working environment for all workers.[18]

Most corporate leaders agree. Eighty-six percent of the respondents in the Liz Claiborne survey felt that companies do have a responsibility for the general well-being of their employees. In fact, 58 percent of these corporations sponsor domestic violence awareness or survivor support programs, and nearly 75 percent offer domestic violence counseling or assistance programs to employees. Specific components of these programs include referrals (87%), counseling (72%), and company-paid benefits to cover physical or psychological care (70%).[19]

The most effective workplace responses to domestic violence are proactive and build on a company's commitment to safety and support. Companies that are proactive in these areas are able to protect lives and save millions of dollars in medical costs, lost productivity, damaged property, and avoided lawsuits.

While domestic violence is a complex issue, workplace responses to domestic violence need not be. By modifying existing programs and policies to demonstrate a sensitivity to domestic violence, employers may well be able to effectively address this issue in the workplace.[20] Some policies and programs that need to be reviewed, and either modified or created, are those that deal with human resource issues, workplace safety, and employee training.

Specific steps that can be taken in the workplace to address domestic violence have been recommended by a special council commissioned by the Clinton administration. The Advisory Council on Violence Against Women consists of forty-seven experts from various fields and is co-chaired by Attorney General Janet Reno and Secretary of Health and Human Services Donna E. Shalala. A draft report from the council, that will eventually be distributed to employers, employees, and unions, recommends many of the steps outlined in this section as a means of addressing domestic violence in the workplace.[21]

Company Policies of Intolerance to Domestic Violence

The first step in creating a proactive response to domestic violence involves the creation of an interdisciplinary management team. The management team's mission is to review existing policies and programs to determine their sensitivity to employees experiencing domestic violence. The management team, with the cooperation of the CEO, should adopt policies and programs that clearly communicate the company's commitment to establishing a workplace that is intolerant of domestic violence.[22]

The team should include a variety of individuals, including representatives from human resources (including the employee assistance program), benefits, legal, medical, and security divisions. Employees who have experienced domestic violence should be invited to participate as well.

Findings should be reported to senior management along with recommendations for changes and additions. Guidelines concerning domestic violence should be clearly communicated to all employees and should complement existing personnel and grievance procedures.[23]

Human Resource Policies

All human resource policies should recognize and be sensitive to the special needs of employees experiencing domestic violence. Policies that should be reviewed include those relating to employee absences and supervisory procedures.[24]

Women who are trying to escape abusive partners need time to plan, make necessary arrangements, and act. Policies should permit employees to take time off for court appearances and meetings with agencies and individuals that are offering help.

If there is a high risk of death or physical assault, an employee may need to leave the area to escape the batterer. The length of time an employee needs to stay away will depend on the situation. A policy that permits an employee to take an unpaid leave of absence under special circumstances can be lifesaving.

There may also be occasions when an employee is at such serious risk that she may need to relocate to escape her abusive partner. If a company has a policy of transferring employees to other job sites, employees at risk of life-threatening assault should be considered for relocation. This type of relocation requires special safety precautions, which include not disclosing the new location to coworkers at the original worksite except on a need-to-know basis and removing the employee's name and other identifying information from all company directories and organizational charts.

Battered employees may require sick leave for special medical treatment of the physical trauma they have suffered. Physical therapy and reconstructive surgery are two of the disability services abused employees may require. In addition, while domestic violence occurs between intimate partners, others in the household are often affected by the abuse as well. An employee may need medical leave to care for a family member or other member of the household who has been hurt by the batterer.

Many performance problems, including those caused by domestic violence, can be addressed through existing personnel policies and programs. The complex nature of domestic violence may, however, cause some continued performance problems until the violence is stopped and the employee receives the help she needs. While supervisory guidelines should be consistently applied to all employees, a special effort should be made to consider all aspects of the battered employee's situation. Supervisors should attempt to make every accommodation possible within the framework of that guideline. Company policy usually describes the process supervisors must use to address performance problems. That process should include referral to an employee assistance program or other source of assistance.

Employee Assistance Programs

If a company provides an employee assistance program, program staff should receive in-service training, in collaboration with local shelters, in order to provide information and referrals to employees who are experiencing domestic violence. EAP staff can assist employees in several areas including crisis intervention, problem solving, dealing with work issues, and accessing other internal corporate services.[25]

EAP staff should have information about local battered women's shelters and other helpful service agencies in the community. In addition, they should be able to help employees create safety plans (see Appendix I for examples of safety plans).

Workplace Safety

In a recent survey of 248 corporate security and safety directors conducted by the National Safe Workplace Institute, 94 percent of the respondents said that domestic violence is a high-security problem at their companies. More than 90 percent had seen at least three cases of men stalking women. Sixty-four percent reported that their company does not have explicit procedures for encouraging battered employees to report threats of domestic violence, and 61 percent reported that their company does not have established procedures for protecting employees experiencing domestic violence.[26]

If a company has any form of security, it can prove valuable for employees who are being harassed by their abusive partners. Among the safety and security measures that should be examined are the safety of parking areas, full-time or after-hours security guards, monitoring and warning systems, limited-access key cards, and visitor policies.[27]

Batterers can be extremely resourceful in gaining access to buildings and work sites, often simply talking their way in. Security guards should be trained to handle the special safety needs of battered women. In addition, supervisors should be trained in company policy on violence and harassment and instructed to contact the appropriate persons when they know or suspect that an employee is being abused by her partner.

In cases of domestic violence, confidentiality policies should extend beyond personal information and include protecting information about job title, work schedule, dates of service, and work site locations.

Additional safety measures that can help to protect battered employees are the following:[28]

- Relocate the employee's workstation.
- Change the employee's work schedule.
- Show the batterer's photograph to receptionists and security personnel.
- Install security cameras near entrances to the employee's work area.
- Provide escorts to and from the employee's car.
- Place silent alarms at the employee's workstations.

If harassment is persistent, company security can call in local law enforcement, who can further involve the telephone company and others as needed. Some employers have obtained restraining orders on behalf of their abused employees. This may actually help to reduce the possibility of a batterer's retaliation against a woman who requests the order in her own name.[29]

Companies can arrange for a meeting between security personnel and local law enforcement agencies to help facilitate appropriate information sharing and the development of collaborative working relationships. Emphasis should be placed on developing procedures for interaction with law enforcement officials.

Employee Training

Forty-two percent of the respondents in the Liz Claiborne survey said their corporations promote programs to provide employees with information on domestic violence. However, the perceived belief by 57 percent of corporate leaders that companies should have such a program exceeds the levels of assistance actually offered.[30] Many large corporations offer wellness-promotion programs. Domestic violence awareness and prevention programs can easily be incorporated into these efforts.

Workshops can be held as part of the employee training program. For example, a domestic violence survivor can be invited to speak about her experiences and the impact that the violence has had on her life and specifically her work. Staff from local battered women's shelters can be invited to discuss domestic violence.

A training program for all supervisors can be established to offer guidance on how to respond when an employee is experiencing domestic violence. Specialized training can be arranged for company nurses, employee assistance program staff, and others who may be working with abuse survivors.

Employee training can also be conducted in the following ways:

- Sponsor a companywide educational campaign that includes an acknowledgment from the CEO, in the form of a letter or memo to the staff, of the need for heightened awareness of domestic violence.

- Distribute educational materials about domestic violence to all employees.
- Display posters and brochures that examine the issue and send the message that there is no excuse for domestic violence.
- Make safety information available in private places, such as restrooms or paycheck envelopes.
- Include articles on domestic violence in the company newsletter.

Support of Local Domestic Violence Programs

Effectively addressing domestic violence requires a collaborative effort from all institutions in our society, including the business sector. To support community domestic violence programs, companies can consider adopting a local shelter. A drive in the workplace can be conducted to collect monetary donations and such needed items as toys, clothing, diapers, personal hygiene items, baby formula, food, furniture, office equipment, and office supplies, and perhaps company products. Employees can also volunteer their time.

Companies can also work with and support local domestic violence programs by serving on boards, donating a percentage of their profits during National Domestic Violence Awareness Month in October, cosponsoring conferences and workshops on domestic violence, and sponsoring mentoring programs for shelter residents.

Responding to Battered Employees

To effectively respond to employees experiencing domestic violence, organizations must first and foremost take the abuse seriously and treat employees respectfully.

Battered women are often isolated and feel that their situation is unique. A battered employee may be embarrassed to discuss her situation with anyone. Many battered women are afraid that no one will believe them. If she has previously raised the issue with someone and has been blamed or judged, or the abuse has been minimized, she may withdraw. Other women may deny or minimize their abuse in order to make their home situations more tolerable.

Supervisors can be of help by watching for the following warning signs of abuse among their employees.

Warning Signs of Domestic Abuse

- Physical indicators such as bruises, which the employee may attempt to hide with makeup or clothing
- Employees who claim to be "accident-prone," which can be a way to cover up abuse
- Pregnant employees, as abuse often escalates during pregnancy
- Signs of depression, including crying at work
- Employees who mention having stress at home
- Harassing telephone calls at work
- Frequent absences from work, especially taking vacation days sporadically and one to three days at a time
- Frequent doctor appointments
- Employees who frequently refer to partners' anger or temper or who seem to be afraid of their partners
- Decreased productivity
- Inattentiveness
- Employees who have little or no access to such resources as money or a car
- Employees who are isolated from friends, family, and even coworkers

Reaching Out to Battered Employees

People are often reluctant to approach a woman they suspect is being abused. They may feel that to ask questions is to intrude into the woman's personal life. The key is to ask questions and offer comments that let her know you are concerned and that it is not inappropriate for her to bring up important personal issues. A good way to start is to say, "You're such a good employee, but you seem to be depressed lately. I want you to know I'm here if you want to talk." Or, "Can I help in any way?"

It is often very difficult for a battered woman to tell a supervisor or coworker that she is in crisis and is afraid of her partner. If she appears willing to talk, try asking clear, direct questions in a sensitive and caring manner. For example:

- Has your partner ever threatened to hurt you?
- Are you afraid of your partner when he gets mad?
- Does your partner try to control how you dress, whom you associate with, or what you do?
- Has your partner ever hit you or your children?

According to Jim Hardeman, direct questions about family violence should be asked when there is either evidence of abuse or a strong suspicion that the woman is being abused. Employee assistance program and human resources staff should, however, ask indirect questions of all female employees, regardless of whether there is evidence of abuse. Hardeman suggests the following questions to approach the issue:[31]

- I talk to many women who are having problems. Many of these women are being hurt by a loved one. Are you in this situation?
- Many women I talk to are in relationships where their partners are abusing them in some way. Are you in a situation like this?

Certain questions should not be asked, as they tend to shut down the conversation.

- Don't ask why she stays with her partner. Her inability to leave is a part of the crisis she is experiencing.
- Don't ask if she is a "battered woman." Many battered women deny or minimize the abuse they suffer and will not readily identify with the term.
- Don't ask what she has done to provoke the violence or why she thinks her partner is abusive to her. Both questions suggest that she is being blamed for the abuse she is experiencing.

If a battered employee discloses her situation and is comfortable discussing it with you, the following tips may be helpful:

- Encourage her to talk about her abusive situation and her feelings about it.
- Validate all of her feelings, including those of anger, shame, fear, guilt, confusion, and hopelessness.
- Let her know you believe her and that the abuse she is suffering is not only illegal but also unacceptable to you and the company.
- Let her know you do not blame her for what is happening to her and that it is not her fault.
- Let her know that she is not alone and that she has your support and the support of the company.
- Gently remind her that domestic violence usually gets worse without outside intervention. Let her know that there are domestic violence programs that can help.
- Ask her how you can help.
- If she needs help with referrals, a place to stay, someone to talk to, information about battering, or information on creating a safety plan, refer her to appropriate internal divisions such as the company's employee assistance program, a local battered women's shelter, or the state's coalition against domestic violence. You can find out about the state's coalition by calling the National Domestic Violence Hotline, (800) 799-SAFE.

Continue to check in with her as she struggles with her situation, but be aware that she may not be ready to take action. Resist the temptation to make decisions for her. Instead, allow her to make her own decisions, and be supportive whether she leaves or stays. Offering assistance and then stepping back is often the most difficult aspect of helping someone. It is, however, one of the most beneficial and empowering actions you can take.

CHAPTER 10

Battered Women and Their Health: The Response of the Medical Community

When physicians and nurses do nothing, even when the victim/patient knows they know, they magnify the victim's anxiety, hopelessness, fear, and shame—her sense that she alone is responsible for her safety, that she alone is perhaps, after all, to blame.

—Ann Jones, author of *Next Time She'll Be Dead: Battering and How to Stop It*[1]

Many battered women may never call the police, go to court, or flee to a shelter. A great number of battered women do, however, visit doctors and hospitals for treatment of injuries and stress-related illnesses. Each year, more than 1.5 million women seek medical treatment for injuries related to abuse.[2] In fact, more women are treated in emergency rooms for injuries resulting from battering than for (nonmarital) rapes, muggings, and traffic accidents combined.[3]

Edward Gondolf and Ellen Fisher, in their study of women in Texas shelters, found that 42 percent of the women sought hospital care for their injuries.[4] Evan Stark and Anne Flitcraft reviewed the medical records of 3,676 randomly selected women with injury complaints at a major metropolitan hospital. Those identified as battered averaged one injury visit per year to the emergency room. Compare this to nonbattered women, who may make one injury visit to an emergency service in a lifetime.[5]

Medical costs associated with domestic violence are staggering. A study conducted at Rush Medical Center in Chicago found that the average charge for medical services provided to abused women, children, and older adults was $1,633 per person per year. This would amount to a national annual cost of $857.3 million.[6]

Although numerous battered women seek emergency service, an even greater number are found in nontrauma caseloads. For example, 20 to 25 percent of obstetrical patients have a history of battering. Estimates of battered female patients in primary care clinics range from 28 to 38 percent.[7]

Health Risks for Battered Women

In her study of battered women who killed their abusive partners, Angela Browne found that injuries suffered by battered women range from bruises, cuts, black eyes, concussions, broken bones, and miscarriages caused by beatings to such permanent injuries as damage to joints, partial loss of hearing or vision, and scars from burns, bites, or knife wounds.[8]

Lenore Walker, in *The Battered Woman,* states that the injuries of battered women treated in hospital emergency rooms fall into several categories.[9] The first category is serious bleeding injuries, including wounds requiring stitches, especially around the face and head. The second category is internal injuries that cause bleeding and malfunctioning of organs. The women Walker interviewed reported damage to their spleens and kidneys and punctured lungs. The third category is damage to bones, including cracked vertebrae, skulls, and pelvises as well as broken jaws, arms, and legs. The fourth category is burns, including cigarette burns and burns from hot appliances, stoves, irons, acids, and scalding liquids. One battered woman seeking shelter from the Austin Center for Battered Women described how her husband poured drinking alcohol over her and then methodically threw matches at her until she caught on fire.

According to Browne, the force with which an act is carried out, repetitions of the act, and the clustering of various violent acts determine the severity of the injuries. The clustering of violent acts during an assault frequently produces a distinctive pattern of injuries characterized by multiple injury sites. Typically, these injuries are to the face and central areas of the body rather than to the extremities. Battered women are thirteen times more likely than other accident victims to have injuries to the breasts, chest, and abdomen.[10]

Injury frequency is also an indicator of domestic violence. A woman who comes to the emergency room three times with injuries has an 80 percent chance of being a battered woman, whether or not the injuries require sutures. High frequency of injuries and the presence of multiple injury sites increase the likelihood that a woman is being battered.[11]

Richard Gelles and Murray Straus asked battered women to compare their present health with their health prior to being beaten by their partners. Women who had experienced violence, especially severe violence, reported that their health, the amount of stress they were experiencing, the chances of their feeling bad or depressed, and their own drinking and alcohol problems were much worse than before the violence began. Gelles and Straus asked the more than three thousand women in their survey to give a general evaluation of their health. The greater the violence experienced, the more likely women reported their health as fair or poor. Battered women also reported that they stayed in bed due to illness an average of one day each month, which is twice as often as women from nonviolent homes.[12]

The stress of an abusive relationship increases women's risk of depression, suicide, and substance abuse.[13] Battered women have an attempted suicide rate approximately five to eight times that for nonbattered women.[14]

Battered women often experience symptoms of post-traumatic stress disorder not unlike those experienced by soldiers, hostages, and prisoners of war. Headaches, abdominal pains, and atypical chest pains are not uncommon. Physical problems associated with depression, such as backaches, gastrointestinal problems, fatigue, restlessness, loss of appetite, and sleep problems, are also common.[15]

Complications of previous injuries—for example, recurrent sinus infections among women who have suffered fractured facial bones—are another source of medical illness among battered women. Many physicians have also noted that chronic illnesses such as asthma, diabetes, arthritis, hypertension, and heart disease may be exacerbated in women who are being abused.[16]

Abused women frequently experience significant changes in their eating habits. For many women, these changes, that may be relatively short in duration, are concurrent with the violence. Battered women may be unable to eat because of nausea or able to eat but unable to keep their food down.

For some battered women, regulating caloric intake may be the one area in which they feel they can exert influence in a world that otherwise appears beyond their control. *Choice* and *self-control* are terms that women repeatedly use to describe being thin.[17] Battered women's struggles with eating disorders are not simply to achieve thinness, but to gain control over their lives.

The sexual specificity of battering is evident by the frequency of abusive assaults during pregnancy. Between 25 and 60 percent of abused women are assaulted during pregnancy. Stark and Flitcraft found that battered women are three times more likely than nonbattered women to be pregnant when injured. As a result, they experience a greater number of miscarriages.[18] Other effects of battering during pregnancy include separation of the placenta from the uterus; antepartum hemorrhage; fetal fractures; low infant birthweight; and rupture of the uterus, liver, or spleen.[19]

Sexual coercion and assault are common in abusive relationships. Women who have been repeatedly raped frequently experience vaginal discharge, itching, chronic yeast infections, burning sensations when urinating, and general genital discomfort. Vaginal and anal bleeding are not uncommon and often require internal and external suturing.

Victims of sexual assault are also at risk of acquiring sexually transmitted diseases including chlamydia, gonorrhea, syphilis, herpes, trichomoniasis, and HIV, the virus that causes AIDS.[20] Many battered women have been infected with STDs by batterers who force them into unprotected sex. Some batterers deliberately infect their partners to prevent them from having sex with other men. A direct link has been identified between battering and the spread of HIV and AIDS among women.[21]

The batterer's control frequently extends to the medical setting. The batterer may limit the woman's access to routine or emergency medical care, remain with her constantly during her stay, or insist that she be released prematurely. He may also prevent her from taking her medication as prescribed, hide or destroy her birth control, or prevent her from keeping medical appointments.[22]

Ineffective Responses of the Medical Community

The Family Violence Prevention Fund, in collaboration with the San Francisco Injury Center for Prevention and Research, conducted a survey of all California emergency departments to explore the hospitals' capacity to respond to the overwhelming number of battered women seeking medical care. This study clearly demonstrated that battered women are not being identified by emergency department staff and that most ED personnel are not being trained in identification and referral procedures.[23]

In Stark and Flitcraft's study of 481 women seeking emergency medical services, one in four women could be identified as battered, approximately nine times the number identified by emergency service staff.[24] A study conducted by Carol Warshaw found that emergency service staff reported explicit information about abuse in only 21 percent of cases involving identified battered women. Despite guidelines for referral, no social service consultation or shelter information was given in more than 90 percent of the cases.[25]

Even in cases in which battering is not officially recognized, physicians seem to make diagnoses that select battered women from the general population of injured patients and treat them differently. Battered women are more likely to leave the emergency room with prescriptions for pain medications or tranquilizers: only one in ten nonbattered accident victims receive such prescriptions, compared to one in four battered women. In addition, despite the injuries battered women suffer, physicians are less likely to clinically follow them than they are nonbattered women.

When they do receive referrals, battered women are typically sent to detox programs, drug dependency units, mental health clinics, hospitals, and a variety of counseling agencies. Most of these agencies approach alcoholism or depression as the primary problem and domestic violence as secondary.

Abused women are referred to psychiatric staff five times more frequently than nonbattered accident victims. Battered women who complain of frequent headaches, stomach disorders, painful intercourse, and muscle pains, but whose X rays and lab tests are normal, are labeled "neurotic," "hysteric," "hypochondriac," or "a well-known patient with multiple vague complaints." One nonbattered woman in fifty leaves with such a label compared to one battered woman in four.[26] According to Stark and Flitcraft, "This highlights the tension between patient demand for help and medicine's frustration in the absence of overt physiological disorder. The use of such phrases to characterize patients makes it extremely difficult for them to get sympathetic, quality treatment."[27]

Battered women often make repeated trips to the emergency room. At first, these visits are noted simply by recording "repeated trauma." Their injuries are defined as the only object for medical care, and questions are focused primarily on obtaining diagnostic information. Patients are interrupted or redirected when they mention social problems that do not conform to diagnostic reasoning.[28]

Gradually, the accumulation of injuries is supplemented by physician notes about "vague medical complaints." Finally, a set of complex problems is recognized, including alcoholism, drug abuse, attempted suicide, depression, fear of child abuse, and a variety of alleged mental illnesses.

At this point the actual source of women's repeated injuries may be noted, but the abuse is dismissed as a consequence of their problem with drugs or an emotional disorder. In shifting the focus from the women's conditions to the women themselves, labels such as *alcoholic, addict,* and *neurotic* explain their continued suffering in a way that leaves the medical paradigm intact.[29] It appears that it is more convenient to blame the woman than to question the treatment approach.

The Medical Power and Control Wheel on the opposite page outlines how physicians' interactions with battered women often mirror the abusive partners' behavior. Neglect, inappropriate medication, isolation, blaming violence on secondary problems such as alcohol, labeling, and punitive referrals (such as to psychiatric facilities) only serve to undermine battered women. The batterer's strategies of coercion, isolation, and control converge with these discriminatory and ineffective medical responses to make it extremely difficult for women to escape from abusive relationships.

Changing the Medical Paradigm

Effectively changing the medical paradigm, or the way of thinking that emphasizes treating the illness or disease rather than focusing on the patient's well-being, requires adjustments at a variety of levels. Initially, health care providers must recognize and educate themselves about the impact of domestic violence on the lives of millions of women. Second, effective identification and intervention strategies must be developed and utilized. Third, increased cooperation with other societal institutions and community-based organizations must be encouraged and supported. Finally, and perhaps most difficult of all, the attitudes and values surrounding the role of health care provision for women must be redefined in order to encourage the empowerment of female patients.

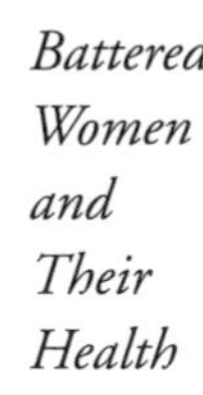

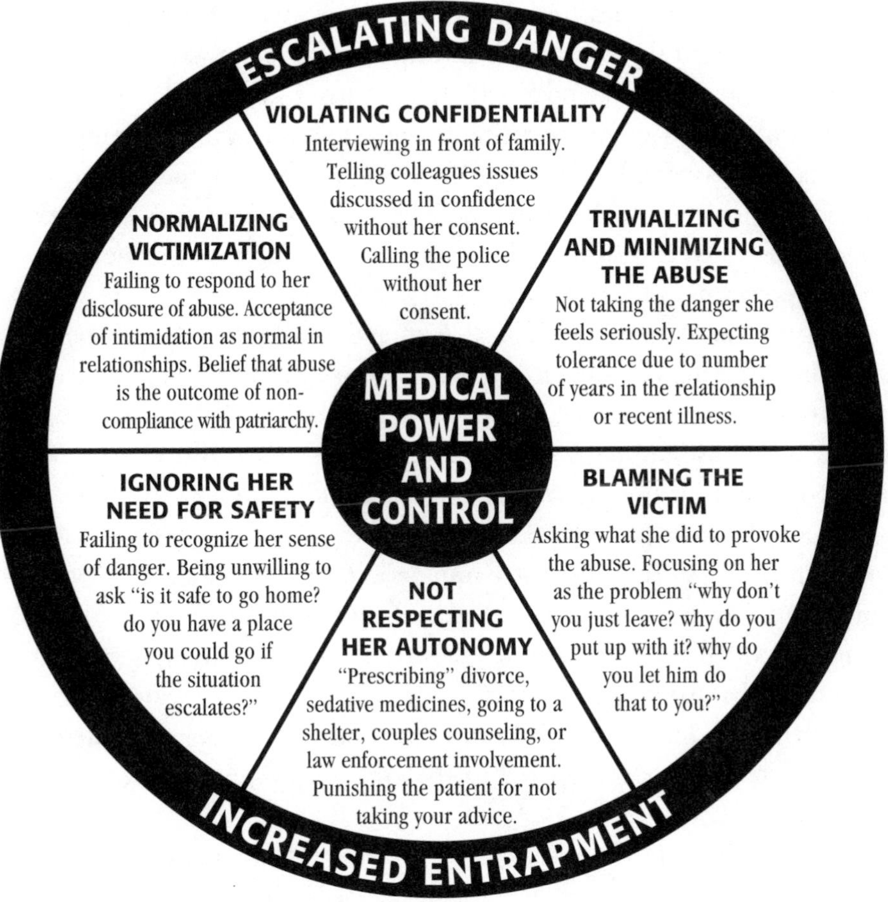

Developed by the Domestic Violence Project, Inc., Kenosha, Wisconsin, modeled after the "Power & Control and Equality Wheels" developed by the Domestic Abuse Intervention Project, Duluth, Minnesota.

Recognition and Education

Despite the medical community's history of inattention to domestic violence, efforts to educate health care providers have dramatically increased in the last few years. Today, medical responses to domestic violence extend from the Office of the U.S. Surgeon General, the Centers for Disease Control, and the Family Violence Prevention Fund (a federally funded center for information on health and domestic violence) to state health departments, professional medical organizations, and public health organizations. Almost every major group of health care professionals has produced comprehensive guidelines, standards of practice, and informational materials to assist medical professionals in improving their practices.[30]

In 1985 Surgeon General Dr. C. Everett Koop suggested that hospitals and trauma centers might prevent further violence by intervening. That same year the Nursing Network on Violence Against Women International was formed. The network fosters the ideal of nursing practice designed to provide assistance and support to women in the process of achieving personal empowerment.[31]

In 1991 the American Medical Association announced the start of a campaign to address family violence as a major health problem. The development of diagnostic and treatment guidelines on child abuse and neglect, child sexual abuse, domestic violence, and elder abuse and neglect served as the backdrop for the AMA's organizational efforts.

The AMA also played a key role in the formation of the National Coalition of Physicians Against Family Violence, with membership from more than seventy-five major medical organizations. The American Women's Medical Association, the American Academy of Family Physicians, the American Nurses' Association, the American College of Obstetricians and Gynecologists, and the American College of Emergency Physicians have also participated in the creation of a medical response to family violence.[32]

Increasingly, state and local medical associations are taking a leadership role in addressing family violence. Medical associations in Texas, California, Florida, Iowa, Minnesota, North Carolina, Oklahoma, and Oregon, among others, have initiated a variety of domestic violence training and educational activities.[33]

In 1992 the Texas Medical Association's Council on Public Health identified family violence as a priority. TMA's council stressed the need for more emphasis on prevention and the importance of the physician's role in addressing family violence. Accordingly, in collaboration with the Texas Council on Family Violence, TMA developed a brochure and packet entitled *Start the Healing Now: What You Can Do About Family Violence*, that was distributed to primary care physicians throughout the state. TMA continues to collaborate with the Texas Council on Family Violence to cosponsor their statewide conference.[34]

Recent initiatives have emphasized the importance of educating medical students about domestic violence. While many medical students now receive some basic information on domestic violence, most medical, nursing, and social work schools have failed to provide students with in-depth information.[35] A recent national study of the 143 accredited medical schools in the United States and Canada revealed that 53 percent did not require medical students to receive instruction about domestic violence.[36] Cognizant of the need for improved education for medical students, the AMA has established a committee to draft guidelines for the integration of domestic violence into the curricula of medical schools.[37]

Identification and Intervention

Since January 1992, the Joint Commission on Accreditation of Healthcare Organizations (JCAHO) has required that all accredited hospitals implement policies and procedures in their emergency departments and ambulatory care facilities for identifying, treating, and referring victims of abuse. The standards require educational programs for hospital staff in domestic violence as well as elder abuse, child abuse, and sexual assault.[38]

The physician's role in the intervention process includes not only identification, but also validation, appropriate medical treatment, mental health assessment, clear documentation, safety assessment, appropriate referrals, and follow-up.[39]

The AMA has developed the following lists of indicators that health care providers can look for as keys to diagnosing domestic violence.[40] In addition, the AMA notes that some experts suggest that a patient's chart be flagged when a partner calls to cancel a woman's appointment.

Physical Indicators of Abuse

Type of or extent of injury is inconsistent with the patient's explanation

Injuries to the head, neck, breasts, chest, and abdomen

Injuries, such as forearm bruises or fractures, are consistent with a defensive posture

Injuries occurring during pregnancy

Repeated or chronic injuries

Multiple injuries or injuries in various stages of healing

Frequent visits for complaints of pain without tissue injury or evidence of disease

Patient presents with symptoms of migraines, backaches, fatigue, sleep or appetite disturbances, chest pains, hyperventilation, gastrointestinal disorders, or gynecological problems

Substantial delay between the time of injury and the presentation for treatment

Patient may see physician at inappropriate times for seemingly minor injuries

Evidence of assault to the genital area indicating rape

Abuse of children and partners frequently occurs simultaneously; therefore, if abuse of one is identified, other family members should be carefully screened

Behavioral Indicators of Abuse

Thoughts about or attempts at suicide

Depression

Alcohol or drug use

Patient appears frightened, nervous, withdrawn, ashamed, evasive, or embarrassed

Patient is accompanied by her partner, who insists on staying close and answering all questions directed to the patient

Patient seems reluctant to speak or disagree in front of her partner

Intense, irrational jealousy or possessiveness is expressed by partner or reported by patient

Partner or patient denies or minimizes violence

Patient exhibits an exaggerated sense of personal responsibility for the relationship including self-blame for her partner's violence

Patient may appear to be noncompliant with a medical regimen prescribed for a chronic condition

Despite the initiatives set forth by JCAHO, many hospitals continue to lack standards of practice for managing domestic violence cases. Standard hospital policy should include asking questions about battering at every hospital unit and as a routine part of every physician's visit.

While ineffective responses contribute to women's increased entrapment in violent relationships, supportive responses enhance women's opportunities for personal empowerment and violence-free lives. The Advocacy Wheel in Appendix II was developed by the Domestic Violence Project in Kenosha, Wisconsin. This wheel outlines the keys to empowerment-based advocacy for battered women and is a useful guide for anyone interested in helping battered women.

Effective assessment begins with a patient-centered interview. Patients should be interviewed in privacy, away from family and friends. The need for patient trust in the physician is especially important. Patient safety may be jeopardized if the physician discloses a diagnosis of abuse to the woman's partner.[41] Interviews should include a history of adult trauma, an overview of the dynamics in the relationship, a review of health and mental health problems that may be associated with abuse, and consideration of risk to children in the family.

In order to survive in battering relationships, women often deny, minimize, or forget incidents of control and violence. Repeated, short interviews and the use of significant events in a woman's life as markers for violent episodes can help physicians obtain more detailed information.[42]

Physicians should routinely ask all women direct, specific questions about abuse. Although women may not bring up the subject of abuse, many will discuss it when asked simple, nonjudgmental questions in a confidential setting. For example:[43]

Because abuse and violence are so common in women's lives, I've begun to routinely ask about it. Are you in a relationship in which you feel you are treated badly?

What happens when you and your partner fight or disagree?

Has your partner ever destroyed things that you cared about?

Has your partner ever forced you to have sex when you didn't want to?

Are you in a relationship in which you have been physically hurt or threatened by your partner?

Has your partner ever threatened or abused your children?

The physician's recognition and validation of the woman's situation is important. Silence, disregard, or disinterest convey acceptance of domestic violence. In contrast, recognition, acknowledgment, and concern confirm the seriousness of the problem and the need to address it.

Physicians may choose to identify someone on their office staff who will be responsible for asking every patient about domestic violence. This staff person should be educated about appropriate questions to ask and knowledgeable about community resources.

Once the diagnosis of battering is established, physicians must convey to their patients concern, respect, and a willingness to offer ongoing support. Let the patient know that she doesn't deserve to be beaten and that she is not alone. Assert that domestic violence is illegal, assure her that it is not her fault and that many others are in the same situation, and ask whether she is interested in community resources. If the patient thinks it is safe to have written materials, offer her written information, including telephone numbers for local shelters, crisis services, and legal options.

Physicians and therapists should not suggest that an abused woman enter couples counseling with her batterer. Family therapy is inappropriate in the presence of domestic violence and may increase the risk of serious harm.[44]

The possibility of life-threatening violence must always be considered, particularly if violence has resulted in hospitalization. This risk is significantly increased if any of the following conditions exist: the woman believes her life is in danger; violence has resulted in previous hospital visits; the batterer has used a gun or knife, stalked her, or threatened to kill her or himself; or the couple is in the process of divorce, separation, or conflict over children.[45]

Routine safety assessment is particularly important for women who have left a violent relationship. In a sample of battered women seeking emergency service, two-thirds were either divorced or separated.[46] Ask a battered woman in this situation if she is safe and encourage her to take steps to protect herself and her children. Do not assure a battered woman of her safety after she has been discharged. The person most qualified to determine whether she will be safe upon leaving the hospital is the battered woman. Only she knows how dangerous her home situation is and when the time is right to leave.

It may be useful to help the patient identify her degree of entrapment by specifying elements of control that might prevent her from defending herself, escaping, or using helping resources when she is threatened or hurt again. Offer to help her develop a safety plan in case violence reoccurs. Sample safety plans can be found in Appendix I.

In addition to shelter and other emergency housing, legal services, and treatment for substance abuse, safety planning with battered women often includes women's support groups, changing jobs, continuing education, applying for Aid to Families with Dependent Children or emergency assistance, counseling for children, and child or adult protective services.

Since medical records assist in documenting the abuse, it is particularly important that they be accurate and legible. Include photographs or use a body map to detail the extent of the injuries. Even if the patient chooses not to proceed with legal action immediately, she might in the future and these records will be helpful.[47]

Around 1994, when some insurance companies began denying coverage to battered women, there was concern that physicians should not write a diagnosis of domestic violence in the medical record as it might be used to deny the women insurance coverage. Substantial pressure on the insurance industry forced them to change their policies of direct denial and charge higher premiums instead. Although there is continued concern that domestic violence documentation could adversely affect a woman's ability to obtain affordable insurance, the benefits of this documentation outweigh that possibility.[48]

The success of each stage of the intervention process depends on accountability achieved through monitoring and feedback, including follow-ups with the patient. It is crucial that the physician support the patient in whatever decision she makes. At the same time, the physician should express concern for her safety and that of her children. Expressing disappointment with her decision reinforces feelings of low self-esteem and lack of control and may also make her less likely to return for help. Even if the woman does not immediately leave her abusive partner, the fact that a health care provider is concerned about her suffering validates her feelings and reinforces her capacity to seek help when she feels ready to do so.

Collaboration and Innovation

For battered women, the hospital can serve as a vital link to other crisis services. Health care providers can smooth the way for frightened women by offering encouragement and support in seeking more specialized help in the form of shelters and battered women's centers. The transition from the hospital to a battered women's center is made even easier when there is a collaboration between these service providers. Every emergency facility should have a paid battered woman's advocate either on staff or on call from a battered women's center. Regrettably, few hospitals have programs of this nature.

Programs such as Advocacy for Women and Kids in Emergencies in Boston, WomanKind in Minneapolis, and Project SAFE in New Haven, Connecticut, are leading models for collaborative intervention programs between health care systems and community-based battered women's programs. Integrating the services of battered women's programs, domestic violence state coalitions, medical associations, medical schools, and hospitals, these groups have designed and implemented innovative programs that have successfully assisted battered women and their children and have helped educate the medical community about domestic violence.[49]

In 1995 the Austin Center for Battered Women (CBW) received funding from the Texas Department of Human Services to develop and initiate a hospital advocacy program in collaboration with Brackenridge Hospital. The goals of the program were twofold: advocates provided support to battered women using hospital services, and they provided in-house training to hospital staff about family violence. Despite its success in strengthening support for victims when they are in most urgent need, the program lost funding in 1997.

Effective advocacy offers battered women two essential types of assistance. Emotional support helps women sort through the confusion and despair that abuse often creates. Practical assistance helps women maintain their safety and, in some cases, escape their abusive partners and rebuild their lives.

Effective advocacy reduces battered women's isolation and increases their safety and the safety of their children. An advocate listens to a woman's story, assesses danger, explores options, develops safety plans, and may try to find the woman shelter. Advocates make contact with the women through in-hospital visits and telephone calls. The key is for the advocate to establish a personal relationship with the battered woman.

Hospital advocacy staff worked diligently to educate the hospital staff about family violence. An information packet, *Domestic Violence: Identification, Intervention, and Nursing Documentation,* and one-hour presentations were regularly offered to nurses.[50] These training programs conveyed information on the dynamics of abusive relationships; indicators of abuse; and how to question, listen, and respond to battered women.

Specialized training programs targeting pregnant battered women were offered to hospital staff in labor and delivery. One particularly innovative aspect of the CBW Hospital Advocacy Program was a four-hour workshop on battered women, elder abuse, child abuse, and women with disabilities. This workshop was offered to all health care professionals within a two-hundred-mile radius of Austin.

While CBW staff collaborated with the entire staff at Brackenridge Hospital, staff members in the children's hospital, the emergency room, and labor and delivery were particularly supportive. According to one CBW staff member, "We're trying very hard to work with each other rather than being combative. Many of the hospital staff are ready and willing to work with us. They really want to see this joint effort succeed."

The CBW Hospital Advocacy Program operated on a shoestring budget with a small staff and a group of well-trained volunteers. The task sometimes seemed overwhelming; one staff member remarked, "Sometimes I feel like I'm trying to scratch a hole in the Berlin Wall with my fingernail." Their successes and their vision, however, kept them going. "We've connected with women who have used our services and that feels good. Bit by bit, through the workshops and just talking, we [were] really beginning to see an increase in staff's awareness and understanding of domestic violence."

Empowerment of Female Patients

The dissolution of effective projects like the CBW Hospital Advocacy Program demonstrates the attitudes of many legislators and health care providers regarding domestic violence. They reflect society's denial of the prevalence and severity of abuse against women and children. An effective response to domestic violence extends well beyond instituting protocols or asking a few questions. It requires that, as individuals, we question the power imbalances in our own lives and of those around us. It is at this point that we can begin to question the institutional and societal traditions that perpetuate and maintain violence against women.

Many battered women have been poorly served by a health care system that too often believes that medicine is a science and forgets that, above all, it is an art of healing. Good health goes beyond a rigid medical definition and is best expressed by the concept of well-being.

The well-being of battered women depends heavily on their empowerment as users of the health care system. How can women receive better health care if they are alienated by the established medical paradigm? Empowerment does not deny the individual woman her dignity nor refute or discount her pain and fear.

According to Jeanne Achterberg, author of *Woman as Healer,* "The growth and change in health care will obviously depend upon the breadth of our energies and the richness of our creative process."[51] Empowerment means eliminating the myths, prejudices, and preconceived notions about women and women's bodies. Empowerment means providing women a safe, confidential environment in which to discuss their health and their lives, to control them and to make decisions about them. The empowerment of battered women involves the sharing of information so that everyone will be equal partners in the patient-doctor relationship.

CHAPTER 11

Battered Women and Communities of Faith

A healthy and creative society cannot tolerate any form of violence. When this violence is based on the erroneous and insidious premise that men are entitled to dominate women, it is particularly abhorrent and dangerous. This attitude and behavior are capable of destroying all that is life-affirming and beautiful in society.

—Canadian Conference of Catholic Bishops
Permanent Council on Violence Against Women[1]

Domestic violence occurs in all types of families, including the nonreligious, the marginally religious, and the devoutly religious. In 1981 the United Methodist General Board of Global Ministries conducted a study of 600 Methodist women to investigate the presence of domestic violence among its congregants. One out of six women in the study reported abuse by their husbands, and for one-fourth of those women the abuse involved physical battering.[2]

Domestic violence is found in families of all religious backgrounds. Many women are pressured by the traditions, attitudes, and values of their religious or cultural groups to remain in abusive marriages. Christian women are often instructed to be submissive to their husbands, while many Jewish women have been taught that divorce just doesn't happen in their community. Muslim women are taught to devote themselves to their husbands and families. For these women, leaving their marriages feels like a betrayal of their religious beliefs as well as of the traditions and hopes of their communities.

For hundreds of years domestic violence has been the unmentionable sin. Historically, communities of faith, not unlike society as a whole, have ignored the problem. Battered women who have strong religious convictions need help not only with ending the abuse they suffer, but also with addressing the religious issues they face.

Religious faith is a primary reference point in the lives of some women. When faced with a personal crisis, these women turn first to their priest, pastor, or rabbi. Their religious leader is a trusted and known resource, and these women may assume that he or she will know what to do. For other women, a religious leader may be the only resource in a small town or rural area. Unfortunately, many communities of faith have responded poorly or not at all to the issue of domestic violence.

In an effort to assess the validity of the claim that pastors hold a patriarchal attitude that predisposes them to respond ineffectively to battered women, James and Phyllis Alsdurf distributed a questionnaire to more than 5,000 Protestant pastors throughout the United States. According to the Alsdurfs, "The opinion that pastors do hold such views was partially confirmed in our study. However, the comments from pastors revealed them to be a group concerned about women but torn by the theological perspectives they hold which conflict with this concern."[3]

Battered women of faith also find themselves in conflict. Any devout woman, no matter what her particular faith, may find herself torn between the teachings of her religion and her own safety. Of the nearly one hundred battered Protestant women in another study conducted by the Alsdurfs, approximately 75 percent stayed with their abusive husbands long after most women would consider it safe. Rather than leave, they prayed for their husbands to change or for the ability to endure the abuse. Those who left generally did so after years of questioning whether or not there was adequate biblical justification for divorcing an abusive partner. Most of the women in the study reported they received little sympathy or support within the church after revealing their abusive situation to others.[4] In addition, many of the women perceived their pastors as naive or afraid to get involved, especially when the batterers held positions of power within the church. Most of the women reported that their pastors focused on getting *them* to change, rather than their abusive partners.[5]

Spiritual Dilemmas

When people are in crisis, they usually rely on their basic beliefs about the world and their role in it. For people with strong religious convictions, these beliefs and values are often principles of faith and religious doctrine. Crisis frequently affects these belief systems.[6]

Religious battered women face a multitude of spiritual dilemmas, including a sense of abandonment by God, the nature of suffering, the value of obedience, and the biblical justification for separation and divorce.[7] When they question their faith, they are trying to make sense of their suffering and find meaning for this experience in their lives. According to Reverend Marie Fortune, executive director of the Center for the Prevention of Sexual and Domestic Violence, these women's theological concerns "are to be seen as a healthy sign because they represent an effort to comprehend and contextualize the experience of family violence and thereby regain some control over their lives in the midst of crisis."[8]

For battered women of faith, religious concerns are often a priority and should be respected, or they will become obstacles that prevent women from addressing their own safety and well-being. The manner in which communities of faith address the concerns of battered women will either jeopardize their lives or help them to transform their experiences. Theological concerns cannot be met with simplistic answers and then dismissed. Efforts at crisis intervention will be thwarted until the crisis of faith is acknowledged and addressed.[9]

Women may find simple explanations for their suffering insufficient. They may feel that their faith has failed them or that their God has abandoned them. It may be, however, that the actions of their particular denomination have failed them. According to Fortune, many religious battered women receive such instructions as the following:

- Keep the commandments and everything will work out.
- Pray more, pray harder.
- Accept Jesus Christ as your Lord and Savior and everything will be fine.
- Go to services every week.
- Bring your husband to services.

While such advice may be a part of the fundamental teachings of religious faith, it does not effectively address the complexity of domestic violence. When offered as simple and complete answers to battered women's crises, such advice leaves women vulnerable and sets up a dynamic that actually blames women for their own suffering.[10]

The way the Bible is interpreted, particularly in relation to Christian women, is crucial for battered women. The misinterpretation and misuse of Scripture to support subordination of women, suffering as virtuous, forgiveness without justice, and divorce as a sin help to keep battered women in their abusive relationships.[11] The misinterpretation of religious scripture contributes to the guilt, self-blame, and suffering that battered women experience and serves as a rationalization for abusers. When batterers misinterpret religious scripture, they are misusing religious teachings to excuse or justify their abusive behaviors.

After careful study of Jewish and Christian Scripture, Fortune has found that it is not possible to use Scripture to justify family violence. It is possible, however, to misuse Scripture and other traditional religious literature for this purpose.[12] According to the U.S. Bishops' Committees on Women in the Church and Society, and on Marriage and Family Life, "As a church, one of the most worrying aspects of the abuse practiced against women is the use of biblical texts, taken out of context, to support abusive behavior. . . . As bishops, we condemn the use of the Bible to condone abusive behavior. A correct reading of the Scriptures leads people to a relationship based on mutuality and love."[13]

It is not uncommon for women who seek help from their pastors, priests, or rabbis to receive advice reflecting a theology of female suffering and submission. For example:[14]

- Marriage is sacred. You must do whatever you can to hold it together.
- Your husband is the head of your household. Obey him and he won't need to resort to violence.
- All of us must suffer. Offer up your suffering to Jesus, and he will give you strength to endure.

That some communities of faith continue to misuse scripture to keep women locked in abusive relationships is evident by the results of the Alsdurfs' survey of conservative Protestant clergy. Twenty-seven percent of the pastors surveyed felt that if a woman submits to her husband, God will eventually honor her and either the abuse will stop or God will give her the strength to endure it. According to the Alsdurfs, "to take such a stance is to acknowledge that the principle of wifely submission preempts other considerations, such as that of a woman's safety. This was evident by the fact that pastors who stressed wifely submission were also opposed to victims using certain protective legal and medical resources and were inclined to discount women's reports of violence."[15]

Many communities of faith minimize the severity of violence reported by women because of traditional attitudes toward marriage that encourage the maintenance of marriage at all costs. Pastors in the Alsdurfs' survey were asked to rate just how intense marital violence would have to be in order to justify a woman leaving. One-third of the respondents felt that the abuse would have to be life-threatening, and almost one-fifth believed that no amount of abuse would justify a woman leaving.[16]

Creating an Effective Pastoral Response to Domestic Violence

Communities of faith have the potential to be a source of direct and indirect support for battered women. To do so, they must begin to accept their responsibility to prevent, recognize, and intervene in cases of domestic violence. To create an effective response to domestic violence, religious leaders and their congregations must work together to acknowledge the problem, learn more about the issue, work with secular resources, and reach out to the community.

Conduct a Self-Evaluation

Self-evaluation is one of the first steps religious leaders need to take to address the issue of domestic violence. First, to become comfortable with this issue, religious leaders should examine their attitudes, feelings, and beliefs about domestic violence, battered women, and women in general.[17]

Religious leaders must also examine their traditions and theologies to determine whether they are a source of comfort and support for all parishioners or oppressive for some. According to Rita-Lou Clarke, author of *Pastoral Care of Battered Women,* "We need to see that the Bible also speaks of healing for sufferers and forgiveness with repentance and reconciliation.

We need to see that divorce can be an option for new life. These views can help to liberate a woman from the bondage of a battering relationship."[18]

Leaders should also evaluate their understanding about domestic violence as well as their strengths and limitations for helping battered women. Many seminaries do not provide instruction regarding ministry in situations of family violence. Some seminarians are not even alerted that they will see family violence in their ministries. One Protestant minister explains that for too many years the need to understand the problem of domestic violence has been overshadowed by the need to maintain the marriage covenant. Religious leaders must begin to understand the dynamics of this issue if they are to effectively respond to battered women and their families.[19]

Many battered women's shelters offer training for volunteers. Religious leaders should try to attend these or other trainings offered by local shelters, state coalitions against domestic violence, or the religious community. In addition, several excellent publications address the religious concerns of battered women. These and other resources are listed on pages 370–373.

Acknowledge and Address the Problem

Religious leaders can break the silence surrounding domestic violence by educating congregations about the realities of the issue and, by example, creating an atmosphere in which battered women feel a sense of belonging and support. When religious leaders communicate that it is acceptable to talk about violence in church, they are giving battered women a clear signal that it is safe to ask for help. Once battered women feel safe, they will begin to reach out to others for the comfort and assistance they so desperately need.

One way religious leaders can educate their congregations and create a safe environment for abused women is through sermons. Several suggested sermon topics are listed below.[20] In addition, a moment of silence or a candlelight service can be offered for victims of domestic violence, perhaps including testimony from a survivor of domestic violence on a topic such as "How God Helped Me Through My Crisis."

Violence against women and repercussions in the community:

2 Samuel 13
Judges 19

Suffering:

I Peter 4:12–19
Jeremiah 29:10–14
Psalm 55

Love and marriage:

Ephesians 5:21–33
I Corinthians 13
I John 4:18

Sin and accountability:

John 7:53–8:11
Ezekiel 18:21–32

Reaching out to others in need:

Luke 10:25–37

Religious leaders might also post fliers advertising such local resources as battered women's shelters and adapt curricula dealing with domestic violence for Sunday school classes. Announcements can be made from the pulpit about local shelters and support groups for battered women and abusers. Speakers can be brought in from local shelters or seminaries to speak to youth groups, adult education classes, couples groups, singles groups, social groups, and women's groups in the church. Religious leaders can support observance of National Domestic Violence Awareness Month in October by including relevant articles in the church newsletter. The congregation can supply resources such as money, referral sources, clothes, food, and child care for families in crisis.[21]

Leaders should be alert for signs of abuse among female parishioners, such as frequent church hopping, intermittent attendance, and very private couples who keep to themselves and rarely socialize or interact with church acquaintances or relatives.[22]

The issue of domestic violence can be raised in marriage preparation sessions by questioning couples regarding how they handle disagreements and their families' problem-solving patterns. Leaders can help couples learn how to increase justice and equality in their marriages. They should also be aware that pregnancy is often a time of increased battering for women, a fact that can be addressed in baptismal preparation programs.[23]

Know About and Use Secular Resources

Religious leaders should familiarize themselves with community resources available to battered women, including talking to the local battered women's shelter to learn about the services that are offered. The National Domestic Violence Hotline, (800) 799-SAFE, can provide the names and telephone numbers of community organizations willing to help battered women.

When resources are available, it is advisable to refer battered women or their abusive partners to shelters or batterers' treatment programs. Staff and volunteers of these agencies are trained to deal with abuse and have the knowledge and experience to provide the needed support and advocacy.

A religious leader's wise use of referrals comes from an awareness of his or her limitations and a clear understanding of what his or her role should be. Seldom do religious leaders have the training or time to provide the long-term advocacy that battered women or their abusive partners need. They can often be most effective by serving as support persons and advocates while the battered woman is getting specialized help.

Some leaders are hesitant to utilize secular resources in response to domestic violence. They often do not trust battered women's advocates to be sensitive to the spiritual needs of their parishioners. Likewise, many battered women's advocates are hesitant to trust religious leaders to know how to help battered women. Unfortunately, it is battered women who suffer most from this mutual mistrust. Such resulting lack of cooperation puts them in a position of choosing either battered women's services or pastoral support.

An effective response develops when religious leaders and secular helpers reach out to each other as peers, share information, offer mutual training, serve on boards together, and provide services when referred to by the other. Working together to meet the needs of battered women begins to build the mutual trust that is needed for effective advocacy.[24]

Several years ago Joel Maiorano, a minister at a Christian church in Austin, called me because concerned parents of a battered woman had just contacted him. Although Maiorano had attended the Center for Battered Women's volunteer training class and was knowledgeable about domestic violence, he decided to refer the callers to me. I contacted the concerned family members and was able to provide them with appropriate assistance. By working together, Maiorano and I were able to address the spiritual, emotional, and informational needs of his acquaintances.

Support Community Outreach

Communities of faith can participate in planning a coordinated community response to domestic violence and take the lead in teaching that male violence against women and children is morally wrong. Religious leaders can participate in community activities that discourage violent behavior and support battered women's shelters. Church groups can be encouraged to support local shelters by volunteering and donating money or needed resources. Religious leaders should also encourage the formation of a committee or task force to educate the congregation and recruit volunteers for service.

Becoming an Advocate for Battered Women

The very nature of ministry makes it difficult to spend more than a few sessions in serious counseling with a parishioner. Battered women are better served when religious leaders recommend resources that can provide the long-term advocacy abused women frequently need. Religious leaders can then continue to offer support to battered women as they struggle to make decisions about their lives. Although a leader's time with a battered woman may be limited, the quality of his or her efforts can make a substantial difference in a battered woman's life.

The Advocacy Wheel in Appendix II is a helpful tool for anyone interested in helping a battered woman. In addition, the following ideas may be beneficial to religious leaders who are approached by battered women for help.

Most battered women are relieved when they feel it is safe to discuss their situation. Encourage the woman to openly share her story and her feelings. Try to listen without assigning blame and without judging her. Be prepared to hear about and validate feelings of anger, shame, isolation, guilt, confusion, fear, powerlessness, and hopelessness.

Hearing horrific stories of abuse can be quite unsettling, and it may seem incomprehensible that a person can do such terrible acts to someone he supposedly loves. Do not deny or minimize what she is sharing with you. Being knowledgeable about domestic violence; knowing what to do; and not allowing personal feelings of anger, disbelief, or discomfort to interfere helps the listener to overcome the tendency to minimize. It is also helpful to remember that, in an attempt to make an intolerable situation more tolerable, many battered women actually minimize, rather than exaggerate, the abuse they suffer.[25]

Some women may be hesitant to admit that they are being abused by their partners. Asking clear, direct questions in a sensitive and caring manner will help to create an environment in which a woman will feel safe to discuss her situation. If you suspect that a woman is experiencing violence, these questions may help:[26]

- Are you in a relationship in which you feel you are treated badly?
- Has your partner ever destroyed things that you cared about?
- Are you afraid of your partner when he gets angry?
- Has your partner ever physically hurt you or threatened you?
- Has your partner ever threatened or hurt your children?

Express your concern about the violence, and be very clear in communicating to the woman that she does not deserve to be beaten. Let her know that not only is domestic violence illegal, it is also a sin. Assure her that it is not her fault. Tell her that she is not alone in her situation and that she has your support and the support of her religious community.

Conduct a Safety Assessment

Safety is the first priority for battered women and their children. Ask the woman if she is safe, and encourage her to take the necessary steps to protect herself and her children. Offer to help her develop a safety plan in case violence reoccurs. Sample safety plans are given in Appendix I.[27]

Make Appropriate Referrals

The battered woman you are helping may find it difficult to assess her situation and to make decisions. You can help her to assess her personal strengths, resources, and support systems. Making decisions for her is not as helpful as offering her information, such as telephone numbers of local resources, and outlining options, such as shelters or other safe locations, support groups, counseling, legal counsel, and continuing education and training.

Let her know that you support her decisions even it means breaking up the family. Her safety and the safety of her children must be secured before work to preserve the family can begin.

Address Pastoral Concerns

A battered woman may struggle to understand her suffering in the context of her religious beliefs. She may believe that she deserves the abuse because of a previous sin or that suffering is the way to salvation. Recognize her inner conflict, and be willing to discuss the religious questions she asks. Stress that religious scripture does not condone or justify the abuse she is suffering. Address her guilt by emphasizing that the responsibility for the abuse lies with the batterer.

Maintain a Connection

Stay in contact with the battered woman as she struggles with her situation. Acknowledge the danger she faces, and let her take the lead as to whether it is safe for you to contact her or whether she should contact you. Ask her how she is doing with the referrals you offered. Continue to reassure her of the ongoing support of her religious community.[28]

Guidelines for Crisis Counseling

There may be occasions when religious leaders receive a call from a woman who has just been beaten. This can be a very dangerous situation for everyone, and special precautions are required.

First, do not go to a home where violence is occurring. It is extremely dangerous. Ask the woman if she is safe and if she would like you to call the police. If the violence is over, ask how she is. Does she need medical attention? Where are her children? Do her children need medical attention? When is her husband returning?

If she is in physical danger, encourage her to find a safe place for herself. Does she want to leave? Explore options available to her, including parents, friends, a church-family refuge, a motel, or a shelter. If the shelter is the only option, give her the telephone number. Whether she decides to leave or stay, encourage her to make contact with the nearest shelter for support and assistance.[29]

Guidelines for Secular Helpers

Secular advocates may encounter a battered woman who has religious questions and concerns. Marie Fortune's booklet, *Keeping the Faith: Questions and Answers for the Abused Woman,* is an excellent resource for both the advocate and the abused woman.[30] In addition, the following recommendations may be helpful:[31]

1. Acknowledge and pay attention to religious questions, comments, and references.
2. Respect any religious concerns the woman may have.
3. Affirm these concerns as appropriate and try to identify how important they are for the woman.
4. If you are uncomfortable or feel unqualified to pursue the discussion, refer the woman to a trusted religious leader who is willing to help her address these particular concerns.
5. If you are comfortable pursuing the conversation, emphasize the ways that her religious beliefs can be a resource for her. Assure her that religious scripture does not justify nor condone domestic violence.

Pitfalls Religious Leaders Should Avoid

Successful advocacy on behalf of battered women and their families means avoiding certain pitfalls. Listed below are some recommendations regarding actions that religious leaders should not take.[35]

1. Do not contact the batterer or disclose any information to him about the woman's discussions with you. You could endanger her life.
2. Do not suggest marriage counseling, mediation sessions, or communications workshops. These avenues will not stop the batterer's violence. Counseling to stop a batterer's violence must be with a helper skilled in domestic violence. Marriage counseling and other intervention strategies may be beneficial only after the batterer has received the treatment he needs.[32]
3. Do not interview a battered woman and her abusive partner as a couple or try to counsel the couple together to stop the batterer's violence. It is important to talk with the battered woman alone. Joint counseling often threatens her safety, and the batterer's presence may hinder her ability to openly discuss the abuse.[33]
4. Do not minimize what a battered woman shares with you. Assume that you are hearing only a part of her story.
5. Do not try to deal with the problem alone. Refer as often as you can to appropriate resources.
6. Do not be manipulated by a batterer's claim of a religious conversion experience, which is a common claim when arrest has already taken place. An experience of religious conversion may be genuine, but should not be used as a reason to avoid the consequences of the batterer's violent behavior.[34]
7. Do not encourage premature reconciliation. Safety is a priority in domestic violence situations. This may mean a marital separation. True reconciliation can occur only when certain conditions have been met. First, the woman must be safe. Next, the batterer must be held responsible for his violence, genuinely repent, and seek help for his abusive behavior. Acceptance of responsibility for the abuse and a firm commitment to change are crucial for authentic repentance. Even when the batterer has expressed regret, he must be encouraged to seek help to change his abusive behavior.[35]

Breaking the Silence

While communities of faith have long ignored the problem of domestic violence, recent years have witnessed a growing change. The Center for the Prevention of Sexual and Domestic Violence, founded by Reverend Marie Fortune, has made exemplary efforts to educate religious communities in the United States and Canada. The center is an interreligious ministry that develops educational programs aimed at preventing sexual and domestic violence for use at all levels of organized religion. In 1994 and 1995, the center provided training and consultation to more than 10,000 clergy, denominational and organizational staff, religious educators, seminarians, and secular professionals.[36]

In addition, the center acts as a bridge between religious and secular communities, preparing and encouraging religious and secular professionals to work cooperatively so that victims, offenders, and their families can receive thorough and meaningful assistance. The center promotes institutional and social change, calling upon religious communities to assume leadership in reforming institutional policies and cultural norms of sexism, racism, anti-Semitism, classism, ableism, heterosexism, and ageism so that all women, children, and men may live free of sexual and domestic violence.

In the United States, the Catholic church has publicly taken a strong stand against domestic violence. In a pastoral letter issued by the United States Bishops' Committees on Women in the Church and Society, and on Marriage and Family Life, the bishops proclaim, "As pastors of the church in the United States, we join bishops in other countries, notably Canada and New Zealand, in stating as clearly and strongly as we can that violence against women, in the home or outside the home, is 'never' justified. Violence in any form—physical, sexual, psychological or verbal—is sinful."[37]

Asking for increased cooperation with secular helpers, the bishops go on to explain, "We agree with the bishops of Quebec, Canada, in calling on the Christian community to 'join forces with and complement the work of those associations and groups which are already involved in preventing and fighting this form of violence.'"[38]

In Austin, Texas, the Catholic Diocese has made an outstanding effort to address and prevent family violence. Working closely with the Center for Battered Women, the Texas Council on Family Violence, and other domestic violence organizations, the diocese has developed a comprehensive educational manual entitled *Breaking the Silence: A Pastoral Response to Domestic Violence Against Women.*[39] A valuable resource for both religious and secular helpers, the manual offers guidelines for preventing domestic violence as well as suggestions for preaching with sensitivity to the issue. It also explores how religious leaders can approach domestic violence in marriage preparation sessions and baptism preparation.

With the knowledgeable assistance of both secular and religious leaders, the diocese sponsored two workshops on domestic violence in 1995. According to Chris Attal, director of parish social ministries in Austin, "Our first conference was so successful that we decided to offer a second one. Since then we continue to work with parishes on an individual basis, offering our support based on their specific needs and referring as often as possible. One of the future options we're exploring is doing broader parish work, perhaps offering another conference for other denominations."

In Austin, individual churches and parishioners have begun to reach out to battered women and their families. Cristo Rey Catholic Church, St. Catherine of Siena, St. Louis, and St. Paul's have formed either a domestic violence committee or an awareness program. At Cristo Rey, Father Larry Mattingly and parishioner Roy Gomez have developed a domestic violence awareness program. Gomez, whose daughter lost her life as a result of domestic violence, feels that educating people about domestic violence is their greatest challenge. "We have to rely on the church to condemn domestic violence from the pulpit," explains Gomez. "We at Cristo Rey Church are very fortunate to have Father Mattingly, who really understands domestic violence and the harm it does."

Gomez works closely with the Austin Center for Battered Women to educate and assist battered women and their families. He has created an information center that contains publications on domestic violence in both Spanish and English. He also recruits speakers—survivors, family members, and battered women's advocates—to address the congregation during mass.

Gomez also runs ads in the church bulletin addressing domestic violence, listing his name and telephone number as a resource. And he is getting calls. "Many of the women I talk to have heard of CBW, but they seem to be more willing to reach out to another church member. They'll call me first and we work from there." Gomez, along with Father Mattingly and other members of the congregation, provide resources to battered women to help them stay safe and rebuild their lives.

The Austin Catholic community serves as an example of the positive impact communities of faith can have on battered women and their families. From the United States bishops to the diocese, individual priests, and parishioners, the Catholic community has demonstrated a willingness to address domestic violence and to work with secular advocates. Ultimately, their efforts not only contribute to the enhanced safety and well-being of battered women and their children, but to a more loving and peaceful society. As Fortune so eloquently puts it, "It is time we began focusing on what is really important—and that is the promise that for each of us God wishes life in all its abundance. Saving the family means ending the violence that is destroying it."[40]

CHAPTER 12

Creating a Community Response to Domestic Violence

We cannot have a healthier community unless we all work together to recognize our strengths, abilities, weaknesses, and needs to achieve the common goal of preventing family violence.

—Caryl Clarke Colburn and Mike Denton
Co-chairs, Travis County Family Violence Task Force

Domestic violence is much more than an individual or family problem: it is a widespread community and societal problem. For more than twenty years the battered women's movement has done a commendable job of advocating for battered women and children and increasing public awareness about domestic violence. However, increased community accountability and collaboration must become the standard if we are to realize our dream of a future without family violence.

Efforts to end family violence must be community driven, as individual communities are in the best position to understand their needs and resources. They are also in the best position to prioritize community needs with respect to family violence and to allocate increasingly scarce resources.

Community Accountability

The ideal community response to domestic violence requires that community opinion strongly state that domestic violence is unacceptable. This unified opinion will lead all social institutions to demand full accountability from batterers by applying appropriate consequences.

Mike Jackson and David Garvin, with the Domestic Violence Institute of Michigan, have developed a Community Accountability Wheel that outlines the actions comprising the ideal institutional responses to domestic violence.[1] Collectively, these responses can have a major impact on both the intervention and prevention of domestic violence.

Ideal Institutional Responses to Domestic Violence

Employers will

1. Condition batterers' continuing employment on remaining nonviolent.
2. Actively intervene against stalking and harassment in the workplace.
3. Support, financially and otherwise, advocacy and services for battered women and their children.
4. Continually educate and dialogue about domestic violence issues.

The justice system will

1. Adopt mandatory arrest policies for batterers.
2. Charge and prosecute batterers in a manner that does not rely on the survivors involvement.
3. Refer batterers exclusively to intervention programs that meet state or federal standards.
4. Never offer a deferred sentence option to batterers. This option withholds sentencing pending a defendant's completion of probation. If the defendant successfully completes probation, the sentence's procedures are dropped.
5. Provide easily accessible protection orders and back them up.
6. Incarcerate batterers for noncompliance with any aspect of their adjudication.

The educational system will

1. Dialogue with students about violence in their homes, the dynamics of domestic violence, and how domestic violence is founded on the oppression of women.

2. Provide a leadership role in research and theoretical development that prioritizes gender justice, equal opportunity, and peace.
3. Intervene in harassment, abuse, violence and intimidation of girls and women in the education system.

The clergy will

1. Conduct outreach within the congregation regarding domestic violence and provide a safe environment for women to discuss their experiences.
2. Develop internal policies for responding to domestic violence.
3. Speak out against domestic violence from the pulpit.
4. Organize multifaith coalitions to educate the religious community.
5. Actively interact with the existing domestic violence intervention community.

The media will

1. Educate the community about the epidemic of violence against women.
2. Prioritize safety, equal opportunity, and justice for women and children over profit, popularity, and advantage.
3. Expose and condemn patriarchal privilege, abuse, and chauvinism.
4. Cease its practice of glorifying violence against women and children.

Social service providers will

1. Become social change advocates for battered women.
2. Refer batterers to accountable intervention programs.
3. Stop blaming batterers' behaviors on myths such as drugs and alcohol, provocation, and loss of control.
4. Design and deliver services that are sensitive to women and children's safety needs.

Enhancing Community Collaboration

In 1994 the American Medical Association invited a broad range of organizations to send interested representatives to the National Conference on Family Violence: Health and Justice. Results of this conference included recommendations for a more coordinated, communitywide approach to reducing both the effects and incidence of family violence.[2]

One conference recommendation is that individual communities should create family violence councils to coordinate efforts to end family violence at the local level. The councils should consist of representatives of all groups and agencies who deal with family violence. There should be no barriers to membership, and all interested parties, including the following, should be encouraged to join:

- Physicians
- Nurses, including clinical and school nurses
- Nurse practitioners
- Midwives
- Medical administrators
- Legislators
- Judges
- Former battered women
- Advocates
- Law enforcement
- Educators
- Social workers
- Clergy
- Pharmacists
- Substance abuse counselors
- Mental health providers
- Prosecutors
- Attorneys

- Probation and parole officials
- Corrections officials
- Researchers
- Community-based organizations
- Rehabilitated offenders of family violence
- Concerned community members

The general purpose of the family violence councils should be as follows:

- To enhance coordination among hospitals, service agencies, police departments, and the courts at both the system and service levels
- To provide opportunities for the various disciplines to educate each other and to facilitate cross-training
- To promote and evaluate interventions that have been found to be effective
- To improve the response to family violence in order to reduce its incidence
- To identify areas where interventions are known to work and need only to be coordinated, and to identify areas lacking effective programs wherein new interventions must be developed
- To promote the development and support of intervention programs by hospitals and health care systems
- To promote the development and replication of family-centered, community-based intervention programs

In addition to providing leadership for intervention and rehabilitation, family violence councils are in an ideal position to address prevention, community education, assessment, media, and the integration of these functions. Specific strategies of the councils should include the following:

- Developing and revising policies and procedures for interagency coordination and cooperation at both the system and service levels
- Sponsoring conferences that focus on family violence in the community
- Promoting educational programs in primary and secondary schools

- Providing professional education
- Identifying health and justice intervention and rehabilitation methods that have been effective in other disciplines and that can be applied to family violence
- Searching for cross-disciplinary approaches

Ann Jones, author of *Next Time She'll Be Dead: Battering and How to Stop It*, reminds us that a crucial element of a coordinated community approach is mutual accountability. "They must build in to their design specific ways to monitor one another's work, collaborate on reviewing and revising programs, hold one another accountable for ineffective policies and practices, provide mutual support, and work to overcome institutionalized sexism, racism, and homophobia. . . . Every aspect of the coordinated community program must aim to protect victims and to hold offenders accountable."[3]

The Travis County Family Violence Task Force

As the problem of domestic violence continues to soar, agencies struggle to meet the demand for services. With few exceptions, current waiting lists are long and service providers often offer prevention and community education cautiously because it is already difficult to serve women and children in need. According to Julia Spann, associate director at the Austin Center for Battered Women, "It's clear that in order to impact the problem in a more comprehensive way, all service providers and community planners must cooperate and collaborate. Even though we desperately need new resources, we also need to ensure that services are being coordinated throughout the community."

Austin, Texas, has historically been deeply concerned about domestic violence. This is evident from the grassroots inception of the Center for Battered Women in 1977, the first shelter for battered women and their children in the state, to the creation of the first Austin/Travis County Family Violence Task Force (FVTF) in 1981. The FVTF developed from the understanding that without a common vision and a united approach, a significant impact on family violence could not be accomplished. The FVTF serves as a good model for other communities.

Organizations and individuals represented on the Family Violence Task Force include the following:

- Austin Police Department—assault, patrol, and victim services units
- Austin Stress Clinic
- Center for Battered Women
- Child and Family Services
- Constable, Pct. 5
- County attorney's office
- County courts
- Criminal Defense Bar
- Criminal Justice Planning
- District attorney's office
- Former battered women
- Legal Aid Society
- Municipal courts
- Pre-trial Services
- Sheriff's department
- Texas Department of Health
- Travis County Counseling Center
- Travis County Probation Department
- Women's Advocacy Project

The FVTF has had a tremendous impact on the Austin community. They have helped to educate sectors of the community about domestic violence and have effected legislative, criminal justice, and law enforcement legal, policy, and procedural changes. Local service providers now better understand each other's expertise, and current services are provided by the most appropriate entity. Duplication of services is avoided so that a continuum of care is now available to survivors, their families, and abusers.

Following is a list of accomplishments attributed to the Travis County Family Violence Task Force.

1. Adoption of a "pro-arrest" policy, which states that police officers are expected (but not required) to make an arrest when they see signs of domestic assault, in 1989.
2. Filing of family violence misdemeanors at the more serious Class A level instead of Class C, meaning offenders are subject to harsher punishments.
3. Establishment of mandated screening for batterers' counseling as a condition of personal recognizance bonds. Personal recognizance means that the offender is released upon posting little or no bond and trusted to reappear on his court date, often under the conditions that he has a home address and a job.
4. Establishment of quality control standards for batterers' intervention programs.
5. Adoption of a "direct file" policy. This requires the arresting officer, rather than the victim, to file charges against the offender.
6. Implementation of procedures for law enforcement to request emergency protective orders on behalf of victims.
7. Creation of a jail-based batterers' intervention program.
8. Establishment of procedures to allow prosecutors to request increased police patrols in cases involving very angry abusers.
9. Establishment of the policy whereby jail personnel now routinely attempt to contact the victim to help insure her safety prior to an abuser's release.
10. Creation of investigation techniques by prosecutors and law enforcement that are more sensitive to victims.
11. Increased number of Austin Police Department Victim Service mobile crisis teams.
12. Creation and implementation of "Project Options," a supportive educational program for victims requesting to drop charges.
13. Creation of collaborative AWAKE (Awareness That Women Are Killed Everyday) Walks that help to commemorate women killed by their abusive partners. Since October 1994, walks have been held for nineteen women.
14. Creation of a VISTA (Volunteers in Service to America) project to provide year-long volunteer projects focused on public education.

This resulted in bringing both the Clothesline and the Witness to Violence projects to Travis County. The Clothesline project, inspired by the AIDS quilt, displays T-shirts painted by family members, friends, and survivors of violence against women. The Witness to Violence project sponsors public performances to heighten domestic violence awareness.

15. Establishment of the periodic review of batterer intervention program content by former battered women.
16. Creation of a family violence public awareness campaign in collaboration with an arts group know as Dance Umbrella. The project, "The Beast," is now traveling nationally.
17. Increased cross-training among system components.

The FVTF has recently been involved in multiple community planning activities to identify the continuum of services that should be in place to effect positive change against violence. The continuum encompasses (1) outreach and primary prevention, (2) intervention and treatment, (3) collaboration, and (4) policy change. This is a systems approach to identifying those abused, helping people to be safe, intervening appropriately, reducing domestic violence, and ultimately fostering a healthier community.

Although current activities of the task force continue to focus on the justice system's response, recent public awareness and survivors' outreach efforts indicate the beginning of a new era. According to Gail Rice, director of community outreach for the Center for Battered Women and former chair of the FVTF, the collaboration with Dance Umbrella serves as a premier example of the FVTF's willingness to expand beyond the justice system. "We really want to branch out," explains Rice. "In addition to some of our other efforts, we also plan to do PSAs [public service announcements] intended to raise awareness about adolescent violence." The task force also intends to broaden active and participatory membership to include health, education, and other community institutions.

FVTF members have been active participants in two substantive community planning efforts, the Community Action Network Master Study and Master Plan for Austin/Travis County Health and Human Services and the Criminal Justice Council Task Force Community Plan. Both efforts were launched in 1994, completed in 1995, and remain as working documents that are being refined, expanded, and enhanced to ensure a comprehensive community justice approach and a comprehensive health and human services plan related to violence and victimization for Austin/Travis County.

The Center for Battered Women's Supportive Housing Program

Families with children are the fastest-growing segment of the homeless population in the United States. Single mothers and their children comprise most homeless families,[4] and 50 percent of all homeless women and children are fleeing domestic violence.[5] These statistics are substantiated by the Center for Battered Women and the Salvation Army, who together provided emergency shelter to 90 percent of all homeless families receiving shelter in Austin in 1993. The mutual effort of these organizations can be an excellent model for programs attempting to address the need for transitional housing in other communities.

A serious effort has been made over the past few years to create a continuum of care in the Austin/Travis County metropolitan area. The Center for Battered Women has been a consistent participant in this process. In 1994 major social service funders, that include the City of Austin, Travis County, United Way, the State of Texas, the Austin Independent School District, and local foundations, joined together to form the Community Action Network. The functions of CAN are to develop a comprehensive assessment of social service needs in the community, to evaluate the effectiveness of current social service programs, to identify gaps in services, and to make recommendations concerning annual funding decisions.

An outgrowth of CAN was the creation of the Homeless Coalition. The coalition works to develop initiatives to address issues facing the homeless, to facilitate collaborative development of funding applications, to create allied ventures among organizations, and to strengthen the collective effectiveness of social service providers.

In 1994 the Center for Battered Women, in collaboration with the Salvation Army, was awarded $2,164,472 of Department of Housing and Urban Development (HUD) funding under the Transitional Housing component of the Supportive Housing Program. Their joint effort, the Supportive Housing Program, addresses a critical gap in the continuum of care for homeless families in Austin, as transitional housing and intensive support services move homeless families from emergency shelters to permanent housing and self-sufficiency. Representing an innovation in service delivery for battered women and their children, the Supportive Housing Program pairs the CBW, a local grassroots organization, with the Salvation Army, a national organization serving homeless people.

Families served by the CBW and the Salvation Army are experiencing multiple problems and barriers that maintain their dependent and homeless situation. Affordable housing is one of the primary barriers they face. In addition, lack of job skills, unemployment, lack of child care, poor parenting skills, lack of confidence and self-esteem, and unresolved issues resulting from abusive relationships must all be addressed before a family can be independent. The Supportive Housing Program addresses these and numerous other obstacles that prevent families from ending their homelessness.

Initially, the CBW and the Salvation Army address safety, shelter, and emergency needs for these families. Once these needs have been met, the families are moved into transitional housing that is owned and operated by the CBW but shared by both agencies' clients. In addition, the agencies participate with the Homeless Coalition to develop and use a collaborative method for sharing available transitional housing.

Services provided by the CBW include outreach, assessment, case management, and life skills training to participants in the transitional housing program, as well as counseling for women and children. Other services are delivered collaboratively by educational and social services organizations to provide child care, substance abuse services, mental health services, specialized services for developmentally delayed children, and transportation.

While transitional shelter providers in the United States offer comprehensive arrays of support services to people in shelters, the provision of therapeutic child care, focused on building parenting skills and developing healthier families, is an innovative addition that is easily replicated.

According to Kelly White Rountree, CBW executive director and abuse survivor, "The foundation has been laid for a strong and lasting influence on our community. Families will have opportunities they never had before and doors will open for them. Lives will be vastly improved by the existence of this program, and many will even be saved. Achievement will replace hopelessness, and broken lives will heal and head in new directions."

Other CBW Collaborations

The Center for Battered Women's willingness to collaborate with the Salvation Army is indicative of the center's belief in the need for a united response to domestic violence. The Supportive Housing Program is the latest in a long line of collaborative ventures with other groups, organizations, and individuals intent on ending family violence. Some of the CBW's other collaborations are listed below.

- *County Attorney's Office and the CBW:* The Early Linkage Program provides on-site advocacy at court that is independent of the legal system. The purpose of the program is to address safety issues and to link battered women with support services.
- *County Attorney's Office, CBW, and the Austin Police Department (APD):* Project Options provides educational classes for survivors requesting to drop criminal charges.
- *Family Violence Diversion Network, CBW, Formerly Battered Women's Task Force, and the Texas Council on Family Violence:* This group periodically reviews curriculum for batterers' intervention programs.
- *APD, CBW, and the University of Texas at Austin:* The Community Policing Project researches the effectiveness of community policing and community-based provision of victim services.
- *Dance Umbrella (local arts group), the CBW, Family Violence Task Force Public Awareness Committee, and the University of Texas at Austin Fine Arts Department:* The group sponsors an arts program intended to broaden public awareness of the impact of violence on families and society.
- *APD Victim Services Unit and the CBW:* This group operates under a COPS grant to provide culturally sensitive outreach efforts and services for battered Latinas. COPS (Community Oriented Policing) is a federal program that funds projects which help team police with domestic violence advocates and agencies.
- *APD and the CBW:* The ADT AWARE (Abused Women's Active Response Emergency) Program provides free alarm systems to survivors of domestic violence who are found to be in danger of being killed by their abusers.

- *Austin Independent School District and the CBW:* The Teen Dating Violence Prevention Program offers educational programs for middle and high schools and provides intervention groups for victims.

• • •

Our ability to end family violence is directly related to our willingness, as individuals and communities, to unite our voices and our efforts. Our society cannot afford to rely solely on the battered women's movement to end this epidemic. While our movement has accomplished incredible feats, we need everyone's participation if we truly want to make our communities and our world a more loving, peaceful place for women and children.

CHAPTER 13

Intervention Strategies for Battered Women and Their Children

Growing
I am the fish which strikes forth into the great blue endless ocean.
My eyes are open and I am travelling ahead, strong and free.
My body, smooth and wet, is surging through waves which splash and lull me on my endless journey.
Openness and freedom are my jewels—
Space is my reward.
Let lightness and airiness carry me on my journey.

—P.M.G.[1]

Intervention on behalf of battered women and their children takes place in a variety of arenas. The battered women's movement has, however, distinguished itself as a leader in this regard. Our experiences with battered women and, for many of us, our experiences as formerly battered women have taught us that women have a variety of needs. First and foremost, battered women need to be safe. This understanding has given rise to the numerous shelters and safe home networks (private residences opened to women in need by concerned citizens) across the country.

Second, battered women need information. They need to know about the resources and options available to them.

Third, battered women need material resources. Initially, they need a safe place to gather whatever material resources they currently have. When those resources are limited or unavailable, they may need to access resources from the city or state. Battered women may need medical assistance, housing, food, clothing, transportation, and money. In addition, they may need child care, education, job training, jobs, or legal assistance. Some women may need to secretly relocate to another area to protect themselves from their abusive partners.

Although battered women need, at a minimum, these material resources, they also need more. Battered women need opportunities to break their isolation. They need opportunities for connecting, for sharing, for being respected, and for healing. Two of the interventions that provide these opportunities are support groups and individual counseling.

Support Groups

Support groups for battered women are an important resource, both in and out of shelters, that offer advantages not available from individual counseling or other services. They are often the best way of providing support and information to battered women while helping to reduce their sense of isolation.

Women who feel isolated and powerless, and who blame themselves for the abuse they suffer, often benefit from exchanging information and expressing their feelings with other women in similar situations. In addition, women who have begun to change their lives are impressive role models for new group members. In some groups women act as advocates for each other, and many eventually go on to join the battered women's movement.

Mutual help groups for battered women are the direct offspring of feminist ideas and the consciousness-raising groups of the 1960s and 1970s. Ginny NiCarthy, Karen Merriam, and Sandra Coffman, in their book *Talking It Out: A Guide to Groups for Abused Women*, outline these feminist ideas as follows:[2]

- Women are the best experts on their own lives. Women are often safer in relying on others who are like themselves.
- Women teach each other that their problems aren't individual, but are social, political, and shared by many others.
- Institutionalized sex roles are damaging to women and the first step in changing them is to understand them.
- Individual women have power, and collectively their power can be great.

- The best place for women to look for emotional support and practical help is often from other women.

Most support groups have a facilitator who provides guidance to enhance the sense of safety and to enable each woman to take as much responsibility for the group as she is willing. Many groups, such as those described by Ellen Pence,[3] build on the work of the adult educator Paulo Freire. Freire's approach is built on a group process of critical reflection and transformative action. The development of critical consciousness starts with the recognition of the problem and moves on to analysis, action and organization. In the Freirian model, the facilitator does not impart knowledge to passive participants, but serves as a partner in a common search for insight about relevant problems.[4]

The facilitator helps women gain a critical consciousness about gender, power, and how violence operates in women's lives. According to Pence, "There is no greater challenge for any social movement than to live the vision of the change it seeks. A women's group does not merely prepare women for a future experience of empowerment or liberation. The group is itself an act of empowerment or liberation."[5]

Such support groups are composed entirely of women, including the facilitator. The absence of men frees women to express feelings and thoughts that they might suppress in a mixed group. This may be especially true for battered women, who have learned to fear men. If battered women are to gain from the support group experience, they need to learn to trust again and to risk intimacy with others.

Support groups help women face the reality of what has happened to them, what might happen, and what their responsibilities are. They provide an opportunity for women to explore feelings and options previously unknown or denied and an environment in which women can make decisions with the support of other participants.

As women begin to experience revelations about their abuse, they may become fearful and retreat into an earlier stage of denial. Women who feel too threatened may decide not to return to the group. The group experience, however, may help them to take action at a later date.[6]

If possible, groups should be divided into two stages. The first stage would be for battered women in crisis or who are trying to get free from abusive relationships. The second stage would be for women who have successfully escaped abusive relationships and who are facing other life issues.

Many communities do not have the luxury of providing groups for specific populations, such as battered women of color or lesbians. Every effort should be made, however, to form groups of whatever type are most needed in the community. If specialized groups are not feasible, facilitators should try to incorporate information and ideas about different populations into the mixed groups (see Chapter 7).

Individual Counseling

In the 1970s, Phyllis Chesler's critique of the ways in which traditional counseling reinforces the oppression of women led the way for alternative approaches to helping women.[7] Articles began appearing that discussed consciousness-raising groups as therapy for women. These were followed by works that specifically used the terms *feminism* and *feminist therapy*.[8]

Feminist therapy has several basic tenets. First, it is a wellness-based rather than a pathological-based approach. The counselor or advocate approaches battered women with respect for their success in surviving. Battered women are not viewed as psychologically impaired or "sick." In her book *In Our Best Interest: A Process for Personal and Social Change*, Ellen Pence reminds advocates, "We must constantly be aware of the tremendous pressure to view women's oppression as a sickness rather than as a political, social and cultural condition.[9]

Second, the feminist approach is based on the principles of individual choice and self-determination. Neither individual counselors nor the battered women's movement know what will work best for any individual battered woman. Instead, battered women themselves know what will work best for them.

Third, the role of the counselor is to provide support, to identify resources, to supply information, and, at times, to serve as an advocate for battered women. Fourth, the relationship between the counselor and the battered woman is characterized by an equality of power. The counselor's actions do not suggest that she is the expert and, instead, affirm the battered woman's power and competence to make decisions and to act. The counselor and the battered woman talk and work together to solve problems. This feature of feminist counseling stands in direct contrast to traditional counseling that operates from a hierarchical structuring of power in which the therapist knows best and directs the counseling process.

Fifth, the techniques of counseling include the identification of battered women with other women, particularly other battered women, and consciousness-raising about institutionalized sexism.[10]

Individual counseling offers battered women a safe environment in which to connect with another woman and begin to explore their personal situations. According to Margaret Bassett, counselor/advocate for the Austin Center for Battered Women, individual counseling coupled with support groups can be doubly rewarding for women. "Women who participate in individual counseling seem to do better in the support groups," explains Bassett. "They seem to have a higher self-awareness and are more willing and better able to focus on themselves instead of their abusive partners."

Intervention with Children of Battered Women

Intervention with children of battered women is closely associated with the battered women's movement. Intervention models specifically designed for children of battered women were developed throughout the 1980s as a response to children's observed difficulties. Just as with their abused mothers, intervention with children must be centered on the issue of their safety. Children who live with ongoing violence need to be protected from the direct and indirect consequences of the violence.

A major focus for shelter staff is to ensure that children and their needs do not become invisible. This may be an ideal opportunity for children to share their feelings and to sense some safety and adult support. Children of battered women are experiencing emotional trauma that requires an outlet for expression.[11] According to Melinda Cantu, director of children's services at the Austin Center for Battered Women, "Our work with these children is not to take away their feelings, but to help them understand them so that they may lead nonviolent, healthy lives. Basically, we're trying to work ourselves out of a job so that future generations will know what it means to live in peace and harmony."

Battered women's shelters provide children with safety and support, but at the same time may be experienced by children as highly stressful environments. The needs of children in battered women's shelters are great and often require crisis intervention and ongoing emotional support, medical attention, and interaction with educational systems and child protection agencies.

Shelter programs for children have become increasingly focused on the crisis state of the child, the special needs at the time of admission to the shelter, and the development of more extensive programs to assist in recovery.[12] Intervention typically consists of individual and group support and falls into four service-delivery areas: children's programs, child abuse intervention, parenting intervention, and academic assistance.

Children's Programs

Stopping the violence does not, by itself, create healing. Children need emotional support both during and after witnessing or experiencing violence. Many children of battered women are traumatized by family violence and require intensive short- or long-term individual therapy. The needs of others may be answered through small groups in which children can break the silence surrounding family violence.

One of the challenges facing shelter staff is providing meaningful services in a limited time. Women and children often average only a week at a shelter, and some stay for only one or two nights. Many shelters have developed programs that are directed to age groups with specific strategies in mind; for example:[13]

- Behavioral techniques to deal with specific behaviors, such as aggression
- Play assessment and play therapy to encourage preschool-age children to express feelings about the violence
- Encouragement of teenagers to develop and act out plays about family violence to foster awareness, self-expression, and a sense of helping others
- Individual counseling for children, including very specific strategies to obtain a better understanding of the children's reaction to the current crisis and to prepare them for possible violence in the future
- Structured group counseling for children and teenagers to assist them in gaining peer support and a sense of not being alone with the problem

- Multifamily groups that include women and children and are open-ended enough to deal with the reality of a brief, time-limited intervention, which encourages mutual support within and among families in crisis

One of the most widely used interventions for children of battered women is group counseling. Although most children require a great deal of individual attention from shelter staff, group programs are an essential service. Groups allow children an opportunity to learn that they are not alone in dealing with their crises and that other children have comparable life experiences. Children can learn helpful coping strategies from other survivors and caring adults who lead the group. For many children, this intervention is their first opportunity to openly discuss the issue of violence in their families. They are often anxious to share their thoughts and feelings and are sometimes surprised to hear about alternative ideas for dealing with family violence.

Most group counseling programs are sixty- to ninety-minute group sessions that meet weekly for six to ten weeks. The number of sessions typically depends on the child's length of stay in the shelter. The age range of participants varies from one to sixteen years, but most groups focus on the ages of four to thirteen. Groups are usually divided according to the children's developmental abilities. Many groups are small, with memberships of from three to six children.[14]

The majority of children's group programs consist of highly structured sessions with specific goals and educational activities. Stated goals include helping children to

- Define violence and responsibility for violence
- Express feelings, including anger
- Improve communication, problem-solving, and cognitive-coping skills
- Increase self-esteem
- Develop social support networks
- Develop safety plans
- Feel safe and develop trust during the group sessions

Programs achieve these goals through a variety of structured educational and play activities that include presentations, discussions, modeling, role-playing, art projects, homework assignments, and perhaps a family night during which children's activities take place either concurrent with a parents' program or with parent participation.[15]

Children's attendance at these sessions may raise uncomfortable issues for their mothers. It is important that group leaders maintain close contact with the mothers, preparing them for the issues that will be and are covered. Initial information and ongoing feedback to mothers is essential. Some group models suggest that mothers be part of the group and that parent-child relationships become a major focus.

According to Peter Jaffe, David Wolfe, and Susan Wilson, authors of *Children of Battered Women*, group counseling programs may be best suited for children with mild to moderate behavioral problems. For children exposed to repeated acts of severe violence over many years, a group will address only a small proportion of their numerous concerns. These children may require more extensive individual work.[16]

Parenting Intervention

Domestic violence often raises parenting challenges for mothers. Problematic relationships are not unusual because of the violence the children have witnessed as well as the fact that their mothers are also in crisis. Children may miss their fathers and quickly forget or minimize the reasons they came to the shelter. The mothers may be blamed for displacing them from their homes and friends.

Parenting groups for battered women can take place in or out of a shelter. Child rearing may be one of the few areas in which battered women perceive they have control. Any parenting intervention with battered women needs to be respectful and acknowledge their struggle to be the kind of parents they want to be.[17]

Through supportive counseling, parenting groups, and some parenting relief, shelter staff can help mothers to empower themselves to become more effective parents. Many battered women have had few role models for effective parenting because of their own childhood sexual and physical abuse. Some mothers residing in shelters may not be able to elevate their parenting skills without very specific educational programs that teach them new ways of relating to their children.

Protecting Children

A major challenge faced by children's advocates is the protection of abused children and coordination with child protection agencies. All staff members of a domestic violence program, but children's staff in particular, must be clear about the appropriate policies and procedures for reporting abuse and neglect and protecting children from further abuse. An appropriate response to child abuse includes protecting the children from further abuse while understanding the abuse in the context of woman battering. Intervention should help the women to empower themselves by highlighting their strengths and encouraging them to take control over their lives and their children's lives.[18]

In families in which the mother continues to reside with the batterer or returns to the batterer after staying in a shelter, realistic goals need to be formulated to assist the children in coping with ongoing violence. The focus should be placed on safety planning for the children in an effort to heighten their safety and to lessen the impact of the exposure to violence.

Melinda Cantu, director of children's services at the Austin Center for Battered Women, recommends that advocates incorporate the following steps when creating a safety plan with the children:

- Identify a safe adult in the neighborhood.
- Identify someone in the school system with whom they can talk.
- Call 911.
- Reach out to any adult with whom they have a trusting relationship.

According to Cantu, "Our primary goal in helping children create a safety plan is to make sure they get safe, then get help."

Academic Assistance

After admission to a shelter, many children may not attend school because of the fear of the fathers kidnapping them. Others face the further disruption of relocating to a new school environment. The temporary stay at a shelter is vital for the children as it may be an opportunity to identify remedial needs, offer individual support, and create some sense of routine and stability. Shelters may offer a variety of school services, including the following:[19]

- Liaison with the existing school placement to assure awareness of the trauma and continuity of education
- Specialized teachers on-site to offer remedial assistance and reintegration into the school system after the crisis period
- Specialized classrooms in schools that have a close relationship with the shelter and are prepared for the unique demands on these students

Safety and Empowerment

Regardless of the type of intervention, any action on behalf of battered women and their children should ensure their safety and help them to empower themselves. As advocates for battered women and their children, we must exercise care in the liberal use of the word *empowerment.* The literal definition of *empower,* granting power to another, presumes an agent who is doing the granting. If we claim to empower battered women, we are claiming to give them power. Using empowerment in this way negates the feminist philosophy of an egalitarian relationship between the advocate and the battered woman, as it speaks of a relationship in which the advocate is seen as having power to impart to the battered woman.

If we are committed to providing services that are aimed at liberating battered women and their children, advocates must thoughtfully consider how they use this word. A truly liberating experience for battered women is not the result of our empowerment of them. We can, however, talk with women about power, how it operates, and the effects of power. We can help women develop strategies and join with them to seize personal and political power. In doing this, we work with women to help them empower *themselves,* and we nurture the concept of the power of women as a group.[20]

CHAPTER 14

Intervention and Prevention Programs for Batterers

Violence against women will cease when men renounce the thinking and practice of dominance. We can begin to do this on an individual basis at home, at work, and in our community. When we begin to speak up, other men will listen and the seeds of change will be planted. I hope men will take the initiative and work with other men to confront sexism and violence, not to get approval from women, but because it is the right thing to do for women and men.

—Michael Paymar, Training Coordinator,
Duluth Domestic Abuse Intervention Project[1] and author of *Violent No More*

The first intervention programs for batterers were organized in the late 1970s by men who wanted to end violence against women. EMERGE in Boston and RAVEN (Rape and Violence End Now) in St. Louis were two of the first programs to offer counseling and educational services for batterers. In their initial efforts to develop these programs, organizers were careful to base their analyses of battering on the experiences of battered women.[2] The safety of battered women and their children is the first priority of profeminist batterers' programs.

The first interagency batterers' intervention programs were organized by advocates in the newly emerging battered women's movement. (Interagency programs exist within or grow out of larger, established programs.) These programs focused on changing the way the judicial system handled individual domestic violence cases. They usually included rehabilitation as an important part of a larger intervention strategy. While these early programs valued education and counseling for men, these strategies were viewed as secondary to criminal justice reform. The Domestic Abuse

Intervention Project (DAIP) in Duluth and the AMEND program in Denver fall into this category.[3]

In the 1980s and throughout the 1990s, batterers' intervention programs have spread across the United States. These programs have very different models, not all of which have the same feminist commitment to battered women as do some of the earlier programs. While some intervention techniques may be similar, very different messages are communicated to men about their responsibility for their violence.

Treatment Models

Most new programs are being started by mental health centers through the efforts of private mental health practitioners. The focuses of these programs vary tremendously. Some programs attempt to restore relationships by viewing violence as a symptom of a dysfunctional relationship. Others work exclusively with batterers on anger management, interpersonal communication skills and stress reduction. Still others adapt the model used by such programs as EMERGE, RAVEN, AMEND, or the DAIP.[4]

Several of these treatment approaches routinely give contradictory messages to men about why they batter and what they, or their partners, must do to stop it. From a feminist perspective, some of these approaches actually collude with batterers by not making their violence the primary issue or by implicitly legitimizing men's excuses for violence.

In his in-depth analysis, David Adams identifies five clinical approaches currently used with batterers: the insight model, the ventilation model, the interaction model, the cognitive-behavioral model, and the profeminist model.[5] Although many batterers' programs consider themselves eclectic, most are predominantly guided by one of these models.

The Insight Model

Although there are many variations of the insight model, the broad theme is that certain intrapsychic problems give rise to violent behavior. The list of intrapsychic problems includes poor impulse control, low frustration tolerance, fear of intimacy, fear of abandonment, dependency, underlying depression, and impaired ego functioning resulting from developmental trauma.

When underlying problems like insecurity are made the central focus of treatment, not only does therapy fail to confront the violence, but it also fails to confront the more immediate causes of the insecurity. Violence increases the man's feelings of insecurity since it also increases the risk that his partner will leave or grow distant from him. He typically reacts to these possibilities with more violence. Thus violence is self-perpetuating unless it is directly confronted.

The Ventilation Model

Proponents of the ventilation model do not provide specialized interventions for batterers, primarily because violence is seen as a symptom of the core problem of emotional repression. Batterers and their partners are usually included in groups for couples or individuals that address repressed feelings and dishonest communication. Domestic violence is usually compared to miscommunication or "game playing," and distinctions between violent and nonviolent men are deemphasized or blurred.

In the ventilation approach, participants are encouraged to "level with one another" while they are also taught to "fight fairly." In some cases, acts of "mock fighting," such as pillow punching or hitting one another with foam clubs, are practiced to facilitate the release of pent-up aggression. Encouragement to "fight fairly" while venting hostile feelings sends a dangerous, contradictory message to men about the acceptability of violent behavior. Ventilation therapy dangerously distorts men's understanding of growth and emotional maturity by selectively promoting certain forms of self-expression without confronting the violence itself.

The Interaction Model

The interaction model is similar to the ventilation approach since treating both the batterer and his partner is considered essential for improving marital communication, resolving conflict, and ending violence. Couples either participate in couples therapy or are included in specialized groups with other "violent couples." Most interaction therapists, however, do not consider ventilation to be an appropriate method of ending violence.

The goal of interaction therapy is for each partner to identify and change how he or she contributes to the problem. The tendency of the counselor to equalize responsibility for violence between the man and the woman is at the heart of the feminist criticism of the interaction model.

Couples counseling gives ambiguous and contradictory messages to batterers about how much responsibility they should take for ending their violent behavior. In addition, although women are expected to be open about their feelings and report their partners' violence, doing any of these things places them in danger of continued abuse.

The Cognitive-Behavioral Model

The cognitive-behavioral approach makes violence the primary focus of treatment. In addition, because violence is seen as having a dominating influence on marital interaction, abusive men are seen separately in specialized groups or in individual therapy to increase the opportunity for them to focus on their own behavior.

According to the cognitive-behavioral model, since violence is a learned behavior, nonviolence can similarly be learned. The psychoeducational therapist points out the damaging and self-defeating consequences of violence and teaches alternative behaviors. Since battering behavior is also seen as reflecting certain social skill deficits, interpersonal skills training is provided as an important element in helping men refrain from violence.

Although sharing a philosophy that identifies skills-learning as fundamental to change, psychoeducational programs vary in terms of which skills are emphasized. They also vary in how explicitly they address battering as an abuse-of-power issue or confront the sexist attitudes of participants.

The psychoeducational programs that do not address sexism tend to view battering as a skills-deficit or a stress-management problem. The majority of interventions are aimed at helping batterers better manage their anger, cope with stress, and improve communication skills.

The cognitive-behavioral model has offered many valuable insights and interventions for battering behavior. From a feminist perspective, however, its major weakness is that when interventions are too broadly aimed at reducing stress or improving interpersonal skills, the important power and control dimensions of domestic violence are minimized or ignored.

Domestic violence is controlling behavior that creates and maintains a power imbalance between the batterer and his partner. This is the feminist insight that directs the profeminist approach to batterers' intervention programs.

Therapeutic interventions directly challenge the batterer's attempts to control his partner through the use of physical force and verbal and nonverbal intimidation. Compared to other models, the profeminist model broadly defines violence as any act that causes a woman to do something she does not want to do, prevents her from doing something she wants to do, or causes her to be afraid.

The profeminist model, like the psychoeducational model, recognizes the need to provide basic education to batterers about caretaking and communication skills. This model, however, also sees the need to challenge the sexist expectations and controlling behaviors of batterers. While the focus of early treatment is on the identification and elimination of violent and controlling behaviors, later interventions focus more on sexist expectations and attitudes.

Programmatic Considerations

A batterer will typically enter a treatment program for at least one of these five reasons: his partner is threatening to leave; his partner has left; the man has recently offended and is feeling particularly remorseful; something was different about his last offense (for example, he reached relatively greater levels of violence or started hitting the children as well); various state or local authorities have become involved and ordered him to do so.[6] A batterer can be referred by a number of agencies and individuals, though state-sanctioned referrals usually carry more influence in providing the initial motivation to attend and in compelling men to stay in the program.

Although programs vary a great deal, the preferred format seems to be small groups of five to fifteen men, the leaders of which may be male, female, or both. Most programs are highly structured, focus on teaching behavior and attitude change, and last from ten to thirty-six sessions.[7]

Most batterers' intervention programs use standardized curricula in which a diverse group of men participate. There is, however, a shortage of culturally sensitive programs for men of color and for gay and lesbian batterers.

Approaches and treatment methods frequently become generic and standardized. Although generic methods may be effective with men of color, or with gay and lesbian batterers, it is important to consider the race and culture of participants when designing intervention programs. Programs that are not sensitive to their particular population can be as ineffective as are those that take a stereotypical approach to working with battered women and their children.[8] Battering intervention programs should establish ways to respectfully account for cultural and racial differences while focusing on participants' personal responsibility and the unacceptability of domestic violence.

The Success of Batterers' Intervention Programs

"Do batterers' intervention programs really work?" is probably one of the most frequently asked questions I hear in my presentations and workshops on domestic violence. Expecting a simple yes or no answer, audiences are often frustrated by my response. It seems the answer to the question depends upon whom you ask and the program's definition of success.

The way in which the term *success* is defined will greatly influence the degree to which these programs are perceived as effective. For example, does success mean that physical abuse is reduced rather than eliminated? Under this criteria, men could be considered successful participants if they have decreased their average violence from four beatings to two beatings a week. This decrease in violent behavior may make little difference, however, to those who continue to receive or witness repeated abuse. Thankfully, most experts working with batterers agree that ending violent behavior is an important success criterion.[9]

In his review of studies evaluating batterers' intervention programs, Jeffrey Edleson reports that, in varying programs, using various methods of intervention, a large proportion of men stop their physically abusive behavior subsequent to involvement in the intervention programs. Rates of successful outcomes range from 53 to 85 percent.[10]

Favorable evidence supporting the success of batterers' programs must be weighed with a degree of caution, however. Lower percentages of success often occur in programs with lengthier follow-up or in cases where researchers rely on the partners' reports rather than on men's self-reports or police reports.[11] For example, one study of the Domestic Abuse Intervention Project found that battered women consistently report that their batterers are significantly more abusive than the batterers themselves report.[12]

Much of the controversy about the success of batterers' programs centers around the issue that many battered women continue to feel unsafe despite the fact that their abusive partners do eliminate their use of physical violence. The continued, and sometimes increased, use of emotional abuse and other forms of manipulation often replaces physical violence while maintaining the system of power and control. Ending physical violence alone will not create true safety for women and children. Evaluations that are more sensitive to the perspectives of battered women may provide further insight into these safety concerns and thus help refine program interventions.[13]

The Search for an Appropriate Model

Much debate has occurred around the question of which model is the most effective, especially the issue of couples counseling and its importance in batterers' programs. In response to this debate, there has been an increase in state guidelines that set parameters for the structure and content of batterers' programs as well as the qualifications of providers offering such programs.[14]

According to the guidelines set forth by the Texas Council on Family Violence, traditional couples counseling, family therapy, and mediation are inappropriate as the initial or primary intervention for batterers. Approaches that see the batterer and partner together are considered detrimental for the following reasons:[15]

1. They tend to avoid fixing responsibility on the batterer and imply that the partner or the relationship is also to blame for the abuse.
2. They may perpetuate the abuse by giving the batterer a sense of support for his actions and placing the partner in the position of self-disclosing information that the batterer may subsequently use against her.
3. They underestimate the real power imbalance between family members and leave the partner at a disadvantage.

There are no guarantees that any program will work. To a large extent, much depends on the batterer's motivation and capacity for change. Some programs do, however, work better than others. The Texas Council on Family Violence offers the following guidelines for women whose partners are in a battering intervention and prevention program.

Your Safety Is the First Priority

Programs should always assess your safety when communicating with you. A program should never disclose information that you have given without your permission. A program should not misrepresent its ability to change your partner's behavior. A program's definition of success is the quality of your life and your children's lives, starting with safety.

The Program Lasts Long Enough

Change takes time. Programs should last at least eighteen weeks and require at least thirty-six hours of participation during that time, in addition to any individual sessions that may be scheduled for orientation or evaluation. The longer the program, the better the chances are that your partner will change. A year or longer in a program is preferable, although that is not always possible.

The Program Holds Him Accountable

The first step of accountability is that your partner takes responsibility for choosing to use violence in the relationship. A program should recognize that his behavior is the problem and not allow him to use your behavior as an excuse. His violence is the problem, not you. Programs should also hold your partner accountable for attendance, participation, and complying with the group's rules.

The Curriculum Addresses the Root of the Problem

The content of the program should challenge your partner's underlying belief system that he has the right to control and dominate you. Programs that address only his anger, communications skills, and stress do not get to the root of his problem.

The Program Makes No Demand on You to Participate

You are not the one with the problem. Some programs offer groups for partners of batterers. Your participation is entirely optional. Don't let anyone lead you to believe that your partner's success in the program is dependent upon your participation.

The Program Is Open to Your Input

If you initiate contact with the program to ask questions or give input you think may be useful, the program should welcome your participation. This is different from requiring you to participate. Also, if a program initiates contact with you to discuss your partner's behavior outside the program, you are not obligated to share information, especially if you feel it might create a risk of violence against you.

The Program Encourages Follow-up Support

Completing a program does not guarantee that your partner will be nonviolent. Staying nonviolent can be a lifelong challenge. A program should promote self-help and social support beyond the duration of the program, in the form of such activities as community service and participation in self-help programs.[16]

Creating a Men's Movement

Regardless of the effectiveness of any batterers' intervention program, we must remember that most programs try for a relatively short period of time to counterbalance much of what men have learned over years of exposure to a sexist culture. According to Jeffrey Edleson, "What is needed . . . is a major social movement in which men take responsibility for their abuses of power, both large and small, and in which they join with a more mature women's movement. Many men would probably welcome a movement that would lessen their emotional isolation from each other and from their intimate partners; ironically, that very isolation among men is probably one factor that inhibits such change."[17]

CHAPTER 15

Loving Ourselves: Self-Care for Helpers

Pleasure is the expression of the true self. —Gloria Steinem[1]

There's a small child running down the hallway looking for his mother. Two women are arguing over who is going to do the dinner dishes. A new resident just walked through the door. An advocate needs to use the van, but it has a flat tire—again. One of the children's advocates just discovered a raccoon in the garbage can. Welcome to shelter life!

While working in the battered women's movement can be incredibly rewarding, it can also take a tremendous toll. The emotional strain of dealing extensively with other human beings, particularly those in crisis, frequently creates a state of emotional exhaustion, frustration, and reduced personal accomplishment known as burnout. Burnout occurs when we give too much energy to others and don't conserve enough for ourselves.[2]

Regrettably, the movement loses a lot of good people to this insidious phenomenon. The connection between burnout and turnover is all too apparent: two years is frequently cited as the first critical point at which burnout will lead people to quit the movement.[3] Susan Schechter, author of *Women and Male Violence: The Visions and Struggles of the Battered Women's Movement,* reflects: "It may well be that helping one battered woman after another for fifty hours a week and realizing that violence is extensive and infinite, heightens burnout."[4]

Burnout appears to be a response to chronic stress rather than to occasional crisis. The emotional pressure of working closely with people is a part of the daily routine. Over time, our tolerance for this stress erodes under constant emotional tension.[5]

Overload is another risk factor for burnout. Too much information is pouring in and too many demands are being made of the individual. Helpers may overextend themselves and feel overwhelmed by the emotional demands imposed by other people. The response to this situation is emotional exhaustion. People feel drained, used up.

The risk for burnout is also high when helpers lack a sense of control over the care they are providing. This lack of control can be a consequence of having no input into how job tasks are accomplished or having no direct input on policy decisions that affect one's job. It can arise when a person receives little or no support from coworkers or has no opportunity to get away from a stressful situation. Whatever the reason for the lack of autonomy, not perceiving control over important outcomes in one's job adds to the emotional strain of the helping relationship.[6]

In addition to external factors, internal factors play an important role in determining a person's susceptibility to burnout. Such psychological characteristics as personal needs, motivation, self-esteem, expressiveness, as well as basic physiological differences, influence how an individual handles external sources of emotional stress. This helps explain why two different people will respond to the same stress in different ways.[7]

Fight or Flight

If we are to take care of ourselves effectively in order to avoid burnout, it is helpful to know exactly what happens to our bodies when we are placed in stressful situations. Our reactions to stress are partly determined by the sensitivity of our sympathetic nervous system, which produces the *fight or flight reaction* in response to stress and excitement.

The human body, when anticipating the necessity of fight or flight, begins to mobilize almost instantly. This biochemical mobilization stands at the very heart of the burnout process. It all starts in the hypothalamus, a bundle of nerve cells at the center of the brain. Messages race from that command post and spread the alarm throughout the nervous system. Muscles tense; blood vessels constrict; the capillaries under the skin shut down altogether. The pituitary gland sends out two hormones that move through the bloodstream to stimulate the thyroid and adrenal glands. Thyroid hormones increase the energy supply we need to cope physically with the stress. The adrenals send some thirty additional hormones to nearly every organ in the body.

The automatic stress response causes the pulse rate to shoot up and the blood pressure to soar. The stomach and intestines stop the activity of digestion. Hearing and the sense of smell grow more acute. Literally hundreds of other physical changes occur without our knowledge.[8]

All types of stress stimulate our biochemical response, so our bodies experience the energy-draining mobilization again and again. It may happen once a day or dozens of times, depending on the amount of stress we experience. And the stress response can be mobilized not only by actual stressors, but by simply thinking about them.[9]

Repeated episodes of the fight or flight reaction can eventually be damaging. If we constantly mobilize energy at the cost of energy storage, we will never store any surplus energy. We will experience fatigue more rapidly and risk developing a form of diabetes. The consequences of chronically overactivating our cardiovascular system are similarly damaging. The repair and remodeling of bone and other tissues can be disrupted.

If we are constantly under stress, a variety of reproductive disorders may ensue. In women, menstrual cycles can become irregular or cease entirely. In men, sperm count and testosterone levels may decline. In both sexes, interest in sexual behavior decreases. The immune suppression brought about by chronic stress may mean that individuals are less likely to resist a variety of diseases. Finally, the same systems of the brain that function more alertly during stress can also be damaged by one class of hormones secreted during stress.[10]

The High Cost of Caring

Exposure to chronic stress can have devastating effects on those ill-prepared to take care of themselves. While stress does not necessarily cause illness, it does make us more susceptible to physical, emotional, mental, and spiritual imbalance. Following is a list of a few of the many symptoms of stress exhaustion.[11]

Physical Symptoms

appetite change
headaches
tension
fatigue
insomnia
colds

muscle aches
digestive upsets
teeth grinding
rash
lower back pain
tension at the base of neck
lowered sex drive
increased alcohol, drug, or tobacco use

Mental Symptoms

forgetfulness
dulled senses
poor concentration
negative attitude
confusion
negative self-talk

Emotional Symptoms

anxiety
frustration
nightmares
irritability
depression
worrying
discouragement
joylessness
isolation
loneliness
lashing out

Spiritual Symptoms

emptiness
loss of meaning
loss of direction
apathy
cynicism

Burnout doesn't just suddenly overwhelm us; it is insidious, chipping away at our ability to resist it. In fact, there appear to be five recognizable stages leading toward burnout.[12] The first stage is a period of high energy and job satisfaction. It is, however, also a time when we use more energy than we realize. This expenditure of energy sets us up for the second stage of burnout. In this stage, the energy drain is more visible and we start to experience inefficiency in our work. Fatigue and procrastination start to take their toll.

If we don't stop to reenergize ourselves, we slip into the third stage. Symptoms that developed in the second stage become habitual. In addition, new symptoms emerge, including chronic exhaustion and physical illness. Physical illness might be a cold that lasts for months or a period when our immune system is not working in our best interest.

Weakened by physical symptoms, we are now set up for the fourth stage. At this point, burnout dominates our lives. We may experience frustration, self-doubt, isolation, loss of enthusiasm, pessimism, and depression.

One of the hallmarks of this stage is a change in the way helpers interact with others. Once emotional exhaustion sets in, people often feel they are no longer able to give of themselves. One way people try to put distance between themselves and others is by emotionally detaching from them. While this detachment may protect the helper from the strain of close involvement with others, it can also prevent any feelings from getting through. With increasing detachment comes an attitude of indifference to others' needs and a disregard for their feelings. The development of this response frequently leads to depersonalization; the helper may begin to view people in more cynical and derogatory terms.[13]

Feeling negatively about others can progress to the point that helpers develop feelings of inadequacy about their ability to relate to others, which may lead to feelings of failure. Many helpers experiencing self-doubt begin to physically isolate themselves from others.

Burnout can affect psychological well-being in another way. The person who feels emotionally exhausted is easily irritated. Even the most minor frustration can provoke an immediate response of anger.[14]

The fifth, and most destructive, stage witnesses individuals who can no longer function in their jobs. Some individuals will seek counseling or therapy while others will change jobs, often to abandon any kind of work that brings them into stressful contact with other people. Regrettably, others try to deal with burnout using alcohol or drugs. Recovery from this final burnout stage is often a long, arduous process.

alancing Our Lives

f you find yourself busily helping others, stop and ask yourself, "Am I reating myself as fairly and lovingly as I treat others?" If your answer is no, be careful. If you are waiting for someone other than yourself to take care of you, you may be heading toward burnout. Don't wait until your world is crumbling around you before you care for yourself. You don't need permission from others to do this: give yourself permission to take care of yourself.

Each of us is valuable and warrants nurturing and love. To care for ourselves does not diminish the support and affection we have to share with others; it actually makes it sweeter. The bottom line is that we do not have to sacrifice ourselves in the pursuit of our passion.

Giving to others must be balanced with giving to ourselves. The concept of balance is probably the single most important factor in developing a lifestyle that can successfully support us over a long period of time. Balance is flexibility, the ability to make decisions from a wide variety of possibilities.

To achieve some level of balance, we should attempt, in any twenty-four-hour period, to address our emotional, mental, spiritual, and physical needs. Consider your satisfaction in all of these areas. While nurturing and maintaining this balance can be difficult, self-questioning will ensure that at least your thinking is balanced. As long as you remind yourself daily of your need for balance, you probably won't stray too far from it.

In terms of balancing your life, consider the following questions:

- Do you usually get six to eight hours of quality sleep each night?
- Do you allow yourself time to touch nature each week, no matter how briefly?
- Do you get some kind of fun exercise each week?
- Do you do something fun at least once a week?
- Are you happy with your sex life?
- Do you give and receive hugs on a regular basis?
- Do you have people who you can honestly talk to and who will listen to you?

- Do you take reasonable risks and seek new experiences?
- Do you ask for what you need?
- Do you forgive yourself when you make a mistake?
- Do you reward yourself for your accomplishments?
- Do you trust yourself?
- Do you do things that give you a sense of purpose, meaning, and joy?
- Do you try to live in the moment?
- Do you laugh at least once a day?
- Do you make time for your friends?
- Do you make time for solitude?
- Do you make time for daily or weekly spiritual nourishment?

The first step toward balancing our lives begins when we attempt to connect with ourselves. This is actually a lifelong quest. To begin this journey, however, we must at some point begin to lovingly and honestly take a look at ourselves. In this introspective process, we should examine who we are, what is meaningful for us, who we want to be, and how we can get there.

Once we begin to address these issues, we can establish the path we want to follow. We all, at least to some extent, create our own lives. Consider the following as you begin your introspective journey.

Self-Concept

Your sense of who you are and how you feel about yourself plays a crucial role in your relationship to yourself and others. Self-care means making a commitment to the creation of a loving and positive attitude toward yourself. This does not mean that you see yourself as perfect or deny your limitations. Instead, it means that you strive to see the positive, to encourage and accept yourself. To know and like yourself is crucial when giving of yourself to others.

Needs

A need is something we require for our well-being. Self-care begins with evaluating what we need, from ourselves and from others. We can then determine whether or not our basic needs are being met and work to fulfill them.

Listen to Yourself

Be sensitive to the emotional and physical signals your body gives you. Trust these signals and use them as guides along your journey.

Goals

Set goals for yourself that you will actually have a reasonable chance to accomplish. If a goal is virtually impossible to accomplish, you are setting yourself up for failure.

Know Your Limits

Setting realistic goals requires that you recognize your limitations as well as your abilities. Failing to recognize your limitations ultimately means that there will be discrepancies between your aspirations and your actual achievements. You are the best judge of the gap between your desire to do something and the personal energy and resources you possess.[15]

Boundaries

Define and consciously set your boundaries.[16] Be very clear to yourself and to others about what you will and will not accept. Not being honest with others about your personal boundaries will leave you feeling betrayed and angry. Begin to gently but clearly tell people in your life what your limits are. Remember, too, that you may change your boundaries at any time.

Seeking Help

Doing this kind of work frequently brings up personal issues that are not addressed in the workplace. Seeking help from a counselor, therapist, or support group often provides a safe environment for personal growth and enhances our longevity in the movement.

Suggestions for Self-Care

This section suggests many strategies you can use to balance your life and address burnout. These strategies can be used after burnout has occurred or as a means of preventing burnout.

Some of these approaches may interest you while others will not; choose those approaches that are meaningful and enjoyable and reflect who you are. These suggestions can be combined to create your own unique balanced pathway. They can also be rejected altogether yet still serve as a catalyst to the discovery of others that will work for you.

Whatever your responses to these activities, trust them. We all innately know what will work best for us. Honor yourself and follow your inner wisdom. We must all find our own balanced path and discover what is right for us. This is one of the beautiful aspects of the individual journey, which is as unique and precious as we are. It is my hope that these suggestions help you find your own special pathway to self-caring and self-discovery.

When at Work

Strategies to address burnout can be implemented at a variety of levels, including the organizational level. The suggestions in this section relate to individual strategies you can use to take care of yourself while at work.

Choose Your Battles

We encounter human needs almost constantly throughout our day, and it is easy to get involved with every struggle to improve services and efforts on behalf of battered women and their children. One of the quickest ways to burnout, however, is trying to do too much and taking on too many tasks.[17] Carefully assess each situation to determine whether it is best for you to fight or let it go.

Take Breaks

As difficult as it may be to get away from your work, try to take a break occasionally, if only for a few minutes.

Monitor Your Overtime

Keep track of your overtime and try not to let it get the best of you.

Take Time Off

Try to take a real vacation every year. A real vacation is more than two or three days or a long weekend; it means one to two weeks.[18]

Take Mental Health Days

Instead of waiting until you have totally run yourself down emotionally and physically, take a mental health day for rest, relaxation, or play. Try to resist any feelings of guilt for taking this time for yourself. Remember, you are using self-care techniques that will help prolong your involvement in the movement.

Personalize Your Environment

Furnish your office with personal objects and mementos to serve as reminders of who you are and your connections, personal convictions, and life outside work.[19]

Relax Your Body

The stress and anxiety we feel at work is often reflected in tired shoulders and a stiff neck. Ultimately, this leads to a heightened state of fatigue. The following exercises may help relax your body and can easily be done at work.[20]

- Sit straight in your chair with feet flat on the floor. Lift arms above your head with elbows locked and palms facing each other. Reach upward until your rib cage lifts. Bend down from the waist, reaching toward your ankles. Relax in the bent position. Repeat five times.
- Sit back in your chair with hands clasped behind your head. Lean forward and touch your right elbow to your left knee. Then touch your left elbow to your right knee. Return to the starting position and repeat five times.

Prioritize and Delegate

If you feel overwhelmed by the tasks you need to finish, try to address your anxiety by prioritizing. List all of the tasks you need to do the next day.

Can any of the tasks be delegated? If yes, delegate them to the appropriate persons, along with a deadline. Can any be dealt with later in the week? Assign a priority date and time to each of these.

Barbara Mackoff, author of *Leaving the Office Behind*, suggests that visualization can be an effective means of addressing anxiety over unfinished tasks. Review each task on your list. After you reach each item, close your eyes and imagine yourself finishing that task. Visualize the best possible outcome. You can end your day with a picture of yourself completing tomorrow's work. This relief from unfinished business can be a powerful tool in your successful passage from work to home.[21]

Leave Work at Work

Try to limit the amount of time you spend at home finishing job tasks.

Remember Why You Do This Work

Remind yourself of the importance and value of the work you do. The loss of meaning and hope can be countered by celebrating your successes with coworkers, friends, and loved ones, and with yourself.[22]

Diet, Exercise, and Sleep

Taking physical care of ourselves allows us to perform at our finest. The following are some ways you can be at your physical best.

Monitor Your Diet

Determine the most healthful diet for you and make sure you have the right foods available. You will be much less susceptible to stress if your body has the nutrients it needs.[23]

Get Sufficient Exercise

Try to get a reasonable amount of exercise. Start slowly, gradually increasing the length and intensity of the exercise you choose. Walking and swimming are both gentle exercises that can be taken at your own pace and are therapeutic for mind as well as body. Once you reach a certain level of fitness, more strenuous exercises such as jogging or low impact aerobics can be started.[24] Be sure to contact your physician before beginning any exercise regimen.

Get Enough Sleep

Although most people require six to eight hours of sleep each night, the quality of sleep is also crucial. Sleeping poorly and insomnia are frequently caused by our inability to relax. If you experience these problems, try doing things that are calming for you immediately before retiring, such as drinking a glass of warm milk, engaging in gentle stretching, relaxing in a warm bath, meditating, listening to soft music, or reading. Above all, try to clear your mind of the day's activities rather than focusing on them.[25]

Monitor Your Negative Thoughts

If you find yourself unable to sleep because you are preoccupied with negative thoughts, try saying *STOP*, either silently or aloud. This command interrupts your negative review and offers you the opportunity to redirect your thinking. Another way to relax and nurture a positive attitude about yourself is through affirmations. Affirmations provide a means of changing negative or punitive beliefs to more empowering and positive thoughts.[26] For example, one might tell oneself, "I am a valuable and loved person." Whatever affirmation you use should hold a special meaning for you.

Practice Moderation

Moderate your engagement in such things as alcohol, cigarettes, sex, socializing, and food. Remember, balance is the key. Every day ask yourself, "Am I doing too much of any one thing?"

Socializing and Solitude

Both solitude and socializing are necessary for addressing burnout. Getting away from people is a common response when we are experiencing emotional overload. Occasional solitude, however, is not the same as isolation. The danger occurs when avoiding others is carried to the extent that individuals isolate themselves from their support systems.

Take Time for Solitude

Insist on having at least thirty minutes each day in which you can be alone without interruption. This can be after everyone has gone to sleep or before everyone has awakened. Use this time to relax, read, meditate, walk, or just reflect.

Schedule Escape

Read a novel in the bath, on the bus, or at lunchtime. See a movie. If your body can't go on a faraway adventure, at least your mind can.

Socialize

Cultivate and nurture close relationships. Have at least one friend with whom you are totally honest.

Join a Group

Look around for a group in which you can share an interest in something with others. If you can't find a group you would like to join, consider creating one of your own. Remember, however, the idea is not to increase your stress level, but to help reduce it. Ask yourself the following questions about the people you are considering spending your free time with: [27]

- Does having this group in your life make you feel more empowered and challenged than you otherwise would?
- Can you be honest inside the group?
- Do you feel accepted as you are?
- Does the group make you stretch and become better than you thought you could be?
- Is there a balance between what you're receiving and what you're giving to others?

Leisure Activities

Don't underestimate the genuine pleasure that can come from the simple things in life. We would all do well to remember and emulate the way children have fun. Consider a few of the characteristics of children's play:[28]

- Children are curious and usually eager to try something at least once.
- Children smile and laugh a lot.
- Children are creative and innovative.
- Children learn enthusiastically.

- Children dream and imagine.
- Children seek out fun things to do or else find a way to have fun at what they are doing.
- Children jump from one interest to another, leaving an activity whenever they feel forced or become more interested in something else.
- Children are constantly growing, mentally and physically.

Play Games

Take up crossword puzzles, backgammon, chess, pool, or any other game that you find relaxing and enjoyable.

Engage in Everyday Activities

Leisure activities such as dancing, movies, frolicking with a pet, traveling, gardening, cooking, and reading help guard against stress buildup.

Nurture Your Creativity

Take up painting, drawing, pottery, sculpting, woodworking, weaving, or whatever lets your creative side come through.

Keep a Journal

A private journal is a safe place for you to express your feelings, explore your world, and say whatever you want to say. Include humorous stories as well as the painful ones.

Sing, Hum, Whistle

It doesn't matter if you can't carry a tune; embrace yourself and your world with the music of your spirit.[29]

Start a Dream Journal

Keep a journal by your bed and record your dreams. You might be surprised by what you learn from them.[30]

Laughter

Laughter brightens faces, relaxes muscles, restores objectivity, and enhances hope. It also produces endorphins, the body's natural shield against pain.[31]

While humor can be helpful, it does have a harmful side. If we laugh at people instead of with them, humor becomes cruel. Humor that disrespects people adds to the callousness of burnout.

Barbara Mackoff suggests that one of the easiest way to lighten your thoughts about work is to add an imaginary soundtrack to accompany your recollections of the day. As you review your workday, you can think of it as a movie or a television show that needs a musical score. You don't need a large musical repertoire for this, simply a willingness to see yourself with humor.[32] You'll be surprised at the number of songs you can bring to mind that befit your everyday experiences.

Relaxation Techniques

One simple way you can begin to relax is by simply not rushing your life unnecessarily. Practice eating, drinking, and driving at a slower pace. This can help to reduce your sense of urgency and lower irritation.[33]

Relaxation techniques can help you create a sense of peace. The key to the effectiveness of these techniques is practice: it does not matter what you do as long as you actually do it. This means setting aside time to practice the technique until it becomes second nature.

While the following techniques can be part of a general relaxation program, true relaxation follows from an attitude toward life rather than a particular activity. Relaxation must engage the mind as well as the body. If you are interested in learning more about these techniques, consider enrolling in a community education class or visiting the library to find one of the many excellent books currently available.

Meditation

Meditation helps you to create a state of deep relaxation that is healing to the entire body. Set aside some time on a daily basis to sit quietly in your own space. You can also try meditating just before going to sleep to help you relax.[34]

Deep Breathing

These techniques can have a major impact on feelings of stress and anxiety. Deep breathing helps to relax the entire body, strengthens muscles in the chest and abdomen, and heightens energy levels.

A simple method is to sit or lie in a darkened room and concentrate on breathing in and out. At first it may be difficult to sit for any length of time, but with practice, the time can gradually be lengthened. The beauty of this technique is that it can be used at the point of stress.[35]

Muscle Relaxation

Muscle tension is frequently associated with high levels of stress. The following exercise will help you get in touch with your areas of muscle tension and learn to release them.

Lie on your back in a comfortable position. Allow your arms to rest at your sides, palms down. Inhale and exhale slowly and deeply. Clench your hands into fists and hold them tightly for fifteen seconds. As you do this, relax the rest of your body. Visualize your fists contracting, becoming tighter and tighter. Then let your hands relax, and visualize all your muscles becoming soft and relaxed. Now tense and relax the following parts of your body in this order: face, shoulders, arms, back, stomach, pelvis, legs, feet, and toes. Hold each tensed for fifteen seconds, and then relax your body for thirty seconds before moving to the next part. Finish the exercise by shaking your hands and imagining the remaining tension flowing out of your fingertips.[36]

Visualization

Visualization can be an excellent method of de-stressing ourselves. Susan Lark, author of *Anxiety and Stress*, recommends visualization using colors. Color therapy has been shown to have a profound effect on health and well-being. Lark recommends visualizing the color blue to provide a calming and relaxing effect. The color blue lessens the fight or flight response and calms such physiological functions as pulse rate, breathing, and perspiration.[37]

Yoga

Yoga is an excellent way to promote a deep sense of peace and calm. Unlike fast-paced aerobic exercise, yoga actually slows the pulse, heart rate, and breathing. Yoga exercises gently stretch every muscle in the body, relaxing tense muscles and improving their suppleness and flexibility. They also promote better circulation and oxygenation to tense and contracted areas throughout the body. The stress-reduction and physiological effects of yoga benefit all body systems.[38]

Tai Chi

This Chinese system of movements engages the mind, body, and spirit. While there are many martial arts, Tai Chi is the most gentle and soothing. It is far less physical and more of a combination of all the senses. The slow movements strengthen each part of the body in a series of coordinated exercises.[39]

Hydrotherapy

People have used warm water as a way to calm themselves and relax their muscles for centuries. You can create your own home spa by adding relaxing ingredients, such as bath oils and salts, to your bath water. While you're at it, try combining your spa with candlelight and music.

Music

Music can have an incredibly relaxing effect on our minds and bodies. Classical music and quiet music, such as that set to nature sounds, are particularly good for relaxing. Music can have a pronounced effect on your physiological functions, slowing your pulse and heart rates, lowering your blood pressure, and decreasing your levels of stress hormones.[40]

Massage

Gentle touching—by a trained massage therapist, your intimate partner, and even you—can be very relaxing. Tension often fades away quickly with gentle, relaxed touching. The kneading and stroking movements of a good massage relax tense muscles, improve circulation, and induce a feeling of relaxation and well-being.[41]

Aromatherapy

Combine massage oils with flower and herbal extracts and you have aromatherapy, a relaxation technique designed to please the senses while treating the body. Scented oils, lotions, and bath products are excellent complements to your massage or hydrotherapy. While making these products can be fun and relaxing in itself, they can also be purchased.[42]

Reflexology

This is basically foot massage, but much more. The pressure points of the foot represent the parts of the body that can be treated by massaging the relevant areas of the foot. Reflexology can help to increase blood circulation and relax tension.[43]

The Organization's Commitment to Self-Care

The self-care strategies explored up to now are used by individuals to take care of themselves. The organization, however, also has a responsibility in helping to minimize burnout.[44] First, the organization must recognize that people working in the battered women's movement are at risk. Organizations should periodically examine their goals, structure, and division of labor. Providing workers with opportunities for job rotation promotes growth and continued enthusiasm.

Understanding the effects of working with so much pain and violence is also crucial. Having ongoing opportunities to openly discuss frustrations, pain, and anger contributes to advocates' empowerment and longevity.

Encouraging and respecting the self-care boundaries that workers have established for themselves should be a standard. Providing adequate opportunities for time away from work will have positive long-term effects for both the individual and the organization.

Finally, opportunities for workers to learn more about their own self-care should be offered. Both the Texas Council on Family Violence and the Center for Battered Women have sponsored a self-care workshop entitled "Healing the Healers." This inspirational and empowering workshop addresses how workers can explore their power as healers and learn to practice healthful, functional ways to address stress. According to workshop facilitator Lorena Monda, "It is crucial that we look at the things about our work which affect us individually and as a community of healers."

If we are to maintain credibility in voicing our philosophy of helping battered women to empower themselves, we must empower ourselves through self-care and self-discovery. As individuals, organizations, and a movement, we can support and encourage each other on this journey.

CHAPTER 16

The National Domestic Violence Hotline

This is high-tech grassroots.

—Sara Slater, Volunteer Coordinator, Austin Center for Battered Women, after touring the NDVH headquarters

On February 21, 1996, President Bill Clinton announced the opening of the National Domestic Violence Hotline, a project of the Texas Council on Family Violence. The NDVH connects individuals residing in all fifty states, the District of Columbia, Puerto Rico, and the U.S. Virgin Islands with services by way of a nationwide database developed and maintained at offices in Austin, Texas. The system stores up-to-date information on domestic violence, battered women's shelters, legal advocacy, assistance programs, and social service programs.

Hotline telephones are answered twenty-four hours a day, seven days a week by English- and Spanish-speaking advocates who provide assistance and information to battered women, their friends, their families, and other concerned individuals. Specific assistance includes the following:

- *Crisis Intervention:* Helping callers identify problems and possible solutions, including making safety plans in an emergency
- *Information:* Sharing information about resources that can provide assistance to individuals; information about domestic violence, child abuse, and sexual assault; intervention programs for batterers; working through the criminal justice system and related issues
- *Referrals:* Making referrals to battered women's shelters and programs, social service agencies, legal programs, and other organizations willing to help

The NDVH is committed to meeting the needs of diverse communities. A toll-free telecommunications device for the deaf and hearing impaired (TDD) is available as well as access to translators in 139 languages. In addition, the NDVH distributes information in a variety of formats and languages.

History of the NDVH

The realization of a dream does not occur without dedication and effort. President Clinton's announcement represented more than three years of extensive planning and organizing to revive the NDVH.

From September 1988 to January 1992, a national hotline for victims of domestic violence had actually existed. A lack of funding, however, forced its closure. Calls to this hotline had reached approximately 10,000 per month. Now those calls were going unanswered. After the hotline closed, the National Victim Center, which operates a national information and referral service called Infolink, began receiving calls from domestic violence victims. In 1992 and 1993, Infolink accepted three requests to broadcast their number following the airing of television programs on this subject. At Infolink's request, staff of the Texas Council on Family Violence (TCFV) helped answer an astonishing 13,025 calls following these programs.

In November 1992, concerned about the future of the NDVH and other challenges facing the national battered women's movement, Deborah Tucker, then TCFV executive director, and Ellen Rubenstein Fisher, TCFV associate director, along with representatives from the National Coalition Against Domestic Violence, the Pennsylvania Coalition Against Domestic Violence, the National Women Abuse Prevention Project, the Domestic Violence Coalition on Public Policy, the Family Violence Prevention Fund, and other national leaders joined together to discuss the future of the movement. Recognizing the TCFV's leadership capabilities, organizational structure, and accomplishments, the national battered women's movement requested that they consider opening and operating a national hotline for victims of domestic violence.

By June 1993, the TCFV had the support of both staff and their board of directors to pursue this project. That summer, and well into the fall of 1993, the TCFV began fundraising for the feasibility and research phases of the hotline project.

When the TCFV Board of Directors unanimously approved working to establish a national hotline, one board member became more than excited; she saw her destiny. According to Anna Belle Burleson, hotline program director, "When we were discussing the creation of the NDVH, I said to myself, 'I want to be a part of this. This is what I want to do.'" So committed was she to seeing the NDVH get off the ground that Burleson volunteered her time for seven months, including several months of full-time volunteering. During this time she spent countless hours contacting coalitions across the United States seeking support for the NDVH. She was eventually hired on staff in the winter of 1993.

Burleson has a long history of commitment to serving battered women and their children. A survivor of domestic violence, she is a former shelter resident at the Austin Center for Battered Women. Burleson has been volunteering with CBW since 1987 and is a cofounder and past chair of the Formerly Battered Women's Task Force of Central Texas. She is a CBW board member and a former board member of the TCFV. She is also the recipient of numerous local, state, and national awards for her outstanding service to battered women, including her latest award from the National Association of Social Workers recognizing her as "Public Citizen of the Year."

Beginning in the winter of 1993, the TCFV began recruiting members for the Professional Advisory Board and the National Development Council. Members include national and regional leaders in the battered women's movement as well as other public figures committed to domestic violence prevention.

In July 1994, the debut issue of *HotLines* newsletter was published to inform donors, supporters, and interested individuals and organizations of the progress of the TCFV's hotline project.

On September 13, 1994, the Violence Against Women Act (see *Additional Resources*), including funding for five years for a national hotline for victims of domestic violence, was signed into law by President Clinton as part of the crime bill. That same fall, the TCFV received one hundred percent support from all the state domestic violence coalitions, more than 650 local service providers, and 29 national domestic violence and other organizations to establish and operate the NDVH. In the winter, a prototype computer and telecommunications system for the hotline pilot project was installed.

On March 6, 1995, the U.S. Department of Health and Human Services announced its request for proposals to "operate a national, toll-free telephone hotline to provide information and assistance to victims of domestic violence." On June 5, 1995, the TCFV submitted its proposal to establish and operate the National Domestic Violence Hotline. According to Burleson, "It was an incredible amount of work getting to that point. All of us were so excited about finishing the proposal that we asked Christina Walsh [TCFV public relations director] to take a picture of Ellen Rubenstein Fisher, Cyndy Perkins [TCFV development director], and me mailing the proposal in front of the post office. I think people thought we were tourists!"

Their heartfelt efforts proved fruitful, for on August 17, 1995, Texas Congressman Lloyd Doggett announced that the TCFV was awarded the $1 million grant from U.S. Department of Health and Human Services to establish and operate the country's only national domestic violence hotline. Subject to the availability of funds, Congress has authorized the distribution of additional dollars not to exceed $850,000 annually through fiscal year 1999 for the operation of the hotline.

In the fall of 1995 staff were hired to work specifically for the hotline. Staff immediately set to work collecting referral information from more than two thousand domestic violence service providers across the country to establish the hotline's comprehensive referral database.

During that same period, the CBW and the NDVH began a collaborative venture in which volunteers are jointly recruited and trained. We maintain that, rather than competing for volunteers, this partnership is the most effective means of providing volunteers for both organizations.

On December 18, 1995, the NDVH office opened in Austin, Texas. On January 8, 1996, hotline advocates who answer calls to the NDVH began an intensive four-week training on domestic violence issues, cultural sensitivity issues, and computer and telecommunications equipment. That same month, the NDVH and the CBW began the first collaborative forty-hour training class for new volunteers.

The annual operating cost of the National Domestic Violence Hotline will be approximately $1.2 million. Money needed to match available federal funds must be raised from private sources each year and will be sought from foundations, corporations, organizations, and individuals across the country. The plan is to support the hotline through a broad-based mix of private and public funds.

The Texas Council on Family Violence

The National Domestic Violence Hotline is a direct result of the careful stewardship of the Texas Council on Family Violence. That the TCFV was chosen and supported in their effort to revive the NDVH is no surprise. The battered women's movement in Texas has made tremendous progress, and the TCFV has played a significant leadership role. When the TCFV first advocated for state funding for battered women's shelters in 1979, six shelters shared $200,000 from the state. In 1996, sixty-four shelters shared $10 million in state funding.

The Texas Council on Family Violence is a nonprofit, statewide membership association representing sixty-four shelters for battered women, thirty battering intervention and prevention programs for abusive men, and several other family violence service providers. It was founded in 1978 by determined, visionary women who, in 1977, established the Austin Center for Battered Women, the first shelter for battered women and their children in Texas.

Every year the TCFV provides support and assistance in a variety of ways. It responds to literally thousands of technical assistance requests; offers on-site consultation for family violence programs across the state; sponsors innovative training opportunities throughout the year; distributes tens of thousands of brochures and other printed items on a variety of subjects related to family violence; leads successful efforts to pass all of the Texas laws related to domestic violence (many of these laws have been used as models by other states in passing their own domestic violence legislation); provides extensive resource files and a lending library; and creates public awareness that leads to social pressure and cultural values that forbid rather than support violence against women.

Although the TCFV is a statewide organization, their leadership over the years has extended to the national and international levels. For example, the TCFV had a three-year contract with the U.S. Department of Defense to provide domestic violence training to family advocacy staff in all branches of the military. Internationally, the TCFV has provided training, technical assistance, and public education materials to battered women's organizations in Peru, Argentina, Brazil, and Spain. It has also copresented a domestic violence conference in Monterrey, Mexico, in conjunction with the Crime Victim Assistance Center of Monterrey.

TCFV staff serve in key leadership roles of the National Network to End Domestic Violence, which was formed to specifically advocate for passage of laws in Congress that impact battered women and their children. The network's major success to date was the 1994 passage of the Violence Against Women Act (see *Additional Resources*).

The TCFV staff have served on numerous advisory boards, including the board of the National Resource Center on Domestic Violence and the Family Violence Prevention Fund's "There's NO Excuse" public awareness campaign sponsored by the National Advertising Council. This campaign educated the public about domestic violence by distributing printed materials and bumper stickers and producing public service announcements.

The TCFV publishes the national newsletter *Nexus* for state domestic violence coalitions, national domestic violence organizations, and other supporters of the national battered women's movement. In addition, the TCFV staff have served on the NCADV board for several years.

The Human Connection

Nestled among the computers and other high-tech equipment at the NDVH headquarters are signs of our movement's humanity. Pictures of smiling women, children, and men; teddy bears; and symbols of diverse spirituality watch over hotline advocates as they answer calls from women and children in pain and from loved ones concerned about them. Each small cubicle reflects the personality of its resident. It is very obvious that each cubicle represents someone's home. This suits Ellen Rubenstein Fisher, NDVH executive director, just fine. According to Fisher, "This is the best of technology with a human voice."

Fisher understands the strength in the human connection. A long-time advocate for battered women and their children, Fisher has worked in the field of violence against women since 1974, including a six-year tenure as executive director of the CBW. For Fisher, it is an "honor to do this work."

Fisher is particularly excited about the potential impact the NDVH can have on public policy at the national level. She explains, "The hotline represents the entry point that impacts everyone along the way. We are talking to so many women and these women are going someplace. We can use the hotline to increase local support for battered women's programs.

We can go back to the federal government and say this area has no services for battered women or this area needs more services. We have the potential to make a major difference in the way communities respond."

Hotline advocates are talking to a lot of women. In fact, the numbers are staggering. During the first three months in operation, NDVH staff answered more than 24,000 calls. While the majority of calls are from battered women, 19 percent are from family or friends of battered women. According to Diane Perez, hotline advocate, "Calls from family members are often the hardest. Hearing Mom and Dad crying, really wanting to help their child and not knowing what to do. This can be really hard."

Perez says that the type of calls she receives varies from moment to moment. "I've gotten calls from women who were being beaten while they were on the phone with me, calls from batterers being abusive, and calls from women living underground who were lonely and just wanted someone to talk to who would understand. I've also gotten quite a few calls from children. Come to think of it, all of these calls, in some way or another, are difficult."

Difficult is probably an understatement. Suicide, child abuse, incest, depression, rape, and torture are just a few of the issues hotline advocates face every day. Their challenge is to help people in pain, people who are afraid, confused, and in need.

The magic happens when they are able to help someone. According to Hotline Advocate Sonia Benavides, "The most rewarding thing for me is when I've reached someone. We click and the caller really begins to understand. They know we're here for them no matter whether they stay or leave. You can hear the relief in their voice." Karen Buck echoes these sentiments. "I can't tell you how many women I've talked to that told me I was the very first person they've ever talked to about this. They are so grateful for my help. I can't tell you how good that makes me feel."

The NDVH is committed to making sure that—whatever the need—women who need help are made aware of where to find it. It is through the NDVH's partnership with literally thousands of advocates across the United States that battered women can get the help they need as they consider their options and plan for a violence-free future. And what a future that can be, for, according to a sign at the NDVH, "Who knows what women can be when they are finally free to become themselves."

CHAPTER 17

A History of Violence Against Women

If I want I may clean my shoes on you. —Wife batterer, 1934[1]

Who knows, in the end the entire modern women's movement may be nothing but a revolt against the vicious thrashing of women, and its aim may be none other than the emancipation of woman from the cane.

—Hedwig Dohm
Nineteenth Century German Feminist[2]

Violence against women has its roots in a patriarchal system dating back thousands of years. It is a system that has historically viewed women as inherently inferior to men. This perceived inferiority extends to women's intellectual, spiritual, physical, sexual and emotional lives. In fact, at the height of misogynous attitudes during the Middle Ages, women were actually perceived as evil incarnate. The male tendency to devalue women and view them as property has lead to the creation of a variety of cruel practices against women, including femicide, infanticide, rape, battering, torture, widow burning, veiling, foot-binding, witch burning, chastity belts, clitoridectomies, and infibulation.[3]

At the very heart of wife battering is the subordination of women and their subjection to male control and authority. This subordination has been institutionalized in the structure of the patriarchal family and is supported by such societal institutions as economics, politics, religion, medicine, education, and culture.

In the Beginning . . .

Women have not always been subordinated by a patriarchal society. Ample archaeological evidence from the Paleolithic, Neolithic, and Bronze Ages supports the contention that women were actually once held in high esteem.[4] According to Frederick Engels, author of *The Origin of the Family, Private Property, and the State*, "It is one of the most absurd notions derived from eighteenth century enlightenment, that in the beginning of society woman was the slave of man."[5]

Archaeological evidence in the form of wall paintings, cave sanctuaries, burial sites, and female figures of fertility goddesses depict women with dignity and signs of high status.[6] By far, most of the evidence consists of female figurines that emphasize breasts, hips, and buttocks. These figurines have been discovered across Europe, the Mediterranean, and Eastern Asia. Approximately thirty thousand of these miniature sculptures in clay, marble, bone, copper and gold have been excavated from some three thousand sites in southeastern Europe alone.[7]

One of the reasons women were so highly esteemed may be the fact that it was only through women that lineage could be traced. Early civilizations lived in extended families, making any knowledge of paternity impossible. Women were the only apparent parents. Women's power of creation resulted in their association with the divine.[8]

Gerda Lerner, author of *The Creation of Patriarchy*, argues that the establishment of patriarchy consisted not of one event but of a series of events occurring over a period of nearly 2500 years, from approximately 3100 to 600 B.C.E., at different paces and at different times in several societies. Lerner emphasizes that single-cause explanations for the rise of patriarchy are insufficient.[9]

At some point during the agricultural revolution, egalitarian societies with a sexual division of labor developed into societies in which both private property and the exchange of women based on incest taboos were common. These earlier societies were often matrilineal and matrilocal while the later surviving societies were predominantly patrilineal and patrilocal. The later, more complex societies contained a division of labor no longer based only on biological distinctions, but also on hierarchy and the power of some men over other men and all women. Numerous researchers have reported that this move coincided with the formation of archaic states.[10]

Susan Brownmiller, in her book *Against Our Will: Men, Women, and Rape,* reports that "Female fear of an open season of rape, and not a natural inclination toward monogamy, motherhood or love, was probably the single causative factor in the original subjugation of woman by man, the most important key to her historic dependence, her domestication by protective mating."[11] The price woman paid was a precious one, however. In trying to obtain security she relinquished much of her power. Those who assumed her protection, be it a husband, father, brother, or uncle, began to perceive her as nothing more than chattel. The earliest permanent, protective monogamous relationships took the form of bride capture. A man took possession of a woman and staked a claim on her body by raping her. Bride capture was considered an acceptable means of acquiring women and actually existed in England as late as the fifteenth century.[12] Man's forcible extension of his boundaries to his mate and their children was the beginning of his concept of property and ownership.

This view of women as property is inherent in the very definition of family. Engels explains that the word *family* is derived from the Latin word *familia.* "The word familia did not originally signify the composite idea of sentimentality and domestic strife in the present day philistine mind. Among the Romans it did not even apply in the beginning to the leading couple and its children, but to the slaves alone. Famulus means domestic slave and familia is the aggregate number of slaves belonging to one man. . . . The expression was invented by the Romans in order to designate a new social organism, the head of which had a wife, children and a number of slaves under his paternal authority and according to Roman law the right of life and death over all of them."[13]

Along with the notion of women as property was born the concept of male privilege. This ideology asserted that a man was expected to protect his mate and that the primary purpose of this protection was to secure her faithfulness and the reliability of his paternal lineage. In assuming this responsibility, a man also became responsible for her behavior. He was, therefore, expected to control that behavior by whatever means possible. According to Engels, "the women are delivered absolutely into the power of the men; in killing his wife, the husband simply exercises his right."[14]

Violence Against Women in the Archaic States

Ancient Babylonian and Mosaic laws provide the earliest written documentation illustrating that slavery, private property, and the subjugation of women were facts of life. During this period the practice of buying one's wife became common.[15] According to Brownmiller, "A payment of money to the father of the house was a much more civilized and less dangerous way of acquiring a wife. And so the bride price was codified, at fifty pieces of silver."[16]

Once exchanged, women were no longer seen as equal human beings. Rather, women's sexuality and reproductive potential became commodities to be exchanged or acquired for the service of families. Women were thus perceived to have less autonomy than men. While men belonged to a household or lineage, women belonged to males who had acquired rights to them. The domestic subordination of women was the model out of which slavery evolved.

The development of slavery involved the refinement of the concept that permanent powerlessness of one group and total power of another were acceptable conditions of social interaction. Historical evidence suggests that the process of enslavement was first developed and perfected upon female war captives and reinforced by already known practices of woman exchange and concubinage.[17]

Lerner explains that "By experimenting with the enslavement of women and children, men learned to understand that all human beings have the potential for tolerating enslavement and they developed the techniques and forms of enslavement which would enable them to make of their absolute dominance a social institution."[18] By the time slavery had become widespread, the subordination of women was a historical fact.

The archaic states in the ancient Near East emerged in the second millennium B.C.E. from both men's sexual dominance over women and the exploitation by some men of others. Male heads of households allocated the resources of society to their families the way the state allocated the resources of society to them. The husbands' control over their female kin and minor sons was vital and was reflected in the various Mesopotamian laws, especially in the great number of laws dealing with the regulation of female sexuality.

Women in Mesopotamia depended on the males in their lives for any power they had. Women, even those from the upper class, thought of themselves as persons depending on the protection of a man. The daughters of the poor were sold into marriage or prostitution in order to advance the economic interests of their families. The daughters of men of property could command a bride price, paid by the family of the groom to the family of the bride, which frequently enabled the bride's family to secure more financially advantageous marriages for their sons, thus improving the family's economic position.[19]

As was the case in Mesopotamia and Israel, Greece of the eighth through the fifth century B.C.E. was a thoroughly patriarchal society. Women's legal and social subordination was undisputed. The main function of wives was to produce male heirs and to supervise their husbands' households. Women were defined by the family and, within the family, by their relationship to the men of the group. The Greek philosopher Aristotle expresses the generally held view of women when he writes,

> The male is by nature superior, and the female inferior; and the one rules, and the other is ruled; this principle, of necessity, extends to all mankind . . . the courage of a man is shown in commanding, of a woman in obeying.[20]

Laws rewarded and institutionalized women's dependence and subordination. All of these early cultures explicitly excluded women from activities outside the family, activities these cultures valued most. Powerful cultural messages reinforced this division of roles and activities and excluded women from the important areas assigned to men including government, philosophy, science, law, and in some cases religion.[21] Double standards prevailed for both divorce and adultery.[22]

In early Rome conditions for women were little better. Every Roman family was autocratic.[23] The head of the household, whether father, grandfather, uncle, or slave owner, under the title of *paterfamilias,* occupied the position of petty absolute monarch. His authority, designated the *patria potestas,* extended to life-and-death decisions. A new recruit to the household, whether a newborn infant, a bride, a servant, or a slave, had to gain the formal acceptance of the paterfamilias. The newborn was laid before him. If he picked the child up, he or she was admitted into the family and given a name. If not, the child was "exposed," that is, abandoned with the chance that it might be rescued.[24]

Infanticide, especially of female children, was an accepted practice in these early cultures. The decision over the fate of female infants was always made by the male head of household. Infants were rarely killed outright; instead, they were left on garbage heaps or in public places in the hope that a passerby might rescue them. Brothel owners collected infant girls and raised them to be prostitutes.

In Rome there is ample evidence for the routine exposure of female infants. The Law of the Twelve Tables required a father to raise all his sons, but only one daughter. Written evidence in the early third century A.D. states that "there were far more males than females" among the Roman nobility of Augustus's era.[25] Outside Greece and Rome, infanticide and exposure were condemned, but girls and women continued to be valued less than boys and men.[26]

Early Roman husbands had the legal right to chastise, divorce, or kill their wives for engaging in behavior that they themselves engaged in. A woman could legally be beaten for drinking from the family wine cellar, attending public games without the husband's permission, and walking outdoors with her face uncovered.[27]

Although the earliest writings of Greece, Rome and Israel contain and justify female subordination, they are not misogynous. This attitude came later in the Greek poetry of the seventh and sixth centuries B.C.E., in the satires and poetry of the first century A.D. in Rome, and in the Jewish and Christian interpretations of the Old Testament from the second century B.C.E. to the third century A.D. Women would then be stigmatized as innately evil. The creation of woman would be seen as a punishment for man, and woman would be identified as the enemy of both men and civilization. She would be seen as the source of trouble and be equated with all things despised.[28] According to Euripides,

> Terrible is the force of the waves of the sea, terrible the rush of river and the blasts of hot fire, terrible is poverty, and terrible are a thousand other things; but none is such a terrible evil as woman. No painter could adequately represent her: no language can describe her; but if she is the creation of any of the gods, let him know that he is a very great creator of evils and a foe to mortals.[29]

These early writings created the foundation for later European culture. The works of many of the Greek philosophers, the laws of Rome, and the first five books of the Bible shaped the views of later European generations and remained revered long after the Greeks, Romans, and Hebrews had ceased to dominate their regions. They transmitted images, morals, and values based on the assumption that women are inferior to men and are subordinate to them, ideologies inherited by later generations of European women and men.[30]

The Impact of Christianity

In the fourth century A.D., after struggling through three centuries of persecution and indifference, the Christian religion matured into a position of status and authority. As the Barbarians and Romans mingled and adapted to each other, the Christian community aligned itself into history's first great church organization.

Church intellectuals created doctrines designed both to answer esoteric theological questions and to provide rules of conduct for everyday Christian life. In this latter area, St. Augustine and his fellow church theologians were confronted by the marriage and family customs of the Roman and Barbarian worlds. In several significant respects these theologians offered a new perspective. The church soundly condemned abortion, infanticide, and contraception, including the rhythm method advocated by the Greek physician Hippocrates. In other areas, Christian teaching accepted existing custom or law.[31]

The idea of original sin was used to subjugate women to the authority of the church, state, and men. Original sin was a misogynous interpretation of other creation myths that predate the book of Genesis by at least seven thousand years.[32]

This dogma was reinforced by the philosophy of St. Augustine, who believed that only the church could absolve one of this sin. It was an ingenious power play that kept people tied to the Church with guarantees of forgiveness and eternal life. According to Jeanne Achterberg, author of *Woman as Healer,* "Women lost on all counts. In order to maintain the logic underlying the Church's hold on power, women's inherent sinfulness also had to be sustained. If there had been no evil temptress, no sin would exist, and the promised deliverance would wield no control over the masses. The doctrine of Original Sin was critical: any established church dependent on an economic power-base of unquestioned obedience would collapse if it were not considered the gateway to heaven by significant numbers of people."[33]

In St. Augustine's view, women assume a threefold role of temptress, wife, and mother. As temptress, woman is the instrument of the devil. As wife, woman is the instrument of her husband who oversees the peacefulness of the family. As mother, woman is the instrument of God's creativity. This doctrine would later be used to justify wife beating. If women were inherently evil, they deserved to be beaten. According to St. Augustine,

> And if any member of the family interrupts the domestic peace by disobedience, he is corrected either by word or blow, or some kind of just and legitimate punishment, such as society permits, that he may himself be the better for it and be readjusted to the family harmony from which he had dislocated himself.[34]

Women healers who tried to soothe the pangs of childbirth were severely punished because, according to the church, these pains existed to remind women of their original sinful nature. Women began to see themselves as unclean and impure. They hid in shame, especially during menstruation, pregnancy, and childbirth. Women's role in creation became not a blessing, but a curse.

The Witch Craze

Following the lead of St. Paul and St. Augustine, the thirteenth-century medieval church had long since solidified its thinking about women. As a justification for the brutalization of women, the doctrine of Original Sin was expanded upon by the forefathers of modern science in order to demonstrate women's inferiority.

Summa Theologica, the multivolume work St. Thomas Aquinas wrote between the years 1266 and 1272, reflects official attitudes. This important work was destined to provide the Roman Catholic Church with its official theological and philosophical dogma for many centuries. According to Aquinas, "woman is naturally subject to man, because in man the discretion of reason predominates."[35]

The period from the sixteenth to the eighteenth century illustrates the level to which the church and state condoned and perpetuated the abuse, torture, and murder of women. The femicidal mania of the witch craze spanned from approximately 1560 to 1760 and swept across Europe and even into the American colonies.[36]

During this period there were thousands of executions, usually live burnings at the stake, in Germany, Italy, and other countries. In the mid–sixteenth century the mania spread to France and England.[37] By far, the greatest number of crimes against women were committed in the Holy Roman Empire, which was centered in Germany. The second heaviest concentration of European witch hunts was in the French-speaking regions.[38]

Although the actual number of women killed during this period is unknown, researchers estimate that from two hundred thousand to ten million women were brutally tortured and killed as heretics and witches.[39] The authority figures in witch trials were entirely male, including the majority of accusers, ministers, priests, constables, jailers, judges, doctors, witch prickers, torturers, jurors, executioners, and the courts of appeal. Women made up approximately 85 percent of those executed.[40]

The women accused and murdered were typically single women living alone, older women living alone (especially widows), healers, and midwives. Still other women were accused because they were considered obnoxious, needy, deformed, or mentally disabled.[41] Many women were burned at the stake for threatening their husbands; talking back to or refusing a priest; stealing; prostitution; adultery; bearing a child out of wedlock; permitting sodomy; masturbation; lesbianism; child neglect; scolding and nagging; and even miscarrying, even if the miscarriage was caused by a blow from the husband.[42]

"Wise women," such as healers and midwives, were useful and popular members of society before 1550. By attacking the female-centered world of healing, the church cut at the very heart of female power. Anne Llewellyn Barstow, author of *Witchcraze*, writes, "The witch hunt records speak eloquently of the fear of the wise women that developed, especially in men. The role of healer, long respected and even seen as essential, became suspect."[43] Certain women were suspected of witchcraft not because they were powerless, but precisely because they were seen to have a great deal of power.

In the century preceding the beginning of the European witch craze, the field of medicine became firmly established as a profession. Being in the medical profession required university training, thus making it easy to legally ban women from practice. With few exceptions, universities were closed to women and licensing laws were established to prohibit all but university-trained doctors from practice.[44]

Since women were not allowed to study medicine, it was widely accepted that the only way they could obtain the information for their skill was from the devil. The position of the church was that "if a woman dare to cure without having studied, she is a witch and must die."[45]

It is noteworthy that witch-hunting in Europe was a lucrative business. In most cases, the woman was required to pay fees for the witch finder; her confinement; the activities of the torturers; the torture equipment; and for the beer, meals, and banquets of the torturers, judges, clerics, and others involved in her arrest. According to Barstow, "Even more disturbing are the bizarre entertainments and banquets for the judges and priests that often preceded the executions—all of which had to be paid for by the family of the victim."[46]

As women in the Middle Ages were allowed to own property, the accused woman's estates were confiscated. Finally, all costs of her murder were charged to her heirs. If she was boiled in oil, a favorite means of death in France, the fees were particularly high.[47]

The witch-hunts were well-orchestrated campaigns that were initiated and executed by the church and state. To Catholic and Protestant witch-hunters, the unquestioned authority on how to conduct a witch-hunt was the *Malleus Maleficarum,* written in the 1480s by the German Dominican friars Kramer and Sprenger. Using biblical, classical, and medieval sources, this misogynous book explains that women were more likely to be witches because they were more stupid, weak, superstitious, and fickle than men. Additionally, they were sensual and insatiably carnal.[48] All of these stereotypes rendered women as less than human, thereby justifying the inhuman treatment inflicted upon them.

A woman could be arrested on the most minimal evidence. Finding a "devil's teat" from which animal familiars or demons could suck was sufficient evidence to convict a person.[49] Such a mark was a mole or other skin blemish or any place that didn't bleed when pricked with a needle. Modern researchers have discovered that many of these surviving "needles" were fake and simply retracted under pressure.[50] About this mark, the Franciscan theologian Lodovico Maria Sinistrari explains,

> The Demon imprints on them some mark, especially on those whose constancy he suspects. That mark, moreover, is not always of the same shape or figure. . . . It is imprinted on the most hidden parts of the body . . . with women, it is usually on the breasts or the privy parts.[51]

Finding the devil's teat on an accused woman's body was one of the chief proofs of witchcraft. Although the searches were normally done by women, they were often witnessed by male court officials. In Scotland the searcher, called the witch pricker, was always male.[52] Women were stripped and shaved and their genitals were probed for marks. When the witch's mark was found, as it usually was, the charges against the woman were validated.

The process in the secular courts followed methods used during the Inquisition. It was not necessary to inform the accused of her crimes and no defense was allowed. Communication with the accused was forbidden and torture was repeatedly used. Promises of lighter torture were traded for the naming of accomplices, virtually assuring that more trials would ensue. Priests worked closely with the courts to obtain confessions.

Officials actually went beyond what inquisitional procedures prescribed. Women were often tortured even after conviction, and their bodies were repeatedly examined by the executioner. Two male guards were usually stationed in the cell with the woman, exposing her to the possibility of constant sexual harassment.[53]

The following is from a report of the first day's torture of a woman accused of witchcraft in Prossneck, Germany, in 1629.

> First, she was put on the "ladder," alcohol was thrown over her head and her hair was set fire. Strips of sulfur were placed under her arms and ignited. Then the torturer tied her hands behind her back and hoisted her to the ceiling, where she hung for four hours while he went to breakfast. On his return, he threw alcohol over her back and set fire to it. Placing heavy weights on her body, he jerked her up to the ceiling again. Then he squeezed her thumbs and big toes in a vise, trussed her arms with a stick, and kept her hanging until she fainted. Then he whipped her with rawhide. Once more to the vises, and he went to lunch. After his lunch she was whipped until blood ran through her shift.[54]

Torture often had strong sexual angles. Performed on women by men, legal torture permitted sadistic experimentation and sexual advances.

When a woman was whipped, she was stripped to the waist, exposing her breasts to the public.

When the executioner Jehan Minart of Cambrai prepared the condemned Aldegonde de Rue for the stake, he examined her mouth and *parties honeuses* (shameful parts). In another recorded incident, a priest applied hot fat repeatedly to an accused woman's eyes, armpits, thighs, elbows, the pit of her stomach, and *dans sa nature* (in her vagina).[55]

The ultimate form of torture was to be burned alive. According to Barstow, "the most horrifying symbol of some men's power over all women and over some other men was public execution at the stake. That this ferocious type of punishment was commonly carried out on witches added to the sadistic nature of their treatment, compounding the sexual torture that many had already been subjected to. That this torture was carried out in the presence of large crowds often numbering in the thousands gave it a ritual meaning beyond that of simple punishment."[56]

Gradually, women ceased to be burned. The last witch officially hanged in England was in 1684, and the last witch burned at the stake in Germany was in 1775. The madness began to diminish when Christianity began to lose its stronghold on the governing bodies of Europe. Thus this particular violence against women ended not because of changed attitudes about women, but because the power base of governments had shifted.[57]

When we narrow the focus from the national level to the local level, we can see the absolute horror of this period for women. Women basically found themselves afraid and alone. With few exceptions, families did not speak up for them and, in many cases, husbands and other family members actually turned against them. Women learned not to trust and that the safest route was to mind one's business and obey one's husband.

Domestic Violence in the Middle Ages

The large-scale abuse and murder of women had become institutionalized and served to reinforce and promote a husband's control and abuse of his wife. The husband's right to beat his wife derived from God's command and was grounded in European family law.

Men were encouraged from the pulpit to beat their wives, and wives were encouraged to kiss the rod that beat them. A medieval theological manual, *Gratian's Decretum,* explains that "a man must castigate his wife and beat her for her correction, for the lord must punish his own." The church approved these methods of keeping women in subjection and advised abused wives to try to win their husbands' goodwill by increased devotion and obedience.[58]

Late medieval law in Christian Saxony allowed a squire to whip any woman of his domains who displayed pride and self-respect, called "immodesty" in the wording of the law.[59] The thirteenth-century French law code, Customs of Beauvais, stated:

> In a number of cases men may be excused for the injuries they inflict on their wives, nor should the law intervene. Provided he neither kills nor maims her, it is legal for a man to beat his wife when she wrongs him.[60]

In sixteenth-century Russia under Ivan the Terrible, the murder of one's wife was legal as long as it was done for disciplinary purposes. In fact, wife battering was so well accepted and so common that the Russian Church issued an edict entitled the "Household Ordinance." This edict was a handbook outlining when and how best to beat one's wife.

Samuel Collins, an English physician to Tsar Alexei from 1660 to 1669, described a merchant who beat his wife with a whip two inches thick. Whipping her until he was exhausted, he then forced his wife into a smock dipped in brandy and set her on fire. She died in the flames and the man went unpunished.[61]

In the following narrative the knight Geoffrey de la Tour de Landry educates his daughters about the consequences of women's "misbehavior":

> Here is an example to every good woman that she suffer and endure patiently, nor strive with her husband nor answer him before strangers, as did once a woman who did answer her husband before strangers with short words; and he smote her with his fist down to the earth; and with his foot he struck her in her visage and broke her nose, and all her life after she had her nose crooked, which so shent [spoiled] and disfigured her visage after, that she might not for shame show her face, it was so foul blemished. And this she had for her language that she was wont to say to her husband. And therefore the wife ought to suffer, and let the husband have the words, and to be master, for that is her duty.[62]

The question of obedience dominates the manual composed by the Ménagier of Paris for his fifteen-year-old wife. According to the Ménagier, she should obey her husband's rules and act according to his desires rather than her own because his pleasure should come before hers. She should not contradict him or shame him in public because "it is the command of God that women should be subject to men . . . and by good obedience a wise woman gains her husband's love and at the end hath what she would of him."[63]

In Germanic village law, which was not replaced by Roman law until the sixteenth century, the right to administer corporal punishment was a part of the guardianship ("Munt") of the husband over the wife.[64] In many regions the husband who did not observe the right to practice physical punishment was threatened with repercussions. One such punishment was practiced in Germanic parishes. Wilhelm Heinrich Riehl describes the punishment as follows:

> The men of the neighboring villages solemnly came in with an ass, upon which the woman was set, and she was driven around the town, so that the men according to God's commandment should remain the masters and keep the upper hand. The husband who had put up with it is punished as well as the wife who commits the outrage and only by the donation of an Ohm [137.4 liters] of beer to the allied communities could the guilty married couple buy their way free from the punishment.[65]

In an effort to maintain women's chastity, many European men during this period performed infibulation on their wives. The European form of infibulation consisted of fastening together the labia majora by means of a ring, buckle, or padlock. As late as 1871, a European woman complained to her doctor that the weight of the padlock her husband had imposed on her was tearing the lips of her vagina and causing great pain and bleeding. On examination, the doctor found that the husband had bored holes in her labia through which he had inserted two metal rings, which he had drawn together and fastened securely with a padlock.

A similar case involving a German immigrant couple was reported in New York in 1894 and another in Eastern Europe in 1906. According to Elizabeth Gould Davis, author of *The First Sex,* "This sort of thing was probably a great deal more common in Europe than is generally supposed, the few cases which have come to light having been discovered purely accidentally. The sewing up of the labia over the vaginal opening . . . also occurred spasmodically in Europe, though probably less frequently than the padlock type of infibulation."[66]

The surgical procedure Davis describes involves the removal of the clitoris, labia minora, and at least two-thirds of the labia majora. The raw edges are then sewn together, leaving a small opening for the flow of urine and menstrual fluid. The suturing is done so that the remaining skin of the labia majora will heal together and form a bridge of scar tissue over the vaginal opening. Incredibly, this horrific procedure is still practiced today in parts of Egypt, Africa, Iraq, Iran, and Latin America.[67]

In Medieval Europe, infibulation was performed on women of the lower classes while the chastity belt was used on women of the upper classes. The chastity belt, like that of infibulation, was brought from the East by the Crusaders and became common in Europe during the thirteenth century.

The device consisted of an iron or silver corset with, curving between the legs, a tight-fitting metal bar perforated with a narrow opening surrounded by rows of tiny, sharp teeth. Into this instrument of torture the woman was locked, with her husband usually possessing the only key. As men were frequently gone to war for months and even years, women suffered from incredible infection and disease resulting from their inability to properly tend to their personal hygiene.[68]

The Pennsylvania Dutch settlers in the colonial United States used a version of the chastity belt known as "day belts." As late as 1946 a man in Atlantic City forced his wife to wear one of these infamous belts, padlocking her into the belt each day as he left for work. The man was eventually arrested for assault and battery, and he stated upon his arrest that he had fashioned the belt in his spare time and used it on his wife to "keep her from running around."[69]

The Common Scold

Once I had a scolding wife
She wasn't very civil
I clapped a plaster on her mouth
And sent her to the Devil

"Haul Away Joe"
American whaling ballad[70]

During this period, instruments of torture and punishment were used in England against women convicted as "scolds." Scolds, as defined by Jacob's *Law Dictionary,* are "troublesome and angry women, who, by their brawling and wrangling amongst their neighbors, break the public peace."[71] A scold was a crime that consisted basically of speaking one's mind, and it was a crime that could be committed only by a woman.

One of the punishments for this offense was a public ducking in a local body of cold water using a "ducking stool." One version of the ducking stool was an armchair fastened to the ends of two beams held parallel to each other. The chair hung between the beams on a type of axle, allowing it to move freely and remain in the horizontal position so that the woman could be raised up and down. A post was set up on the bank of a pond or river. Over this post two pieces of wood were laid, at one end of which the chair hung over the water. Some ducking stools could be wheeled to and from the water while others were stationary. The woman was tied to the chair and plunged into the water, the number of times dependent upon her sentence. In some instances the ducking was carried to such an extreme as to cause death.[72]

Writing in 1780, Benjamin West of Weedon Beck, Northamptonshire, England describes the fate of the common scold:

There stands, my friend, in yonder pool,
An engine called the ducking-stool,
By legal pow'r commanded down,
The joy and terror of the town,
If jarring females kindle strife,
Give language foul or lug the coif;
If noisy dames should once begin
To drive the house with horrid din,
Away, you cry, you'll grace the stool,
We'll teach you how your tongue to rule.
The fair offender fills the seat,
In sullen pomp, profoundly great,
Down in the deep the stool descends,
But here, at first, we miss our ends;
She mounts again, and rages more
Than ever vixen did before.
So, throwing water on the fire

Will make it but burn up the higher;
If so, my friend, pray let her take
A second turn into the lake,
And, rather than your patience lose,
Thrice and again repeat the dose.
No brawling wives, no furious wenches,
No fire so hot, but water quenches.
In Prior's skilful lines we see
For these another recipe:
A certain lady, we are told
(A lady, too, and yet a scold),
Was very much reliev'd you'll say
By water, yet a different way;
A mouthful of the same she'd take,
Sure not to scold, if not to speak.[73]

The latest recorded instance of the ducking stool being used in England was in 1809, although it began to fall out of favor as early as the 1770s.[74]

Another instrument used to punish scolds was the "brank" or "scold's bridle." The brank was an iron frame that was placed on the head of the woman, enclosing her in a kind of cage. It had a iron mouthpiece that was either sharpened or covered with spikes. If the woman attempted to move her tongue in any way, she was sure to be injured. With the brank on her head, she was lead through the streets on a chain held by one of the town's officials. In some towns it was the custom to chain the victim to a pillory, whipping post, or market cross.

In some houses a hook was attached to the side of large, open fireplaces. When a woman was accused of being a scold, her husband sent for the town jailer to bring the brank and had her confined and chained. There she remained until her husband instructed the jailer to release her.[75]

The Common Scold Law and these torturous devices were brought from England to Connecticut by the Puritans and early settlers. From Connecticut they were carried into New Jersey and other colonies.

A Virginia act of 1662 ordered each county to erect a pillory, stocks, a whipping post, and a ducking stool. Declaring that "brabling women often slander and scandalize their neighbors for which their poore husbands are often brought into chargeable and vexatious suites, and cast in greate damages," it provided that in actions of slander by the wife, if the husband refused to pay the damages, the wife was to be punished by ducking. If the slander were so great as to call for damages greater than five hundred pounds of tobacco, the wife was to be ducked one time for every five hundred pounds fined against her husband. Later acts of the Virginia and Maryland assemblies made it compulsory for counties to build ducking stools, and county court minutes show many court orders for the erection of such devices.[76]

It was not until 1967 that the Common Scold Law was declared obsolete in England by the Criminal Law Act. The last woman convicted of being a common scold in the United States was a journalist named Ann Royall in 1829. However, the last woman to be indicted as a scold was in 1971 in New Jersey. At that time the law was still on the books, but the state's superior court threw the case out the following year.[77]

Riding the Stang

Traditional community sanctions against unacceptable levels of domestic violence included rituals of public shaming. Known by such names as "charivari," "skimmington rides," "riding the stang," "rough music," and "misrules," these rituals involved costumes, floats, dancing, singing, rude songs, and sometimes physical punishment. Common from the fifteenth through the nineteenth century, these punishments were also used on men who allowed themselves to become "henpecked."[78]

To begin the ceremony, a trumpeter blew his horn and the villagers gathered around him. A pole or ladder was obtained, and the most witty man in the village was placed in a chair atop the ladder, raised shoulder high, and carried through the streets. In one hand he held a large key or stick and in the other a pan, which he banged together to lead the music and the crowd. Men, women, and children joined the jovial procession, beating pots and pans. Tin whistles, horns, and trumpets were blown. About every fifty yards the procession stopped and the mounted man loudly proclaimed a rhyme. One such rhyme reads as follows:

> Here we come with a ran, dan, dang:
> It's not for you, nor for me, we ride this stang;
> But for ___________, whose wife he did bang.
> He banged her, he banged her, he banged her indeed:

He banged her, poor creature, before she stood need.
He took up neither tipstaff nor stower,
But with his fist he knocked her backwards ower;
He kicked her, he punched her, till he made her cry,
And to finish all, he gave her a black eye.
Now, all you good people that live in this row
We would have you take warning, for this is our law:
If any of you, your wives you do bang,
We're sure, we're sure, to ride you the stang.[79]

The house of the wife beater was visited several times each night, and the proceedings were kept up three nights in succession. If the offense was considered a serious one, the batterer was burnt in effigy in front of his door. In some areas the batterer was compelled to ride the stang himself. Such was the punishment for men accused of beating their wives.

Cross-cultural Misogynous Practices

Women's formal oppression has been common to different cultures between and within geographic boundaries. Cultural distinctions may delineate the character and means of a woman's forced subjection, but the tactics—popular culture, law, and religious or social traditions—remain the same.

Footbinding

Footbinding began in China during the tenth century as an innovation of palace dancers of the Imperial harem. A symbol of gentility, bound feet were considered an asset in the marriage market. In effect, they reinforced women's oppressed existence, as Chinese tradition dictated that a woman should not appear in public or be seen in the company of men.[80] The objective of binding and deforming the foot was to achieve what was known as an "A-1 Golden Lotus." The golden lotus was a foot no bigger than 3 inches in length.[81]

Manufacturing this deformity required the application of a bandage, about two inches wide and ten feet long, around each foot. One end was placed within the instep and pulled over the small toes to force the toes in and towards the sole. The large toe was left unbound. The bandage was then forcefully wrapped around the heel so that the heel and toes were drawn together. This process was repeated until the entire bandage had been applied.[82] The torture usually began for young girls between the ages of 5 and 7 years.

Footbinding was an excruciatingly painful and crippling practice. A woman had to walk on the outside of her toes, which had been bent into the sole of her foot. Hard calluses formed and toenails grew into her skin. The woman's feet became infected and bloody. Circulation was virtually stopped.

Walking unassisted was almost impossible. To keep her balance, a woman would need to lean against a cane or a servant and take very short steps. She was actually falling with every step and catching herself with the next. According to Andrea Dworkin, author of *Woman Hating,*

> Footbinding was a visible brand. Footbinding did not emphasize the differences between men and women—it created them, and they were then perpetuated in the name of morality. Footbinding functioned as the Cerberus of morality and ensured female chastity in a nation of women who literally could not "run around". Fidelity, and the legitimacy of children, could be reckoned on.[83]

Footbinding remained a popular practice in China until it was outlawed after the 1911 Revolution. By then, however, Chinese immigrants had brought this horrendous practice with them to the U.S. In 1904 a Chinese entrepreneur put a Chinese woman with bound feet on display at the St. Louis World's Fair.[84]

Sati

The original definition of the Indian word sati meant a virtuous or pious woman. Indian tradition holds chastity, purity, and loyalty to the husband as the highest ideals for women. To voluntarily throw her body upon her husband's funeral pyre came to be considered an example of a woman's loyalty and devotion.[85] Sati evolved to define a woman who burns herself along with the body of her deceased husband.

Greek visitors to North India wrote accounts of sati as early as the fourth century B.C.E.[86] Evidence suggests that it was an encouraged practice by 700 A.D.[87] The importance of maintaining a woman's chastity was given as an excuse for the continuation of sati.

The usual form that sati took was that of burning the wife alive on her husband's funeral pyre. Scriptural rules prohibited the ceremony while the woman was menstruating (which was equated with uncleanness) or pregnant. When this occurred, or when the husband's death occurred during an absence from home, some women would burn themselves with an article of her husband's clothing or other personal effect.

In the most common form of the ceremony, the widow or her eldest son was required to light the fire. On her way to the pyre, the widow would distribute money and jewelry to the crowd of on-lookers. The richer she was, the more valuable the gifts. No woman who was unfaithful to her husband could be burnt. Sati did not make the woman virtuous; it proved that she had been virtuous all her life.[88]

Basically, widows had two choices. They could choose a painful but heroic death or they could live, viewed as a sinner, in poverty and loneliness. Widows were not allowed to remarry. They were forbidden to turn to religious instruction, to hold jobs, or to maintain interests outside the home. For many women, sati became an escape from a seemingly bleak and hopeless future. The Widow Remarriage Act made such weddings legal in 1856. However, it did not readily eliminate the centuries of prejudices against remarriage for women. Even today, remarriage for a widow is not seen in the same favor as remarriage for a widower.[89]

Within Indian borders, the incidence of sati was subject to great regional variations. By the early nineteenth century, however, most satis occurred in the province of Bengal. From 1815 to 1828, Bengal officially recorded the occurrence of 7,941 sati rites. An 1829 study profiling widows who burned themselves in this province found that many came from impoverished families. According to Sakuntala Narasimhan, author of *Sati: Widow Burning in India,* "For many widows in the early nineteenth century, the virtue of becoming a sati lay in the deliverance that is promised from a life of certain misery."[90]

The practice of burning a widow along with her husband's body was outlawed in British India in 1829. Nevertheless, cases continued to be reported long after the practice was legally abolished.

By 1987, the Rajasthan Sati (Prevention) Act stated that an attempted sati was punishable with imprisonment ranging from one to five years and a fine of five thousand to twenty thousand rupees. By abetting a sati, directly or indirectly, one became subject to a death sentence or life imprisonment along with a fine.[91]

Domestic Violence in the Colonies

Women in the American colonies were without political rights, and wives were generally considered legal nonentities. Single women, however, were considered fully competent persons for all the purposes of private law. As soon as a woman married, her legal existence was suspended or incorporated into that of her husband, who was regarded as her head and master.[92]

Writing in the late 1700s, Samuel Jennings, in his book *The Married Lady's Companion,* was to echo what generations of men before him had argued:

> It is in your interest to adapt yourself to your husband, whatever may be his peculiarities. Again, nature has made man the stronger, the consent of mankind has given him superiority over his wife, his inclination is, to claim his natural and acquired rights. He of course expects from you a degree of condescension, and he feels himself the more confident of the propriety of his claim, when he is informed, that St. Paul adds his authority to its support. "Wives submit yourselves unto your own husbands, as unto the Lord, for the husband is the head of his wife." In obedience then to this precept of the gospel, to the laws of custom and of nature, you ought to cultivate a cheerful and happy submission.[93]

Wife beating was an accepted male right in the colonies although it was not a legal privilege. If the husband exceeded his legal prerogatives, the woman could take him to court. Many cases appear in the colonial records of a wife's appealing to the court for protection against her husband's battering. The justices usually ordered the husband to appear in court and promise his good behavior, but on occasion they fined or gave him corporal punishment.

Judges did recognize, however, the husband's right to batter his wife. An order of a Maryland court in 1681 expresses what appears to have been an orthodox opinion. The order was to the sheriff of Charles County and explained that Jane, wife of John Bread, had made supplication to the court complaining that she had been "grievously and manifestly threatened" by her husband of her life and of "mutilation of her members." It instructed the sheriff to summon the husband and have him give bond not to do "any damage or evil" to his wife "otherwise than what to a husband, by cause of government and chastisement of his own wife, lawfully and reasonably belongeth."[94]

Evidence suggests that in some cases in which the court was convinced that a woman's life was endangered by her abusive husband, it allowed her to live away from him and required him to furnish her a separate maintenance.

The acceptance of wife battering became a part of the American tradition through the borrowing of English common law by the colonists. The only exception was in Massachusetts where, in 1655, men convicted of beating their wives were fined a maximum of ten pounds and/or given corporal punishment.[95]

Under English common law the notion of chastisement in moderation prevailed. The "rule of thumb" is a good example of this perceived moderation. This law, which modified the weapons a man could legally use in beating his wife, was created as an example of compassionate reform. The old law authorized a husband to "chastise his wife with any reasonable instrument." The new law stipulated that the reasonable instrument be only "a rod not thicker than his thumb."[96]

In 1765 Sir William Blackstone published the *Commentaries of the Law of England,* that provided the colonists with the primary source of information about English common law. Blackstone approved of chastisement and wrote,

> For, as [the husband] is to answer for her misbehavior, the law thought it reasonable to intrust him with this power of chastisement, in the same moderation that a man is allowed to correct his apprentices or children.[97]

While Blackstone's work was quickly discredited in England, it was influential in the United States for the next hundred years. Not until the women's movement of the 1800s was a serious challenge made to Blackstone's ideas concerning the legal status of women.[98]

In 1824 the Mississippi Supreme Court became the first state to acknowledge the wife-beating right, and other states soon followed. By the 1870s, however, states began rejecting the legal justification of wife beating.[99] In 1871 both Alabama and Massachusetts rescinded the wife-beating privilege.[100]

In 1874 the North Carolina Supreme Court disavowed a husband's right to beat his wife; however, the court went on to state,

> If no permanent injury has been inflicted, nor malice, cruelty nor dangerous violence shown by the husband, it is better to draw the curtain, shut out the public gaze and leave the parties to forget and forgive.[101]

Twelve years later, as a result of this ruling, a lower court in North Carolina declared that a criminal indictment could not be brought against a husband unless the assault was so great as to result in permanent injury, endanger life and limb, or be malicious beyond all reasonable bounds.

Between 1876 and 1906 bills to punish wife beaters with the whipping post were introduced in twelve states and the District of Columbia. The idea of whipping wife beaters originated in England during a period of public concern about armed robbery. It was believed that a man who battered his wife would also assault his neighbors or strangers. Well-known lawyers, judges, and other law enforcement officials led the campaign, but opponents of the whipping post far outnumbered its supporters. Whipping-post bills were defeated except in Maryland in 1882, Delaware in 1901, and Oregon in 1905. Maryland's law provided a whipping of not more than forty lashes, a one-year jail term, or both.[102]

It was not until 1890 that the North Carolina Supreme Court eliminated the last remaining restrictions on a husband's liability and prohibited a man from committing even a minor assault against his wife.[103] By 1910 only eleven states still did not permit divorce by reason of cruelty by one spouse to the other.[104]

The Early Feminists

The popular eighteenth-century writer Jean Jacques Rousseau was adamant in his belief that women were inferior and subordinate beings who should be nurtured for the sole purpose of serving men and providing them pleasure. He argued that women should be restricted to domestic chores and excluded from liberal education. Like others before him, Rousseau insisted that the patriarchal structure of the family was natural. Writing in *Paternity and the Origin of Political Power,* Rousseau explains,

> In the family, it is clear, for several reasons which lie in its very nature, that the father ought to command. In the first place, the authority ought not to be equally divided between father and mother; the government must be single, and in every division of opinion there must be one preponderant voice to decide. Secondly, however lightly we may regard the disadvantages peculiar to women, yet, as they necessarily occasion intervals of inaction, this is a sufficient reason for excluding them from this supreme authority. . . . Besides, the husband ought to be able to superintend his wife's conduct, because it is of

importance for him to be assured that the children, whom he is obligated to acknowledge and maintain, belong to no one but himself.[105]

In 1792 British writer Mary Wollstonecraft published *A Vindication of the Rights of Woman* as a rebuttal to Rousseau's then popular work, *Emile.*[106,107] Although an early disciple of Rousseau's egalitarian views, she objected to his assumption that man's nature and virtues differ from woman's, the essence of this distinction lying in the belief that women are deficient in reason. Since reason is the fundamental human characteristic, Wollstonecraft argued, to deny women a full measure of rationality amounts to denying their humanity. Ultimately, she explained, such beliefs and practices damaged not only women, but the family and society as well. Wollstonecraft urged equal rights for women, although she primarily addressed the problems of middle- and upper-class women.[108]

Wollstonecraft's book is one of the first sociopolitical manifestos demanding equal treatment for women. In the mid 1800s her book became the bible for the early feminist movement in both England and the United States. These early feminists supported Wollstonecraft's contention that women were not inherently inferior, but rather were victims of life-long subjugation that was encouraged and perpetuated by social forces.[109]

It was out of a concern for others that American women found a concern for themselves. In the 1820s and 1830s, especially in New York, Pennsylvania, and New England, a spirit of reform was in the air. It started in the churches and was involved at first with such humanitarian issues as temperance, peace, capital punishment, and education. Through their churches, women became part of the reform movement. The cause that attracted these white, middle-class feminists the most was the antislavery movement.

The antislavery cause gave middle-class women an opportunity to expand their roles as wives and mothers. They developed public-speaking and fund-raising skills, they learned how to distribute literature and how to call meetings, and they became adept in the use of the petition. In addition, women learned how to challenge male supremacy.[110]

Participation in the antislavery movement led white women to realize their own oppression and inequality. As a result of the frustrations caused by their awakening, American women began the first organized effort to change the condition of their lives. Only when women decided to work together did the "women's movement" begin in the United States. This officially occurred in July 1848 in Seneca Falls, New York, with the first women's rights meeting. Five women, Lucretia Mott, Martha C. Wright, Jane Hunt, Elizabeth Cady Stanton, and Mary Ann McClintock, planned the meeting to discuss "the social, civil and religious condition and rights of women."[111]

From this point until well into the new century, reform became associated with women. Millions participated in a variety of reform movements. While some women demanded the right to vote, others organized themselves in order to reform America in a multitude of areas including legal and educational systems, employment, marriage, temperance, health, and birth control.[112] Some of these early reformers were Lucy Stone, Susan B. Anthony, Carrie Chapman Catt, Harriet Tubman, Angelina and Sarah Grimké, Sojourner Truth, Ida B. Wells, Lucretia Mott, Mary Church Terrell, Margaret Sanger, Emma Goldman, Lucy Parsons, "Mother" Ella Reeve Bloor, Jane Addams, and "Mother" Mary Harris Jones.[113] Wendell Phillips, W. E. B. Du Bois, William Lloyd Garrison, and Frederick Douglass were some of the men who joined women in these early reform movements.[114]

John Stuart Mill's *The Subjection of Women* was published in England in 1869, during the formative years of the feminist movement. Mill was one of the few men to actively call for equal rights for women and an end to their mistreatment by their husbands. According to Mill,

> The vilest malefactor has some wretched woman tied to him, against whom he can commit any atrocity except killing her, and, if tolerably cautious, can do that without much danger of the legal penalty.[115]

Mill's analysis of the physical, psychological, and legal subjection of women proved highly controversial and helped to bring the issue to the attention of the British Parliament.[116]

British suffragist Frances Power Cobb, an opponent of the whipping post, persuaded its supporters to favor instead a protection bill for battered wives. Her bill provided a battered woman with legal separation from her husband, legal custody of her children, and an order requiring her husband to pay her and her children support. Her bill, known as the Matrimonial Causes Act, was passed by the British Parliament in 1878.[117] In her successful campaign in support of this legislation, Frances Power Cobb wrote,

> The notion that a man's wife is his property . . . is the fatal root of incalculable evil and misery. Every brutal-minded man, and many a man who in other relations of life is not brutal, entertains more or less vaguely the notion that his wife is his thing, and is ready to ask with indignation . . . of any one who interferes with his treatment of her, "May I not do what I will with my own?"[118]

Cobb sent a copy of the bill to the American suffragist Lucy Stone, who introduced a similar bill into the Massachusetts legislature in 1879. Opposition to the bill came from legislators who believed that its passage would make it too easy for women to secure legal separation and thus create disharmony in the family. Stone made two more attempts to pass the bill, each of which failed.[119]

The Medical Solution

One of the effects of the murder of thousands of wise women during the witch craze was the virtual elimination of female healers and the creation of a new male medical profession. Since women had been barred from universities and the midwives had been murdered, it became the responsibility of male doctors to attend to women and their health. It was during this period, from the late 1700s to the late 1800s, that male midwives became identified by the name *gynecologist.*

One commonly diagnosed female illness during this period was "female hysteria," also known as "female insanity." Female hysteria encompassed a vast array of physical and emotional symptoms including fits, fainting, vomiting, choking, sobbing, laughing, and paralysis. [120] Not only did the management of female hysteria play a major role in the work of leading English, American, French, and German physicians of this period, it also became the starting point for psychoanalysis.[121]

The British doctor Isaac Baker Brown actively practiced a particularly brutal and extreme form of surgery, known as clitoridectomy, to cure female hysteria. A respected member of the Obstetrical Society of London, Brown became convinced that female hysteria was caused by masturbation and that the surgical removal of the clitoris would stop the disease.

Brown conducted his sexual surgery in his private clinic in London from 1859 to 1866. In the 1860s he began to expand his surgery to include the removal of the labia. As he grew more confident, he operated on patients as young as ten and even on women with eye problems. He operated on five women whose "madness" consisted of their wish to take advantage of the new Divorce Act of 1857 and found that, in each case, the patient returned humbly to her husband. In no case, Brown claimed, was he so certain of a cure as in nymphomania, for he had never seen a recurrence of the disease after surgery.

In 1867 Brown was expelled from the Obstetrical Society, primarily because his patients had complained of being tricked and coerced into the treatment. Some had been threatened that if they refused to have surgery, their condition would worsen and they would become hopelessly insane.[122]

Clitoridectomy was enthusiastically accepted as a cure for female masturbation by some American gynecologists. In the 1860s Dr. Isaac Ray and his contemporaries proclaimed that women were susceptible to hysteria, insanity, and criminal impulses by reason of their sexual organs. The year 1873 marked Dr. Robert Battey's practice of "female castration," the removal of the ovaries to cure insanity. For the next several decades ovariectomy became the gynecological craze. Doctors claimed the surgery elevated the moral sense of women, making them orderly, industrious, and cleanly.[123]

Although middle and upper middle class women suffered most from the doctor's practice, the pioneering work in gynecological surgery had been performed by Marion Sims on black female slaves whom he kept for the sole purpose of surgical experimentation. After moving to New York, Sims continued his experiments on impoverished Irish women in the wards of the New York Women's Hospital.[124]

Doctors noticed that hysteria was likely to appear in young women who were especially rebellious. Dr. F. C. Skey observed that his hysterical patients were likely to be more independent and assertive than "normal" women. Other doctors had seen a high percentage of unconventional women, such as artists and writers. From these observations, they concluded that rebelliousness could produce nervous disorders such as hysteria.

Elaine Showalter, writing in *The Female Malady: Women, Madness, and English Culture,* explains that "during an era when patriarchal culture felt itself to be under attack by its rebellious daughters, one obvious defense was to label women campaigning for access to the universities, the professions, and the vote as mentally disturbed, and of all the nervous disorders . . . hysteria was the most strongly identified with the feminist movement."[125]

It was not until hysteria became a widespread malady of men that the notion of a "talking cure" entered English psychiatric practice. It was not feminism that initiated the new era of psychiatric practice, but the new name given to female hysteria during World War I: shell shock.

Gradually, psychologists and medical personnel came to agree that the real cause of shell shock was the emotional disturbance created by chronic conditions of fear, tension, horror, disgust, and grief and that the neurosis shell shock caused was an escape from an intolerable situation.[126]

Societies for the Prevention of Cruelty to Children

In the 1870s the United States witnessed the first attempt to confront domestic violence. Societies for the prevention of cruelty to children were the first social agencies devoted to family violence problems. These agencies originally focused only on child abuse, but were soon drawn into other forms of family violence. By the end of the decade, there were thirty-four of these societies in the United States.[127]

From approximately 1875 to 1910, family violence agencies were part of the general reform movement, which was heavily influenced by the feminism of the era.[128] Societies for the prevention of cruelty to children originally tried to avoid intervention between husbands and wives, but their clients virtually dragged the child protection workers into wife abuse problems.

Few battered women kept their problems to themselves. Close neighbors, landladies, and relatives were asked for child care, credit, or food. Women often requested places to stay or money to help maintain their own households. Battered women turned to child welfare agencies when their informal networks could not protect them, adding these agencies to their collection of survival strategies.

These early social workers tried to help battered women secure the help they needed in the form of monetary assistance, safety, and housing. They also helped to bring domestic violence to an heightened state of public awareness.

Battered women also turned to child protection agencies because of the inadequacy of police protection. During this period the police frequently identified with the husband and, while urging him to moderate his violence and to sober up, sympathized with his frustration and trivialized his assaults. The police often removed men from their homes for a while in order to calm them, and they sometimes threatened men with arrest and jail.[129]

In the early years of child protection, caseworkers actually tried to reform men. They heckled, threatened, and cajoled. They made frequent home visits, surprise visits, and visits to employers and relatives, and they pursued nonsupporting men for money.

During the 1920s and 1930s, the women's movement began to shrink in size and effectiveness. The reform spirit, with its discontent and insistence on change, was at odds with the national mood. So was the women's movement. Since the turn of the century women had begun to gain more personal freedom. There was, consequently, less interest in collective activities and social reform.[130]

During the Progressive era, from approximately 1910 to 1930, family violence work was incorporated into professional social work and a reform program relying heavily on state regulation. Social work was becoming professionalized and "scientific," and a new group of middle-class "experts" replaced upper-class reform workers as those who set standards for family life.

The Progressive era produced a cover-up of wife beating as a form of family violence. The feminist outcries against drunken, brutal men were seen as moralistic and unscientific. Instead, marital violence was portrayed as mutual, resulting from environmental stress, lack of education, or lack of mental hygiene. During this period women actually began to be blamed for much of the abuse they suffered.

One of the major characteristics of Depression-era social work was a policy of defending the "conventional" nuclear family. Depression-era family violence agencies continued to deemphasize wife battering as a significant family problem. Women were consistently held responsible for the treatment of children and the general mood of the family; men were not. The treatments of preference for family violence were reconciliation and economic aid. The very meaning of family violence had shifted. It was seen as resulting from extrafamilial events. Indeed, violence altogether was deemphasized, and the societies for the prevention of cruelty to children devoted themselves almost exclusively to child neglect.[131]

During the 1930s violence against women, their poverty, and their frustrations were submerged in the troubles of the whole nation. As the country began to recuperate from the Depression, people turned their attention and energies toward Europe and Asia. From 1930 to 1945, and during a decade of adjustment after the war, the women's movement was silent.[132]

Women's complaints about wife beating escalated just as feminism was at its low point. After the 1930s, records from child protection societies indicate that the majority of women clients complained directly rather than indirectly about wife beating. Women continued to allege child abuse in order to get agency help, but in the investigations they tended to protest about their own abuse more strongly.

Through the 1940s and 1950s, family casework was no longer reluctant to inquire into the roots of family conflict. Psychiatric categories and profamily values, however, now dominated the social work approach to family problems.

The most notorious example of the psychiatric influence in family violence work was in the blaming of wives for abuse by their husbands. According to Linda Gordon, author of *Heroes of Their Own Lives,* "The 'nagging wife' of traditional patriarchal folklore was now transformed into a woman of complex mental ailments: failure to accept her own femininity and attempting to compete with her husband; frustration as a result of her own frigidity; a need to control resulting from her own sexual repression; masochism. These neuroses required diagnosis and treatment by professionals. . . . Moreover, these neuroses indicated treatment not of the assailant but of the victim."[133]

These years were a low point in the public awareness of domestic violence. It was during this period that the notion of defending and maintaining the conventional family prevailed. Until the revival of feminism and the establishment of battered women's shelters in the 1970s, victims of domestic violence had three basic resources: their own individual survival strategies; the help of relatives, friends, and neighbors; and the child welfare agencies. While a woman's survival strategies certainly may have kept her alive, they did not guarantee that she would live violence free. Friends and relatives were often intimidated by abusive husbands and by the sanctity of marriage itself. Lastly, child welfare agencies did not represent the interests of battered women.

The Reemergence of Feminism

True emancipation . . . begins in woman's soul. History tells us that every oppressed class gain[s] true liberation from its masters through its own efforts. It is necessary that woman learn that lesson, that she realize that her freedom will reach as far as her power to achieve her freedom reaches.

Emma Goldman, Early Twentieth-Century Feminist[134]

The rediscovery and redefinition of domestic violence in the 1960s and 1970s resulted from women's involvement with the civil rights, antiwar, antirape, student, and women's movements. From their experience in reform activities, these women, like feminists in the nineteenth century, learned about their own oppression and inequality. Once again, their concern with the needs of others led to a concern for themselves.

These movements all challenged family norms, but in different ways. Critical questions were raised about the sanctity of family privacy, the privileged position of the male head of the family, and the importance of family togetherness at any price. Together these movements created an atmosphere in which child abuse and wife beating could again be exposed. Linda Gordon explains that "Defining wife-beating as a social problem, not merely a phenomenon of particular violent individuals or relationships, was one of the great achievements of feminism. Women always resisted battering, but in the last hundred years they began to resist it politically and ideologically, with considerable success."[135]

Radical feminism had its roots in the civil rights movement of the 1950s and 1960s. After leaving the South, many of these young women returned to their colleges and universities, where they later demonstrated against the war in Vietnam and joined various groups of the new left.

Examining the social roots of feminism, Sara Evans, in her book *Personal Politics,* suggests the following preconditions for an insurgent revolt:[136]

1. Social spaces within which members of an oppressed group can develop an independent sense of worth in contrast to their received definitions as second-class or inferior citizens
2. Role models of people breaking out of patterns of passivity

3. An ideology that can explain the sources of oppression, justify revolt, and provide a vision of a qualitatively different future
4. A threat to the newfound sense of self that forces a confrontation with the inherited cultural definitions
5. A communication or friendship network through which a new interpretation can spread, activating the insurgent consciousness into a social movement

These preconditions evolved and strengthened as more and more women participated in the various reform movements. When women in the Student Non-Violent Coordinating Committee and Students for a Democratic Society voiced their concerns regarding the unequal treatment of men and women within their ranks, they were either ignored or laughed at. Taking literally the admonition to "look to your own oppression," many women made their final break with the new left in 1967 when they declared that feminism was their first priority.[137]

By the late 1960s and early 1970s, feminism had developed two major branches. One branch was the women's rights movement, exemplified by organizations like the National Organization for Women; the other was the women's liberation movement. NOW had been founded in 1966 to focus on legal inequalities and gaining access to the rights and opportunities held by men.[138] The women's liberation movement was embodied in radical feminist groups working on such issues as abortion, women's schools, day care, and prisoners' rights.

The women's liberation movement believed that the campaigns these moderate groups waged were important; however, radical feminists wanted more. Crucial to the women's liberation movement was the rejection of middle-class standards and lifestyles and a focus on such personal issues as the unequal gender division of labor and women's lack of control over their bodies, sexuality, and lives. Radical feminists were urging a transformed society in which neither women nor men would be assigned or restricted to roles based on their sex.[139] Their demands went beyond equal rights to a demand for equality of power.

Radical feminists agreed that their first task was to awaken women by helping them explore their own experiences and how those experiences conformed to assigned social roles. The instinctive sharing of personal experiences soon became a political instrument called "consciousness-raising."[140]

When feminists met in small consciousness-raising groups, they talked about their backgrounds, their experiences, and their feelings. Very quickly they discovered that the problems they thought were uniquely their own were actually common to other women. Carol Hymowitz and Michaele Weissman state in their book, *A History of Women in America,* that "The idea that the personal is political was the most important insight of modern feminism. It led to the understanding that women were a caste or class, linked together by their sex. Regardless of the many differences among groups of women—class, race, age, education, life style—all women were subject to sexism."[141] These consciousness-raising groups inspired not only an analysis of personal experiences, but a thorough critique of both internal and external oppression.

Soon the radical ideas and cooperative forms of the women's liberation movement were reshaping the more conservative, tightly structured women's rights branch of the movement. Within a few years NOW had strengthened its positions on such issues as abortion and lesbianism and had considerably changed its style. In several cities NOW became the primary instigator of new consciousness-raising groups.[142]

By 1970 consciousness-raising groups had become the heart of the women's liberation movement. The format of these groups reflected the grassroots style of women's liberation. Groups developed wherever several women decided to meet and talk about their experiences. From these groups such words as *sexism, chauvinism, oppression,* and *liberation* became common.

The idea that through personal testimony women could make political changes became a reality. Women began to make changes in their lives that would not only impact their families, friends, and coworkers, but would also literally change the country.[143]

Sisterhood Is Powerful: The Birth of the Battered Women's Movement

Prior to the revival of feminism in the 1960s and 1970s, women's organized resistance to battering occasionally occurred, both in the United States and internationally. In 1875 Martha McWhirter opened a shelter in Belton, Texas, for battered women and women whose husbands spent the crop money on Saturday-night drinking binges. The shelter became so prosperous that the group donated money for Belton civic causes and thrived well into the 1890s.[144]

In 1916 Rokeya Sakhawat Hossain organized the Muslim Women's Association to offer assistance to widows and shelter for battered women in Calcutta's slums. In the years following the Russian Revolution, women in villages near the Caspian Sea set up special community centers to provide assistance to women, and the centers soon became shelters for those escaping battering husbands. Later that same decade, a women's shelter in the Hupeh province in China was established by one of the many women's unions set up during the Nationalist Revolution. These unions assisted women trying to divorce abusive husbands.[145]

Religious organizations in the United States were sheltering battered women long before the movement mobilized in the 1970s. Closely allied with Al-Anon, programs like Rainbow Retreat in Phoenix, Arizona, and Haven House in Pasadena, California, sheltered women abused by alcoholic husbands as early as the 1960s.[146]

In most cases, however, battered women had nowhere to go. Shelters were almost nonexistent, and medical, social service, and law enforcement agencies rarely provided battered women with the kind of support they needed.

Worldwide, women stopped hiding the violence in their lives and started helping each other during the 1970s. The British battered women's movement, that began a few years before the movement in the United States, was led by Erin Pizzey. Pizzey founded the first English shelter, Chiswick Women's Aid, in 1971.[147] Demonstrating an unrelenting determination in the battle to secure shelters for battered women, Pizzey brought international attention to the problem in her groundbreaking work, *Scream Quietly or the Neighbors Will Hear.*[148]

Women everywhere began to tell their stories. As they began to break the walls of isolation and shame, it became apparent that there was a worldwide epidemic of violence against women. Not only were women living with daily threats to their lives, but little was being done to guarantee their safety. Outraged at society's failure to address this problem, activists began to take matters into their own hands.

In Amsterdam, six women grew tired of waiting for social services to aid battered women. In September 1974, they occupied an abandoned house and established the shelter "Bliff van m'n Liff" (Hands off My Body).

That same year feminists in Sydney, Australia, took over two abandoned houses and refused to move out. These houses became Elsie, shelters for battered women. Feminists in Glasgow, Scotland, converted a three-bedroom apartment into the shelter Interval House. Across the Atlantic Ocean, Transition House opened in Vancouver, British Columbia.

On November 2, 1979, Danish feminists stormed the dilapidated Danner House demanding that the nineteenth-century palace be used to shelter women in need. After battling with the government, the women finally gained the right to the building. Even before renovations began battered women and their children were streaming through the doors.

Thereafter, wherever women began to speak the truth of what happened in the privacy of their homes, they discovered other women willing to unite with them in their pain. Crisis centers opened in Berlin and Barcelona, in Bogota and Tokyo. Battered women sought the help of their sisters in New Delhi and Jerusalem.

In 1981 in Thailand, Kanitha Wichiencharoen, an active member of the Women Lawyers' Association, founded that country's first shelter for battered women when she turned her home into a refuge. In 1989 the African country of Zimbabwe opened its first counseling service for survivors of rape and battering in the city of Harare.[149]

The Battered Women's Movement in the United States

Inspired by the feminist and antirape movement's analysis of male violence against women as a social and political issue, battered women in the United States began to speak out. The feminist assertion that women had the right to control their own bodies and lives resulted in the creation of women's hotlines and crisis centers, services that provided a context for battered women to ask for help.

Women's right to verbalize their pain without blame created an environment in which discussing violence was less shameful. The women's liberation movement helped create an atmosphere in which women could understand and speak about battering.

Formerly battered women and women who had witnessed violence in their families of origin were among the first to reach out to battered women. Whatever specific political label, if any, these women used, they brought a heartfelt commitment to the movement. Their experiences and strength were the force that started the movement.

Like their sisters who continue the work today, they were determined and persistent change agents who saw themselves as improving the world for women, children, and for their communities.[150] According to Susan Schechter, author of *Women and Male Violence: The Visions and Struggles of the Battered Women's Movement,* "Far from being monolithic or homogeneous, the battered women's movement incorporates differences among women in ideology, class, race, ethnicity, education, skill and knowledge level and sexual preference. The fight against battering, like those waged against other forms of male domination, bonds together diverse groups of women."[151]

In St. Paul, Minnesota, in March 1972, members of the Women's Advocates Collective started a legal information telephone service. They were surprised when most of the calls were from battered women. Advocates decided to provide shelter in their own homes, and for the next two years battered women and their children slept on their living-room floors. Finally, in October 1974, they moved into a shelter they had obtained.[152]

In 1975 a feminist women center, Women's Center South in Pittsburgh, evolved into a shelter for battered women. In 1976 Chris Womendez and Cherie Jimenez opened up their five-room apartment in Boston as a refuge for battered women. At the time they supported Transition House as well as themselves and two children on their welfare checks and small contributions from friends.[153]

In Austin, Texas, a grassroots coalition of women opened the Center for Battered Women in 1977. They quickly discovered, however, the magnitude of the problem and the lack of adequate shelter space. In 1980 the CBW was adopted by the Austin Association of Homebuilders, who proceeded to construct the first shelter in the United States specifically designed for battered women and their children.[154]

In the early 1970s the battered women's movement did more than create and expand a network of shelters and services for battered women and their children. Equally important was their role in heightening community awareness about domestic violence and promoting changes in the criminal justice system and other institutions.[155]

Operating on shoestring budgets, battered women's advocates began to open up formal programs around the United States. Only a handful of such programs existed in the mid 1970s. Today, there are more than twenty-five hundred shelters, hotlines, and safe home networks nationwide.[156] Individual programs may differ in philosophy and approach, but all share the conviction that no one deserves to be beaten and that battered women need special resources to end the violence in their lives.

Battered women's programs vary in size, type of services, and sources and levels of funding. Their most critical functions are to provide crisis intervention and safety provision for battered women and their children. Most programs operate twenty-four-hour hotlines. Typical shelter services include legal, economic, housing, and medical advocacy; court accompaniment; education and job-training assistance; support groups for residents and nonresidents; and child care and counseling programs for children. Some shelters now operate separate programs for abusive men.[157]

Although the growth in the number of battered women's programs over the last twenty years has been remarkable, many communities still have minimal or no services available to battered women. Programs are often inadequately funded and must turn away as many women as they help. Most rely heavily on donations and the continued grassroots efforts of volunteers.

Community support is an essential component of a successful shelter program. Generating this support can be difficult as many communities refuse to acknowledge the existence of domestic violence. In addition, advocates often struggle against the widely held misconception that shelters try to break up families, even though it is actually the violence that destroys families. Most shelters operate from a philosophy of supported self-help: women are given the opportunity to explore their options and resources in a safe environment to help them empower themselves to make their own decisions.

Gaining National Attention

In 1976 NOW announced the formation of a task force, cochaired by Del Martin, to examine the problem of battering. That same year, Martin published *Battered Wives,* the first American feminist publication illustrating that violence against wives is deeply rooted in sexism.[158] Her work proved to be a major source of information and validation for the movement.

The first national conference on battered women, held in Milwaukee, was sponsored by the Milwaukee Task Force on Battered Women.[159] Since then literally hundreds of conferences have been held by the battered women's movement, some of them serving as internal political and educational forums and others reaching out to educate the community. In all kinds of forums, grassroots service providers have found one another, shared information, worked on problems, and, through mutual support, lessened the pain of daily service delivery and organizing work.

Although providing shelter for abused women is a top priority of the battered women's movement, groups in the movement have organized in other ways too. In some cities, women representing a variety of organizations form coalitions. In 1976 Pennsylvania established the first state coalition against domestic violence. Services provided by these coalitions include workshops, educational materials, lobbying efforts, and support services for battered women's shelters and advocates. Coalitions are the vehicles through which lobbying and organizing have proceeded. As a result of their capacity to mobilize hundreds of women in lobbying efforts, state coalitions often prove their strength in legislative campaigns.

In 1977 the National Communications Network for the Elimination of Violence Against Women (NCN) published the first national newsletter on battered women. The following year, NCN merged with the Feminist Alliance Against Rape to publish *Aegis: The Magazine on Ending Violence Against Women,* a grassroots feminist forum on rape, battering, and other issues of violence affecting women.[160]

Aegis fulfilled many needs. It alleviated women's sense of isolation and offered inspiration. It provided insight and direction so that women could define their community as national rather than local. The magazine offered information and resources about legislation as well as political articles that provided the focal points for local, state, and regional discussions.[161]

At the same time these resources were being published and conferences were being held around the country, the idea of a national coalition was becoming a reality. As the grassroots battered women's movement gained public attention, a government response set the stage for further attempts at national organizing.

On July 20, 1977, the first White House meeting on battered women opened with the testimony of battered women followed by twelve carefully prepared statements by advocates. These advocates offered suggestions about how specific federal agencies and legislation could be improved. Although no substantial decisions were made, the movement used this meeting to build trust and support among an ever-increasing number of grassroots activists.

The International Women's Year conference in Houston in November 1977 provided the next opportunity for grassroots groups from all over the United States to organize themselves. A caucus on battered women met and decided again to develop a national feminist coalition based in local, autonomous grassroots programs.[162]

In 1978 the United States Commission on Civil Rights held "A Consultation on Battered Women" in Washington, D.C. These hearings brought together hundreds of concerned activists to clarify and define the needs of battered women and their children. The result of these two-day proceedings was the publication of *Battered Women: Issues of Public Policy*, which offered more than seven hundred pages of written and oral testimony.[163]

During the consultation the National Coalition Against Domestic Violence was formed. NCADV is the grassroots organization that serves as the voice of the battered women's movement on the national level. This national group established the vision and philosophy that guide the development of hundreds of local battered women's programs and state coalitions.[164]

NCADV remains the only national organization of grassroots shelter and service programs for battered women in the United States. Their efforts include coalition building at the local, state, regional, and national levels; support for the provision of safe homes and shelter programs for battered women and their children; public education; technical assistance; and public policy development.

The 1978 Civil Rights Commission hearings did far more than create the space for women to start a national organization. The hearings legitimized the needs of battered women, educated some federal agencies, and introduced those agencies to a new constituency. A movement had been born and was now recognized.

On April 27, 1979, President Carter created the Interdepartmental Committee on Domestic Violence, composed of representatives of twelve federal agencies and staff from the Office on Domestic Violence, formed on that same day. Many in the battered women's movement supported the establishment of the Office on Domestic Violence because it was seen as a potential federal advocate for battered women. During its brief existence, ODV worked hard for the passage of federal legislation. Activists and ODV staff worked together on legislative lobbying strategy, with ODV lending the legitimacy of its office to the struggle. This collaboration was short-lived, however. With the election of President Reagan in 1980, the ODV was dismantled.[165]

The same year a three-year dream came true as six hundred women from forty-nine states came to Washington, D.C., for NCADV's first official membership conference.[166] The conference gained federal recognition of critical issues facing battered women and witnessed the birth of several state coalitions.

As this grassroots movement continued to gain momentum, so did the heightened awareness of the problem of domestic violence. As a result of grassroots lobbying efforts, the Family Violence Prevention and Services Act was passed in 1984. This act earmarked federal funding for programs serving victims of domestic violence. In 1985 the United States Surgeon General issued a report identifying domestic violence as a major health problem.[167]

In 1987 NCADV established the first national toll-free domestic violence hotline. The hotline closed in 1992; however, because of the unrelenting efforts of the Texas Council on Family Violence, the National Domestic Violence Hotline received federal funding and reopened on February 21, 1996.

The Violence Against Women Act was passed in 1994 and provided millions of dollars of funding for a variety of programs and services, including shelters, child abuse, rape prevention, judicial training, community programs, youth education, and campus assault (see *Additional Resources*).

The many changes that have occurred in the last twenty years can be attributed to the battered women's movement. Some of these important changes include improved data collection about domestic violence, laws in all fifty states that identify domestic violence as a criminal act, availability of civil protection orders, increased reporting of domestic violence cases in police departments and hospitals, and recognition of the problem on a national level.

While much has been accomplished in the last twenty years, there is more work to be done. Sheltering battered women and their children, effecting systematic changes, educating the community about domestic violence, and promoting victims' rights remain ongoing challenges. The incredible people that make up this movement are ready for the task, however, and continue to unselfishly share themselves, their time, their energy, and their money to assure that no woman or child need ever cry out in fear and pain.

Appendix I: Safety

Safety When Preparing to Leave

1. Make arrangements to go to a place that is safe. This may be with trusted friends, relatives, or at a hotel.
2. Keep a bag packed and hidden that contains clothes and personal hygiene items. You should also pack money; extra checks or a checkbook; charge cards; important papers such as a protective order; birth certificates; marriage license; children's immunization records; titles to property or cars; and telephone numbers of friends, relatives, and shelters. You may want to pack anything which has personal value to you, such as photographs, that you do not want destroyed. If you have space, pack one or two of your children's toys.
3. To avoid jeopardizing your safety, hide the bag where it will not be discovered by your partner, perhaps leaving it with trusted friends, relatives, or at work.
4. Hide an extra set of house keys and car keys in a place that is easily accessible to you.

Safety During a Violent Episode

1. Make a safety plan in advance, in case you need to leave your home quickly.
2. If an argument seems unavoidable, try to have it in a room from which you can easily get away. Try to stay away from rooms where weapons might be available, including the bathroom, kitchen, and bedroom.
3. Identify in advance the doors, windows, or stairways that would allow you to get out of your home quickly and safely.

4. Identify trusted neighbors that you can tell about the violence, and ask that they call the police if they hear a disturbance coming from your home.
5. Devise a code word to use with your children, trusted family members, friends, and neighbors when you need them to call the police.

Workplace Safety

1. Decide who at work you will inform of your situation. This can include a supervisor, a staff person in the employee assistance program or human resource department, and security personnel.
2. Provide a picture of your batterer to the appropriate persons.
3. Ask for help screening your telephone calls at work.
4. Review your work schedule with your supervisor and ask about changing your work hours.
5. Ask your supervisor about changing your workstation.
6. Review the parking situation. If possible, try to park close to the building for easy entry and exit.
7. Ask someone to escort you to and from your vehicle. Ask them to wait until you are safely on your way.
8. Try to use a variety of routes to and from your home. Plan what you would do if something happened while you were going home.
9. Provide your contacts at work with the name and telephone number of an emergency contact person in case you cannot be reached. This person should be someone other than your abusive partner and should be someone you trust.
10. If you need to take a leave from work, provide your address or telephone number to a trusted company contact person.
11. If you need to permanently leave your community, ask whether your company has a relocation program and how it operates.

Appendix II: The Advocacy Wheel

Developed by the Domestic Violence Project, Inc., Kenosha, Wisconsin, modeled after the "Power & Control and Equality Wheels" developed by the Domestic Abuse Intervention Project, Duluth, Minnesota.

Notes

Chapter 1

1. National Coalition Against Domestic Violence, "Fact Sheet," Washington D.C., 1993.
2. Walker, L., *The Battered Woman,* Harper and Row, NY, 1979, p. 21.
3. National Woman Abuse Prevention Project, "Domestic Violence Fact Sheet: Men Who Batter," Washington D.C., no date.
4. Herman, J., *Trauma and Recovery,* BasicBooks, NY, 1992, pp. 74-95.
5. Pence, E., *In Our Best Interest: A Process for Personal and Social Change,* Minnesota Program Development, Duluth, MN, 1987.
6. Pence, E. and Paymar, M., *Education Groups for Men Who Batter: The Duluth Model,* Springer Publishing Company, NY, 1993, p. 2.
7. Graham, D.L., Rawlings, E. and Rimini, N., "Survivors of Terror: Battered Women, Hostages and the Stockholm Syndrome," in K. Yllo and M. Bogard (eds.), *Feminist Perspectives on Wife Abuse,* Sage Publications, Newbury Park, CA, 1988, pp. 217-233.
8. Rich, A., *On Lies, Secrets, and Silence,* W.W. Norton and Company, NY, 1979, p. 122. See also Pence, E., 1987.
9. Ferraro, K.J., "Rationalizing Violence: How Battered Women Stay," *Victimology,* 1983, 8, pp. 203-212.
10. Walker, L., 1979, pp. 49-61.
11. Project for Victims of Family Violence, Inc., "Warning Signs: How to Spot a Potential Batterer," Fayetteville, Arkansas, no date.
12. National Coalition Against Domestic Violence, 1993.
13. National Woman Abuse Prevention Project, "Domestic Violence Fact Sheet: The Lethality of Domestic Violence," Washington D.C., no date.

Chapter 2

1. Carlson, B.E., "Children's Observations of Interparental Violence," in A.R. Roberts (ed.), *Battered Women and Their Families,* Springer, New York, 1984, pp. 147-167.
2. National Coalition Against Domestic Violence, Fact Sheet, Washington D.C., 1993.
3. Martin, D., *Battered Wives,* Volcano Press, Volcano, CA, 1981, pp. 22-24.
4. National Coalition Against Domestic Violence, 1993.

5. Jaffe, P.G., Wolfe, D.A. and Wilson, S.K., *Children of Battered Women,* Sage Publications, Newbury Park, CA, 1990, pp. 26-42.
6. Ibid, pp. 28-29.
7. Sroufe, L.A. and Fleeson, J., "Attachment and the Construction of Relationships," in W.W. Hartup and Z. Rubin (eds.), *Relationships and Development,* Lawrence Erlbaum, Hillsdale, NJ, 1986, pp. 51-72.
8. Wolfe, D.A., Zak, L., Wilson, S. and Jaffe, P., "Child Witnesses to Violence Between Parents: Critical Issues in Behavioral and Social Adjustment," *Journal of Abnormal Child Psychology,* 1986, 14(1), pp. 95-104.
9. Hughes, H.M., "Research With Children in Shelters: Implications for Clinical Services," *Children Today,* 1986, pp. 21-25.
10. Hyde, M., *Cry Softly!: The Story of Child Abuse,* The Westminister Press, Philadelphia, 1986, pp. 28-29.
11. Jaffe, P.G., et al., 1990, pp. 27-31.
12. Matthews, R. and Richmond, S. (eds.), *What Will Happen Next?*
13. American Psychiatric Association, Diagnostic and Statistical Manual of Mental Disorders, Washington, D.C., 1987.
14. Garmezy, N., "Stressors in Childhood," in N. Garmezy and M. Rutter (eds.), *Stress, Coping and Development in Children,* McGraw Hill, New York, 1983, pp. 43-84.
15. Hess, R.D. and Camara, K.A., "Post-divorce Family Relationships as Mediating Factors in the Consequences of Divorce for Children," *Journal of Social Issues,* 1979, 35, pp. 79-96.
16. Kurdek, L.A., "An Integrative Perspective on Children's Divorce Adjustment," *American Psychologist,* 1981, 36, pp. 856-866.

Chapter 3

1. From *In Touch with Teens: A Relationship Violence Prevention Curriculum for Youth Ages 12-19,* Los Angeles Commission on Assaults Against Women, Los Angeles, 1993, 1995. "Eddie's Got a Fast Car" is reprinted with permission.
2. Levy, B. (ed.), *Dating Violence: Young Women in Danger,* Seal Press, Seattle, WA, 1991, p. 3.
3. See Cate, R.M., Henton, J.M., Koval, J., Christopher, F.S. and Lloyd, S., "Premarital Abuse: A Social Psychological Perspective," *Journal of Family Issues,* 3, 1982, pp. 79-91. See also Henton, J., Cate, R., Koval, J., Lloyd, S. and Christopher, S., "Romance and Violence in Dating Relationships," *Journal of Family Issues,* 4, 1983, pp. 467-482; Makepeace, J.M., "Courtship Violence Among College Students," *Family Relations,* 30,

1981, pp. 97-102; Roscoe, B. and Callahan, J.E., "Adolescents Self Report of Violence in Families and Dating Relations," *Adolescence,* 20, 1985, pp. 545-553.

4. Levy, B., 1991, p. 4.
5. Kanin, E.J., "Male Aggression in Dating-Courtship Relations," *Journal of Sociology,* 63, 1957, pp. 197-204.
6. Henton, J., et al., 1983, pp. 467-482. See also Laner, M.R. and Thompson, J., "Abuse and Aggression in Courting Couples," *Deviant Behavior,* 3, 1982, pp. 229-244.
7. Cate, R.M., et al., 1982, pp. 79-91. See also Henton, J., et al., 1983, pp. 467-482.
8. Malamuth, N.M., "Rape Proclivity Among Males," *Journal of Social Issues,* 37, 4, 1981, pp. 138-157.
9. Sugarman, D.B. and Hotaling, G.T., "Dating Violence: A Review of Contextual and Risk Factors," in Levy, B. (ed.), *Dating Violence: Young Women in Danger,* Seal Press, Seattle, WA, 1991, pp. 106-107.
10. Dutton, D.G., "Wife Assaulter's Explanation for Assault: The Neutralization of Self-Punishment," *Canadian Journal of Behavioral Science,* 18, 4, 1986, pp. 381-390.
11. Levy, B., 1991, pp. 8-9.
12. Nicarthy, G., *Getting Free,* Seal Press, Seattle, WA, 1986, p. 269.
13. Giggans, P.O., "Youth in Jeopardy," *Livewire,* 4, 1, Fall, 1992, p. 1.
14. Nicarthy, G., "Addictive Love and Abuse: A Course for Teenage Women," in Levy, B. (ed.), *Dating Violence: Young Women in Danger,* Seal Press, Seattle, WA, 1991, pp. 241-243.
15. Johnson, S.A., *When "I Love You" Turns Violent: Abuse in Dating Relationships,* New Horizon Press, Far Hills, NJ, 1993, pp. 75-83.
16. Kessner, E., "Sweetheart Murders: When Teen Boyfriends Turn into Killers," *Redbook,* March, 1988, pp. 130-189.
17. Gamache, D., "Domination and Control: The Social Context of Dating Violence," in Levy, B. (ed.), *Dating Violence: Young Women in Danger,* Seal Press, Seattle, WA, 1991, pp. 76-77.
18. Makepeace, J.M., 1981, pp. 97-102. See also Roscoe, B. and Callahan, J.E., 1985, pp. 545-553; Roscoe, B. and Kelsey, T., "Dating Violence Among High School Students," *Psychology,* 23, 1, 1986, pp. 53-59.
19. Lane, K.E. and Gwartney-Gibbs, P.A., "Violence in the Context of Dating and Sex," *Journal of Family Issues,* 6, 1, 1985, pp. 45-59.
20. Levy, B., 1991, p. 9.
21. Fisher, G.J., "College Student Attitudes Toward Forcible Date Rape," *Archives of Sexual Behavior,* 15, 6, 1986, pp. 457-467.

22. Miller, B. and Marshall, J., "Coercive Sex on the University Campus," *Journal of College Student Personnel,* 28, 1, 1987, pp. 38-47.
23. Levy, B., 1991, pp. 4-5.
24. Gamache, D., p. 74.
25. Pirog-Good, M.A. and Stets, J.E., "The Help Seeking Behavior of Physically and Sexually Abused College Students," in Pirog-Good, M.A. and Stets, J.E. (eds.), *Violence in Dating Relationships: Emerging Social Issues,* Praeger Publishers, New York, 1989, pp. 108-125. See also Henton, J., et al., 1983, pp. 467-482; Makepeace, J.M., 1981, pp. 97-102; Stets, J.E. and Pirog-Good, M.A., "Patterns of Physical and Sexual Abuse for Men and Women in Dating Relationships: A Descriptive Analysis," *Journal of Family Violence,* 4, 1, 1989, pp. 63-76.
26. Levy, B., 1991, p. 5.
27. McFarlane, J., "Battering in Pregnancy: The Tip of the Iceberg," *Women and Health,* 15, 3, 1989, pp. 69-84. See also Campbell, J., "Nursing Assessment for Risk of Homicide with Battered Women," *Advances in Nursing Science,* 8, 4, 1986, pp. 36-51.
28. McFarlane, J., "Violence During Teen Pregnancy: Health Consequences for Mother and Child," in Levy, B. (ed.), *Dating Violence: Young Women in Danger,* Seal Press, Seattle, WA, 1991, pp. 136-137. See also Stark, E. and Flitcraft, A., *Women at Risk: Domestic Violence and Women's Health,* Sage Publications, Thousand Oaks, CA, 1996, p. 17.
29. Bullock, L. and McFarlane, J., "A Program to Prevent Battering of Pregnant Students," *Response,* 11, 1, 1988, pp. 18-19.
30. Stark, E. and Flitcraft, A., p. 11; 204. See also McFarlane, J., 1991, pp. 137-141.
31. See White, E.C., *Chain Chain Change: For Black Women Dealing With Physical and Emotional Abuse,* Seal Press, Seattle, WA, 1985.
32. White, E.C., "The Abused Black Woman: Challenging a Legacy of Pain," in Levy, B. (ed.), *Dating Violence: Young Women in Danger,* Seal Press, Seattle, WA, 1991, pp. 85-86.
33. Levy, B., 1991, pp. 6-7.
34. Yoshihama, M., Parekh, A. and Boyington, D., "Dating Violence in Asian/Pacific Communities," in Levy, B. (ed.), *Dating Violence: Young Women in Danger,* Seal Press, Seattle, WA, 1991, p. 192.
35. Symonds, M., "Victims of Violence: Psychological Effects and After-Effects," *American Journal of Psychoanalysis,* 35, 1975, pp. 19-26.
36. Yoshihama, et al., pp. 188-193.
37. Ibid., pp. 189-190.

38. Levy, B. and Lobel, K., "Lesbian Teens in Abusive Relationships," in Levy, B. (ed.), *Dating Violence: Young Women in Danger,* Seal Press, Seattle, WA, 1991, pp. 205-206.
39. Ibid., pp. 206-207.
40. Roscoe, B. and Callahan, J.E., pp. 545-553. See also Lane, K.E. and Gwartney-Gibbs, P.A., pp. 45-59.
41. Henton, J., et al., 1983, pp. 467-482. See also Makepeace, J.M., "Gender Differences in Courtship Violence Victimization," *Family Relations,* 35, 1986, pp. 383-388.
42. National Victim Center and Crime Victims Research and Treatment Center, "Rape in America: A Report to the Nation," Arlington, VA, April, 1992.
43. Steketee, M.S.S. and Foa, E.B., "Rape Victims: Post-Traumatic Stress Responses and Their Treatment," *Journal of Anxiety Disorders,* 1, 1987, pp. 69-86.
44. Gallers, J. and Lawrence, K.J., "Overcoming Post-Traumatic Stress Disorder in Adolescent Date Rape Survivors," in Levy, B. (ed.), *Dating Violence: Young Women in Danger,* Seal Press, Seattle, WA, 1991, p. 172.
45. Ibid., p. 174.
46. Ibid., pp. 173-174.
47. Sousa, C., Bancroft, L. and German, T., *Preventing Teen Dating Violence: Three Session Curriculum for Teaching Adolescents, Dating Intervention Project,* Cambridge, MA, 1989.
48. Texas Council on Family Violence and the Bridge Over Troubled Waters, *Dating Violence: An Anti-Victimization Program,* Austin, TX, no date. See also Johnson, S., pp. 175-176.
49. Schechter, S., *Guidelines for Mental Health Practioners in Domestic Violence,* National Coalition Against Domestic Violence, Denver, CO, 1987.
50. Nicarthy, G., 1986, pp. 274-275.
51. Bartels, D., "What Teens Do and Don't Need From Adults and Peers," Austin Center for Battered Women, Austin, TX, no date.
52. Levy, B., 1991, p. 7.
53. Sugarman, D.B. and Hotaling, G.T., pp. 116-117.
54. See Levy, B., "Support Groups: Empowerment for Young Women Abused in Dating Relationships," in Levy, B. (ed.), *Dating Violence: Young Women in Danger,* Seal Press, Seattle, WA, 1991, pp. 232-239.
55. See Rosenbluth, B., *Expect Respect: A Support Group Curriculum for Preventing Teenage Dating Violence and Promoting Healthy Relationships,* Teen Dating Violence Project, Austin Center for Battered Women, Austin, TX, August, 1995.

Chapter 4

1. Gelles, R.J., "Alcohol and Other Drugs Are Associated With Violence—They Are Not Its Cause," in Gelles, R.J. and Loseke, D.R. (eds.), *Current Controversies on Family Violence,* Sage Publications, Newbury Park, CA, 1993, p. 184.
2. Byles, J.A., "Violence, Alcohol Problems and Other Problems in the Disintegrating Family," Journal of Studies on Alcohol, 39, 1978, pp. 551-553. See also Coleman, D.H. and Straus, M.A., "Alcohol Abuse and Family Violence," in Gottheil, E., Druley, K., Skoloda, T. and Waxman, H. (eds.), *Alcohol, Drug Abuse and Aggression,* Charles C. Thomas, Springfield, IL, pp. 104-124; Leonard, K.E., Bromet, E.J., Parkinson, D.K., Day, N.L. and Ryan, C.M., "Patterns of Alcohol Use and Physically Aggressive Behavior," *Journal of Studies on Alcohol,* 46, 1985, pp. 279-282; Kaufman Kantor, G. and Straus, M.A., "Substance Abuse as a Precipitant of Wife Abuse Victimization," *American Journal of Alcohol Abuse,* 15, 1989, pp. 173-189; Martin, S.E., "The Epidemiology of Alcohol-Related Interpersonal Violence," *Alcohol Health and Research World,* 16, 1992, pp. 230-237.
3. Roy, M., "Four Thousand Partners in Violence: A Trend Analysis," in Roy, M. (ed.), *The Abusive Partner: An Analysis of Domestic Battering,* Van Nostrand Reinhold, New York, 1982, pp. 17-35. See also Rosenbaum, A. and O'Leary, K.D., "Marital Violence: Characteristics of Abusive Couples," *Journal of Consulting and Clinical Psychology,* 49, 1981, pp. 63-71; Browne, A., When Battered Women Kill, The Free Press, New York, 1987, pp. 12-71; Fagan, J.A., Stewart, D.K. and Hansen, K.V., "Violent Men or Violent Husbands: Background Factors and Situational Correlates," in Finkelhor, D., Gelles, R.J., Hotaling, G.T. and Straus, M.A. (eds.), *The Dark Side of Families,* Sage Publications, Beverly Hills, CA, 1983, pp. 49-67; Gondolf, E.W. and Fisher, E.R., Battered Women as Survivors: An Alternative to Treating Learned Helplessness, Lexington Books, Lexington, Massachusetts, 1988, pp. 6-7; Eberle, P., "Alcohol Abusers and Non-Users: A Discriminant Analysis of Differences Between Two Subgroups of Batterers," *Journal of Health and Social Behavior,* 23, 3, September, 1982, pp. 260-271; Fitch, F. and Papantonio, A., "Men Who Batter: Some Pertinent Characteristics," *Journal of Nervous and Mental Diseases,* 171, 3, March, 1983, pp. 190-192.
4. Browne, A., pp. 12-73. See also Eberle, P., pp. 260-271; Flanzer, J.P., "Alcohol and Family Violence: Double Trouble," in Roy, M. (ed.), *The Abusive Partner: An Analysis of Domestic Battering,* Van Nostrand Reinhold, New York, 1982, pp. 136-141; Fagan, J.A., et al., pp. 49-67.

5. Fitch, F., et al., pp. 190-192. See also Browne, A., pp. 12-71.
6. Miller, M.M. and Potter-Efron, R.T., "Aggression and Violence Associated With Substance Abuse," in Potter-Efron, R.T. and Potter-Efron, P.S. (eds.), *Aggression, Family Violence and Chemical Dependency,* Haworth Press, New York, 1990, pp. 1-36. See also Gelles, R.J. and Straus, M.A., *Intimate Violence,* Simon and Schuster, New York, 1988, pp. 46-48.
7. Gelles, R.J., 1993, pp. 187-188. See also Nicholi, A., "The Non-Therapeutic Use of Psychoactive Drugs," *New England Journal of Medicine,* 308, 1983, pp. 925-933; Taylor, S. and Leonard, K.E., "Alcohol and Human Physical Aggression," in Green, R. and Donnerstein, E. (eds.), *Aggression: Theoretical and Empirical Reviews, Vol. 2,* Academic Press, New York, 1983, pp. 77-111; Miller, M.M., et al., 1988, pp. 46-48.
8. Martin, D., *Battered Wives,* Volcano Press, Volcano, CA, 1981, p. 57.
9. Gondolf, E.W., "Alcohol Abuse, Wife Assault and Power Needs," in *The Relationship Between Substance Abuse and Domestic Violence,* compiled by the Texas Council on Family Violence, Austin, Texas, July, 1994, pp. 42-43. See also Gelles, R.J. and Straus, M.A., 1988, pp. 45-46.
10. See MacAndrew, C. and Edgerton, R.B., *Drunken Comportment: A Social Explanation,* Aldine, Chicago, 1969.
11. Lang, A.R., Goeckner, D.J., Adesso, V.J. and Marlatt, G.A., "Effects of Alcohol on Aggression in Male Social Drinkers," *Journal of Abnormal Psychology,* 84, 1975, pp. 508-518.
12. Bard, M. and Zacker, J., "Assaultiveness and Alcohol Use in Family Disputes," *Criminology,* 12, 1974, pp. 281-292.
13. See Flanzer, J.P., "Alcohol and Other Drugs are Key Causal Agents of Violence," in Gelles, R.J. and Loseke, D.R. (eds.), *Current Controversies on Family Violence,* Sage Publications, Newbury Park, CA, 1993, pp. 171-179.
14. Martin, D., p. 57. See also Browne, A., p. 73.
15. Gondolf, E.W., p. 40.
16. Zubretsky, T.M. and Digirolamo, K.M., "Adult Domestic Violence: The Alcohol Connection," *Violence Update,* 4, 7, March, 1994, pp. 1-2.
17. Gondolf, E.W., p. 40.
18. Lemle, R. and Mishkind, M., "Alcohol and Masculinity," *Journal of Substance Abuse Treatment,* 6, 1989, pp. 213-222. See also Lisansky Gomberg, E.S., "Learned Helplessness, Depression and Alcohol Problems of Women," in Russianoff, P. (ed.), *Women in Crisis,* Human Science Press, New York, 1981, pp. 41-42.
19. Gelles, R.J., 1993, p. 194.
20. DiMona, L. and Herndon, C. (eds.), *The 1995 Women's Sourcebook,* Houghton Mifflin Company, Boston, 1994, p. 204. See also Texas

Commission on Alcohol and Drug Abuse, New View, Austin, TX, September, 1992, pp. 4-5.

21. National Council on Alcoholism, Inc., "Alcoholism and Alcohol-Related Problems Among Women," Washington, D.C., December, 1985. See also DiMona, L. and Herndon, C. (eds.), pp. 203-204.
22. Lisansky Gomberg, E.S., pp. 41-42. See also National Institute on Drug Abuse (NIDA), "Women and Drug Abuse," Rockville, Maryland, March, 1994, p. 2.
23. Stark, E. and Flitcraft, A., *Women at Risk: Domestic Violence and Women's Health,* Sage Publications, Thousand Oaks, CA, 1996, pp. 8-18/162-163. See also Gelles, R.J. and Straus, M.A., pp. 136-137.
24. National Woman Abuse Prevention Project, "Domestic Violence Factsheet: Alcohol Abuse and Domestic Violence," Washington, D.C., no date.
25. Ibid; See also Stark, E. and Flitcraft, A., p. 185; Thorne-Finch, R., *Ending the Silence,* University of Toronto Press, Toronto, Canada, 1992, p. 41.
26. Herman, J.L., *Trauma and Recovery,* Basic Books, New York, 1992, pp. 42-45.
27. Stark, E. and Flitcraft, A., pp. 95-102. See also Jones, A., *Next Time She'll Be Dead,* Beacon Press, Boston, 1994, pp. 145-152.
28. Friedman, C., "Alcohol and Other Drug Abuse in the Lives of Battered Women and Their Children," *NCADV Voice, Special Edition: Chemical Dependency, Co-Dependency and Battered Women,* National Coalition Against Domestic Violence, Denver, CO, Summer, 1988, p. 16.
29. Herman, J.L., p. 78. See also NIDA, "Women and Drug Abuse," p. 2.
30. Beckman, L. and Amaro, H., "Patterns of Women's Use of Alcohol Treatment Agencies," in Wilsnack, S. and Beckman, L. (eds.), *Alcohol Problems in Women,* Guilford Press, New York, 1984, p. 342. See also Zubretsky, T.M. and Digirolamo, K.M., p. 3.
31. Herman, J.L., p. 161.
32. Haven House and the Alcoholism Center for Women, "Double Jeopardy: A Two Day Training for Those Working in the Alcohol or Domestic Violence Fields," California State University, Los Angeles, CA, March 20-21, 1987, pp. 17-24.
33. Ibid, pp. 1-14. See also Black, C., *It Will Never Happen To Me,* Ballantine Books, New York, 1981, pp. 149-151.
34. Black, C., p. 150.
35. Grusznski, R.J. and Carrillo, T., "Who Completes Batterer's Treatment Groups?: An Empirical Investigation," *Journal of Family Violence,* 3, 1988, pp. 141-150. See also Cocozzelli, C. and Hudson, C., "Recent Advances in

Alcoholism Diagnosis and Treatment Assessment Research: Implications for Practice," Social Science Review, 37, 1989, pp. 533-552.

36. Battered women's advocates may want to attend an AA, NA or Al-Anon meeting. It would also be helpful to familiarize yourself with AA's Twelve Steps and Twelve Traditions. Likewise, substance abuse counselors may want to read more about the battered women's movement and the philosophies upon which we are based. There are several excellent books about battered women listed throughout this book; however, an excellent introductory reference is Del Martin's *Battered Wives.*
37. See Alcoholics Anonymous World Services, Inc., Alcoholics Anonymous, New York, 1976.
38. Gondolf, E.W., p. 48.
39. Ibid, pp. 49-50.
40. Ibid, p. 49.
41. Black, C., p. 163.
42. See Al-Anon Family Group Headquarters, Inc., Al-Anon Family Groups, New York, 1986.
43. Zubretsky, T.M. and Digirolamo, K.M., p. 3.
44. Texas Council on Family Violence, "Points to Remember in Working With Battered Women," Austin, TX, no date.
45. DiMona, L. and Herndon, C., p. 204.
46. Blume, S., "Women, Alcohol and Drugs," in Miller, N.S. (ed.), *Comprehensive Handbook of Drug and Alcohol Addiction,* Marcel Dekker, Inc., New York, 1991, pp. 147-177.
47. Austin Women's Addiction Referral and Education Center (AWARE), "Things to Ponder," Austin, TX, no date.
48. Zubretsky, T.M. and Digirolamo, K.M., p. 3.
49. Hortensia, A., Beckman, L. and Mays, V., "A Comparison of Black and White Women Entering Alcoholism Treatment," Journal of Studies on Alcohol, 48, 1987, pp. 220-228.
50. AWARE, "Things to Ponder."
51. DiMona, L. and Herndon, C., p. 203.
52. NIDA, "Women and Drug Abuse," p. 3.
53. National Council on Alcoholism, Inc., "Alcoholism and Alcohol-Related Problems Among Women."
54. See Unterberger, G., "Twelve Steps for Women Alcoholics," The Christian Century, December 6, 1989, pp. 1150-1152. See also Clemmons, P., "Feminists, Spirituality, and the Twelve Steps of Alcoholics Anonymous," *Women and Therapy,* 11, 2, 1991, pp. 97-109.

Chapter 5

1. Buzawa, E.S. and C.G., *Domestic Violence: The Criminal Justice Response,* Sage Publications, Thousand Oaks, CA, 1996, p. 243.
2. Texas Council on Family Violence, *Working Together for Change: Battered Women's Advocates and the Criminal Justice System,* Austin, TX, 1994, Section III, p. 2.
3. Deller Ross, S., Katz Pinzler, I., Ellis, D.A. and Moss, K.L., *The Rights of Women: The Basic ACLU Guide to Women's Rights,* Southern Illinois University Press, Carbondale, IL, 1993, p. 155.
4. Ibid, p. 156. See also Finn, P. and Colson, S., *Civil Protection Orders: Legislation, Current Court Practice and Enforcement,* National Institute of Justice, Office of Justice Programs, U.S. Department of Justice, Washington, D.C., March, 1990, pp. v-1; Buzawa, E.S. and Buzawa, C.G., *Domestic Violence: The Criminal Justice Response,* Sage Publications, Thousand Oaks, CA, 1996, p. 188.
5. Deller Ross, S., et al., p. 156.
6. Finn, P. and Colson, S., pp. 2-3.
7. Ibid, p. 3.
8. National Institute of Justice, *Domestic Violence, Stalking, and Antistalking Legislation: Annual Report to Congress,* Office of Justice Programs, U.S. Department of Justice, Washington, D.C., March, 1996, p. 9.
9. Finn, P. and Colson, S., p. 15.
10. Ibid, p. 2.
11. Newmark, L. and Harrell, A., "Study on Civil Protection Orders," *NCADV Voice,* Winter, 1994, pp. 16-17.
12. Finn, P. and Colson, S., p. 2.
13. Ibid, p. 15.
14. Nickum, L.L., "The Protective Order Experience," *The River,* Summer/Fall, 1994, p. 5.
15. Finn, P. and Colson, S., p. 63.
16. Ibid, p. 49.
17. Ibid, p. 4.
18. National Institute of Justice, p. 9.
19. Lardner, G., "The Stalking Game," *The Washington Post,* June 2, 1996.
20. National Institute of Justice, p. 1.
21. Ibid, p. 9.
22. Ibid, pp. 3-4.
23. Ibid, pp. 6-7.
24. Ibid, p. 6.

25. Herman, K., "Anti-Stalking Law Rejected by State Court," *The Austin American Statesman,* September 12, 1996.
26. National Institute of Justice, p. 4.
27. Ibid, p. B-2.
28. Walls, L.F., "Stalked!," *NCADV Voice,* Winter, 1994, pp. 2-5.
29. Deller Ross, S., et al., pp. 157-158.
30. Ibid, pp. 158-159.
31. Ibid, p. 160.
32. National Council of Juvenile and Family Court Judges, Family Violence: Improving Court Practice, Washington, D.C., 28, 1990.
33. Deller Ross, S., et al., pp. 160-161.
34. Ibid, p. 161. See also Robson, R., *Lesbian (Out)Law: Survival Under the Rule of Law,* Firebrand Books, Ithaca, NY, 1992, pp. 157-167.

Chapter 6

1. Bryant, D., *The Promise of a New Day: A Book of Daily Meditations,* Hazelden Educational Materials, Center City, MN.
2. See Culligan, J., *When In Doubt Check Him Out: A Woman's Survival Guide for the '90s,* Hallmark Press, Incorporated, 1993.
3. Girdner, L.K. and Hoff, P.M., *Obstacles to the Recovery and Return of Parentally Abducted Children: Research Summary,* Office of Juvenile Justice and Delinquency Prevention, Office of Justice Programs, U.S. Department of Justice, Washington, D.C., March, 1994, p. 4.
4. National Center on Women and Family Law, Inc., "Battered Women: Procedure for Change of Name and Social Security Number," New York, 1995, p. 1.
5. Ibid, pp. 1-2.
6. Culligan, J., pp. 2-35.
7. Ibid, pp. 51-73.

Chapter 7

1. Lorde, A., "An Open Letter to Mary Daly," in Lorde, A., *Sister Outsider,* The Crossing Press, Freedom, CA, 1984, p. 70.
2. See Pence, E., *In Our Best Interest: A Process for Personal and Social Change,* Minnesota Program Development, Inc., 1987.
3. Comas-Di'az, L. and Greene, B., "Overview: An Ethnocultural Mosaic," in Comas-Di'az, L. and Greene, B. (eds.), *Women of Color: Integrating Ethnic and Gender Identities in Psychotherapy,* NY, 1994, p. 7.
4. White, E.C., *Chain Chain Change: For Black Women Dealing With Physical and Emotional Abuse,* The Seal Press, Seattle, WA, 1985, pp. 20-21.

5. Ibid, pp. 61-62.
6. Ibid, pp. 63-65.
7. Ibid, p. 25.
8. Greene, B., "African American Women," in Comas-Di'az, L. and Greene, B. (eds.), *Women of Color: Integrating Ethnic and Gender Identities in Psychotheraphy,* NY, 1994, p. 15.
9. White, E.C., p. 44.
10. Zambrano, M.M., *Mejor Sola Que Mal Acompanada: For the Latina in an Abusive Relationship,* The Seal Press, Seattle, WA, 1985, p. 226.
11. Ibid, pp. 225-227.
12. Ibid, p. 227.
13. Ibid, p. 131.
14. Lum, J., "Battered Asian Women," *Rice,* March, 1988, pp. 50-52.
15. Ibid.
16. Ibid.
17. Das Dasgupta, S. and Warrier, S., *In Visible Terms: Domestic Violence in the Asian Indian Context,* Manavi, PO Box 614, Bloomfield, NJ 07003, 1995, p. 3.
18. Ibid, pp. 11-12.
19. Ibid, pp. 7-8.
20. DasGupta, K., "Asian Indian Women: Guidelines for Community Intervention in the Event of Abuse," *Family Violence and Sexual Assault Bulletin,* 9, 4, 1993, pp. 27-28.
21. Das Dasgupta, S. and Warrier, S., p. 20.
22. DasGupta, K., p. 26.
23. Ibid, pp. 27-28.
24. Chester, B., Robin, R.W., Koss, M.P., Lopez, J. and Goldman, D., "Grandmother Dishonored: Violence Against Women by Male Partners in American Indian Communities," *Violence and Victims,* 9 ,3, 1994, pp. 249-258.
25. Ibid.
26. Mousseau, M. and Artichoker, K., *Domestic Violence is Not Lakota/Dakota Tradition,* South Dakota Coalition Against Domestic Violence and Sexual Assault and Project Medicine Wheel, no date, p. 2.
27. Chester, B., et al., pp. 249-258.
28. Ibid.
29. Mousseau, M. and Artichoker, K., p. 3.
30. Chester, B., et al., pp. 249-258.
31. Ibid.
32. State Bar of Texas, *Violence Against Women Act (VAWA): Implications for Battered Immigrant Spouses and Children,* Austin, Texas, 1995, p. 9.

33. Ibid, p. 2.
34. Ibid, pp. 3-4.
35. See Department of Human Services Family Violence Advisory Committee, *Survey on Undocumented Battered Women,* Texas Department of Human Services, Austin, TX, 1992.
36. Nyakabwa, K. and Harvey, C.D.H., "Adaptation to Canada: The Case of Black Immigrant Women," in Dhruvarajan, V. (ed.), *Women and Well-Being,* McGill-Queen's University Press, Montreal, Canada, 1990, p. 143.
37. State Bar of Texas, pp. 4-5.
38. Nyakabwa, K. and Harvey, C.D.H., p. 144.
39. Renzetti, C.M., *Violent Betrayal: Partner Abuse in Lesbian Relationships,* Sage Publications, Newbury Park, CA, 1992, p. 115.
40. Pharr, S., "Two Workshops on Homophobia," in Lobel, K. (ed.) for the National Coaltion Against Domestic Violence Lesbian Task Force, *Naming the Violence: Speaking Out About Lesbian Battering,* The Seal Press, Seattle, WA, 1986, p. 204.
41. Pharr, S., *Homophobia: A Weapon of Sexism,* Chardon Press, Inverness, CA, 1988, p. 1.
42. Hart, B., "Lesbian Battering: An Examination," in Lobel, K. (ed.) for the National Coalition Against Domestic Violence Lesbian Task Force, *Naming the Violence: Speaking Out About Lesbian Battering,* The Seal Press, Seattle, WA, 1986, pp. 183-185.
43. Benowitz, M., "How Homophobia Affects Lesbians' Response to Violence in Lesbian Relationships," in Lobel, K. (ed.) for the National Coalition Against Domestic Violence Lesbian Task Force, *Naming the Violence: Speaking Out About Lesbian Battering,* The Seal Press, Seattle, WA, 1986, p. 199.
44. Renzetti, C.M., p. 131.
45. Hammond, N., "Lesbian Victims and the Reluctance to Identify Abuse," in Lobel, K. (ed.) for the National Coalition Against Domestic Violence Lesbian Task Force, *Naming the Violence: Speaking Out About Lesbian Battering,* The Seal Press, Seattle, WA, 1986, p. 194.
46. Renzetti, C.M., p. 127.
47. Ibid, p. 123.
48. United States Senate Special Committee on Aging, the American Association of Retired Persons, the Federal Council on the Aging and the United States Administration on Aging, *Aging America: Trends and Projections,* United States Department of Health and Human Services, Washington, D.C. 20201, 1991, p. xix.
49. Vinton, L., "Abused Older Women: Battered Women or Abused Elders," in *Women's Initiatives, American Association of Retired Persons, Abused Elders or*

Older Battered Women?, AARP, 601 E St. NW, Washington, D.C. 20049, 1992, p. 51.

50. Pillemar, K.A. and Finkelfor, D., "The Prevalence of Elder Abuse: A Random Sample Survey," The Gerontological Society of America, 28, 1, 1988, pp. 51-57.
51. Breckman, R.S. and Adelman, R.D., *Strategies for Helping Victims of Elder Mistreatment,* Sage Publications, Newbury Park, CA, 1988, p. 29.
52. See Brandl, B., "Older Battered Women in Milwaukee," Community Care Organization of Milwaukee, Milwaukee Foundation, Wisconsin Coalition Against Domestic Violence, 1991.
53. Brandl, B., "Older Abused/Battered Women: An Invisible Population," *Wisconsin Coalition Against Domestic Violence Newsletter,* 14, 3, 1995, pp. 7-8.
54. Ibid, p. 7.
55. Mixon, P., "Older Battered Women: The Forgotten Victims," *The River,* Texas Council on Family Violence, Winter, 1995, p. 3.
56. United States Senate Special Committee on Aging, e.al., pp. xx-xxi.
57. Brandl, B., 1995, p. 8.
58. Mixon, P., p. 3.
59. Women's Initiative, American Association of Retired Persons, *Abused Elders or Older Battered Women?,* AARP, 601 E Street NW, Washington D.C. 20049, 1992, p. 16.
60. Brandl, B., 1995, p. 8.
61. Ibid, pp. 8-9.
62. Adams, C.J. and Engle-Rowbottom, M., "A Commentary on Violence Against Women and Children in Rural Areas," in Fortune, M.M., *Violence in the Family: A Workshop Curriculum for Clergy and Other Helpers,* The Pilgrim Press, Cleveland, OH, 1991, p. 170.
63. Graveline, M.J., "Threats to Rural Women's Well-Being: A Group Response," in Dhruvarajan, V. (ed.), *Women and Well-Being,* McGill-Queens University Press, Montreal, Canada, 1990, p. 173.
64. Adams, C.J. and Engle-Rowbottom, M., p. 169.
65. Ibid, pp. 166-167.
66. Graveline, M.J., pp. 171-172.
67. Ibid, p. 171.
68. Adams, C.J. and Engle-Rowbottom, M., pp. 168-169.
69. Ibid, p. 167.
70. Krueger-Pelka, F., "Abuse: A Hidden Epidemic," *Mainstream,* March, 1988.
71. Melling, L., "Abuse in the Deaf Community," Center for Women Policy Studies, Jan/Feb, 1984.

72. Ibid.
73. Ibid.
74. Krueger-Pelka, F.
75. Donovan, S., "What Can We Do To Help?", *The River,* Texas Council on Family Violence (TCFV), Winter, 1995, p. 5.
76. Ibid.
77. Osthoff, S., "When Battered Women Become Defendants: Should We Advocate?", *NCADV Voice,* Winter, 1989, pp. 6-7.
78. "National Estimates and Facts About Domestic Violence," *NCADV Voice,* Winter, 1989, p. 12.
79. Ibid.
80. Donovan, S., "A View From the Inside," *The River,* TCFV, Winter, 1995, p. 7.
81. "National Estimates and Facts About Domestic Violence."
82. Edwards, L., "My Story," *The River,* TCFV, Winter, 1995, p. 6.
83. "National Estimates and Facts About Domestic Violence."
84. DuBow, T., "Getting the 'Inside' Story Out," *NCADV Voice,* Winter, 1989, p. 8.
85. Ibid.
86. "National Estimates and Facts About Domestic Violence."
87. Wardlow, B., "Why Clemency Now?", *The River,* TCFV, Winter, 1995, p. 7.

Chapter 8

1. Gelles, R.J. and Straus, M., *Intimate Violence,* Simon and Schuster, Inc., New York, 1988, pp. 156-159. See also Gondolf, E.W. and Fisher, E.R., *Battered Women As Survivors: An Alternative to Treating Learned Helplessness,* Lexington Books, Lexington, MA, 1988, pp. 28-31.
2. Herman, J.L., *Trauma and Recovery,* Basic Books, New York, 1992, p. 61.
3. Texas Council on Family Violence, "What a Battered Woman Faces If She Leaves," Austin, TX, no date. See also Browne, A., *When Battered Women Kill,* The Free Press, New York, 1987, pp. 109-130.
4. Herman, J.L., pp. 142-143.
5. Schechter, S., *Women and Male Violence: The Visions and Struggles of the Battered Women's Movement,* South End Press, Boston, 1982, p. 253.
6. McEvoy, A.W. and Brookings, J.B., *Helping Battered Women: A Volunteer's Handbook for Assisting Victims of Marital Violence,* Learning Publications, Inc., Holmes Beach, FL, 1982, p. 9.
7. Jones, A., *Next Time She'll Be Dead: Battering and How to Stop It,* Beacon Press, Boston, 1994, p. 234.

8. McEvoy, A.W. and Brookings, J.B., p. 10.
9. Rice, G., "Some Ideas on Helping a Battered Woman," Austin Center for Battered Women, Austin, TX, no date.
10. Ellin, J., *Listening Helpfully: How to Develop Your Counseling Skills,* Souvenir Press, Ltd., London, 1994, pp. 104-105.
11. Clarke, R.L., *Pastoral Care of Battered Women,* The Westminster Press, Philadelphia, PA, 1986, pp. 98-99.
12. Herman, J.L., p. 162.
13. Rice, G., "Some Ideas of Helping A Battered Woman."
14. Texas Department of Human Services in cooperation with the Texas Council on Family Violence, "Counseling Battered Women," Austin, TX, no date.
15. Ellin, J., pp. 40-51.
16. Small, J., *Becoming Naturally Therapeutic: A Return to the True Essence of Helping,* Bantam Books, New York, 1989, pp. 27-30.
17. McEvoy, A.W. and Brookings, J.B., p. 12.
18. Texas Council on Family Violence, "Five Things to Say to a Victim Who is Not Ready to Leave Her Abuser," Austin, TX, no date.
19. Johnson, S.A., *When 'I Love You' Turns Violent: Emotional and Physical Abuse in Dating Relationships,* New Horizon Press, Far Hills, NJ, 1993, p. 33.
20. Ibid, p. 169-170. See also Browne, A., pp. 42-54; Walker, L., *The Battered Woman,* Harper and Row Publishers, New York, 1979, pp. 223-224; Jones, A. and Schechter, S., *When Loves Goes Wrong,* HarperCollins Publishers, New York, 1992, pp. 300-301.
21. Jones, A., p. 236.
22. Center for Battered Women, "Warning Signs of Abuse," Austin, TX, no date.

Chapter 9

1. Family Violence Prevention Fund, "57 Percent of Corporate Leaders Believe Domestic Violence is a Major Social Problem According to Survey by Liz Claiborne," San Francisco, CA, September 30, 1994.
2. Texas Council on Family Violence (TCFV), "Workplace Domestic Violence," Austin, TX, no date.
3. Ibid.
4. Ibid.
5. See Stark, E. and Flitcraft, A., *Women At Risk: Domestic Violence and Women's Health,* Sage Publications, Thousand Oaks, CA, 1996.
6. Bell, C.A., "Female Homicides in United States Workplaces, 1980-1985," *American Journal of Public Health,* 81, 6, 1991, pp. 729-732.

7. TCFV, "Workplace Domestic Violence."
8. Texas Council on Family Violence (TCFV), "What a Battered Woman Faces If She Leaves," Austin, TX, no date.
9. Ibid.
10. Roper Starch Worldwide Inc., *Addressing Domestic Violence: A Corporate Response,* prepared for Liz Claiborne, New York, August, 1994.
11. Family Violence Prevention Fund, "57 Percent of Corporate Leaders Believe Domestic Violence Is a Major Social Problem According to Survey by Liz Claiborne."
12. Family Violence Prevention Fund, "Violence At Home Has Effect on the Workplace," San Francisco, CA, no date.
13. Ibid.
14. Family Violence Prevention Fund, "57 Percent of Corporate Leaders Believe Domestic Violence is a Major Social Problem According to Survey by Liz Claiborne."
15. See Scholder, A. (ed.), *Critical Condition: Women on the Edge of Violence,* City Lights Books, San Francisco, CA, 1993.
16. Liz Claiborne, "Liz Claiborne Women's Work Program Fact Sheet 1991-1995," New York, no date.
17. Polaroid Corp., "Polaroid Corporation and the Domestic Violence Issue," Cambridge, MA, no date.
18. National Institute for Occupational Safety and Health, *Preventing Homicide in the Workplace,* Cincinnati, OH, September, 1993, p. 3.
19. Roper Starch Worldwide Inc., *Addressing Domestic Violence: A Corporate Response.*
20. See Moskey, S.T., *Domestic Violence Policy Checklists for the Workplace: A Guide for Employers,* Kettle Cove Press, Cape Elizabeth, ME, 1996.
21. Bulletin to Management, "Guidance Calls for Action Against Domestic Violence," July 25, 1996, p. 234.
22. Minor, M., *Preventing Workplace Violence: Positive Management Strategies,* Crisp Publications, Menlo Park, CA, 1995, pp. 21-22.
23. Moskey, S.T., p. 2.
24. Ibid, pp. 4-6.
25. Minor, M., p. 25.
26. Family Violence Prevention Fund, "Domestic Violence—A Workplace Security Problem," San Francisco, CA, no date.
27. Kelley, S.J., "Making Sense of Violence in the Workplace," Risk Management, 42, 10, October, 1995, pp. 50-57. See also Mattman, J.W., "What's Growing in the Corporate Culture?", *Security Management,* 39, 11, November, 1995, pp. 42-46.

28. Kelley, S.J., pp. 50-57.
29. Moskey, S.T., pp. 18-19.
30. Roper Starch Worldwide Inc., *Addressing Domestic Violence: A Corporate Response.*
31. Hardeman, J., "Intervention Strategies," Polaroid Corp., Cambridge, MA, no date.

Chapter 10

1. Jones, A., *Next Time She'll Be Dead: Battering and How to Stop It,* Beacon Press, Boston, 1994, p. 148.
2. American Medical Association Council on Scientific Affairs, "Violence Against Women: Relevance for Medical Practitioners," *Journal of the American Medical Association,* 267, 1992, pp. 3184-3189.
3. Jones, A., p. 87.
4. Gondolf, E. and Fisher, E., *Battered Women as Survivors: An Alternative to Treating Learned Helplessness,* Lexington Books, Lexington, MA, 1988, pp. 29-30.
5. Stark, E. and Flitcraft, A., "Spouse Abuse," in Last, J.M. (ed.), *Maxcy-Rosenau: Public Health and Preventive Medicine,* Appleton-Century-Crofts, New York, 1991, pp. 1040-1043.
6. Meyer, H. "The Billion Dollar Epidemic," *American Medical News,* January 6, 1992.
7. Helton, A.S. and Snodgrass, F.G., "Battering During Pregnancy: Intervention Strategies," *Birth,* 14, 1987, pp. 142-147. See also Rath, G.D., Jarratt, L.G. and Leonardson, G., "Rate of Domestic Violence Against Adult Women by Male Partners," *Journal of the American Board of Family Practice,* 2, 1989, pp. 227-233; Hamberger, L.K., Saunders, D. and Harvey, M., "Prevalence of Domestic Violence in Community Practice and Rate of Physician Inquiry," *Family Medicine,* 24, 1986, pp. 283-287.
8. Browne, A. *When Battered Women Kill,* The Free Press, New York, 1987, p. 69.
9. Walker, L., *The Battered Woman,* Harper and Row, Publishers, New York, 1979, pp. 196-199.
10. Browne, A., p. 69. See also Stark, E. and Flitcraft, A., *Women At Risk: Domestic Violence and Women's Health,* Sage Publications, Thousand Oaks, CA, 1996, p. 17.
11. Stark, E. and Flitcraft, A., 1991, pp. 1040-1043.
12. Gelles, R.J. and Straus, M.A., *Intimate Violence,* Simon and Schuster, Inc., New York, 1988, pp. 136-137.

13. Stark, E. and Flitcraft, A., 1996, pp. 162-163. See also Gelles, R.J. and Straus, M.A., pp. 136-137.
14. Stark, E. and Flitcraft, A., 1996, pp. 8-18;162-163.
15. Gelles, R.J. and Straus, M.A., pp. 132-133.
16. Stark, E. and Flitcraft, A., 1996, p. 196. See also Flitcraft, A.H., Hadley, S.M., Hendricks-Matthews, M.K., McLeer, S.V. and Warshaw, C., "American Medical Association Diagnostic and Treatment Guidelines on Domestic Violence," in *Strengthening the Health Care Response to Domestic Violence* prepared by the Family Violence Prevention Fund's Health Resource Center on Domestic Violence, San Francisco, no date.
17. Currie, D., "Women's Liberation and Women's Mental Health: Towards a Political Economy of Eating Disorders," in Dhruvarajan, V. (ed.), *Women and Well-Being,* McGill-Queens University Press, Montreal, Canada, 1990, pp. 32-33.
18. Stark, E. and Flitcraft, A., 1996, pp. 11-17. See also McFarlane, J., "Violence During Teen Pregnancy: Health Consequences for Mother and Child," in Levy, B. (ed.), *Dating Violence: Young Women in Danger,* Seal Press, Seattle, WA, 1991, pp. 136-137.
19. American Medical Association Council on Scientific Affairs, pp. 3184-3189.
20. Thorne-Finch, R., *Ending the Silence: The Origins and Treatment of Male Violence Against Women,* University of Toronto Press, Toronto, Canada, 1992, pp. 42-44.
21. Jones, A., p. 87.
22. Flitcraft, A.H., et al., "American Medical Association Diagnostic and Treatment Guidelines on Domestic Violence." See also Stark, E. and Flitcraft, A., 1996, p. 204.
23. Family Violence Prevention Fund, Health Alert: Medical Care System's Response to Domestic Violence, 1, 1, Summer, 1993 in *Strengthening the Health Care Response to Domestic Violence* prepared by the Family Violence Prevention Fund's Health Resource Center on Domestic Violence, San Francisco.
24. Stark, E. and Flitcraft, A., 1996, p. 9.
25. Warshaw, C., "Limitations of the Medical Model in the Care of Battered Women," *Gender and Society,* 3, 1989, pp. 506-517.
26. Stark, E. and Flitcraft, A., 1996, pp. 20-23.
27. Ibid, p. 13.
28. Waitzkin, H., "Information Giving in Medical Care," *Journal of Health and Social Behavior,* 26, 1985, pp. 81-101. See also Stark, E. and Flitcraft, A., 1996, pp. 16-17.

29. Stark, E. and Flitcraft, A., 1996, pp. 16-18.
30. Ibid, p. 202. See also Buel, S.M., "Family Violence: Practical Recommendations for Physicians and the Medical Community," *Women's Health Issues,* 5,4, Winter, 1995, pp. 158-172.
31. Jones, A., p. 147. See also Campbell, J., "Nurses Have Been Saying It," *NCADV Voice,* Winter, 1994, pp. 5-7; Stark, E. and Flitcraft, A., 1996, p. 216.
32. Salber, P.R., "Domestic Violence: How to Ask the Right Questions and Recognize Abuse," in *Strengthening the Health Care Response to Domestic Violence,* prepared by the Family Violence Prevention Fund's Health Resource Center on Domestic Violence, San Francisco, no date. See also, Buel, S.M., pp. 158-172; Flitcraft, A., "Project SAFE: Domestic Violence Education for Practising Physicians," *Women's Health Issues,* 5, 4, Winter, 1995, pp. 183-188; Stark, E. and Flitcraft, A., 1996, p. 216.
33. Buel, S.M., pp. 158-172.
34. Texas Medical Association, *Domestic Violence: Start the Healing Now,* Austin, TX, no date, pp. 1-2.
35. Flitcraft, A., 1995, pp. 183-188. See also Buel, S.M., pp. 158-172.
36. Family Violence Prevention Fund, "The Health Care Response to Domestic Violence—Fact Sheet," in *Strengthening the Health Care Response to Domestic Violence* prepared by the Family Violence Prevention Fund's Health Resource Center on Domestic Violence, San Francisco, no date.
37. Buel, S.M., pp. 158-172.
38. Flitcraft, A.H., et al., "American Medical Association Diagnostic and Treatment Guidelines on Domestic Violence."
39. Texas Medical Association, p. 19.
40. Ibid., pp. 9-12. See also Flitcraft, A.H., et al., "American Medical Association Diagnostic and Treatment Guidelines on Domestic Violence"; Salber, P.R., "Domestic Violence: How to Ask the Right Questions and Recognize Abuse."
41. Texas Medical Association, p. 16.
42. Stark, E., "Discharge Planning with Battered Women," in *Strengthening the Health Care Response to Domestic Violence* prepared by the Family Violence Prevention Fund's Health Resource Center on Domestic Violence, San Francisco, no date.
43. Flitcraft, A.H., et al., "American Medical Association Diagnostic and Treatment Guidelines on Domestic Violence." See also Salber, P.R., "Domestic Violence: How to Ask the Right Questions and Recognize Abuse."
44. Ibid.

45. Stark, E., "Discharge Planning with Battered Women."
46. Rounsaville, B.J. and Weissman, M., "Battered Women: A Medical Problem Requiring Detection," *International Journal of Psychiatry in Medicine,* 8, 2, 1977-1978, pp. 191-202.
47. Salber, P.R., "Domestic Violence: How to Ask the Right Questions and Recognize Abuse."
48. See National Coalition Against Domestic Violence, *NCADV Voice,* Winter, 1994, p. 19.
49. Flitcraft, A., 1995, pp. 183-188. See also Schechter, S. with Gary, L.T., *Health Care Services for Battered Women and Their Abused Children: A Manual About AWAKE,* Children's Hospital, Boston, MA, 1992; Hadley, S.M., Short, L.M., Lezin, N. and Zook, E., "WomanKind: An Innovative Model of Health Care Response to Domestic Abuse," *Women's Health Issues,* 5, 4, Winter, 1995, pp. 189-198.
50. Austin Center for Battered Women, *Domestic Violence: Identification, Intervention and Nursing Documentation,* Austin, TX, no date.
51. Achterberg, J., *Woman as Healer,* Shambhala, Boston, 1991, p. 204.

Chapter 11

1. Canadian Conference of Catholic Bishops Permanent Council on Violence Against Women, "To Live Without Fear," June 13, 1991, in *Diocese of Austin, Breaking the Silence: A Pastoral Response to Domestic Violence Against Women,* Austin, TX, 1995.
2. Halsey, P., "Women in Crisis: Out There or In Here?", *Response,* June, 1981, p. 5.
3. Alsdurf, J. and Alsdurf, P., *Battered into Submission: The Tragedy of Wife Abuse in the Christian Home,* InterVarsity Press, Downers Grove, Illinois, 1989, p. 153.
4. Ibid, p. 77.
5. Ibid, p. 23.
6. Herman, J.L., *Trauma and Recovery,* Basic Books, New York, 1992, pp. 51-52.
7. Clarke, R.L., *Pastoral Care of Battered Women,* The Westminister Press, Philadelphia, 1986, pp.. 61-85. See also Fortune, M.M., "Ministry in Response to Violence in the Family: Pastoral and Prophetic," in Fortune, M.M., *Violence in the Family: A Workshop Curriculum for Clergy and Other Helpers,* The Pilgrim Press, Cleveland, OH, 1991, pp. 198-199; Fortune, M.F., "The Transformation of Suffering: A Biblical and Theological Perspective," in Brown, J.C. and Bohn, C.R. (eds.), *Christianity, Patriarchy, and Abuse,* The Pilgrim Press, New York, 1990, pp. 139-147.

8. Fortune, M.M., "A Commentary on Religious Issues in Family Violence," in Fortune, M.M., *Violence in the Family: A Workshop Curriculum for Clergy and Other Helpers,* The Pilgrim Press, Cleveland, OH, 1991, pp. 137-138.
9. Fortune, M.M., *Sexual Violence: The Unmentionable Sin,* The Pilgrim Press, New York, 1983, pp. 191-193.
10. Fortune, M.M., "A Commentary on Religious Issues in Family Violence," pp. 138-139.
11. Clarke, R.L., pp. 61-85. See also Fortune, M.M., *Keeping the Faith: Questions and Answers for the Abused Woman,* Harper, San Francisco, 1987.
12. Fortune, M.M., "A Commentary on Religious Issues in Family Violence," p. 138.
13. U.S. Bishops' Committees on Women in the Church and Society, and on Marriage and Family Life, "When I Call for Help: A Pastoral Response to Domestic Violence Against Women," November, 1992, in *Diocese of Austin, Breaking the Silence: A Pastoral Response to Domestic Violence Against Women,* Austin, TX, 1995.
14. Bohn, C.R., "Dominion to Rule: The Roots and Consequences of a Theology of Ownership," in Brown, J.C. and Bohn, C.R. (eds.), *Christianity, Patriarchy and Abuse,* The Pilgrim Press, New York, 1990, p. 107.
15. Alsdurf, J. and Alsdurf, P., p. 156.
16. Ibid, pp. 157-158.
17. Fortune, M.M., *Sexual Violence: The Unmentionable Sin,* pp. 128-129.
18. Clarke, R.L., p. 62.
19. Fortune, M.M., "Ministry in Response to Violence in the Family: Pastoral and Prophetic," p. 193.
20. Clarke, R.L., pp. 89-92. See also U.S. Bishops' Committees on Women in the Church and Society, and on Marriage and Family Life, "When I Call for Help: A Pastoral Response to Domestic Violence Against Women"; Texas Department of Human Services, "Family Violence and the Clergy," Austin, TX, November, 1990.
21. Alsdurf, J. and Alsdurf, P., pp. 130-131.
22. Clarke, R.L., pp. 91-92.
23. Ibid, pp. 88-89. See also Fortune, M.M., *Sexual Violence: The Unmentionable Sin,* pp. 131-133.
24. Texas Department of Human Services, "Family Violence and the Clergy," p. 6. See also Clarke, R.L., pp. 96-101.
25. Salber, P.R., "Domestic Violence: How to Ask the Right Questions and Recognize Abuse," in Strengthening the Health Care Response to

Domestic Violence prepared by the Family Violence Prevention Fund's Health Resource Center on Domestic Violence, San Francisco, no date.

26. Texas Department of Human Services, "Family Violence and the Clergy," p.7.
27. Clarke, R.L., p. 97.
28. Ibid, pp. 101-102.
29. See Fortune, M.M., *Keeping the Faith: Questions and Answers for the Abused Woman,* Harper, San Francisco, 1987.
30. Fortune, M.M., "A Commentary on Religious Issues in Family Violence," p. 140.
31. Clarke, R.L., p. 97. See also Fortune, M.M., *Keeping the Faith,* p. 85.
32. Texas Department of Human Services, "Family Violence and the Clergy," p.6.
33. Fortune, M.M., "Forgiveness: The Last Step," in Fortune, M.M., *Violence in the Family: A Workshop Curriculum for Clergy and Other Helpers,* The Pilgrim Press, Cleveland, OH, 1991, p. 177.
34. Canadian Conference of Catholic Bishops' Permanent Council on Violence Against Women, "To Live Without Fear."
35. Center for the Prevention of Sexual and Domestic Violence, 1994-1995 Annual Report, 936 North 34th Street, Suite 200, Seattle, WA 98103.
36. U.S. Bishops' Committees on Women in the Church and Society, and on Marriage and Family Life, "When I Call for Help: A Pastoral Response to Domestic Violence Against Women."
37. Ibid.
38. See Diocese of Austin, *Breaking the Silence: A Pastoral Response to Domestic Violence Against Women,* Austin, TX, 1995.
39. Fortune, M.M., "Saving the Family: When is Covenant Broken?" in Fortune, M.M., *Violence in the Family: A Workshop Curriculum for Clergy and Other Helpers,* The Pilgrim Press, Cleveland, OH, 1991, p. 241.
40. Texas Council on Family Violence, "Suggested Sermon Topics and Biblical Readings," Austin, Texas, no date. See also Diocese of Cleveland, "Five Suggestions for Preaching with a Sensitivity to Issues Relating to Domestic Violence," in Diocese of Austin, *Breaking the Silence: A Pastoral Response to Domestic Violence Against Women,* Austin, TX, 1995.

Chapter 12

1. Jackson, M. and Garvin, D., "Community Accountability Wheel," Domestic Violence Institute of Michigan, PO Box 130107, Ann Arbor, MI 48113-0107, no date. Inspired and adapted from the "Power and Control Wheel" developed by the Domestic Abuse Intervention Project, 206 West 4th Street, Duluth, MN 55806.

2. See Witwer, M.B. and Crawford, C.A., *A Coordinated Approach to Reducing Family Violence: Conference Highlights,* United States Department of Justice, Office of Justice Programs, National Institute of Justice, Washington D.C. 20531, October, 1995.
3. Jones, A., *Next Time She'll Be Dead: Battering and How to Stop It,* Beacon Press, Boston, 1994, pp. 213-214.
4. Velsor-Friedrich, B., "Homeless Children and Their Families, Part I: The Changing Picture," *Journal of Pediatric Nursing,* 8, 1993, p. 122.
5. Sheehan, M.A., "An Interstate Compact on Domestic Violence: What are the Advantages," *Juvenile and Family Justice Today,* 1993.

Chapter 13

1. P.M.G., "Growing," in *Northern Ireland Women's Aid Federation,* The Foam Sprite, Belfast, Ireland, 1993.
2. NiCarthy, G., Merriam, K. and Coffman, S., *Talking It Out: A Guide to Groups for Abused Women,* Seal Press, Seattle, WA, 1984, pp. 25-26.
3. See Pence, E., *In Our Best Interest: A Process for Personal and Social Change,* Minnesota Program Development, Inc., Duluth, MN, 1987.
4. See Freire, P., *Pedagogy of the Oppressed,* Continuum, NY, 1970. See also Freire, P., *Education for Critical Consciousness,* Continuum, NY, 1973.
5. Pence, E., p. 20.
6. NiCarthy, G., et al., pp. 27-29.
7. See Chesler, P., *Women and Madness,* Doubleday, Garden City, NY, 1972.
8. Whalen, M., *Counseling to End Violence Against Women: A Subversive Model,* Sage Publications, Thousand Oaks, CA, 1996, p. 31.
9. Pence, E., p. 5.
10. Whalen, M., pp. 51-52.
11. Jaffe, P.G., Wolfe, D.A. and Wilson, S.K., *Children of Battered Women,* Sage Publications, Newbury Park, CA, 1990, pp. 96-97.
12. Ibid, p. 86.
13. Ibid, p. 98.
14. Edleson, J.L. and Peled, E., "Small Group Intervention with Children of Battered Women," *Violence Update,* 4, 9, May, 1994, p. 1.
15. Ibid, p. 2.
16. Jaffe, P.G., et al., p. 89.
17. Peled, E., "'Secondary' Victims No More: Refocusing Intervention With Children," in Edleson, J.L. and Eisikovits, Z.C. (eds.), *Future Interventions with Battered Women and Their Families,* Sage Publications, Thousand Oaks, CA, 1996, pp. 145-147.
18. Ibid, p. 144.

19. Jaffe, P.G., et al., p. 99.
20. For a discussion of empowerment as depoliticization see Mann, B., "Working With Battered Women: Radical Education or Therapy" in Pence, E., *In Our Best Interest: A Process for Personal and Social Change,* Minnesota Program Development, Inc., Duluth, MN, 1987, pp. 104-155.

Chapter 14

1. Paymar, M., *Violent No More: Helping Men End Domestic Abuse,* Hunter House, Alameda, CA, 1993, p. 26.
2. Schechter, S., *Women and Male Violence: The Visions and Struggles of the Battered Women's Movement,* South End Press, Boston, 1982, pp. 261-262.
3. Ritmeester, T., "Batterers' Programs, Battered Women's Movement, and Issues of Accountability," in Pence, E. and Paymar, M., *Education Groups for Men Who Batter: The Duluth Model,* Springer Publishing Company, New York, 1993, p. 169.
4. Pence, E. and Paymar, M., *Education Groups for Men Who Batter: The Duluth Model,* Springer Publishing Company, New York, 1993, p. 171.
5. See Adams, D., "Treatment Models of Men Who Batter: A Profeminist Analysis," in Yllo, K., and Bograd, M. (eds.), *Feminist Perspectives on Wife Abuse,* Sage, Beverly Hills, CA, 1988, pp. 176-199.
6. Thorne-Finch, R., *Ending the Silence: The Origins and Treatment of Male Violence Against Women, University of Toronto Press,* Toronto, Canada, 1992, pp. 138-139.
7. Eisikovits, Z.C. and Edleson, J.L., "Intervening With Men Who Batter: A Critical Review of the Literature," *Social Service Review,* 63, 1989, pp. 384-414.
8. See Williams, O.J., "Ethnically Sensitive Practice to Enhance Treatment Participation of African American Men Who Batter," *Families in Society: The Journal of Contemporary Human Services,* December, 1992, pp. 588-595.
9. Edleson, J.L., "Controversy and Change in Batterers' Programs," in Edleson, J.L. and Eisikovits, Z.C. (eds.), *Future Interventions with Battered Women and Their Families,* Sage Publications, Thousand Oaks, CA, 1996, p. 156.
10. Ibid, p. 159.
11. Ibid, pp. 159-160.
12. Pence, E. and Paymar, M., p. 166.
13. Edleson, J.L., pp. 164-165. See also Petrik, N.D., Gildersleeve-High, L., McEllistream, J.E. and Subotnik, L.S., "The Reduction of Male Abusiveness as a Result of Treatment: Reality or Myth?", *Journal of Family Violence,* 9, 4, 1994, pp. 307-308.

14. See Texas Department of Criminal Justice, Community Justice Assistance Division and the Texas Council on Family Violence, *Battering Intervention and Prevention Project Guidelines,* Austin, TX, March, 1996.
15. Ibid, pp. 5-6.
16. Texas Council on Family Violence, "Is He Really Going to Change This Time?", Austin, TX, August, 1995.
17. Edleson, J.L., p. 162.

Chapter 15

1. Steinem, G., *Revolution From Within: A Book of Self-Esteem,* Little, Brown and Company, Boston, p. 283.
2. Corrigan, M., "Burnout: How to Spot It and Protect Yourself Against It," *The Journal of Volunteer Administration,* Spring, 1994, p. 24-31.
3. Maslach, C., *Burnout: The Cost of Caring,* Prentice Hall Press, New York, p. 81.
4. Schechter, S., *Women and Male Violence: The Visions and Struggles of the Battered Women's Movement,* South End Press, Boston, p. 293.
5. Maslach, C., p. 11.
6. Ibid, pp. 38-40.
7. Veninga, R.L. and Spradley, J.P., *The Work/Stress Connection: How to Cope with Job Burnout,* Little, Brown and Company, Boston, pp. 28-35; See also Maslach, C., p. 57.
8. Veninga, R.L. and Spradley, J.P., pp. 20-21.
9. Sapolsky, R.M., *Why Zebras Don't Get Ulcers: A Guide to Stress, Stress-Related Diseases and Coping,* W.H. Freeman and Company, New York, p. 8.
10. Ibid, pp. 13-14.
11. Fronk, R., *Creating a Lifestyle You Can Live With,* Whitaker House, 1988.
12. Veninga, R.L. and Spradley, J.P., pp. 39-73.
13. Maslach, C., p. 4.
14. Ibid, pp. 75-76.
15. Ibid, pp. 64-65.
16. Pearlman, L.A. and Saakvitne, K.W., *Trauma and the Therapist,* W.W. Norton and Company, New York, p. 386.
17. Veninga, R.L. and Spradley, J.P., pp. 253-254.
18. Pearlman, L.A. and Saakvitne, K.W., p. 393.
19. Ibid, p. 390.
20. Mackoff, B., *Leaving the Office Behind,* Dell Publishing Company, New York, p. 59.
21. Ibid, p. 23.
22. Pearlman, L.A. and Saakvitne, K.W., pp. 390-391.

23. See Lark, S.M., *Anxiety and Stress: A Self-Help Program,* Westchester Publishing Company, Los Altos, CA, 1993.
24. Saunders, C., *Women and Stress,* Crescent Books, New York, pp. 10-11.
25. Ibid, p. 65.
26. See Lark, S.M., pp. 171-174.
27. Steinem, G., p. 180.
28. McGee-Cooper, A., *You Don't Have to Go Home From Work Exhausted,* Bantam Books, New York, 1992.
29. See Steinem, G., pp. 175-176.
30. See Reed, H., *Dream Solutions: Using Your Dreams To Change Your Life,* New World Library, San Rafael, CA, 1991.
31. See Steinem, G., pp. 173-175.
32. Mackoff, B., p. 36.
33. Witkin-Lanoil, G., *The Female Stress Syndrome,* New Market Press, New York, p. 129.
34. See Lark, S.M., pp. 161-164.
35. Saunders, C., p. 19; See also Lark, S.M., pp. 177-184.
36. Lark, S.M., pp. 164-166.
37. Ibid., pp. 169-171.
38. Ibid., pp. 201-217.
39. Saunders, C., pp. 253-254.
40. Lark, S.M., p. 175.
41. Saunders, C., p. 260.
42. See Wildwood, C., *Creative Aromatherapy,* Thorsons, San Franciso, 1993.
43. Saunders, C., p. 261.
44. See Schechter, S., p. 294.

Chapter 17

1. Gordon, L., *Heroes of Their Own Lives: The Politics and History of Family Violence,* Penguin Books, New York, 1988, p. 250.
2. Janssen-Jurreit, M., *Sexism: The Male Monopoly on History and Thought,* Farrar, Straus and Giroux, New York, 1982, p. 223.
3. See Daly, M., *Gyn/Ecology: The Metaethics of Radical Feminism,* Beacon Press, Boston, 1978, pp. 109-313. See also McAllister, P., *This River of Courage: Generations of Women's Resistance and Action,* New Society Publishers, Philadelphia, PA, 1991, pp. 149-161; Lightfoot-Klein, H., *Prisoners of Ritual: An Odyssey into Female Genital Circumcision in Africa,* Harrington Park Press, New York, 1989; Narasimhan, S., *Sati: Widow Burning in India,* Anchor Books, New York, 1990.

4. Johnson, B., *Lady of the Beasts: Ancient Images of the Goddess and Her Sacred Animals,* Harper, San Francisco, 1988, p. 3.
5. Engels, F., *The Origin of the Family, Private Property and the State* (C.H. Kerr and Co., Chicago, 1902), in Agonito, R., *History of Ideas on Woman,* Perigee Books, New York, 1977, p. 274.
6. Lerner, G., *The Creation of Patriarchy,* Oxford University Press, New York, 1986, p. 31.
7. Ibid., p. 39; pp. 125-147. See also Janssen-Jurreit, M., pp. 70-71; Johnson, B.; Eisler, R., *The Chalice and the Blade,* Harper and Row, Publishers, San Francisco, 1987, pp. 2-28.
8. Chevillard, N. and Sebastien, L., "The Dawn of Lineage Societies," in Coontz, S. and Henderson, P. (eds.), *Women's Work, Men's Property: The Origins of Gender and Class,* Verso, London, 1986, p. 101. See also Martin, D., *Battered Wives,* Volcano Press, Volcano, CA, 1981, p. 25; Johnson, B., pp. 348-349.
9. Lerner, G., p. 8.
10. Ibid., p. 53.
11. Brownmiller, S., *Against Our Will: Men, Women and Rape,* Simon and Schuster, New York, 1975, pp. 16-19.
12. Ibid., p. 17. See also Engels, F., pp. 273-274; Scott, G.R., *Curious Customs of Sex and Marriage,* Senate, London, 1995, pp. 53-57. Originally published 1953.
13. Engels, F., pp. 279-280.
14. Ibid., p. 280.
15. Mill, J.S., *The Subjection of Women,* AHM Publishing Corp., Arlington Heights, Illinois, 1980, p. 29. Originally published 1869.
16. Brownmiller, S., p. 18. See also Scott, G.R., pp. 64-69.
17. Lerner, G., pp. 77-213.
18. Ibid., pp. 81-100.
19. Ibid., pp. 212-216.
20. Aristotle, "The Differences Between Men and Women," (Claredon Press, Oxford, 1912), in Agonito, R., *History of Ideas of Woman,* Perigee Books, New York, 1977, pp. 51-54.
21. Anderson, B.S. and Zinsser, J.P., *A History of Their Own: Women in Europe from Prehistory to the Present, Volume I,* Harper and Row, New York, 1988, p. 31.
22. Donaldson, J., *Woman: Her Position and Influence in Ancient Greece and Rome, and Among the Early Christians,* Longmans, Green and Co., New York, 1907, pp. 87-88. See also Gies, F. and Gies, J., *Women in the Middle Ages,* Barnes and Noble Books, New York, 1978, p. 13.

23. Dobash, R.E. and Dobash, R.P., *Violence Against Wives: A Case Against the Patriarchy,* Free Press, New York, 1979, pp. 34-40.
24. Gies, F. and Gies, J., *Marriage and the Family in the Middle Ages,* Harper and Row, New York, 1987, pp. 18-19.
25. Ibid., p. 27. See also Scott, G.R., pp. 145-150.
26. Anderson, B.S. and Zinsser, J.P., pp. 30-31. See also Janssen-Jurreit, M., p. 261.
27. Dobash, R.E. and Dobash, R.P., p. 37.
28. Anderson, B.S. and Zinsser, J.P., pp. 23-49.
29. Donaldson, J., p. 10.
30. Anderson, B.S. and Zinsser, J.P., pp. 15-23.
31. Gies, F. and Gies, J., pp. 37-41. See also Donaldson, J., pp. 188-190.
32. Achterberg, J., *Woman as Healer,* Shambhala, Boston, 1991, p. 66. See also Davidson, T., "Wifebeating: A Recurring Phenomenon Throughout History," in Roy, M. (ed.), *Battered Women: A Psychosociological Study of Domestic Violence,* Van Nostrand Reinhold Co., New York, 1977, pp. 6-10.
33. Achterberg, J., pp. 66-68.
34. Augustine, "Woman as Auxiliary and Subject to Man," (T. & T. Clark, Edinburgh, 1871), in Agonito, R., *History of Ideas on Woman,* Perigee Books, New York, 1977, p. 79.
35. Aquinas, T., "Woman as Derived Being," (R. and T. Washbourne, Ltd., London, 1912), in Agonito, R., *History of Ideas on Woman,* Perigee Books, New York, 1977, p. 85.
36. Barstow, A.L., *Witchcraze,* Pandora, San Francisco, 1994, p. 21.
37. Ehrenreich, B. and English, D., *Witches, Midwives and Nurses: A History of Women Healers,* The Feminist Press, New York, 1973, pp. 7-8.
38. Achterberg, J., pp. 85-86. See also Barstow, A.L., pp. 58-69.
39. Barstow, A.L., pp. 20-21.
40. Ehrenreich, B. and English, D., p.8. See also Barstow, A.L., p. 142.
41. Achterberg, J., p. 88.
42. Davis, E.G., *The First Sex,* Penguin Books, New York, 1979, p. 257.
43. Barstow, A.L., p. 109.
44. Ehrenreich, B. and English, D., pp. 15-19.
45. Achterberg, J., p. 81.
46. Barstow, A.L., p. 54.
47. Achterberg, J., p. 84.
48. Ehrenreich, B. and English, D., p. 9. See also Barstow, A.L., pp. 62-63; pp. 171-172; Williams, S.R. and Adelman, P.W., *Riding the Nightmare: Women and Witchcraft from the Old World to Colonial Salem,* HarperPerennial, New York, 1992, pp. 35-45.

49. Barstow, A.L., pp. 129-130. See also Williams, S.R. and Adelman, P.W., p. 83.
50. Achterberg, p. 84.
51. Sinistrari, L.M., *Demoniality*, Dover Publications, Inc., New York, 1989, p. 10. Originally published The Fortune Press, London, 1927. See also Williams, S.R. and Adelman, P.W., p. 99.
52. Barstow, A.L., pp. 129-130.
53. Ibid., p. 54. See also Williams, S.R. and Adelman, P.W., p. 19.
54. Achterberg, J., p. 83.
55. Barstow, A.L., p. 131.
56. Ibid, p. 143. See also Williams, S.R. and Adelman, P.W., p. 62.
57. Achterberg, J., p. 98.
58. Davis, E.G., pp. 252-255. See also Dutton, D.G., *The Domestic Assault of Women,* UBC Press, Vancouver, 1995, p. 19.
59. Ibid., p. 253.
60. Gies, F. and Gies, J., 1978, p. 46.
61. Martin, D., p. 30.
62. Janssen-Jurreit, M., p. 225.
63. Tuchman, B.W., *A Distant Mirror,* Ballantine Books, New York, 1978, pp. 213-214.
64. Janssen-Jurreit, M., p. 225.
65. Ibid., p. 227.
66. Davis, E.G., pp. 163-165. See also Dingwall, E.J., *The Girdle of Chastity: A History of the Chastity Belt,* Dorset Press, New York, 1992, pp. 2-4.
67. Janssen-Jurreit, M., pp. 243-254. See also Daly, M., pp. 153-170; Lightfoot-Klein, H., *Prisoners of Ritual.*
68. Davis, E.G., pp. 165-166. See also Scott, G.R., pp. 132-133; Dingwall, E.J., pp. 4-91.
69. Scott, G.R., p. 133.
70. Luria, G. and Tiger, V., *Everywoman,* Random House, New York, 1976, p. 15.
71. Adams, A., *An Uncommon Scold,* Simon and Schuster, New York, 1989, p. 9.
72. Andrews, W., *Old Time Punishments,* Dorsett Press, New York, 1991, pp. 1-4. Originally published 1890.
73. Ibid., pp. 13-14.
74. Ibid., pp. 22-35.
75. Ibid., pp. 38-42.
76. Spruill, J.C., *Women's Life and Work in the Southern Colonies,* W.W. Norton and Co., Inc., New York, 1972, pp. 330-331.

77. Adams, A., pp. 9-12.
78. Gordon, L., p. 279. See also Davidson, T., pp. 12-13; Scott, G.R., pp. 151-152.
79. Andrews, W., pp. 180-181.
80. Dubois, E.C. and Ruiz, V.L., *Unequal Sisters: A Multi-Cultural Read in U.S. Women's History,* Routledge, NY, 1990. p. 197.
81. Dworkin, A., *Woman Hating,* Plume, NY, 1974, pp.96-97.
82. Levy, H.S., *Chinese Footbinding: The History of a Curious Erotic Custom,* W. Rawls, NY, 1966, pp. 25-26.
83. Dworkin, A., pp. 101-103.
84. Dubois, E.C. and Ruiz, V.L., p. 197.
85. Narashimhan, S., *Sati: Widow Buring in India,* Anchor Books, NY, 1990. p. 11.
86. Stein, D.K., "Women to Burn: Suttee as a Normative Institution," in Radford, H. and Russell, D.E.H. (eds), *Femicide: The Politics of Woman Killing,* Twayne Publishers, NY, 1992, p. 62.
87. Narashimhan, S., p. 18.
88. Stein, D.K., p. 63.
89. Narashimhan, S., p.43.
90. Ibid., pp. 52-53.
91. Ibid., pp. 61-73.
92. Spruill, J.C., pp. 340-341. See also Hymowitz, C. and Weissman, M., *A History of Women in America,* Bantam Books, New York, 1978, pp. 22-23.
93. Jennings, S., "Proper Conduct of the Wife Towards Her Husband," (Lorenzo Dow, New York, 1808), in Cott, N.F. (ed.), *Root of Bitterness,* E.P. Dutton, New York, 1972, p. 113.
94. Spruill, J.C., pp. 341-343.
95. Stacey, W.A. and Shupe, A., *The Family Secret: Domestic Violence in America,* Beacon Press, Boston, 1983, p. 12.
96. Martin, D., p. 31. See also Stacey, W.A. and Shupe, A., pp. 12-13.
97. Davidson, T., pp. 18-19.
98. Hymowitz, C. and Weissman, M., p. 25.
99. Stacey, W.A. and Shupe, A., p. 13. See also Davidson, T., p. 4.
100. Davidson, T., p. 19.
101. Martin, D., p. 32.
102. Pleck, E., "The Whipping Post for Wife Beaters, 1876-1906," in Moch, L.P. and Stark, G.D. (eds.), *Essay on the Family and Historical Change,* pp. 127-129.
103. Martin, D., p. 32.
104. Stacey, W.A. and Shupe, A., p. 13.

105. Rousseau, J.J., *Paternity and the Origin of Political Power*, (J.M. Dent and Sons, Ltd., London, 1913), in Agonito, R., *History of Ideas on Woman,* Perigee Books, New York, 1977, p. 119.
106. See Wollstonecraft, M., *A Vindication of the Rights of Woman,* Everyman's Library, New York, 1992. Originally published J. Johnson, London, 1792.
107. See Rousseau, J.J., *Emile,* Barron's Educational Series, Inc., New York, 1964. First original English translation published 1768.
108. Agonito, R., pp. 145-146.
109. Hymowitz, C. and Weissman, M., pp. 76-77.
110. Davis, A., *Women, Race and Class,* Vintage Books, New York, 1981, p. 39. See also Hymowitz, C. and Weissman, M., p. 79.
111. Papachristou, J., *Women Together,* Alfred A. Knopf, New York, 1976, p. 23.
112. Hymowitz, C. and Weissman, M., pp. 218-220.
113. Davis, A., pp. 144-171. See also Hymowitz, C. and Weissman, M., pp. 79-114; pp. 218-263.
114. Papachristou, J., p. 29.
115. Mill, J.S., pp. 34.
116. Agonito, R., pp. 223-224. See also Davidson, T., pp. 16-17.
117. Pleck, E., p. 142.
118. Cobbe, F.P., "Wife Torture in England," in Radford, J. and Russell, D.E.H., (eds.), *Femicide: The Politics of Woman Killing,* Twayne Publishers, New York, 1992, p. 47. Originally published London, 1878. See also Stark, E. and Flitcraft, A., *Women at Risk,* Sage Publications, Thousand Oaks, CA, 1996, pp. 43-45.
119. Pleck, E., pp. 142-143.
120. Showalter, E., *The Female Malady,* Penguin Books, New York, 1985, p. 129.
121. See Masson, J.M., *A Dark Science,* Farrar, Straus and Giroux, New York, 1986.
122. Showalter, E., pp. 74-78.
123 Daly, M. pp. 224-228.
124. Ehrenreich, B. and English, D., *For Her Own Good: 150 Years of the Experts Advice to Women,* Doubleday, New York, 1978, pp. 123-125.
125. Showalter, E., p. 145.
126. Ibid., pp. 164-170.
127. Gordon, L., p. 27, 115
128. Ibid., p. 19.
129. Ibid., pp. 252-281. See also Feldberg, M., "Police Discretion and Family Disturbances: Some Historical and Contemporary Reflections," in Newberger, E.H. and Bourne, R., (eds.), *Unhappy Families.*

130. Papachristou, J., pp. 196-197.
131. Gordon, L., pp. 20-23.
132. Papachristou, J., p. 212.
133. Gordon, L., p. 23.
134. Goldman, E., *The Traffic in Women and Other Essays on Feminism,* Times Change Press, Ojai, CA, 1970, p. 14. Originally published 1917 by Mother Earth Publishing Association, New York.
135. Gordon, L., p. 251.
136. Evans, S., *Personal Politics,* Vintage Books, New York, 1979, pp. 219-220.
137. Hymowitz, C. and Weissman, M., pp. 347-349.
138. Cohen, M., *The Sisterhood,* Fawcett Columbine, New York, 1988, pp. 390-391.
139. Hymowitz, C. and Weissman, M., p. 349.
140. Evans, S., pp. 214-216.
141. Hymowitz, C. and Weissman, M., p. 350.
142. Evans, S., p. 215, 130.
143. Hymowitz, C. and Weissman, M., pp. 351-355. See also Cohen, M., pp. 175-176.
144. Texas Council on Family Violence, *Working Together for Change,* Austin, Texas, 1992, p. 5.
145. McAllister, P., pp. 132-151.
146. Schechter, S., *Women and Male Violence: The Visions and Struggles of the Battered Women's Movement,* South End Press, Boston, 1982, p. 5.
147. Ibid., p. 154.
148. See Pizzey, E., *Scream Quietly or the Neighbors Will Hear,* Ridley Enlow Publishers, Short Hills, NJ, 1974.
149. McAllister, P., pp. 134-135.
150. Schechter, S., pp. 29-51.
151. Ibid., p. 258.
152. McAllister, P., pp. 133-134. See also Schechter, S., pp. 62-63.
153. Schechter, S., pp. 56-57.
154. Austin Center for Battered Women, "History of the Austin Center for Battered Women," Austin, TX, no date.
155. National Woman Abuse Prevention Project (NWAPP), "Domestic Violence Factsheet: The Battered Women's/Shelter Movement," Washington, D.C., no date.
156. National Coalition Against Domestic Violence (NCADV), "Organizational Background," Denver, CO, no date.
157. NWAPP, "Domestic Violence Factsheet: The Battered Women's/Shelter Movement."

158. See Martin, D., Battered Wives.
159. NWAPP, "Domestic Violence Factsheet: Highlights of Major Events of the Battered Women's Movement," Washington, D.C., no date.
160. Ibid.
161. Schechter, S., pp. 133-135.
162. Ibid., pp. 136-137.
163. See United States Commission on Civil Rights, Battered Women: Issues of Public Policy, Washington, D.C., January 30-31, 1978.
164. NWAPP, "Domestic Violence Factsheet: Highlights of Major Events of the Battered Women's Movement."
165. Schechter, S., pp. 192-195.
166. Ibid., p. 143.
167. NWAPP, "Domestic Violence Factsheet: Highlights of Major Events of the Battered Women's Movement."

Additional Resources

State Domestic Violence Coalitions

Alabama	(334) 832-4842
Alaska	(907) 586-3650
Arizona	(602) 279-2900
Arkansas	(501) 812-0571
California	(415) 457-2464
Colorado	(303) 573-9018
Connecticut	(860) 524-5890
Delaware	(302) 658-2958
District of Columbia	(202) 783-5332
Florida	(904) 668-6862
Georgia	(770) 984-0085
Hawaii	(808) 486-5072
Idaho	(208) 384-0419
Illinois	(217) 789-2830
Indiana	(317) 543-3908
Iowa	(515) 244-8028
Kansas	(913) 232-9784
Kentucky	(502) 875-4132
Louisiana	(504) 542-4446
Maine	(207) 941-1194
Maryland	(301) 942-0900
Massachusetts	(617) 248-0922
Michigan	(517) 484-2924
Minnesota	(612) 646-6177
Mississippi	(601) 981-9161
Missouri	(573) 634-4161
Montana	(406) 256-6334
Nebraska	(402) 476-6256
Nevada	(702) 358-1171
New Hampshire	(603) 224-8893
New Jersey	(609) 584-8107
New Mexico	(505) 246-9240

New York	(518) 432-4864
North Carolina	(919) 956-9124
North Dakota	(701) 255-6240
Ohio	(614) 784-0023
Oklahoma	(405) 557-1210
Oregon	(503) 223-7411
Pennsylvania	(717) 545-6400
Puerto Rico	(809) 722-2857
Rhode Island	(401) 467-9940
South Carolina	(803) 750-1222
South Dakota	(605) 945-0869
Tennessee	(615) 386-9406
Texas	(512) 794-1133
Utah	(801) 538-9886
Vermont	(802) 223-1302
Virginia	(804) 221-0990
Washington	(360) 352-4029
West Virginia	(304) 765-2250
Wisconsin	(608) 255-0539
Wyoming	(307) 235-2814

Domestic Violence

Domestic Violence Reading Material

Bograd, Michele and Kersti Yllo, eds. *Feminist Perspectives on Wife Abuse.* Newbury Park, CA: Sage Publications, 1988.

Brownmiller, Susan. *Against Our Will: Men, Women and Rape.* New York: Simon and Schuster, 1975.

Cole, Johnnetta B., ed. *All American Women: Lines That Divide, Ties That Bind.* New York: The Free Press, 1986.

Evans, Patricia. *The Verbally Abusive Relationship: How to Recognize It and How to Respond.* Holbrook, MA: Bob Adams, Inc., 1992.

Ferrato, Donna. *Living with the Enemy.* New York: Aperture Publishing Co., 1991.

Finkelhor, David and Kersti Yllo. *License to Rape: Sexual Abuse of Wives.* New York: Holt, Rinehart and Winston, 1985.

Fisher, Ellen and Edward Gondolf. *Battered Women as Survivors: An Alternative to Treating Learned Helplessness.* Lexington, MA: D.C. Heath and Co./Lexington Books, 1988.

Gondolf, Edward. *Man Against Woman: What Every Woman Should Know About Violent Men.* Bradenton, FL: Human Services Institute, 1989.

Hale, Katherine and M'Liss Switzer. *Called to Account.* Seattle: Seal Press, 1987.

Johnson, Scott. *When "I Love You" Turns Violent: Emotional and Physical Abuse in Dating Relationships.* Far Hills, NJ: New Horizon Press, 1993.

Jones, Ann. *Next Time, She'll Be Dead: Battering and How to Stop It.* Boston: Beacon Press, 1994.

Jones, Ann and Susan Schechter. *When Love Goes Wrong: Strategies for Women with Controlling Partners.* New York: HarperCollins Publishers, 1992.

Martin, Del. *Battered Wives.* New York: Pocket Books, 1983.

NiCarthy, Ginny. *The Ones Who Got Away: Women Who Left Abusive Partners.* Seattle: Seal Press, 1987.

Pence, Ellen. *In Our Best Interest: A Process for Personal and Social Change.* Duluth, Minnesota: Minnesota Program Development, 1987.

Pizzey, Erin. *Scream Quietly or the Neighbors Will Hear.* Short Hills, NJ: Ridley Enslow Publishers, 1977.

Schechter, Susan. *Women and Male Violence: The Visions and Struggles of the Battered Women's Movement.* Boston: South End Press, 1982.

Walker, Lenore. *The Battered Woman.* New York: Harper and Row, 1979.

Domestic Violence Resource Agencies

Another Way / End Violence Now
192 Sarann Ct.
Lilburn, GA 30247
(770) 717-9447
FAX: 770-729-1224

Austin Center for Battered Women
PO Box 19454
Austin, TX 78760
(512) 385-5181

Center For Nonviolence
235 W. Creighton Ave.
Fort Wayne, IN 46807

Center for the Prevention of Sexual and Domestic Violence
936 N. 34th St., Suite 200
Seattle, WA 98103
(206) 634-1903

Clearinghouse on Femicide
PO Box 12342
Berkeley, CA 94701-3342
(510) 845-7005

Clothesline Project
Box 727
East Dennis, MA 02641
(508) 385-7004
http://www.cybergrrl.com/dv/orgs/cp.html

Community United Against Violence
973 Market St., #500
San Francisco, CA 94103
(415) 577-5500
(415) 777-5565
http://www.xq.com/cuav/index.html

Commission For Prevention of Violence Against Women
915 Cedar St.
Santa Cruz, CA 95060
(408) 454-2772

Defensa De Mujeres
406 Main St., # 326
Watsonville, CA 95076
(408) 722-4532

National Clearinghouse for the Defense of Battered Women
125 S. 9th St., Suite 302
Philadelphia, PA 19107
(215) 351-0010

National Clearinghouse on Domestic Violence
PO Box 2309
Rockville, MD 20852

National Coalition Against Domestic Violence
PO Box 34013
Washington, D.C. 20043-4103
(202) 638-6388

National Coalition Against Domestic Violence
PO Box 18749
Denver, CO 80218

National Domestic Violence Hotline
3616 Far West Blvd., Suite 101-297
Austin, TX 78731-3074
800-799-SAFE (7233)
800-787-3224 (TDD)
(512) 453-8117 (Administration)

National Network to End Domestic Violence—Administrative Office
c/o Texas Council on Family Violence
8701 North Mopac Expressway, Suite 450
Austin, TX 78759

National Resource Center on Domestic Violence
Pennsylvania Coalition Against Domestic Violence
6400 Flank Dr., Suite 1300
Harrisburg, PA 17112

Powerful Choices
PO Box 30918
Seattle, WA 98103
(206) 782-5662
http://home.earthlink.net/~takecharge

PrePARE (Protection, Awareness Response, Empowerment)
147 W. 25th
New York, NY 10001
(800) 442-7273
FAX: (212) 225-0505

The Purple Ribbon Project
6053 Mooretown Rd.
Williamsburg, VA 23185
(757) 220-9274
http://www.cs.utk.edu/~bartley/other/prp.html

Silent Witness National Initiative
7 Sheridan Ave. S.
Minneapolis, MN 55405
(612) 377-6629
FAX: (612) 374-3956
http://www.cybergrrl.com/dv/orgs/sw.html

Standing Together Against Rape
1057 W. Firewood Ln. # 230
Anchorage, AK 99503
(907) 276-RAPE

Women Against a Violent Environment (WAVE)
PO Box 15650
Rochester, NY 14615
(716) 234-9709
http://www.rochester.edu/SBA/95-75/wave.html

Families and Children

Families and Children Reading Material

Adams, Caren, Jennifer Fay, and Loreen Martin. *No Is Not Enough: Helping Teenagers Avoid Sexual Assault.* San Luis Obispo, CA: Impact Publishers, 1984.

Bateman, Py and Gayle Stringer. *Where Do I Start? A Parent's Guide for Talking to Teens About Acquaintance Rape.* Dubuque, IA: Kendall/Hall Publishing Co., 1984.

Crary, Elizabeth. *Without Spanking or Spoiling: A Practical Approach to Toddler and Preschool Guidance.* Seattle: Parenting Press, 1979.

Dreikurs, R., M.D. *Children the Challenge.* New York: Dutton, 1987.

Faber, Adele and Elaine Mazlish. *How to Talk So Kids Will Listen and Listen So Kids Will Talk.* New York: Avon Books, 1980.

Gale, Jay. *A Parent's Guide to Teenage Sexuality.* New York: Henry Holt Publishing Co., 1989.

Garbarino, James, Edna Guttman and Janis Wilson Seeley. *The Psychologically Battered Child.* San Francisco: Jossey-Bass Publishers, 1986.

Garbarino, James and Gwen Gilliam. *Understanding Abusive Families.* Toronto: Lexington Books, 1980.

Germane, Charlotte, Margaret Johnson and Nancy Lemon. *Mandatory Custody Mediation and Joint Custody Orders in California: The Danger for Victims of Domestic Violence.* Berkeley Women's Law Journal, vol.1, no.1, Fall 1985.

Gil, Eliana. *Outgrowing the Pain: A Book for and About Adults Abused as Children.* New York: Dell, 1983.

Hyde, Margaret. *Cry Softly!: The Story of Child Abuse.* Philadelphia: Westminister Press, 1986.

Johnson, Kendall. *Trauma in the Lives of Children: Crisis and Stress Management Techniques for Counselors, EMTs, and Other Professionals.* Alameda, CA: Hunter House, 1997.

Johnson, Scott A. *Man to Man: When Your Partner Says No—Pressured Sex and Date Rape.* Orwell, VT: Safer Society Press, no date.

Johnston, Janet R. *High Conflict and Violent Parents in Family Court: Findings on Children's Adjustment, and Proposed Guidelines for the Resolution of Custody and Visitation Disputes.* Center for the Family in Transition, 5725 Paradise Dr., Building B, #300, Corte Madera, CA 94925, 1992.

Johnson, Scott A. *When "I Love You" Turns Violent: Emotional and Physical Abuse in Dating Relationships.* Far Hills, NJ: New Horizon Press, 1993.

Justice, Blair and Rita Justice, *The Abusing Family.* New York: Human Science Press, no date.

Kaufman, Bobbie and Agnes Wohl. *Silent Screams and Hidden Cries: An Interpretation of Artwork by Children from Violent Homes.* New York: Brunner-Hazel Publishers, 1985.

Kosf, Anna. *Incest: Families in Crisis.* New York: Franklin Watts, 1985.

Lindsay, Jeanne Warren. *Teenage Marriage.* Buena Park, CA: Morning Glory Press, 1984.

McDermott, Judith and Frances Wells Burck. *Children of Domestic Violence: A Guide for Moms.* Rockland Family Shelter, 1990.

Miedzian, M. *Boys Will Be Boys: Breaking the Link Between Masculinity and Violence.* New York: Anchor Books, 1991.

Mones, Paul A. *When a Child Kills: Abused Children Who Kill Their Parents.* New York: Pocket Books, 1991.

Muller, Ann. *Parents Matter: Parents' Relationship with Lesbian Daughters and Gay Sons.* Tallahassee, FL: Naiad Press, 1987.

Rafkin, Louise, ed. *Different Daughters: A Book by Mothers of Lesbians.* Pittsburgh: Cleis Press, 1987.

Schwartz, Pepper. *Peer Marriage: How Love Between Equals Really Works.* New York: Free Press, 1994.

Warren, Andrea and Jay Wiedenkeller. *Everybody's Doing It: How to Survive Your Teenagers' Sex Life (and Help Them Survive It Too).* New York: Penguin Books, 1993.

Whitlock, Katherine. *Bridges of Respect: Creating Support for Lesbian and Gay Youth.* Philadelphia: American Friends Service Committee, 1989.

Children's Reading Material

Ancona, George E.P. *I Feel: A Picture Book of Emotions.* New York: Dutton, 1977.

Davis, Diane. *Something Is Wrong at My House.* Seattle: Parenting Press, 1985.

Paris, Susan. *Mommy and Daddy Are Fighting.* Seattle: Parenting Press, 1986.

Stinson, K. *Mom and Dad Don't Live Together Anymore.* Willowdale, Ontario: Amich Press, 1984.

Wachter, Oralee. *No More Secrets for Me.* Boston: Little Brown & Co., 1983.

Teens' Reading Material

Borhek, Mary. *Coming Out to Parents: A Two Way Survival Guide for Lesbians and Gay Men and Their Parents.* Cleveland: Pilgrim Press, 1993.

Gittelsohn, Roland B. *Love in Your Life: A Jewish View of Teenage Sexuality.* New York: UAHC Press, 1991.

Herdt, Gilbert. *Gay and Lesbian Youth.* Binghampton, NY: Harrington Park Press, 1989.

Gordon, Sol. *The Teenage Survival Book.* New York: Book Times, 1981.

Hipp, Earl. *Feed Your Head: Some Excellent Stuff on Being Yourself.* Center City, MN: Hazelden, 1991.

Hyde, Margaret O. *Teen Sex.* Philadelphia: Westminster Press, 1988.

Kuklin, Susan G.P. *Speaking Out: Teenagers Take on Race, Sex, and Identity.* New York: Putnam's Sons, 1993.

Levy, Barrie. *In Love and in Danger: A Teen's Guide to Breaking Free of Abusive Relationships.* Seattle: Seal Press, 1993.

NiCarthy, Ginny. *Assertion Skills for Young Women.* Seattle: New Directions for Young Women, 1981.

Parrot, Andrea. *Sexual Assault on Campus.* Lexington, MA: Lexington Books, 1993.

Pritchard, Carol. *Avoiding Rape On and Off Campus.* Millburn, NY: American Focus Publishers, 1988.

Rue, Nancy N. *Coping with Date Violence.* New York: Rosen Publishing Group, 1989.

Silverstein, Herma. *Date Abuse.* Hillside, NJ: Enslow Publishers, 1994.

Families and Children Curricula

Bancroft, Lundy, Carole Sousa, and Ted German. *Preventing Teen Dating Violence: Three Session Curriculum for Teaching Adolescents.* Dating Violence Intervention Project, Cambridge, MA, (618) 868-8328, 1989.

Bridge Over Troubled Waters, Inc. and Texas Council on Family Violence. *Dating Violence: An Anti-Victimization Program.* Austin: Texas Council on Family Violence and Bridge Over Troubled Waters, Inc., 1990.

Cantor, Ralph with Paul Kivel, Allan Creighton, and Oakland Men's Project. *Days of Respect: Organizing a School-Wide Violence Prevention Program.* Alameda, CA: Hunter House, 1997.

Creighton, Allan and Paul Kivel, Battered Women's Alternatives with Oakland Men's Project. *Helping Teens Stop Violence: A Practical Guide for Counselors, Educators, and Parents.* Alameda, CA: Hunter House, 1990.

Edwards, Susan H. and Maria Moscaritolo. *Violence Is a Choice: A Curriculum of Violence Prevention Activities.* South Shore Women's Center, 225 Water Street, Suite 412, Plymouth, MA 02360, 1989.

Family Violence Curriculum Project. *Preventing Family Violence: A Curriculum for Adolescents.* Boston: Massachusetts Department of Public Health, 1984.

Harris, Cathy A. and Toby B. Simon. *Sex Without Consent, Volume I: A Peer Education Training Manual for Secondary Schools.* Holmes Beach, FL: Learning Publications, 1993.

Kivel, Paul. *Young Men's Work.* Center City, MN: Hazelden Educational Materials, 1994.

Kivel, Paul and Allan Creighton. *Making the Peace: A 15-Session Violence Prevention Curriculum for Young People.* Alameda, CA: Hunter House, 1997.

Levy, Barrie. *Skills for Violence-Free Relationships: A Curriculum for Young People, Ages 13–18.* Southern California Coalition for Battered Women, Box 5036, Santa Monica, CA 90405, 1984.

Minnesota Coalition for Battered Women. *My Family and Me—Violence Free: Domestic Violence Curriculum for Grades 4–6.* St. Paul: Minnesota Coalition for Battered Women, 1988.

Progressive Youth Center and Women's Self Help Center. *Project H.A.R.T.: Healthy Alternatives for Relationships Among Teens.* University City, MO: Progressive Youth Center and Women's Self Help Center, 1989.

Rosenbluth, Barri. *Expect Respect: A Support Group Curriculum Manual for Preventing Teenage Dating Violence and Promoting Healthy Relationships.* Austin: Teen Dating Violence Project, Austin Center for Battered Women, 1995.

Families and Children Videos

Someone You Know: Acquaintance Rape, 30 minutes, Coronet MTI, 4350 Equity Dr., PO Box 2649, Columbus, OH 43216.

Heart on a Chain: The Truth About Dating Violence, 17 minutes, Coronet MTI, 4350 Equity Dr., PO Box 2649, Columbus, OH 43216.

Pregnant Teen, video plus copies of brochures, "Are You in a SAFE Relationship?: Prevention of Battering During Pregnancy" (English/Spanish) and "Is Someone Hurting You?", Judith McFarlane, Texas Women's University, 1130 M.D. Anderson Blvd., Houston, TX 77030.

When Good Times Go Bad: Teenage Dating Violence, Turning Point and Columbus Service League, PO Box 103, Columbus, OH, 47202.

Scoring: A Story About Date Rape, 19 minutes, Coronet MTI, 4350 Equity Dr., P.O. Box 2649, Columbus, OH 43216.

Date Rape, Intermedia, Inc., 1300 Dexter North, Seattle, WA 98109, 1989.

Breaking the Chain: Building Healthy Relationships, Lori Lynette Mumford, Massachusetts Department of Public Health, 150 Tremont St., Third Floor, Boston, MA 02111.

Dating Violence: The Hidden Secret, Intermedia, Inc., 1300 Dexter North, Seattle, WA 98109, 1993.

My Girl: Battering in Teen Relationships, Battered Women's Alternatives, Youth Education and Support Services, PO Box 6406, Concord, CA 94524, 1987.

Teen Sex: Drawing the Line, Alternatives to Fear, 2811 East Madison, Suite 208, Seattle, WA 98112.

Families and Children Resource Agencies

Center for the Study of Anorexia and Bulimia
1 West 91st St.
New York, NY 10024
(212) 595-3449
http://www.social.com/health/nhic/data/hr2100/hr2111.html

Child Welfare League America
440 First St. NW, #520
Washington, D.C. 20001
(202) 833-2850

Children's Defense Fund
25 E St. NW
Washington, D.C. 20001
(202) 628-8787
http://www.tmn.com/cdf/index.html

Committee for Mother and Child Rights
Rt 1 Box 256 A
Cleark Brook, VA 22624
(703) 722-3652

Families First
250 Baltic St.
Brooklyn, NY 11201
(718) 855-3131

Family Violence Prevention Fund
383 Rhode Island St.
San Francisco, CA 94103
(800) 313-1310
(415) 252-8900

Mothers Without Custody
PO Box 27418
Houston, TX 77227-7418
(800) 457-6962

National Association of Mothers Centers
129 Jackson St.
Hempstead, NY 11550
(800) 645-3828

National Clearinghouse on Child Abuse and Neglect
10530 Rosehaven St., Suite 400
Fairfax, VA 22030

National Clearinghouse on Child Abuse and Family Violence
1155 Connecticut Ave., NW, Suite 400
Washington, D.C. 20036
(202) 505-3422

National Clearinghouse on Marital/Date Rape
2325 Oak St.
Berkeley, CA 94708
(510) 524-1582
http://www.emf.net/~cheetham/gna-pe-1.html

National Organization for Victim Assistance
1757 Park Road NW
Washington, D.C. 20010
(202) 232-6682

National Organization of Single Mothers
PO Box 68
Midland, NC 28107
(704) 888-2337
FAX: (704) 888-1752
http://cosmos.netgate.net/~pleiades/org/NOSMI.1.html

National Victim Center
2111 Wilson Blvd., Suite 300
Arlington, VA 22201
(703) 276-2880/(800) 877-3355

Parents, Families, and Friends of Lesbians and Gays (P-FLAG)
1012 14 St. NW, Suite 700
Washington, D.C. 20005
(202) 638-4200

Resource Center on Child Custody and Child Protection
NCJFCJ
PO Box 8970
Reno, NV 89507

Young Women's Project
923 F St. NW, Floor 3
Washington, D.C. 20004
(202) 393-0461

Sexual Abuse

Sexual Abuse Reading Material

Bass, Ellen and Laura Davis. *The Courage to Heal: A Guide for Women Survivors of Child Sexual Abuse.* New York: Harper and Row, 1988.

Blume, Sue E. *Secret Survivors: Uncovering Incest and Its After Effects in Women.* New York: Ballatine Books, 1990.

Crewdson, John. *Silence Betrayed: Sexual Abuse of Children in America.* Boston: Little, Brown and Company, 1988.

Finklehor, David. *Sexually Victimized Children.* New York: Free Press, 1979.

Hunter, Mic. *Abused Boys: The Neglected Victims of Sexual Abuse.* New York: Fawcett Columbine, 1990.

Woititz, Janet. *Healing Your Sexual Self.* Deerfield Beach, Florida: Health Communications, Inc., 1989.

Incest Survivors Education Project
United Ministries of Higher Education
1118 S. Harrison Rd.
East Lansing, MI 48823
(517) 332-2338

Incest Survivors Resource Network International
PO Box 7375
Las Cruces, NM 88006
(505) 521-4260

Moms, Mothers Opposed to Molestation Situations
PO Box 70665
Eugene, OR 97401
(541) 484-7252

National Center for Redress of Incest and Sexual Abuse
1858 Park Rd. NW
Washington, D.C. 20010
(202) 667-1160

RAINN: Rape, Abuse & Incest National Network
252 Tenth St. NE
Washington, D.C. 20002
(800) 656-HOPE
FAX: (202) 544-1401
http://www.cs.utk.edu/~bartley/other/RAINN.html

Substance Abuse and Recovery

Substance Abuse and Recovery Reading Material

Al-Anon Family Group Headquarters. *Al-Anon Faces Alcoholism,* New York: 1986.

Alcoholics Anonymous World Services. *Alcoholics Anonymous,* New York: 1976.

Beckman, Linda and Sharon Wilsnack, eds. *Alcohol Problems in Women* edited. New York: Guilford Press, 1984.

Black, Claudia. *It Will Never Happen to Me.* Ballantine Books, New York: 1981.

Flitcraft, Anne and Evan Stark. *Women At Risk: Domestic Violence and Women's Health.* Thousand Oaks, CA: Sage Publications, 1996.

Potter-Efron, P. S. and R.T. Potter-Efron, eds. *Aggression, Family Violence, and Chemical Dependency.* New York: Haworth Press, 1990.

Robertson, Nan. *Getting Better: Inside Alcoholics Anonymous.* New York: William Morrow and Company, 1988.

Russianoff, Penelope, ed. *Women in Crisis.* Human Science Press, New York: 1981.

Sandmaier, Marian. *The Invisible Alcoholics: Women and Alcohol Abuse in America.* New York: McGraw Hill, 1980.

Schaef, Anne Wilson. *Co-Dependence: Misunderstood, Mistreated.* Minneapolis, MN: Winston Press, 1986.

Swallow, Jean, ed. *Out from Under: Sober Dykes and Our Friends.* San Francisco: Spinsters Ink, 1983.

Woodside, Migs. *Childen of Alcoholics* (booklet). Available from State of New York: Division of Alcoholism and Alcohol Abuse, 1994 Washington Ave., Albany, NY, 12210.

Substance Abuse and Recovery Newsletters

The Healing Woman
PO Box 3038
Moss Beach, CA 94038
(408) 246-1788

Sobering Thoughts
PO Box 618
Quakerstown, PA 18951
(800) 333-1606 or (215) 536-8026

Women and Recovery
c/o Woman to Woman Communications
PO Box 151947-8
Cupertino, CA 95015
(408) 865-0472

Women's Recovery Network
PO Box 141554
Columbus, OH 43214
(614) 268-5847

Substance Abuse and Recovery Cross-Training Material

Haven House and the Alcoholism Center for Women. *Double Jeopardy.* Available from ACW, 1147 S. Alvarado, Los Angeles, CA 90006.

Wright, Janet. *Chemical Dependency and Violence: Working with Dually Affected Families.* Available from Wisconsin Clearinghouse, 1954 E. Washington Ave., Madison, WI 53704.

Substance Abuse and Recovery Resource Agencies

Coalition on Alcohol and Drug Dependent Women and Their Children
National Council on Alcoholism and Drug Dependence.
12 W. 21st St. 8th Floor
New York: NY 10010
(800) 423-4673 or (212) 206-6770

The Galano Club
Recovery and Social Club for Gay, Lesbian, Bisexual, and Transexual People
2408 N. Farwell
Milwaukee, WI 53211
(414) 276-6936
http://www.execpc.com/~reva

National Clearinghouse for Alcohol and Drug Information
PO Box 2345
Rockville, MD 20852
(301) 468-2600

Woman to Woman
Retreat for Women in Recovery
PO Box 30344
Sea Island, GA 31561
http://www.gacoast.com/recovery/w2w.html

WomanFocus
656 Elmwood Ave., #300
Buffalo, NY 14222
(716) 884-3256

Women in Transition
21 S. 12th St. 6th Floor
Philadelphia, PA 19107
(215) 564-5301
http://www.libertynet.org/~wit

Women's Alcohol and Drug Education Project
Women's Action Alliance
370 Lexington Ave. NW
Suite 603
New York, NY 10017

Women for Sobriety
PO Box 618
Quakerstown, PA 18951
(800) 333-1606 or (215) 536-8026

Legal Resources

Legal Reading Material

Anderson, Ken. *Texas Crime Victim's Handbook.* Georgetown, TX: Georgetown Press, 1995.

Browne, Angela. *When Battered Women Kill.* New York: The Free Press, 1987.

Buzawa, Carl G. and Eve S. Buzawa. *Domestic Violence: The Criminal Justice Response.* Thousand Oaks, CA: Sage Publications, 1996.

Ellis, Deborah A., Isabelle Katz Pinzler, Susan Deller Ross, and Kary L. Moss. *The Rights of Women: The Basic ACLU Guide to Women's Rights.* Carbondale, IL: Southern Illinois University Press, 1993.

Geller, Gloria. *Justice for Women Victims and Survivors of Abuse.* Social Administration Research Unit Faculty of Social Work, University of Regina. Regina, Saskatchewan, 1991.

Jones, Ann. *Women Who Kill.* New York: Holt, Rinehart and Winston, 1980.

Kuehl, Sheila James, and Lisa G. Lerman. *Mediator's Response to Abusive Men and Battered Women.* 2000 P St. NW, #508, Washington, D.C. 20036: National Woman Abuse Prevention Project, 1988.

Lardner, George, Jr. *The Stalking of Kristin.* New York: Atlantic Monthly Press, 1996.

Pence, Ellen. *The Justice System's Response to Domestic Violence Assault Cases.* Duluth, MN: Minnesota Program Development, 1985.

Richie, Beth E. *Compelled to Crime: The Gender Entrapment of Battered Black Women.* New York: Routledge, 1996.

Robson, Ruthann. *Lesbian (Out)Law: Survival Under the Rule of Law.* Ithaca, NY: Firebrand Books, 1992.

Project to Develop a Model Antistalking Code for States, National Criminal Justice Association, Department of Justice, National Institute of Justice, Washington, D.C., 1993.

Walker, Lenore E. *Terrifying Love: Why Battered Women Kill and How Society Responds.* New York: Harper Perennial, 1989.

Working Together for Change: Battered Women's Advocates and the Criminal Justice System, Texas Council on Family Violence, 8701 North Mopac Expressway, Suite 450, Austin, TX 78759, 1994.

Violent Crime Control and Law Enforcement Act of 1994, Public Law 103-322.

Legal Resource Agencies

AARP Legal Counsel for the Elderly
601 E. St. NW
Fourth Floor
Washington, D.C. 20049
(202) 434-2120

ACLU National Prison Project
1875 Connecticut Ave. NW
Suite 400
Washington, D.C. 20036
(202) 234-4830

Aid to Incarcerated Mothers
32 Rutland Rd.
Boston, MA 02138
(617) 536-0058

Center on Battered Women's Legal Services
105 Chambers St.
New York, NY 10007
(212) 349-6009

Custody Action for Lesbian Mothers
PO Box 281
Narberth, PA 19072
(215) 667-7508

Indian Law Support Center
Native American Rights Fund
1506 Broadway
Boulder, CO 80302
(303) 447-8760

Lambda Legal Defense and Education Fund
666 Broadway, #1200
New York. NY 10012
(212) 995-8585
http://www.gaysource.com/gs/ht/oct95/lambda.html

Legal Aid Society Domestic Violence Victim Assistance
322 E. 300 S, Suite 230
Salt Lake City, UT 84111
(801) 355-2804

Legal Services for Prisoners with Children
100 McAllister St.
San Francisco, CA 94102
(415) 255-7036

Migrant Legal Action Program
PO Box 53308
Washington, D.C. 20009
(202) 462-7744

National Bar Association
Black Elderly Legal Assistance Project
1225 11th St. NW
Washington, D.C. 20001
(202) 842-3900

National Battered Women's Law Project
799 Broadway
Room 402
New York, NY 10003
(212) 674-8200

National Center for Lesbian Rights
870 Market St., #570
San Francisco, CA 94102
(415) 392-6257

National Center on Women and Family Law
275 7th Ave., #1206
New York: NY 10001
(212) 741-9480

National Clearinghouse for the Defense of Battered Women
125 S. 9th St. Suite 302
Philadelphia, PA 19107
(215) 351-0010

National Criminal Justice Reference Service
Washington, D.C.
(800) 851-3420

National Domestic Violence Hotline
3616 Far West Blvd., Suite 101-297
Austin, TX 78731
(800) 799-SAFE (hotline)
(512) 453-8117 (administration)

National Legal Center for the Medically Dependent and Disabled
50 S. Meridian, Suite 605
Indianapolis, IN 46204
(317) 632-6245

National Women's Law Center Prison Project
1616 P St. NW
Washington, D.C. 20036
(202) 328-5160

NOW Legal Defense and Education Fund
99 Hudson St., Suite 12th Floor
New York, NY 10013
(212) 925-6635
http://www.nowldef.org/

Women's Law Project
125 S. Ninth Ave., Suite 401
Philadelphia, PA 19107
(215) 928-9801

Women's Prison Association
110 Second Ave.
New York: NY 10003
(212) 674-1163

Women of Color

Women of Color Reading Material

Allen, Paula Gunn. *The Sacred Hoop: Recovering the Feminine in American Indian Traditions.* Boston: Beacon Press, 1992.

Angelou, Maya. *I Know Why the Caged Bird Sings.* New York: Bantam Books, 1969.

Agtuca, Jacqueline R. *A Community Secret: For the Filipina in an Abusive Relationship.* Seattle: Seal Press, 1994.

Balzer, Roma, Genevieve James, Liz LaPraire, Tina Olson, Sandra L. Goodsky, and Eileen Hudon. *Full Circle: Coming Back to Where We Began.* Duluth, Minnesota: Minnesota Program Development, 1994.

Bataille, Gretchen M. and Kathleen Mullen-Sands. *American Indian Women.* Lincoln: University of Nebraska Press, 1984.

Bumiller, Elisabeth. *May You Be the Mother of a Hundred Sons: A Journey Among the Women of India.* New York: Fawcett Columbine, 1990.

Cornwell, Anita. *Black Lesbian in White America.* U.S.: Naiad Press, 1983.

Dasgupta, Shamita Das and Sujata Warrier. *In Visible Terms: Domestic Violence in the Asian Indian Context.* PO Box 614, Bloomfield, NJ 07003: Manavi, 1995.

hooks, bell. *Ain't I a Woman?: Black Women and Feminism.* South End Press, Boston: 1981.

Hungry Wolf, Beverly. *The Ways of My Grandmother.* New York: Quill, 1982.

Jelin, Elizabeth, ed. *Women and Social Change in Latin America.* Atlantic Highlands, NJ: Zed Books, 1990.

Levinson, David. *Family Violence in Cross Cultural Perspective.* Newbury Park, CA: Sage Publications, 1989.

Moraga, Cherríe and Gloria Anzaldúa, ed. *This Bridge Called My Back: Writings by Radical Women of Color.* New York: Kitchen Table: Women of Color Press, 1983.

Mousseau, Marlin and Karen Artichoker. *Domestic Violence Is Not Lakota/Dakota Tradition.* Medicine Wheel: South Dakota Coalition Against Domestic Violence and Sexual Assault Project, 1997.

Narasimhan, Sakuntala. *Sati: Widow Burning in India.* New York: Doubleday, 1990.

Ratti, R. *A Lotus of Another Color: An Unfolding of the South Asian Gay and Lesbian Experience.* Los Angeles, CA: Alyson Publications, 1993.

Richie, Beth E. *Compelled to Crime: The Gender Entrapment of Battered Black Women.* New York: Routledge, 1996.

Tsuchida, Nobuya, ed. *Asian and Pacific American Experiences: Women's Perspectives.* Minneapolis, MN: University of Minnesota Press, 1982.

Walker, Alice. *Possessing the Secret of Joy.* New York: Harcourt Brace Jovanovich, 1992.

White, Evelyn C. *Chain Chain Change: For Black Women Dealing with Physical and Emotional Abuse.* Seattle: The Seal Press, 1985.

Zambrano, Myrna M. *Mejor Sola Que Mal Acompañada: For the Latina in an Abusive Relationship.* Seattle: The Seal Press, 1985.

Zambrano, Myrna. *No Más: Gúia Para la Mujer Golpeada.* Seattle: The Seal Press, 1996.

Women of Color Resource Agencies

American Indian Women's Circle Against Domestic Violence
1929 S. 5th St.
Minn, MN 55454
(612) 340-0470

Asian American Legal Defense and Education Fund
99 Hudston St.
New York, NY 10013
(212) 966-5932

Asian Indian Women in America
RD 1, Box 98
Palisades, NY 10964
(914) 365-1066

Asian Task Force Against Domestic Violence
PO Box 120108
Boston, MA 02112
(617) 338-2350

BIHA: Black Indian Hispanic Asian Women in Action
122 W. Franklin Ave., #306
Minneapolis, MN 55404
(612) 870-1193

Cambodian Women for Progress
8102 Bonair Ct.
Silver Springs, MD 20910
(301) 386-0202

Indigenous Women's Network
PO Box 174
Lake Elmo, MN 55042
(612) 770-3861

Manavi (advocates for battered Asian women)
PO Box 614
Bloomfield, NJ 07003
(908) 687-2662

Mexican American Women's National Association
1101 17th St. NW, #803
Washington, D.C. 20036
(202) 833-0060

National Association of Cuban-American Women
2119 Webster St.
Fort Wayne, IN 46802
(219) 745-5421

National Council of Negro Women
1001 G St. NW, #800
Washington, D.C. 20006
(202) 628-0015

National Institute for Women of Color
3101 20th St. NW, #702
Washington, D.C. 20001
(202) 828-0735

National Political Congress of Black Women
282 w. 137th St.
NY, NY 10030
(212) 926-5388

Organization of Pan Asian American Women
PO Box 39128
Washington, D.C. 20016
(202) 659-9370

Revolutionary Sisters of Color
PO Box 191021
Roxbury, MA 02119
(617) 445-3432

Saheli (advocates for battered Asian women)
PO Box 3665
Austin, TX 78704
(512) 703-8745

Immigrant Women

Immigrant Women Reading Material

Violence Against Women Act (VAWA): Implications for Battered Immigrant Spouses and Children. The State Bar of Texas, 1414 Colorado, Austin, TX, 1995.

Immigrant Women. Maxine Seller, Temple University Press, Philadelphia, PA, 1981.

Immigrant Women Resource Agencies

Advocates for Immigrant Women
3094 Kaloaluiki St.
Honolulu, HI 96822
(808) 988-6026

Cosmopolitan Associates
PO Box 1491
West Caldwell, NJ 07007
(201) 992-2232

Refugee Women's Alliance
3004 S. Alaska St.
Seattle, WA 98108
(206) 721-6243

Lesbians and Gays Reading Material

Berzon, Betty. *Permanent Partners: Building Gay and Lesbian Relationships That Last.* New York: Plume, 1990.

Blumenfeld, Warren J. *Homophobia: How We All Pay the Price.* Boston: Beacon Press, 1992.

Island, David and Patrick Letellier. *Men Who Beat the Men Who Love Them: Battered Gay Men and Domestic Violence.* Binghampton, NY: Harrington Park Press, 1991.

Lesbian Battering Intervention Project. *Confronting Lesbian Battering: A Manual for the Battered Women's Movement.* St. Paul: Minnesota Coalition for Battered Women, 1990.

Lobel, Kerry, ed. *Naming the Violence: Speaking Out About Lesbian Battering.* Seattle: Seal Press, 1986.

Pharr, Suzanne. *Homophobia: A Weapon of Sexism.* Inverness, CA: Chardon Press, 1988.

Renzetti, Claire M. *Violent Betrayal: Partner Abuse in Lesbian Relationships.* Newbury Park, CA: Sage Publications, 1992.

Taylor, Joelle and Tracey Chandler. *Lesbians Talk Violent Relationships.* London: Scarlet Press, 1995.

Lesbians and Gays Resource Material

Custody Action for Lesbian Mothers
PO Box 281
Narbeth, PA 19072
(215) 667-7508

Human Rights Campaign Fund Federal Advocacy Network
1101 14th St. NW, #200
Washington, D.C. 20005
(202) 628-4160

Lambda Legal Defense and Education Fund
666 Broadway, 1200
New York: NY 10012
(212) 995-8585

Lesbian Mother's National Defense Fund
PO Box 21567
Seattle, WA 98111
(206) 325-2643

Lesbian Mothers Resource Network
PO Box 21567
Seattle, WA 98111
(206) 325-2643

Lesbian Support Services
PO Box 7164
Santa Rosa, CA 95407

National Gay and Lesbian Task Force
2320 17th St. NW
Washington, D.C. 20009
(202) 332-6483

Older Women

Older Women Reading Material

AARP Women's Initiative. *Abused Elders or Older Battered Women: Report on the AARP Forum.* Washington, D.C.: American Association of Retired Persons, 1992.

Adelman, Ronald D. and Risa S. Breckman. *Strategies for Helping Victims of Elder Mistreatment.* Newbury Park, CA: Sage Publications, 1988.

The Boston Women's Health Collective. *Ourselves Growing Older.* Boston: The Boston Women's Health Collective, 1987.

Chaney, Elsa M., ed. *Empowering Older Women: Cross-Cultural Views.* Women's Initiative, American Association of Retired Persons, 601 E Street N.W., Washington, D.C. 20049, 1990.

The Committee on the Status of Women. *STOP Violence Against Women: A Report and Recommendations from the Committee on the Status of Women.* New York: Episcopal Church Center, August 1994.

Decalmer, Peter and Frank Glendenning, eds. *The Mistreatment of Elderly People.* Newbury Park, CA: Sage Publications, 1993.

Goldman Institute on Aging. *Serving the Older Battered Woman: A Conference Planning Guide.* San Francisco: San Francisco Consortium for Elder Abuse Prevention, 1997.

Goodman, Jane and Elinor B. Waters. *Empowering Older Adults.* San Francisco: Jane Jossey-Bass Publishers, 1990.

Martz, Sandra, ed. *When I Am an Old Woman I Shall Wear Purple.* Watsonville, CA: Papier-Mache Press, 1987.

Nerenberg, Lisa. *Older Battered Women: Integrating Aging and Domestic Violence.* Washington, D.C.: National Center on Elder Abuse, January 1996.

Older Women's League. *Ending Violence Against Midlife and Older Women.* Washington, D.C.: Older Women's League, 1994.

Rosenthal, Evelyn R., ed. *Women, Aging, and Ageism.* Binghampton, NY: Harrington Park Press, 1990.

Vinton, L. "Battered Women's Shelters and Older Women: The Florida Experience." *Journal of Family Violence.* (January 1992): 63-71.

Older Women Resource Agencies

AARP Women's Initiative
601 E St. NW
Washington, D.C. 20049
(202) 434-2640

National Action Forum for Midlife and Older Women
Box 816
Stony Brook, NY 11790

National Aging Resource Center on Elder Abuse
810 First St. NE, Suite 500
Washington, D.C. 20002
(202) 682-2470

Older Women's League
666 11th St. NW, #700
Washington, D.C. 20001
(202) 783-6686

Women with Disabilities

Women with Disabilities Reading Material

Browne, Susan E., Debra Conners and Nanci Sterne. *With the Power of Each Breath: A Disabled Women's Anthology.* San Francisco: Cleiss Press, 1985.

Fine, Michelle and Adrienne Asch. *Women with Disabilities.* Philadelphia: Temple University Press, 1988.

Finger, Anne. *Past Due: A Story of Disability, Pregnancy, and Birth.* Seattle: The Seal Press, 1990.

Rousso, Harilyn with Susan Gusher O'Malley and Mary Severance. *Disabled, Female, and Proud.* Westport, CT: Bergin and Garvey, 1993.

Women and Disability Awareness Project. *Building Community: A Manual on Women and Disability.* New York: Educational Equity Concepts, Inc., 1984.

Women with Disabilities Resource Agencies

American Speech-Language-Hearing Assoc.
10801 Rockville Pike
Rockville, MD 20852
800-638-8255 (V/TDD)
(301) 897-5700 (V) or (301) 897-0157 (TDD)

Disabled Women's Alliance
510 16th St., #100
Oakland, CA 94612
(510) 251-4355

Domestic Violence Initiative/Women with Disabilities
PO Box 300535
Denver, CO 80203
(303) 839-5510

Women's Issues Task Force
United Handicapped Foundation
1821 University Ave.
St. Paul, MN 55104
(612) 645-8922

National Clearinghouse on Women and Girls with Disabilities
Educational Equity Concepts
114 E. 32nd, Room 701
New York: NY 10016
(212) 725-1803

Caretakers Resources

Caretakers Reading Material

Dass, Ram and Mirabai Bush. *Compassion in Action: Setting Out on the Path of Service.* New York: Bell Tower, 1992.

Ellin, Jeanne. *Listening Helpfully: How to Develop Your Counseling Skills.* London: Souvenir Press, Ltd., 1994.

Evans, Patricia. *The Verbally Abusive Relationship.* Holbrook, MA: Bob Adams, Inc., 1992.

Herman, Judith. *Trauma and Recovery.* New York: BasicBooks, 1992.

Jackson, Donna. *How to Make the World a Better Place for Women in Five Minutes a Day.* New York: Hyperion, 1992.

Maslach, Christina. *Burnout: The Cost of Caring.* New York: Prentice Hall Press, 1982.

Murdock Maureen. *The Heroine's Journey.* Boston: Shambhala, 1990.

Parry, Danaan. *Warriors of the Heart.* Cooperstown, New York: Sunstone Publications, 1989.

Small, Jacquelyn. *Becoming Naturally Therapeutic: A Return to the True Essence of Helping.* New York: Bantam Books, 1989.

Caretaker's Resource Agencies

National Assault Prevention Center
606 Delsea Dr.
Sewell, NJ 08080
(908) 369-8972

National Organization for Victim Assistance
1757 Park Rd. NW
Washington, D.C. 20010
(202) 232-6682

Workplace Related Resources

Workplace Reading Material

Bensimon, Helen Frank. "Violence in the Workplace." *Training and Development,* 48, January 1994, pp. 27–32.

Kelley, Sandra J. "Making Sense of Violence in the Workplace." *Risk Management,* 42,10, October, 1995, pp. 50–57.

Ketterman, Grace. *Verbal Abuse.* Ann Arbor, Michigan: Servant Publications, 1992.

Kinney, Joseph A. and Dennis L. Johnson. *Breaking Point: The Workplace Violence Epidemic and What to Do About It.* Chicago: National Safe Workplace Institute, 1993.

Minor, Marianne. *Preventing Workplace Violence: Positive Management Strategies.* Menlo Park, CA: Crisp Publications, 1995.

Moskey, Stephen T. *Domestic Violence Policy Checklists for the Workplace: A Guide for Employers.* Cape Elizabeth, ME: Kettle Cove Press, 1996.

National Institute for Occupational Safety and Health, Publications Dissemination. *Preventing Homicides in the Workplace.* DSDTT, 4676 Columbia Parkway, Cincinnati, OH 45226, September 1993.

Scholder, Amy, ed. *Critical Condition: Women on the Edge of Violence.* San Francisco: City Lights Books, 1993.

Shepard, Melanie. "The Effect of Battering on the Employment Status of Women." *Women and Social Work,* May 1988.

Workplace Resource Agencies

National Association of Working Women, 9 to 5
614 Superior Ave. NW
Cleveland, OH 44113
(216) 566-9308

National Workplace Resource Center on Domestic Violence
383 Rhode Island St., Suite 304
San Francisco, CA 94103
(415) 252-8900

Publications Dissemination, DSDTT
National Institute for Occupational Safety and Health
4676 Columbia Parkway
Cincinnati, OH 45226-1998
(800)-35-NIOSH

Texas Council on Family Violence
8701 N. MoPac Expressway, Suite 450
Austin, TX 78759
(512) 794-1133

Women's Bureau
Department of Labor
Washington, D.C. 20210
(202) 219-6652

Workplace Programs

Employee Assistance Program
Polaroid Corporation
549 Technology Square
Cambridge, MA 02139
(617) 386-2000

Women's Work
c/o PT & Co.
320 West 13th Street 7th Floor
New York: NY 10014
(212) 229-0500

Health Resources

Health Reading Material

The Boston Women's Health Book Collective. *The New Our Bodies, Ourselves: A Book by and for Women.* New York: Simon and Schuster, 1984.

Campbell, Jacquelyn and Janice Humphreys. *Nursing Care of Victims of Family Violence.* Englewood Cliffs, NJ, Reston Publishing Company, 1984.

Chernin, Kim. *The Hungry Self: Women, Eating, and Identity.* New York: Times Books, 1985.

Orbach, Susie. *Fat Is a Feminist Issue.* New York: Berkeley Publishers, 1982.

Salber, Patricia R. and Ellen Taliaferro. *The Physician's Guide to Domestic Violence: How to Ask the Right Questions and Recognize Abuse . . . Another Way to Save a Life.* Volcano, CA: Volcano Press, 1995.

Schechter, Susan with Lisa Tieszen Gary. *Health Care Services for Battered Women and Their Abused Children: A Manual About AWAKE.* Boston: Children's Hospital, 1992.

Stark, Evan and Anne Flitcraft. *Women at Risk: Domestic Violence and Women's Health.* Thousand Oaks, CA: Sage Publications, 1996.

White, Kathleen, et al. *Treating Child Abuse and Family Violence in Hospitals: A Program for Training and Services.* Lexington, MA: Lexington Books, 1989.

Health Care Protocols and Training Material

Domestic Violence: A Guide for Emergency Medical Treatment, State of New Jersey, Division on Women, Department of Community Affairs, Trenton, NJ, 1986.

Start the Healing Now: What You Can Do About Family Violence, Texas Medical Association and the Texas Council on Family Violence, Austin, TX, 1992.

Domestic Violence: A Guide for Health Care Providers, Colorado Department of Health and the Colorado Domestic Violence Coalition, Denver, 1991.

Domestic Violence: A Guide for Health Care Professionals, State of New Jersey, Department of Community Affairs, Trenton, NJ, 1990.

Domestic Violence: Identification, Intervention and Nursing Documentation, Austin Center for Battered Women, Austin, TX, 1996.

Health Videos

Amigas Latinas En Acción Pro-Salud, 51 minutes, ALAS, 240a Elm St., Somerville, MA 02114, (617) 776-4161.

Crimes Against the Future, 23 minutes, March of Dimes Foundation, 1275 Mamaroneck Ave., White Plains, NY 10605, (914) 997-4495.

Domestic Violence: Recognizing the Violence, 30 minutes, Colorado Domestic Violence Coalition, 7700 E. Iliff Ave., Unit H, Denver, CO 80237, (800) 368-0406.

In Need of Special Attention, 18 minutes, Select Media, 74 Varick St., Third Floor, New York: NY 10013-1019, (212) 431-8923.

The Battered Women, versions available for RN, MD, Counselor and Emergency Room personnel, New Jersey Department of Community Affairs, Division on Women, Domestic Violence Prevention Program, 101 S. Broad St., Trenton, NJ 08625-0801, (609) 292-8840.

Video for Physicians Only! Battered Women in Your Practice, 17 minutes, Network for Continuing Medical Education, One Harmon Plaza, Secaucus, NJ 07094, (800) 223-0272.

Health Resource Agencies

American College of Obstetricians and Gynecologists
ACOG Resource Center
409 12th St. SW
Washington, D.C. 20024-2188
(800) 673-8444 or (202) 863-2518

American College of Physicians
Department of Public Policy
Independence Mall West
6th St. at Race
Philadelphia, PA 19106
(800) 523-1546

American Medical Association
Department of Mental Health
515 State St.
Chicago, IL 60610
(312) 464-5066

American Medical Women's Association
801 N. Fairfax St., #400
Alexandria, VA 22314
(703) 838-0500
URL: http//www.hygeia.com.amwa/

Association for Women's AIDS Research and Education
San Francisco General Hospital
Building 90, Ward 95
955 Potrero
San Francisco, CA 94110
(415) 476-4092

Black Women's Health Project
5021 Baltimore
Philadelphia, PA 19143
(215) 474-3066

Black Women Physicians Project
3300 Henry St.
Philadelphia, PA 19129
(215) 842-7124

Boston Women's Health Book Collective
240 A Elm Street
Somerville, MA 02144
(617) 625-0271

Cambodian Women's Health Project
150 Tremont St., 7th Floor
Boston, MA 02111
(617) 727-7222

Canadian Women's Health Network
419 Graham Ave., 2nd Floor
Winnipeg, Manito,
(204) 947-2422 x134
Fax: (204) 943-3844
E-Mail: cwhn@cwhn.co

Caribbean Women's Health Association
2725 Church Ave.
Brooklyn, NY 11226
(718) 826-2942

Center for Women Policy Studies
National Resource Center on Women and AIDS
1211 Connecticut Ave. NW, Suite 312
Washington, D.C. 20036
(202) 872-1770

Children's Safety Network
Education & Development Center
55 Chapel St.
Newton, MA 02158
(617) 969-7100

Coalition for the Medical Rights of Women
558 Capp St.
San Francisco, CA 94110
(415) 567-2674

Federation of Feminist Health Centers
633 E. 11th St.
Eugene, OR 97401
(541) 344-0966

Indian Health Service
Federal Women's Program
Parklawn Building, Room 6A14
5600 Fishers Ln.
Rockville, MD 20857
(301) 443-2700

International Women's Health Coalition
24 # 21st St., 5th Floor
New York, NY 10010
(212) 979-8500

Health Resource Center on Domestic Violence
383 Rhode Island, # 304
San Francisco, CA 94103
URL: http://www.fvpf.org/fund/healthcare/

Hispanic Health Council
175 Main St.
Hartford, CT 06106
(860) 527-0856

March of Dimes Birth Defects Foundation
Material and Supply Division
1275 Mamaroneck Ave.
White Plains, NY 10605
(914) 428-7100

National Association of Women's Health Professionals
175 W. Jackson Blvd., #A1711
Chicago, IL 60604
(312) 786-1468
Fax: (312) 786-0376
URL: http/www.healthwire.com/nawhp/

National Black Women's Health Project
1237 Ralph David Abernathy Blvd. SW
Atlanta, GA 30310
(800) 275-2947 or (404) 758-9590

National Coalition of Physicians Against Domestic Violence
c/o AMA
515 State Street
Chicago, IL 60610
(312) 464-5000

National Council on Women's Health
1300 York Ave., Box 52
New York, NY 10021
(212) 746-6967

National Latina Health Organization
PO Box 7567
Oakland, CA 94601
(510) 534-1362

National Institute of Mental Health
Violence and Traumatic Stress Research Office
5600 Fishers Ln., Room 10-C-24
Rockville, MD 20857
(301) 443-3728

National Minority AIDS Council
1931 13th St., NW
Washington, D.C. 20009
(202) 483-6622

National Resource Center for Women and AIDS
710 I St., SE
Washington D.C., 20003
(202) 547-1155

National Women's Health Network
514 10th St. NW, Suite 400
Washington, D.C. 20004
(202) 347-1140

National Women's Health Resource Center
2425 L St. NW, 3rd Floor
Washington, D.C. 20037
(202) 293-6045

Native American Women's Health Education Resource Center
PO Box 572
Lake Andes, SD 57356
(605) 487-7072

Nursing Network on Violence Against Women
Oregon State University
School of Nursing
SN-FAM
3181 SW Sam Jackson Park Rd.
Portland, OR 97201-3098
(503) 494-7207

Pregnancy and Infant Loss Center
1421 Wayzata Blvd., #30
Wayzata, MN 55391
(612) 473-9372

Women and Wellness
150 Omega Dr., Building K
Newark, DE 19713
(302) 368-9625

Women's Health Action and Mobilization (WHAM)
PO Box 733
New York, NY 10009
(212) 560-7177

Women's Health Initiative
650 Pennsylvania Ave. SE
Washington, D.C. 20003
(202) 675-4770

Health Advocacy Programs

AWAKE, Children's Hospital
300 Longwood Ave.
Boston, MA 02115
(617) 355-7979

WomanKind
Fairfield Southdale Hospital
6401 France Ave. South
Edina, MN 55435
(612) 924-5775

Religious Resources

Religious Reading Material

Alsdurf, James and Phyllis Alsdurf. *Battered into Submission: The Tragedy of Wife Abuse in the Christian Home.* Downers Grove, Illinois: InverVarsity Press, 1989.

Brown, Joanne Carlson and Carole R. Bohn. *Christianity, Patriarchy, and Abuse: A Feminist Critique.* New York: The Pilgrim Press, 1989.

Bussert, Joy M.K. *Battered Women: From a Theology of Suffering to an Ethic of Empowerment.* New York: Division for Missions in North America, Lutheran Church in America, 1986.

Clarke, Rita-Lou. *Pastoral Care of Battered Women.* Philadelphia: The Westminster Press, 1986.

Fortune, Marie M. *Keeping the Faith: Questions and Answers for the Abused Woman.* San Francisco: Harper, 1987.

Fortune, Marie M. *Violence in the Family: A Workshop Curriculum for Clergy and Other Helpers.* Cleveland, OH: The Pilgrim Press, 1991.

Horton, Anne L. and Judith A.Williams, eds. *Abuse and Religion: When Praying Isn't Enough.* Lexington, MA: Lexington Books, 1988.

Ketterman, Grace H. *Verbal Abuse.* Ann Arbor, MI: Servant Publications, 1992.

Mathews, Alice. *A Woman God Can Use.* Grand Rapids, MI: Discovery House Publishers, 1990.

Spitzer, Julie. *When Love Is Not Enough: Spousal Abuse in Rabbinic and Contemporary Judaism.* New York: National Federation of Temple Sisterhoods, 1985.

Religious Resource Agencies

Center for Women and Religion
Graduate Theological Union
2400 Ridge Rd.
Berkeley, CA 94709
(510) 649-2490

Church Women United
475 Riverside Dr.
New York, NY 10115
(212) 870-2347

Coalition on Women and Religion
4759 15th Ave. NE
Seattle 98105
(206) 525-1213

Evangelical and Ecumenical Women's Caucus International
PO Box 9989
Oakland, CA
(510) 635-5098

Institute of Women Today
7315 S. Yale
Chicago, IL 60621
(312) 651-8372

National Assembly of Religious Women
529 S. Wabash Ave., #404
Chicago, IL 60605
(312) 663-1980

Priests for Equality
PO Box 5243
West Hyattville, MD 20782
(301) 699-0042

Resource Center for Women and Ministry in the South
331 W. Main St., Suite 608
Durham, NC 27701
(919) 687-0408

Task Force on Equality of Women in Judaism
838 5th Ave.
New York, NY 10021
(212) 249-0100

The Religious Network for Equality for Women
475 Riverside Dr., Room 812A
New York, NY 10115
(212) 870-2995

Women's Alliance for Theology, Ethics, and Ritual
8035 13th St., Suite 3
Silver Spring, MD 20910
(301) 589-2509

Women in Mission and Ministry
Episcopal Church Center
815 2nd Ave.
New York, NY 10017
(800) 334-7626

Prevention Additional Resources

Prevention Reading Material

Chesler, Phyllis. *Women and Madness.* Garden City, NY: Doubleday, 1972.

Colodzin, Benjamin. *How to Survive Trauma.* Barrytown, NY: PULSE, 1993.

Family Violence Prevention Fund. *A Study of Family and Domestic Violence: Homicide Cases in San Francisco.* San Francisco: San Francisco Commission on the Status of Women, 1993.

Freire, Paulo. *Pedagogy of the Oppressed.* NY: Continuum, 1970.

Herman, Judith Lewis. *Trauma and Recovery.* NY: BasicBooks, 1992.

Jordan, Judith V., Alexandra G. Kaplan, Jean Baker Miller, Irene P. Stiver and Janet L. Surrey. *Women's Growth In Connection: Writings from the Stone Center.* NY: The Guilford Press, 1991.

Lerner-Robbins, Helene. *Our Power as Women: Wisdom and Strategies of Highly Successful Women.* Berkeley, CA: Conari Press, 1996.

Miller, Jean Baker. *Toward a New Psychology of Women.* Boston: Beacon Press, 1976.

NiCarthy, Ginny, Karen Merriam and Sandra Coffman. *Talking It Out: A Guide to Groups for Abused Women.* Seattle: Seal Press, 1984.

NiCarthy, Ginny. *Getting Free: You Can End Abuse and Take Back Your Life.* Seattle: Seal Press, 1986.

Pence, Ellen. *In Our Best Interest: A Process for Personal and Social Change.* Duluth, MN: Minnesota Program Development, 1987.

Schaef, Anne Wilson. *Women's Reality: An Emerging Female System in a White Male Society.* NY: Harper, 1981.

Stone, Maria Fradella. *Domestic Violence Fatality Reviews: One Step Closer to a Solution.* Berkeley: Boalt Hall School of Law, University of California at Berkeley, 1995.

Tavris, Carol. *The Mismeasure of Woman.* NY: Simon and Schuster, 1992.

Whalen, Mollie. *Counseling to End Violence Against Women: A Subversive Model.* Thousand Oaks, CA: Sage Publications, 1996.

Prevention Agencies

National Network to End Domestic Violence – Policy Office
701 Pennsylvania Ave. NW, Suite 900
Washington, D.C. 20004

Center for the Prevention of Sexual and Domestic Violence
936 North 34th St. Suite 200
Seattle, WA 98103
(206) 634-1903

Travis County Family Violence Task Force
Project Courage
PO Box 1748
Austin, TX 78767
(512) 708-4423

Batterers Resources

Batterers Reading Material

Culligan, Joseph J. *When In Doubt Check Him Out.* Miami, FL: Hallmark Press, 1993.

Edleson, Jeffrey L. and Richard M. Tolman. *Intervention for Men Who Batter: An Ecological Approach.* Seattle: Sage Publications, 1992.

Gil, Eliana. *Outgrowing the Pain: A Book for and About Adults Abused as Children.* NY: Dell, 1983.

Gondolf, Edward. *Men Who Batter: An Integrated Approach for Stopping Wife Abuse.* Holmes Beach, FL: Learning Publications, 1985.

Gondolf, Edward. *Men Against Women: What Every Woman Should Know About Violent Men.* Blue Ridge Summit, PA: TAB Books, Inc., 1989.

Gondolf, Edward W. and David M. Russell. *Man to Man: A Guide for Men in Abusive Relationships.* Bradenton, Florida: Human Services Institute, 1987.

Johnson, Scott Allen. *Man to Man: When Your Partner Says No-Pressured Sex and Date Rape.* Orwell, VT: Safer Society Press, 1992.

Kivel, Paul. *Men's Work: How to Stop the Violence that Tears Our Lives Apart.* NY: Hazelden/Ballantine, 1992.

Paymar, Michael and Ellen Pence. *Education Groups for Men Who Batter: The Duluth Model.* NY: Springer Publishing Company, 1993.

Paymar, Michael. *Violent No More: Helping Men End Domestic Abuse.* Alameda, CA: Hunter House, 1993.

Russell, Mary Nomme and Jobst Frohberg. *Confronting Abusive Beliefs: Group Treatment for Abusive Men.* Seattle: Sage Publications, 1995.

Sonkin, Daniel Jay. *The Counselor's Guide to Learning to Live Without Violence.* Volcano, CA: Volcano Press, 1995.

Stordeur, Richard A. and Richard Stille. *Ending Men's Violence Against Their Partners: One Road to Peace.* Seattle: Sage Publications, 1989.

Thorne-Finch, Ron. *Ending the Silence: The Origins and Treatment of Male Violence Against Women.* Toronto: University of Toronto Press, 1992.

Batterers Resource Agencies

EMERGE
2380 Massachusetts Ave.
Cambridge, MA 02140
(617) 422-1550

National Training Project
206 W. Fourth St.
Duluth, MN 55806
(218) 722-2781

The Oakland Men's Project
1203 Preservation Parkway, Suite 200
Oakland, CA 94612
(510) 835-2433

Texas Council on Family Violence
8701 N. Mopac Expressway, Suite. 450
Austin, TX 78759
(512) 794-1133

Self-Help Reading Materials

Davis, Martha, Elizabeth Robbins Eshelman, and Matthew McKay. *The Relaxation and Stress Reduction Workbook.* Oakland, CA: New Harbinger Publications, 1982.

Dowrick, Stephanie. *Intimacy and Solitude.* New York: W.W. Norton and Company, 1991.

Dowrick, Stephanie. *The Intimacy and Solitude Workbook: Self-Therapy for Lasting Change.* New York: W.W. Norton and Company, 1993.

Francis, Cindy. *Life Lessons for Women.* Austin, TX: Newport House, Inc., 1992.

Fanning, Patrick. *Visualization for Change.* Oakland, CA: New Harbinger Publications, 1988.

Folan, L. *Lilias, Yoga, and Your Life.* New York: MacMillan, 1981.

Gawain, Shakti. *Creative Visualization.* San Rafael, CA: New World Library, 1978.

Goldstein, Joseph. *Insight Meditation: The Practice of Freedom.* Boston: Shambhala, 1994.

Johnson, Robert A. *Inner Work: Using Dreams and Active Imagination for Personal Growth.* San Francisco: Harper and Row Publishers, 1986.

Karpinski, Gloria D. *Where Two Worlds Touch: Spiritual Rites of Passage.* New York: Ballantine Books, 1990.

Kauz, Herman. *Tai Chi Handbook: Exercise, Meditation, and Self-Defense.* Dolphin Books, 1974.

Lark, Susan M. *Anxiety and Stress: A Self-Help Program.* Los Altos, CA: Westchester Publishing Company, 1993.

Moore, Thomas. *Care of the Soul: A Guide for Cultivating Depth and Sacredness in Everyday Life.* New York: HarperCollins Publishers, 1992.

Phelps, Stanlee, and Nancy Austin. *The Assertive Woman.* San Luis Obispo, CA: Impact Publishers, 1975.

Reed, Henry. *Dream Solutions: Using Your Dreams to Change Your Life.* San Rafael, CA: New World Library, 1991.

Steinem, Gloria. *Revolution from Within: A Book of Self-Esteem.* Boston: Little, Brown, and Company, 1992.

Saunders, Charmaine. *Women and Stress.* New York: Crescent Books, 1990.

Wildwood, Christine. *Creative Aromatherapy.* San Francisco: Thorsons, 1993.

Wildwood, Chrissie. *Erotic Aromatherapy.* New York: Sterling Publishing Company, 1994.

Women's History and Politics Resources

Women's History and Politics Reading Material

Agonito, Rosemary. *History of Ideas of Woman: A Source Book.* New York: Perigee Books, 1977.

Anderson, Bonnie, and Judith Zinsser. *A History of Their Own.* New York: Harper and Row, 1989.

Barstow, Anne Llewellyn. *Witchcraze: A New History of the European Witch Hunts.* San Francisco: Pandora Books, 1994.

Davis, Angela. *Women, Race and Class.* New York: Vintage Books, 1981.

Ehrenreich, Barbara, and Deirdre English. *For Her Own Good: 150 Years of the Experts' Advice to Women.* New York: Doubleday Books, 1978.

Evans, Sara. *Personal Politics.* New York: Vintage Books, 1979.

Gordon, Linda. *Heroes of Their Own Lives: The Politics and History of Family Violence.* New York: Penguin Books, 1988.

Humm, Maggie, ed. *Modern Feminisms: Political, Literary, Cultural.* New York: Columbia University Press, 1992.

Hymowitz, Carol, and Michaele Weissman. *A History of Women in America.* New York: Bantam Books, 1978.

Lerner, Gerda. *The Creation of Patriarchy.* New York: Oxford University Press, 1986.

Lightfoot-Klein, Hanny. *Prisoners of Ritual: An Odyssey into Female Genital Circumcision in Africa.* New York: Harrington Park Press, 1989.

Martin, Del. *Battered Wives.* Volcano, CA: Volcano Press, 1981.

Masson, Jeffrey Moussaieff. *A Dark Science: Women, Sexuality and Psychiatry in the Nineteenth Century.* New York: The Noonday Press, 1986.

McAllister, Pam. *This River of Courage: Generations of Women's Resistance and Action.* Philadelphia, PA: New Society Publishers, 1991.

Narasimhan, Sakuntala. *Sati: Widow Burning in India.* New York: Anchor Books, 1990.

Radford, Jill, and Diana E.H. Russell, eds. *Femicide: The Politics of Woman Killing.* New York: Twayne Publishers, 1992.

Schechter, Susan. *Women and Male Violence: The Visions and Struggles of the Battered Women's Movement.* Boston: South End Press, 1982.

Showalter, Elaine. *The Female Malady: Women, Madness and English Culture, 1830-1980.* New York: Penguin Books, 1985.

Williams, Selma R., and Pamela Williams Adelman. *Riding the Nightmare: Women and Witchcraft from the Old World to Colonial Salem.* New York: Harper Perennial, 1992.

Wollstonecraft, Mary. *A Vindication of the Rights of Woman.* New York: Everyman's Library, 1992. Originally published J. Johnson, London, 1792.

Women's History and Politics Resource Agencies

American Civil Liberties Union
Women's Rights Project
132 W. 43rd St.
New York, NY 10036
(212) 944-9800
http://www.aclu.org/issues/women/hmwo.html

Amnesty International USA
Women and Human Rights Project
322 Eighth Ave.
New York, NY 10001
(212)775-5161

Bethune Museum and Archives
National Archives for Black
Women's History
1318 Vermont Ave. NW
Washington, D.C. 20005
(202) 332-1233

Challenging Media Images of Women
PO Box 902
Framingham, MA 01701
(508) 879-8504

Clearinghouse on Women's Issues
PO Box 70603
Friendship Heights, MD 20813
(202) 362-3789

Elizabeth Cady Stanton
Foundation
PO Box 603
Seneca Falls, NY 13148
(315) 568-2703

Lesbian Herstory Archives
Lesbian Herstory Educational Foundation
484 14th St.
Brooklyn, NY 11215
(718) 768-DYKE

National Organization for Women
1000 16th St. NW, #700
Washington, D.C. 20036
(202) 331-0066
http://now.ord/now/home.html

National Women's History Project
7738 Bell Rd.
Windsor, CA 95492
(707) 838-6000
URL: http://www.nwhp.org

NWSA: National Women's Studies Association
7100 Baltimore, #501, University of Maryland
College Park, MD 20740
(301) 403-0525
E-Mail: nwsa@umail.edu
URL: http://www.feminist.com/nwsa.htm

Redstockings of the Women's
Liberation Movement and ARC
PO Box 744
Stuyvesant Sta.
New York, NY 10009
(212) 777-9241

Smithsonian Institution Museum
of American History
National Women's History Collection
Washington, D.C. 20560
(202) 357-2008

United Federation of Teachers
Women's Rights Committee
260 Park Ave. S.
New York: NY 10010
(212) 598-7738

Upper Midwest Women's History
Center for Teachers
1536 Hewitt Ave.
St. Paul, MN 55104
(612) 928-6750
URL:http://www.hamline.edu

Women's Action Alliance, Inc.
370 Lexington Ave., Suite 603
New York, NY 10017
(212) 532-8330
http://www.womenconnect.com/wco/or20550j.html

Women's History Research
2325 Oak St,
Berkeley, CA 94708
(510) 524-1582
E-Mail: laurax@igc.apc.org
URL: http://www.emf.net/cheetham/gna-pe-l.html

Index

A

D

T

U

V

W

Y

Z

DOMESTIC VIOLENCE

VIOLENT NO MORE: Helping Men End Domestic Abuse

by Michael Paymar, Trainer at Duluth Domestic Abuse Intervention Project

Based on the model domestic abuse intervention program in Duluth, Minnesota, VIOLENT NO MORE addresses abusive men directly, taking them step-by-step through the process of recognizing their abusive behaviors, taking a time out when necessary, and learning how to express anger without violence. The changes are illustrated with the often shocking stories of several previously abusive men—and of women who were abused.

VIOLENT NO MORE offers a self-help option to men, as well as a blueprint for organizations that work with them. It shows the way through rage, fear, and insecurity to self-respect, communication, and negotiation.

> **"I asked men in the domestic violence program groups that I lead to use the book and give some feedback. The consensus was positive, in that the men believed that the book was supportive of them while encouraging change . . . . As one man said, the book gave him a map but the journey is still his to undertake." — Anne L. Ganley, Ph.D., from *Violence Update***

Michael Paymar is Training Coordinator for the Domestic Abuse Intervention Project in Duluth. He has worked with abusive men for over 15 years and conducts seminars and training sessions throughout the world.

224 pages ... Paperback $12.95 ... Hard cover $21.95

LIVING WITH MY FAMILY—*A Workbook for Children*

by Wendy Deaton, MFCC, and Kendall Johnson, Ph.D.

Part of the *Growth and Recovery Workbooks for Children* series, LIVING WITH MY FAMILY is for working one-on-one with children traumatized by domestic violence. Created by an award-winning team of authors and illustrators, it helps children ages 6 to 12 express their fears and confusion. Tasks are balanced between writing and drawing, thinking and feeling. They are keyed to the phases and goals of therapy: creating a therapeutic alliance; "unpacking" traumatic memories; exploring delayed reactions; teaching coping strategies and strength-building. Each is formatted to become the child's own book, with plenty of space to write and draw, friendly line drawings, and a place for the child's name right on the colorful cover. Each also comes with a removable four-page Professional's Guide with page-by-page thumbnail explanations of each activity and helpful references to *Trauma in the Lives of Children* (see next page) for more detailed information on each area. A selection of the Behavioral Science Book Service.

Other workbooks in the series include:

- No More Hurt
- Someone I Love Died
- A Separation in My Family
- Drinking and Drugs in My Family
- My Own Thoughts and Feelings (for Girls/Boys)
- My Own Thoughts on Stopping the Hurt

32-page workbook $8.95 ... Workbook Library (All 8 in the series) $50.00

YOUTH VIOLENCE PREVENTION

MAKING THE PEACE: A 15-Session Violence Prevention Curriculum for Young People *by* Paul Kivel & Allan Creighton with the Oakland Men's Project

This essential curriculum presents a dynamic structure for working with today's youth to break the cycle of violence. Teachers, administrators, and youth group leaders are given all the information they need to implement a 15-session core curriculum, together with step-by-step instructions to create a climate of safety and anticipate difficult situations. Through exercises, roleplays, homework assignments, posters, and class discussions, students are shown how to: understand the social and economic roots of violence; deal with dating violence, fights, suicide, and sexual harassment; develop leadership and learn practical techniques for stopping the violence.

> **"Violence is usually dealt with as a question of managing offenders and protecting everyone else from their acts. It is therefore refreshing and wonderful to come upon a curriculum that tackles the root causes of violence while at the same time trying to help violent people come to terms with their actions." — Herbert Kohl, from *Rethinking Schools***

192 pages ... Paperback ... $24.95

DAYS OF RESPECT: Organizing a School-Wide Violence Prevention Program *by* Ralph Cantor with Paul Kivel, Allan Creighton, and the Oakland Men's Project

A multiday, school-wide program that brings young people, parents, teachers, and the community together to solve social problems and encourage respect for differences. It cultivates a community and school commitment to nonviolent behavior and promotes integrity, support for others, and student leadership. As part of the Making the Peace program, DAYS OF RESPECT can be used as a follow-up or a precursor to implementing the core curriculum—or as a completely independent project. Drawing on successful presentations in several schools, this manual gives step-by-step instructions for setting up the program, from presenting the idea to parents and administrators, to conducting planning meetings and facilitation groups, to staging the event and establishing ongoing campaigns to reduce violence and promote respect. Written with an experienced teacher and program director, it includes checklists, timetables, training exercises, handouts, sample press releases, and final evaluations.

80 pages ... Paperback ... $14.95

HELPING TEENS STOP VIOLENCE: A Practical Guide for Counselors, Educators, and Parents *by* Allan Creighton with Paul Kivel

Based on programs developed by Battered Women's Alternatives and the Oakland Men's Project, this book offers a proactive, multicultural approach for getting at the roots of violent behavior. It includes activities and workshops that explore how violence manifests in families and dating; how issues of race, gender, and age are involved; and how teens can work to stop the violence.

> **"This book pictures adults and young people finding a common cause, common language, and common understanding to face the very real conditions that limit us all." — *Family Violence & Sexual Assault Bulletin***

176 pages ... 12 illus. ... Paperback $14.95 ... Spiral $17.95

SPECIAL: Youth Violence Prevention Package

***Making the Peace, Days of Respect,* and *Helping Teens Stop Violence* for $53.95**

ORDER FORM

10% DISCOUNT on orders of $50 or more —
20% DISCOUNT on orders of $150 or more —
30% DISCOUNT on orders of $500 or more —
On cost of books for fully prepaid orders

NAME

ADDRESS

CITY/STATE ZIP/POSTCODE

PHONE COUNTRY (outside U.S.)

TITLE	QTY	PRICE	TOTAL
When Violence Begins at Home (paperback)		@ $ 19.95	
When Violence Begins at Home (hard cover)		@ $ 29.95	
Living with My Family		@ $ 8.95	
Workbook Library (8 workbooks)		@ $ 50.00	
Youth Violence Prevention Package (3 books)		@ $ 53.95	
List other titles below			
		@ $	
		@ $	
		@ $	
		@ $	
		@ $	
		@ $	
Check here to receive our book catalog	☐		FREE

Shipping costs:
First book: $3.00 by book post ($4.50 by UPS or to ship outside U.S.)
Each additional book: $1.00
For bulk shipments call us at (510) 865-5282

SUBTOTAL
Less discount @_____% ( )
TOTAL COST OF BOOKS
Calif. residents add sales tax
Shipping & handling
TOTAL ENCLOSED
Please pay in U.S. funds only

☐ Check ☐ Money Order ☐ Visa ☐ M/C ☐ Discover

Card # ____________________ *Exp date* _______

Signature ____________________________

Complete and mail to:

Hunter House Publishers
P.O. Box 2914, Alameda CA 94501-0914
ordering@hunterhouse.com … www.hunterhouse.com
Phone (510) 865-5282 Fax (510) 865-4295
(800) 266-5592

WVB 9/97